CINEMA AND THE CITY

Studies in Urban and Social Change

Published by Blackwell in association with the *International Journal of Urban and Regional Research*. Series editors: Chris Pickvance, Margit Meyer and John Walton.

Published

Forthcoming

CINEMA AND THE CITY

FILM AND URBAN SOCIETIES IN A GLOBAL CONTEXT

Edited by
Mark Shiel and Tony Fitzmaurice

Copyright © Blackwell Publishers Ltd 2001
Editorial matter and arrangement copyright © Mark Shiel and Tony Fitzmaurice 2001

First published 2001

2 4 6 8 10 9 7 5 3 1

Blackwell Publishers Ltd
108 Cowley Road
Oxford OX4 1JF
UK

Blackwell Publishers Inc.
350 Main Street
Malden, Massachusetts 02148
USA

British Library Cataloguing in Publication Data

A CIP catalogue record for this book is available from the British Library.

Library of Congress Cataloging-in-Publication Data

Cinema and the city : film and urban societies in a global context /
edited by Mark Shiel and Tony Fitzmaurice.
        p.   cm. — (Studies in urban and social change)
Includes bibliographical references and index.
        ISBN 0–631–22243–X (acid-free paper) — ISBN 0–631–22244–8 (pbk. : acid-free paper)
    1. Cities and towns in motion pictures.   2. Motion pictures—Social aspects.   3. City and town life.   I. Shiel, Mark.   II. Fitzmaurice, Tony, 1953–   III. Series.
        PN1995.9.C513 C45   2001
        791.43'621732—dc21

                                                                                                00–010767

Typeset in 10½ on 12 pt Baskerville
by Ace Filmsetting Ltd, Frome, Somerset
Printed in Great Britain by TJ International, Padstow, Cornwall

This book is printed on acid-free paper.

From Mark, to Alyce

From Tony, to Mary and Fionn

Contents

Part 4: Urban Reactions on Screen 229

Idealism and Defeat 231

Escape and Invasion 255

Illustrations

Illustrations Acknowledgments

We would like to express our thanks to the following for illustrations and permissions: British Film Institute Stills Library, London; Film Institute of Ireland, Dublin; Eastern California Museum, Independence, CA; Ehrenkrantz Eckstut & Kuhn Architects, Los Angeles, CA; George Cott/Chroma Inc.; Greater Philadelphia Film Office; Houston Metropolitan Research Center, Houston Public Library; Les Films Lazennec, Paris; Loews Cineplex (US), New York; Los Angeles County Museum of Art; News Limited, Sydney; Roadshow Film Distributors, Melbourne; Specta Films CEPEC, Paris; Thin Man Films Ltd, London; Working Dog Pty. Ltd, Melbourne.

While every effort has been made to identify and contact copyright holders, it has not been possible to do so in every case. Any rights not acknowledged here will be acknowledged in subsequent editions if notice is given to the publisher.

Contributors

Gary Baines is Senior Lecturer in History at Rhodes University. He completed his Ph.D. at Cape Town University and has published primarily on Port Elizabeth's African population and South African urban history and culture. He is currently working on a study of jazz in postwar South Africa.

Mike Davis teaches urban and social history and theory in the Department of History at the State University of New York, Stony Brook. He is the author of numerous books including *Ecology of Fear: Los Angeles and the Imagination of Disaster* (1998), *City of Quartz: Excavating the Future in Los Angeles* (1992), and *Prisoners of the American Dream* (1986). His most recent book is entitled *Magical Urbanism: Latinos Reinvent the US Big City* (2000).

Leo Enticknap recently completed his Ph.D. thesis at the University of Exeter on the non-fiction film in postwar Britain. He has articles forthcoming on the newsreel series *This Modern Age* and the implications for film scholars of archival restoration projects, with reference to the recent re-release of *Vertigo*.

Adrian Fielder is currently completing his doctorate at Northwestern University on trends of globalization and urban cultures in postcolonial France and North Africa. His most recent publications include "The Tactical Poetics of Urban Nomadism," in *Les Enfants de l'immigration*, ed. Ernstpeter Ruhe

(1999), and "Articulating the Hip-Hop Nation in the US and France" (in *disClosure*, vol. 8, Summer 1999).

Tony Fitzmaurice is College Lecturer at the Centre for Film Studies, University College Dublin, where he specializes in postwar American cinema and European – particularly Italian – modernist cinema. A graduate of UCD in English and in Film Studies, he previously taught at the National College of Art and Design, Dublin. He has published articles on Hollywood in the 1970s and on Irish and international contemporary art.

James Hay is an Associate Professor in Speech Communication, the Graduate Program in Cultural Studies, the Unit for Criticism and Interpretive Theory, and the Unit for Cinema Studies at the University of Illinois, Champaign-Urbana. His books include *Popular Film Culture in Fascist Italy*, *The Audience and its Landscape*, and numerous essays about screen media and social space. He is currently completing a book (related to his essay in this volume) on cultural technology, advanced liberalism, and the production of social space.

Janna Jones is Assistant Professor of Interdisciplinary Studies at the University of South Florida. She received her Ph.D. in Communication at the University of South Florida. Her research and publications focus on how people understand and negotiate public and private space. She is currently writing a book entitled *Let's Go Downtown: The Return to the Southern Picture Palace*.

Justine Lloyd is Postdoctoral Research Fellow in the Faculty of Humanities and Social Sciences, University of Technology, Sydney. She is the author of numerous articles on popular culture and identity, most recently "A Sublime Indifference," in *Impossible Selves: Cultural Readings of Identity* (ed. J. Lo et al., 1999). She is coeditor of *Planet Diana: Cultural Studies and Global Mourning* (with Ien Ang et al., 1997, and recently completed her doctoral thesis at the University of West Sydney Nepean on technology, travel, and the imagination of modernity in twentieth-century Sydney.

Laurent Marie lectures in French at University College Dublin and completed his Ph.D., on the relationship between the French Communist Party and French cinema, at the University of Warwick. His recent published articles include "La nostalgie est toujours ce qu'elle était: *Germinale* de Claude Berri et le Parti Communiste Français," in *Excavatio*, Spring 1998, and "La réception critique de *L'amour d'une femme*," in *1895*, special issue on Jean Grémillon, October 1997. His essay "*Le Chêne et le roseau*: French Communist critics and the New Wave," will be published shortly in *Visual Culture and French National Identity*.

Bill Marshall is Professor of Modern French Studies at the University of Glasgow, Scotland. He has written a book on Québec National Cinema (2000), as well as studies of Victor Serge and Guy Hocquenghem, and coedited *Musicals: Hollywood and Beyond* (2000).

Mike Mason is Senior Lecturer in Media Theory at the University of Lincolnshire and Humberside. After a varied career in theater, fashion, and graphic design in Holland he returned to England in the late 1980s to study Media and Film at Sheffield Hallam University, completing his dissertation on masculinity in social realist film. His current research focuses on media education and European film-funding.

J. Paul Narkunas is a doctoral candidate in the Department of English at the University of Pittsburgh completing a dissertation entitled "Surfing the Long Waves of Global Capitalism: Inhuman Flights Through Time." His areas of research include Gilles Deleuze, the English language as commodity, US influence in East Asia, the World Bank and UNESCO, and East Asian Film. He is the author of the article "The Metabolic State: Market English and the World Bank."

Mark Neumann is an associate professor in the Department of Communication at the University of South Florida in Tampa, Florida. His research and teaching interests focus on the study of visual society, popular culture, tourism, consumption, and urban life. He is the author of *On the Rim: Looking for the Grand Canyon* (1999), and has written articles and book chapters on documentary, photography, casino gambling, travel, and bootleg music recording.

Geoffrey Nowell-Smith is Professor of Cinema Cultures at the University of Luton. He is the author of *L'avventura* (1998), and has edited or coedited numerous publications including *The Oxford History of World Cinema* (1996), *Hollywood and Europe: Economics, Culture, National Identity, 1945–95* (1998), and *The Companion to Italian Cinema* (1996). He is currently writing a book on art cinema for publication in 2001.

Obododimma Oha is a lecturer in the Department of English, Gaston Berger University, Saint-Louis, Senegal. His research interests are in semiotics and Nigerian visual culture and politics, subjects on which he has published widely. He is currently working on a study of the impact of military dictatorship on the arts in Nigeria.

Kevin Rockett is Lecturer in Film Studies at Trinity College Dublin, and was previously Postdoctoral Fellow at the Centre for Film Studies, University

College Dublin. One of the foremost scholars on Irish cinema, he is the author of *The Irish Filmography: Fiction Films, 1896–1996* (1996), and *Still Irish: A Century of the Irish in Film* (1995). Additionally, he has coauthored *The Companion to British and Irish Cinema*, with John Caughie (1996) and *Cinema and Ireland*, with Luke Gibbons and John Hill (1987).

Mark Shiel is Lecturer in Film Studies at Sheffield Hallam University, where he specializes in American cinema, politics, and social history, and was previously Faculty of Arts Fellow at the Centre for Film Studies, University College Dublin. He is a graduate of Trinity College Dublin (in English Literature and Drama Studies) and completed his Ph.D., "Radical Agendas and the Politics of Space in American Cinema, 1968–1974," at the British Film Institute in London in 1999.

Josh Stenger is a Ph.D. candidate in the English Department at Syracuse University in Syracuse, New York. He is completing his dissertation, which focuses on the relationship between Hollywood film, consumerism, and the urban landscape of Los Angeles. His previous published work includes essays on Planet Hollywood and Universal CityWalk.

Julian Stringer is Lecturer in Film Studies at the University of Nottingham. He received his Ph.D. from Indiana University, Bloomington. His articles have appeared in numerous film journals, including *Screen*. He has contributed essays to the anthologies *The Road Movie Book* (1997), *The Encyclopedia of Chinese Film* (1998), *Asian-American Screen Cultures* (1999), *Mythologies of Violence in Postmodern Media* (1999), and *Titanic: Anatomy of a Blockbuster* (1999). He is currently working on a study of the cultural politics of international film festivals.

Paul Swann is Associate Professor and Director of the MFA Program in the Department of Film and Media Arts at Temple University. He is the author of *The British Documentary Film Movement, 1926–1946* (1989) and of *The Hollywood Feature Film in Postwar Britain* (1987). He has also published extensively on documentary and on Hollywood's relationship to European cinema markets after World War Two. He is currently working on a study of the reception of American popular television in Asia and British films in the United States.

Rolando B. Tolentino is Assistant Professor of Filipino and Philippine Literature at the University of the Philippines. He completed his Ph.D. at the School of Cinema-Television, University of Southern California, and has published widely on Philippine and Southeast Asian cultural identity and global politics.

John Walton is Professor of Sociology at the University of California, Davis. His recent books include *Free Markets and Food Riots* (Blackwell, 1994), *Western Times and Water Wars: State, Culture, and Rebellion in California* (1992), and *The Power and the Story: Collective Memory in Monterey from Colonial Rule to Cannery Row* (forthcoming).

Series Editors' Preface

In the past three decades there have been dramatic changes in the fortunes of cities and regions, in beliefs about the role of markets and states in society, and in the theories used by social scientists to account for these changes. Many of the cities experiencing crisis in the 1970s have undergone revitalization while others have continued to decline. In Europe and North America new policies have introduced privatization on a broad scale at the expense of collective consumption, and the viability of the welfare state has been challenged. Eastern Europe has witnessed the collapse of state socialism and the uneven implementation of a globally driven market economy. Meanwhile, the less developed nations have suffered punishing austerity programmes that divide a few newly industrializing countries from a great many cases of arrested and negative growth.

Social science theories have struggled to encompass these changes. The earlier social organizational and ecological paradigms were criticized by Marxian and Weberian theories, and these in turn have been disputed as all-embracing narratives. The certainties of the past, such as class theory, are gone and the future of urban and regional studies appears relatively open.

The aim of the series *Studies in Urban and Social Change* is to take forward this agenda of issues and theoretical debates. The series is committed to a number of aims but will not prejudge the development of the field. It encourages theoretical works and research monographs on cities and regions. It explores the spatial dimension of society, including the role of agency and of institutional contexts in shaping urban form. It addresses economic and political change from the household to the state. Cities and regions are understood within an international system, the features of which are revealed in comparative and historical analyses.

The series also serves the interests of university classroom and professional readers. It publishes topical accounts of important policy issues (e.g. global adjustment), reviews of debates (e.g. post-Fordism) and collections that explore various facets of major changes (e.g. cities after socialism or the new urban underclass). The series urges a synthesis of research and theory, teaching and practice. Engaging research monographs (e.g. on women and poverty in Mexico or urban culture in Japan) provide vivid teaching materials, just as policy-oriented studies (e.g. of social housing or urban planning) test and redirect theory. The city is analysed from the top down (e.g. through the gendered culture of investment banks) and the bottom up (e.g. in challenging social movements). Taken together, the volumes in the series reflect the latest developments in urban and regional studies.

Subjects which fall within the scope of the series include: explanations for the rise and fall of cities and regions; economic restructuring and its spatial, class, and gender impact; race and identity; convergence and divergence of the "east" and "west" in social and institutional patterns; new divisions of labour and forms of social exclusion; urban and environmental movements; international migration and capital flows; politics of the urban poor in developing countries; cross-national comparisons or housing, planning and development; debates on post-Fordism, the consumption sector and the "new" urban poverty.

Studies in Urban and Social Change addresses an international and interdisciplinary audience of researchers, practitioners, students, and urban enthusiasts. Above all, it endeavours to reach the public with compelling accounts of contemporary society.

Editorial Committee
John Walton, Chair
Margit Mayer
Chris Pickvance

Preface

This book is entitled *Cinema and the City: Film and Urban Societies in a Global Context* because it is primarily interested not in the cinema *per se* or in the city *per se* but in the relationship or conjunction between the two as it has been played out in a wide range of geographical and historical contexts and, particularly, as it may help us to apprehend and respond to large social and cultural processes such as globalization today.

The book is divided into four parts: three mapping a geographical relationship between key global regions and their respective city types and film cultures (Los Angeles, the cities of a number of former European colonies, and the capital cities of two former European colonial powers); and one mapping the political–economic relationship between film production and consumption, on the one hand, and key urban centers, on the other. Each part has its own brief introduction, relating the various chapters to each other and each part to the others. The book as a whole is introduced by two critical chapters: the first, "Cinema and the City in History and Theory," provides a macro-geographical and broad historical contextualization of the relationship between cinema and urban society and its importance in social and cultural theory; the second, "Film and Urban Societies in a Global Context," introduces in detail the various particular essays and parts of the book through a consideration of their binding interest in power, globalization, and resistance as these are revealed in or practiced through cinema and films in the urban environment.

This book has its practical origins in the *Cinema and the City* conference, organized by us, which was hosted by the Centre for Film Studies at University College Dublin (UCD) in March 1999. The conference brought together a wide range of both eminent and emerging scholars in a number of related fields such as Film Studies, Sociology, Urban Studies, Geography, and Architecture to explore the rich relationship between film and the urban environment through a variety of methodologies. The success of the event, the creativity of the many opinions and ideas expressed, and the interest generated internationally by the conference, testified to the importance and fruitfulness of interdisciplinary collaboration, particularly as a means to the understanding of the crucial interconnectedness of cinema/culture and city/society over the past 100 years.

For their support in the development and hosting of the *Cinema and the City* conference in the first place, we would like to take this opportunity to thank the Faculty of Arts and the Board of Studies of the Centre for Film Studies, UCD. Thanks too to our colleagues and students at UCD for their encouragement and practical assistance. A special thank-you to Susanne Bach.

We are very grateful to the Series Editors of *Studies in Urban and Social Change* – John Walton, Chris Pickvance, and Margit Mayer – for their guidance and support throughout the development of the book. A particular note of thanks should go to John Walton for the warmth of his interest and encouragement from the very outset – both from a distance, in California, and on occasional visits to Dublin.

The editorial staff at Blackwell in Oxford have been of invaluable assistance in the course of our work on the book. In particular, we would like to thank Sarah Falkus, Katherine Warren, Joanna Pyke, Jill Landeryou (formerly of Blackwell), and Juanita Bullough for their attentiveness and patience throughout.

We are also indebted to a number of other people for their practical help in securing illustrations and permissions for the book. We would particularly like to mention: Vanessa Marshall and Ann Haydon at the British Film Institute Stills Library; Shaula Coyl at the Los Angeles County Museum of Art; Sunniva O'Flynn at the Film Institute of Ireland; Mary Jane Dodge, VP IMAX Theaters, Loews-Cineplex, New York City; Deborah Reade at Thin Man Films, London; Noura Aberkane at Lazennec Productions, Paris; and Tara Schroeder at the Tampa Theater, Tampa, Florida.

Finally, we would like to thank our respective families and friends for their love, support, and inspiration.

Mark Shiel
Tony Fitzmaurice

1

Cinema and the City in History and Theory

Mark Shiel

A whole history remains to be written of *spaces* – which would at the same time
be the history of *powers* – from the great strategies of geopolitics to the little
tactics of the habitat.

Michel Foucault, "The Eye of Power"[1]

Cinema and the City

This book is concerned with the relationship between the most important
cultural form – cinema – and the most important form of social organization
– the city – in the twentieth century (and, for the time being at least, the
twenty-first century), as this relationship operates and is experienced in society as a lived social reality.

Since the end of the nineteenth century, the fortunes of cinema and the
city have been inextricably linked on a number of levels. Thematically, the
cinema has, since its inception, been constantly fascinated with the representation of the distinctive spaces, lifestyles, and human conditions of the city
from the Lumière brothers' Paris of 1895 to John Woo's Hong Kong of
1995. Formally, the cinema has long had a striking and distinctive ability to
capture and express the spatial complexity, diversity, and social dynamism of
the city through *mise-en-scène*, location filming, lighting, cinematography, and
editing, while thinkers from Walter Benjamin – confronted by the shocking
novelties of modernity, mass society, manufacture, and mechanical reproduction – to Jean Baudrillard – mesmerized by the ominous glamour of
postmodernity, individualism, consumption, and electronic reproduction –
have recognized and observed the curious and telling correlation between
the mobility and visual and aural sensations of the city and the mobility and
visual and aural sensations of the cinema. Industrially, cinema has long
played an important role in the cultural economies of cities all over the world

in the production, distribution, and exhibition of motion pictures, and in the cultural geographies of certain cities particularly marked by cinema (from Los Angeles to Paris to Bombay) whose built environment and civic identity are both significantly constituted by film industry and films.[2]

The nexus *cinema–city*, then, provides a rich avenue for investigation and discussion of key issues which ought to be of common interest in the study of society (in this case, the city) and in the study of culture (in this case, the cinema) and in the study of their thematic, formal, and industrial relationship historically and today. Indeed, interest in their relationship has been growing significantly of late – particularly with regard to the thematic and formal representation of the city – in the fields of Film Studies, Cultural Studies, and Architecture.[3] The central innovative aim of this book is to contribute to the study of the cinema and to the study of society by focusing on the relationship between cinema and the city as *lived social realities* in a range of urban societies of the present and recent past.

Film Studies and Sociology

One of the fundamental premises of this book is that interdisciplinary contact between Film Studies and Sociology (among other disciplines, including Cultural Studies, Geography, and Urban Studies) can be profoundly useful and fruitful in addressing key issues which the two disciplines share (or ought to share) in common at the beginning of the twenty-first century, and which have either emerged in recent years or which have become especially acute in the contemporary cultural and social context.

These include: the perennial issue of the relationship between culture and society, particularly in what is now commonly referred to as the current global postmodern social, and cultural context; the operation of political, social, and cultural power in the urban centers of the present global system; the historical description ("periodization") of social and cultural change through such categories as "industrialism," "post-industrialism," "modernity" and "postmodernity"; and, as a route to the better understanding of these issues, the concept of spatialization as a means of description and analysis in the study of both culture and society, cinema and the city, today.

As Andrew Tudor and other commentators have pointed out, there has been a paucity of positive contact between the disciplines of Film Studies and Sociology.[4] On the whole, their relationship has been a historically unhappy one, most sociological interest in cinema since the early days of the medium having taken either one of two related forms. One area of sociological interest in cinema has, since the 1920s, focused in a limited and undiscriminating way on "the measurable effects of film" on particular groups in society – typically, young people – and almost always with the conviction that those effects were bad – as, for example, in the case of the age-old debate over links between cinema and crime, youth delinquency, or violence. Since the 1940s, a second area, particularly informed by the cultural elitism and instrumentalism of the Frankfurt School, has emphasized the status of cinema as just another form of mass communications exercising control in a mass society of unintelligent and unindividuated consumers (a view, of Hollywood cinema at least, which has certainly had many adherents in Film Studies too). Both sociological approaches to cinema have been guilty of mechanical and deterministic thinking which has generated little common ground with the central interests of Film Studies since its inception in the 1960s.

The larger part of Film Studies over the years has concerned itself primarily with the language of cinema and with various approaches to cinema as a powerful signifying system which have focused on the individual, the subject, identity, representation – for the most part, with the *reflection* of society in films – with a strong faith in theory and an almost complete distrust of empiricism. Film Studies has been primarily interested in the film as *text* (comprising visual language, verbal systems, dialogue, characterization, narrative, and "story") and with the *exegesis* of the text according to one or other hermeneutic (for example, psychoanalysis, Marxism, myth-criticism, semiotics, formalism, or some combination thereof).[5] Such issues have dominated largely as a result of the discipline's origins in (and continuing close relationship with) literary studies, while newer subjects such as Media Studies and Communications have been better at developing sociological approaches (for example, to television) precisely because of their origins, in large part, within Sociology, at a "safe distance" from close concern with the text.[6]

One of the aims of this book is to recognize this history by proposing something of a challenge to Film Studies and Sociology to work to produce a sociology of the cinema in the sense of a sociology of motion picture production, distribution, exhibition, and consumption, with a specific focus on the role of cinema in the physical, social, cultural, and economic development of cities.[7]

This interdisciplinary challenge makes two interdependent propositions. First, it proposes that Sociology has much to gain by building upon its traditional interests in capital, economy, labor, demographics, and other issues by incorporating a greater interest in "culture," "cinema," and "films" through an investigation of their impact upon urban development, on the one hand, and their informative and influential allegorizing of objective social realities, on the other. Secondly, it proposes that Film Studies has much to gain by building upon its traditional interests in representation, subjectivity, and the text by working harder to develop a synthetic understanding of the objective social conditions of the production, distribution, exhibition, and reception of cinema and the mediated production of urban space and urban identity.

This book and the individual contributions in it, it is hoped, make steps in the direction of such a sociology of the cinema, outlining what such a sociology might look like, and what kind of practical and diverse forms it might take.

Culture and Society

This bringing together of Film Studies and Sociology, then, underpins the aim of this book to examine the relationship between cinema and urban societies and, in doing so, to work against the alienation of the study of culture from the study of society which was traditionally explained through the old opposition of "base" (society, wealth, poverty, work, class, race, income, housing) and "superstructure" (culture, text, image, sign), and which fostered little more than mechanistic understandings of the relationship between the two.

The best antidote to the base-superstructure model, as Fredric Jameson has explained, is that of Althusserian structuralism in which base and superstructure are replaced by "structure" and in which mechanistic notions of causality give way to the concept of "over-determination."[8] This formulation of the relationship between culture and society, which has informed the editorial logic of the book, recognizes the interpenetration of culture, society, and economics as part of "a whole and connected social material process," to use Raymond Williams's terminology.[9] It allows (even requires) a conception of cultural production as simultaneously different from and yet similar to other forms of (industrial) production in a manner which is particularly appropriate to cinema, more particularly to Hollywood cinema, and most particularly to Hollywood cinema in the contemporary global economy. It opens the way for interdisciplinary investigation and communication as natural and indispensable, tending to undermine intellectual compartmentalization and fostering a view of culture as "a whole way of life."[10] Finally, it undermines the reifying tendency to speak of cinema simply in terms of the text and its reflection of urban and social change "on the ground," and fosters instead an understanding of cinema (as a set of practices and activities, as well as a set of texts) as something which never ceases to intervene in society, and which participates in the maintenance, mutation, and subversion of systems of power. Althusserian structuralism identifies the cooperation of Film Studies and Sociology not as a mere academic experiment or interdisciplinary trifle, but as a natural and proper pooling of resources in the name of a synthetic and rounded understanding of culture and society as culture and society can only be properly understood – in their *relation* to each other.

Space and Spatiality

If a significant and stubborn discrepancy between the study of culture and the study of society often remains in evidence today, one crucial and positive area which the two have increasingly held in common in recent years is what has become known as the "spatial turn" in social and cultural theory on the Left (broadly defined) since the 1970s which has involved a growing recognition of the usefulness of space as an organizing category, and of the concept of "spatialization" as a term for the analysis and description of modern, and (even more so) of postmodern, society and culture. This spatial turn has been driven by a wide range of critical thinking from the work of Henri Lefebvre (*The Production of Space*, 1974), Michel Foucault (*Discipline and Punish*, 1977), and Ernest Mandel (*Late Capitalism*, 1975) in the 1960s and 1970s to the work of Marshall Berman (*All That Is Solid Melts Into Air*, 1982), David Harvey (*The Condition of Postmodernity*, 1989), Fredric Jameson (*Postmodernism, or, the Cultural Logic of Late Capitalism*, 1991), Edward Soja (*Postmodern Geographies*, 1989), and Mike Davis (*City of Quartz: Excavating the Future in Los Angeles*, 1990) in the 1980s and 1990s.[11]

On the one hand, in the social sciences, this spatial turn has helped us to understand, as Edward Soja has explained, "how relations of power and discipline are inscribed into the apparently innocent spatiality of social life, how human geographies become filled with politics and ideology."[12] On the other hand, in the study of culture, it has helped us to understand how power and discipline are spatially inscribed into cultural texts and into the spatial organization of cultural production – as, for example, through what Jameson has described as the "geopolitical aesthetic" of contemporary world cinema.[13]

One of the key presuppositions of this book is that the increasing prominence given to space and spatialization in the recent study of culture and society has been a profoundly important development and that cinema is the ideal cultural form through which to examine spatialization precisely because of cinema's status as a peculiarly spatial form of culture.

Cinema is a peculiarly spatial form of culture, of course, because (of all cultural forms) cinema operates and is best understood in terms of the organization of space: both *space in films* – the space of the shot; the space of the narrative setting; the geographical relationship of various settings in sequence in a film; the mapping of a lived environment on film; and *films in space* – the shaping of lived urban spaces by cinema as a cultural practice; the spatial organization of its industry at the levels of production, distribution, and exhibition; the role of cinema in globalization. Thus, one of the major contentions of this book is that cinema is primarily a spatial system and that, notwithstanding the traditional textual emphasis of much Film Studies, it is more a spatial system than a textual system: that spatiality is what makes it different and, in this context, gives it a special potential to illuminate the lived spaces of the city and urban societies, allowing for a full synthetic understanding of cinematic theme, form, and industry in the context of global capitalism.

Geographical Description and Uneven Development

On this basis, the analysis of the relationship between cinema and urban societies in this book in a comprehensive range of global contexts, and with an emphasis on cinema as a social and material practice, may be seen as an exercise in what Jameson, with reference to the peculiar spatial character of cinema, has termed "cognitive mapping" – that is, the attempt to "think" a system (today, postmodern global capitalism) which evades thought and analysis. The book aims to map culture as a lived social reality which enacts and articulates relations of power, as these are evident in core–periphery relations both *within* cities and in the current global system *between* the cities and the cinemas of Los Angeles, of former European colonies, and of former European colonial powers.[14]

The emphasis throughout the book is on international diversity, and a conceptual organization which attempts to map out different relations of power in the geopolitical system in terms of dominance, subordination, mediation, and resistance, and their articulation in cinema and its political economy. This geographical diversity encompasses many types of city and urban society, whether these are classified according to Saskia Sassen's typology of "global," "transnational," and "subnational" cities or according to Mike Savage and Alan Warde's classification of "global cities," "Third World cities," "older industrial cities," and "new industrial districts."[15] It also encompasses many types of cinema, including the dominant commercial forms of Hollywood, the European co-production, IMAX, documentary, and low-budget video in West Africa. As such, the book's large geographical spread – attempting to keep equally in focus at all times the local, regional, and global levels, or micro- and macro-perspectives – serves to highlight the important realities of "uneven development" between various urban societies and various cinemas historically and in the present day, realities which are foregrounded both through the various representations of objective urban social and economic conditions discussed in relation to particular films and cities in the book, and in terms of the uneven development of particular national or metropolitan film industries *vis-à-vis* the global dominance and technological and financial superiority of Hollywood cinema.[16]

This description of urban society and of cinema globally in terms of a relationship between cities (and cities alone) corroborates the view held by large numbers of social commentators today that the city – more so than the "nation," perhaps less so than the "transnational corporation" – is *the* fundamental unit of the new global system which has emerged since the 1960s, of which the mobility of capital and information is the most celebrated feature.[17] Thus the book presents a global portrait of a network of semi-autonomous cities and megacities, many of which (just as Sassen said they would) relate primarily to other cities in the network rather than to the particular national or regional space in which they are physically located.[18]

The positioning of Los Angeles at the beginning of the book, then, endorses the characterization of that city (and its larger metropolitan region) by many social commentators as *the* paradigmatic city space, urban society, and cultural environment of the late twentieth and twenty-first centuries – "the place where it all comes together," as Edward Soja has described it, "a World City, a major nodal point in the ebb and flow of the new global economy" and, almost needless to say, the home of the massively, globally dominant Hollywood cinema and larger US entertainment industry.[19] But this notional positioning of Los Angeles as some kind of global core to which the rest of the world can be viewed as periphery must be balanced by the recognition that if Los Angeles is a paradigm, it is so not merely because it can be proposed as one of the world's most "advanced" urban societies but also because it can be proposed as one of the world's most "backward" urban societies – a tense and often violent combination of First and Third World realities in one (albeit highly segregated) space. Thus, Los Angeles contains uneven development internally while accentuating it on the world stage.

This internal and external unevenness places Los Angeles in an illuminating and problematic relationship with postcolonial cities and film cultures in both the First World and the Third World, all to one degree or another emerging or struggling to emerge from broadly shared histories of colonization, exploitation, dependency, and economic and political instability. On the one hand, postcolonial agendas for self-determination – in cinema as much as in other areas of society – have been expressed primarily in national terms, and the problematization of the concept of "nation" by globalization and the rise of cities is rarely more visible than in the now almost quaint notion of "national cinema." On the other hand, the encounter between cinema and postcolonial urban societies in the Third World which remain beset by massive poverty and endemic social injustice may sometimes seem a strange one, given the natural capital-intensive and technology-intensive character of cinema as a cultural practice, and is often a particularly fraught one, given cinema's ability to intervene in particularly charged social and political environments in frequently unwelcome and even dangerous ways.[20]

The postcolonial urban societies, finally, remain closely related, for better or worse, to the capital cities of former colonial powers of which two – Paris and London – are dealt with in detail in this book. Paris and London, of course, have not only long served as archetypal city environments for cinema (London for Hitchcock or David Lean; Paris for Renoir or Godard) and been important as centers of film production, but in their nineteenth-century imperial heydays were the sites in which the first shocked recognitions were made of the definable features of modern urban society, whether by Dickens or Engels in the case of the former or by Flaubert, Hugo, Balzac, or Baudelaire, in the case of the latter.[21] Though today, in cinematic terms, they occupy an arguably subordinate position to Los Angeles, as urban societies, Manuel Castells and Peter Hall remind us, they "remain among the major innovation and high-technology centers of the world," despite their relative age.[22]

The regional–metropolitan conceptualization of the relation between cinema and urban societies which underpins this book, then, recognizes uneven development, diversity, and local specificity as an important antidote to, or safeguard against, the temptations of totalization – either by way of premature celebration of the benevolent leveling power of free-market capitalism (some form of the post-industrialism thesis or the end-of-ideology argument), or by way of defeatist resignation in the face of its unstoppable homogenizing and neutralizing tendencies. But it also suggests a contingent and always provisional macro-geographical contextualization and synthetic understanding of the relation between cinema and urban societies more generally.[23] The name for that macro-geographical context as it emerges in this book is "globalization," a historical and geographical process in which Film Studies and Sociology ought to be equally and cooperatively interested.

Describing History

If this book is structured spatially according to a model of core–periphery relations between different types of cinemas and urban societies in diverse parts of the world, it is simultaneously structured according to a historical description of the development from monopoly capitalism, imperialism, the nation-state and modernity in the nineteenth and early to mid-twentieth centuries to transnational capitalism, postcolonialism, the city, and postmodernity in the mid- to late twentieth and twenty-first centuries. Thus we have a spatial description (spatiality being central to most theorizations of postmodernity) which is also a historical description (history having long underpinned traditional Marxism) of the development of society and culture through "stages" of capitalism variously identified with the terms modernity, postmodernity, modernism, postmodernism, Fordism, post-Fordism, industrialism, and post-industrialism. "Uneven development," then, reminds us that the recent turn toward geography and spatialization, which in the present context highlights the spatial character of cinema and the distinctive spatial typology of the city, necessarily exists in tension in cultural and social theory with more traditional concerns with and approaches based upon history and temporality.

Of particular relevance to cinema on a number of counts is the important debate in postwar social theory over the concept of "post-industrialism" – that is, the insistence by many liberal and conservative thinkers, from David Riesman to Francis Fukuyama, that since the 1950s, society (either globally or specifically in the West) has moved into a qualitatively new phase of its development, with the displacement of production and manufactured goods by consumption and the sign.

First, of course, an important part of the very thesis of post-industrialism is that culture has become increasingly important in society and, indeed, the development of post-industrialism as a concept in Sociology may now be identified as one of the first steps in what David Chaney has termed "the cultural turn" in social history and theory since the 1950s.[24] Many theorizations of "post-industrialism" have attended to this increasing prominence of culture and have been expressed in primarily spatial terms – for example, the work of theorists as diverse as Daniel Bell ("the post-industrial society"), Marshall McLuhan ("the global village"), or Jean Baudrillard ("the political economy of the sign").[25] Secondly, while post-industrialism as a thesis is based upon a presumption of the increasing dominance of sign and image over manufactured goods, cinema has always been "paradoxically" both sign and image *and* manufactured goods. Thirdly, cinema has mostly been imagined primarily as a collection of filmic texts rather than as a spatially-configured industry comprising banks, multinational corporations, distributors, producers, exhibitors and exhibition spaces, various technology manufacturers, workers, consumers, and so on. The often integrally-related prioritization of sign, image, and text in discussion of cinema, together with the neglect of issues of production, capital, and labor, has always been an inherently conservative operation through which, in a sense, cinema has been thought of "post-industrially" even before "post-industrialization."

In contrast, however, to the implication of the concept of "post-industrialism" that the world has moved beyond such things as modernity, industrial society, ideology, or even history itself, this book understands postmodernity not as the end of something but as a period of even more complete and total modernization than in any preceding period – a period (as proposed by writers such as Lefebvre, Mandel, Harvey, and Jameson) which involves the thorough incorporation of rural space by urban space, the thorough colonization of daily life (including most areas of culture) by capital, and the globalization of urban society, economy, and culture as part of a process which has accelerated *qualitatively* since the late 1960s.[26]

This now global postmodern environment, with all of its uneven development, may best be understood in terms of Nicos Poulantzas's characterization of a "social formation" as a complex and dynamic coexistence of overlapping and contradictory modes of production, or in terms of Raymond Williams's explanation of the importance of perpetual interaction and conflict in society and culture between dominant, residual, and emergent elements.[27] Williams's explanation that any hegemony is in practice "full of contradictions and unresolved conflicts" then brings us to the question of the possibility or not of conflict and resistance in the current global context and its operation in cinema and urban societies.[28]

Globalization

Cultural production, both high and low, both supportive and critical of capitalist values, has now become so commodified that it is thoroughly implicated in systems of monetary evaluation and circulation. Under such conditions, the varieties of cultural output are no different from the varieties of Benetton's colors or the famous 57 varieties that Heinz long ago pioneered. Furthermore, all oppositional culture (and there is plenty of it) still has to be expressed in this commodified mode, thus limiting the powers of oppositional movements in important ways.

David Harvey, *The Condition of Postmodernity*[29]

Cinema, of course, is an excellent means to an understanding of globalization for a number of reasons. Since the early twentieth century, it has always operated through a sophisticated organization of film production, distribution, and exhibition internationally – and, particularly, radiating from Southern California and Hollywood to the rest of the world through the expansionist activities and vision not only of the major American film studios, but also of such agencies as the Motion Picture Association of America and the Motion Picture Export Association. Today, cinema exists as part of a much larger global entertainment industry and communications network, which includes older cultural forms such as music and television, and newer forms of technoculture such as digital, the internet, and information technology. Studies of the political economy of cinema almost invariably begin by pointing out that cinema has long been one of the United States' most important export industries and that debates over cinema and national culture have been critical to globally-felt international negotiations such as those surrounding the 1993 General Agreement on Trade and Tariffs (GATT).[30]

Indeed, if cinema may be said to have been one of the first truly globalized industries in terms of its organization, it may also be said to have long been at the cutting edge of globalization as a process of integration and homogenization. The hugely disproportionate dominance of the United States historically in many areas of culture, economics, and politics has rarely been more tangible and overt than in the dominance of Hollywood cinema, which has for decades now been widely recognized as a threat to discrete national and regional cultures and which, in its frequent articulation of the values of free-market enterprise and individualism, and its formal manifestation of those values in its high production values and visual style, has been described by Jameson as "the apprenticeship to a specific culture" – Western (or, American) consumer capitalism.[31]

In this sense, not only may cinema – particularly Hollywood cinema – be described as having always been postmodern, even before postmodernity, because of its peculiar combination of both sign and image (culture) and manufactured goods (industry, technology, capital), it may also be recognized as central to, rather than merely reflecting, the process known as globalization. In today's context, it isn't that films or the Hollywood film industry *reflect* globalization but that films and the Hollywood film industry *effect* globalization. Films *are* globalization, not its after-effects.

In response to this realization, of course, the conflict between incorporation and autonomy becomes an acutely urgent issue of common interest to both Film Studies and Sociology. For if one of the most important issues in Sociology, particularly in the face of globalization (Americanization), is the ability or inability of social groups (either locally or globally) to challenge or resist dominant social structures, institutions, and cultures, so has Film Studies long been concerned with the ability or inability of historically and geographically diverse types of cinema – say, for example, American underground film, European art cinema, Third World filmmaking – to challenge or resist the dominance and saturation of Hollywood and American popular culture more generally.[32]

Globalization – as most of the chapters in this volume demonstrate almost regardless of their precise geographical and historical contexts – is one of the overriding concerns arising in the relationship between cinema and the city as evident since the 1970s. This is especially evident in the increasing tendency in disparate societies around the world for individuals to be struck more by, and for cultures to demonstrate more, their sameness rather than their difference, and for that sameness, rather than being arbitrary, to appear primarily American.

As such, much of this book is concerned with what Manuel Castells has described as the threatened status of "place" – for example, nation, city, neighborhood, or street – in a world which is more and more defined and experienced in terms of "flow" – for example, the flow of transnational capital, or the flow of information in a highly technological society.[33] The realities of what Don Mitchell explains as "deterritorialization" recur insistently and manifest themselves perhaps most clearly in the increasing ubiquity of what the French cultural theorist Gilles Deleuze, in his major study of the spatial and temporal characteristics of cinema, termed the *espace quelconque* – the *any-space-whatever*. This space, whether taking the form of a shopping mall, a corporate headquarters, a hotel lobby, a downtown street, or, indeed, a multiplex cinema, is not notable simply because of its ubiquity or familiarity but more particularly because if, as Foucault suggests, all space is controlled, the any-space-whatever is a space in which the source of control, the center of power, is curiously difficult to apprehend.[34] It is a space in which the intangibility of global capitalism is particularly apparent.

But if the ubiquity of the *espace quelconque* might appear as a metaphorical justification of the totalizing visions of the various theorists of post-industrialism or consumer capitalism and its supposed global triumph, the diversity of cinematic and urban contexts presented in this book also demonstrates the degree to which globalization remains incomplete and "uneven" and possibly demonstrates the degree to which globalization can be or is resisted.

With regard to the former, this book is particularly concerned with those areas where global capitalism has not yet been quite able to reach or which have fallen out of the global capitalist "loop" altogether – whether these are identified as what Miles, Hall, and Borden call "informal settlements" such as slums, tenements, and temporary communities in Third World cities, or what Marcuse and vanKempen term the "excluded ghettos" of major Western metropolises, or even vast swathes of what Portes, Castells, and Benton have described as the "informal economy" which exists in many cities around the world alongside or in open defiance of official economy.[35] These spaces certainly exist and must be identified as different if not resistant to globalization.

But with regard to the latter, sources of resistance are harder to identify. Most of Film Studies and most of Sociology seem to have now long since lost faith in the possibility that the individual nation or nation-state might be able to significantly resist globalization. This recognition has informed the acknowledgment of the growing importance of cities to Sociology and has underpinned recent theorizations of the demise of the power of national governments and structures in the global system. In Film Studies, it has more or less extinguished debate over "national cinema" (that is, the ability of individual nations to achieve cultural self-determination in cinema), a debate which came to the fore in the "window of opportunity" between the end of colonialism in the 1960s and the full realization of globalization in the 1980s when small national cinemas, most excitingly in the Third World, produced films such as *Battle of Algiers* (Gillo Pontecorvo, 1966) or *Memories of Underdevelopment* (Tomás Gutiérrez Alea, 1968), and were looked to as sources of a utopian and dynamic opposition to the dominance of Hollywood.[36]

Today, resistance is hard to identify. Fredric Jameson, for example, speculating on the possible source of any likely future alternative to the dominant forms of American society and culture which drive globalization, has ruled out Japan, Western Europe, and Eastern Europe as sources of coherent opposition or challenge.[37] Manthia Diawara has lamented the difficulty experienced by African nations and cities in developing a sustained, coherent, and viable "regional imaginary" of its own both because of the legacy of European imperialism and newer problems associated with globalization.[38] Leslie Sklair has proposed that, in the absence of any comprehensive or widespread and coherent alternative to American urbanism and American cinema, "effective opposition to capitalist practices" must manifest itself locally and around specific issues if at all despite the undeniable reality that "capitalism is increasingly organized on a global basis."[39] Manuel Castells has proposed that – despite the absence of any comprehensive, mass movement for substantial social change – resistance to the homogenizing tendencies of global capitalism is possible but only in a limited way, by atomized groups at a grass-roots level with largely defensive agendas or, possibly and more hopefully, through the development of localized networks of individuals, agencies, and communities brought together by the liberatory and democratizing potential of information technology and the internet.[40]

Sameness and Difference

The picture of globalization which recurs insistently in this book, then, consists of an opposition between homogenization and blandness, on the one hand, and pluralism and richness, on the other. While it is certainly important to point to and praise difference and heterogeneity where they appear – especially in resistance to the globalizing homogenizing tendencies of "high concept" Hollywood cinema or Western consumer capitalism – there is often a tendency to confuse "unevenness" with "heterogeneity" or "difference" with "resistance" (perhaps arising out of some felt need, particularly understandable since the 1980s, to believe resistance possible). But there is nothing necessarily radical about unevenness. One has the feeling that those areas in the global economy which are unevenly developed are probably those areas where global capitalism hasn't quite managed to settle in yet or which it has already decided to bypass altogether. Difference is not resistance. Global capitalism will allow heterogeneity, or even foster it, if to do so serves the interests of the free market and wealth generation, but heterogeneity is not an aim of global capitalism.

Although one is reluctant to speak of global capitalism in intentionalist terms as if it were a clear and identifiable thing with a defined plan for the world, one suspects that ultimately it prefers homogeneity because it is easier to manage and more efficient but that it will tolerate difference to the extent to which difference is necessary for the generation of profit – a project which is, after all, the one identifiable and certain characteristic of global capitalism. One thus comes to see global capitalism as a process of constant negotiation between homogeneity and difference, played out locally and globally, which makes itself especially manifest in the changing physical and cultural

geography of cities. Thus, for Manuel Castells, the persistence of local difference is often a function of globalization, one half of a dual process which
simultaneously involves "the globalization of power flows and the tribalization
of local communities," while for Jameson, globalization *both* facilitates difference (cultural diversity) *and* ensures homogenization (the universality of the
free market).[41]

Here, finally, we can find another way in which Film Studies and Sociology might usefully communicate. For in the key concept of "genre" in cinema (a genre being a particular "type" of film such as the Western, the
romantic comedy, the melodrama, or the war film) we find an analogy to this
tension between sameness and difference which may help toward the understanding of global capitalism as a process of constant conflict and negotiation: that is, in those theories of genre which explain it as a process of
negotiation, within the context of industrial film production (particularly in
Hollywood from the 1930s to the 1960s), between the competing interests of
film studios as financiers, producers, and primary investors, on the one hand,
in a rationalized and efficient system of production based upon a limited and
homogenous range of product lines and, on the other hand, the needs of film
audiences as consumers for a constant and regular supply of individuated
and varied entertainment product (individual films such as, let's say, *Stage-
coach, Bringing Up Baby, Written on the Wind*, or *The Guns of Navarone*).

This, of course, is a structural understanding of the political-economic
meaning of genre in cinema, just as the construction of this book in terms of
tension and conflict in globalization between sameness and difference suggests a structural understanding of that larger process. But here, perhaps, we
can strike an appropriate balance between *realism* – the recognition of homogeneity, of the apparent stability of the structures of global capitalism (for
now), of the current relatively unchallenged dominance of Hollywood cinema – and *aspiration* – the recognition of the persistence and potential of
difference, the historical inevitability of challenges (hopefully sooner rather
than later) to global capitalism and future destabilization of the ascendancy
of Hollywood cinema.

Whatever happens, this book has been developed in the certainty that the
processes of globalization, nationalism, identity, inequality, social, economic
and cultural power, domination, and resistance raised throughout it will play
themselves out in particularly dramatic and illuminating ways in the relationship between cinema and urban societies.

Notes

1   Michel Foucault, "The Eye of Power," preface to Jeremy Bentham, *La Panoptique*
    (1977), reprinted in Michel Foucault, *Power/Knowledge: Selected Interviews and Other*

   Writings, 1972–1977, ed. C. Gordon (New York: Pantheon, 1980), p. 149.

2 For a fascinating case study of the social production of the contemporary city, and the crucial role of cinema and popular culture therein, see M. Gottdiener, Claudia C. Collins, and David R. Dickens, *Las Vegas: The Social Production of an All-American City* (Oxford: Blackwell, 1999).

3 A number of important studies of the relationship between cinema and the city have appeared in recent years including, from an architectural perspective, François Penz et al. (eds.), *Cinema and Architecture* (London: BFI, 1997); from the perspective of film aesthetics, David Clarke (ed.), *The Cinematic City* (London: Routledge, 1997); and from a broad cultural studies perspective, James Donald, *Imagining the Modern City* (London: Athlone, 1999).

4 Andrew Tudor, "Sociology and Film," in John Hill and Pamela Church Gibson (eds.), *Film Studies: Critical Approaches* (Oxford: Oxford University Press, 2000), pp. 188–92.

5 Indeed, as theorists such as Richard Maltby and Thomas Schatz have explained, the traditional concern of Film Studies with film as text has become increasingly problematic since the 1980s – particularly where Hollywood cinema is concerned – because Hollywood has become relatively open and fluid in formal, thematic, and industrial terms since the 1960s (during what is known as post-classical cinema), and because many contemporary Hollywood films arguably exist less as cinematic texts than as attenuated and complex commodities across the wider consumer cultural and global economic system as a whole, involving television, video, multimedia or online presentation, popular music, fashion, advertising, and merchandising. See Maltby, "Theses on the Philosophy of Hollywood History," in Steve Neale and Murray Smith (eds.), *Contemporary Hollywood Cinema*; p. 2; and Thomas Schatz, "The New Hollywood," in *Film Theory Goes to the Movies* (London: Routledge, 1993).

6 On the history of the close relationship between Film Studies and film as text, and the strengths and limitations thereof, see also Graeme Turner, "Cultural Studies and Film," in Hill and Church Gibson (eds.), *Film Studies*, pp. 193–9. Also of relevance is Don Mitchell, *Cultural Geography: A Critical Introduction* (Oxford: Blackwell, 2000), pp. 43–9.

7 Of course, it should be said that significant work has been carried out in Film Studies in relation to the economics and socioeconomics of cinema as an industry which can contribute to a social understanding of cinema: see, for example, on Hollywood cinema, Janet Wasko's *Movies and Money: Financing the American Film Industry* (Norwood, NJ: Ablex Publishing Corp., 1982), and *Hollywood in the Information Age: Behind the Silver Screen* (Cambridge: Polity Press, 1988); and Douglas Gomery, *Shared Pleasures: A History of Movie Presentation in the United States* (London: BFI, 1992). On European cinema, see Pierre Sorlin's *European Cinemas, European Societies 1939–1990* (London: Routledge, 1990); and Geoffrey Nowell-Smith and Steven Ricci's *Hollywood and Europe: Economics, Culture, National Identity, 1945–95* (London: BFI, 1998). As Andrew Tudor notes, books arising out of genuine engagement between Sociology and Film Studies have been few and far between: Tudor cites, for example, George Huaco, *The Sociology of Film Art* (New York: Basic Books, 1965); Ian Jarvie, *Towards a Sociology of the Cinema: A Comparative Essay on the Structure and Functioning of a Major Entertainment Industry*

(London: Routledge & Kegan Paul, 1970); Tudor, *Image and Influence: Studies in the Sociology of Film* (London: Allen & Unwin, 1974); and Norman Denzin, *Images of Postmodern Society: Social Theory and Contemporary Cinema* (London: Sage, 1991). See Tudor, "Sociology and Film," p. 191. On the impact of cinema on modern urban society in the early twentieth century, one might add to this list Leo Charney and Vanessa R. Schwartz (eds.), *Cinema and the Invention of Modern Life* (Berkeley and Los Angeles: University of California Press, 1995).

8 See Fredric Jameson, *The Political Unconscious: Narrative as a Socially Symbolic Act* (London: Routledge, 1989), pp. 17–102; Louis Althusser et al., *Reading Capital*, trans. Ben Brewster (London: Verso, 1979 (1970)), pp. 91–118, 158–64; Althusser, *For Marx*, trans. Ben Brewster (London: Verso, 1990); Althusser, "Ideology and Ideological State Apparatuses," in *Lenin and Philosophy and Other Essays* (London: New Left Books, 1971), pp. 123–73.

9 Raymond Williams, *Marxism and Literature* (Oxford: Oxford University Press, 1990), p. 140.

10 Ibid., pp. 11–20.

11 Henri Lefebvre, *The Production of Space*, trans. Donald Nicholson-Smith (Oxford: Blackwell, 1991; orig. Paris: Editions Anthropos, 1974); Michel Foucault, *Discipline and Punish* (London: Allen Lane, 1977); Ernest Mandel, *Late Capitalism*, trans. Joris De Bres (London: Verso, 1978; orig. London: New Left Books, 1975); Marshall Berman, *All That Is Solid Melts Into Air* (London: Verso, 1983); Fredric Jameson, *Postmodernism, or, the Cultural Logic of Late Capitalism* (London: Verso, 1991); Edward W. Soja, *Postmodern Geographies: The Reassertion of Space in Critical Social Theory* (London and New York: Verso, 1989); Mike Davis, *City of Quartz: Excavating the Future in Los Angeles* (London: Vintage, 1992 (1990)).

12 Soja, *Postmodern Geographies*, p. 6.

13 Fredric Jameson, *The Geopolitical Aesthetic: Cinema and Space in the World System* (Bloomington and London: Indiana University Press and BFI, 1995 (1992)).

14 Important in this formulation has been Saskia Sassen's argument that the prominence of the city in the current global system problematizes traditional notions of "centrality and marginality" according to national or regional geographies, and according to the opposition First World–Third World. Sassen argues that "a new geography of centrality and marginality" is now in place, based upon centrality/marginality between cities and centrality/marginality within cities. See Sassen, *Cities in a World Economy* (Thousand Oaks, CA: Pine Forge Press, 1994), pp. 119–24.

15 See ibid., pp. 1–8; and Mike Savage and Alan Warde, "Cities and Uneven Economic Development," in *Urban Sociology, Capitalism and Modernity* (London and New York: Macmillan, 1993), pp. 39–40.

16 For an excellent examination of the political economy of Hollywood cinema and resistance to it by non-industrial cinemas, see David James, *Allegories of Cinema: American Film in the Sixties* (Princeton: Princeton University Press, 1989), pp. 3–28.

17 For an excellent introduction to the rise of the city, and to many of the key texts in Urban Sociology, see Richard T. LeGates and Frederic Stout (eds.), *The City Reader* (London and New York: Routledge, 1996), and Malcolm Miles, Tim Hall, and Iain Borden, *The City Cultures Reader* (London: Routledge, 2000).

18 Sassen, *Cities in a World Economy*, pp. 50–1.
19 See Allen J. Scott and Edward J. Soja, *The City: Los Angeles and Urban Theory at the End of the Twentieth Century* (Berkeley and Los Angeles: University of California Press, 1996), p. 12. See also Davis, *City of Quartz*; Roger Keil, *Los Angeles: Globalization, Urbanization and Social Struggles* (New York: John Wiley & Sons, 1998); Norman Klein, *The History of Forgetting: Los Angeles and the Erasure of Memory* (London and New York: Verso, 1997); Soja, *Postmodern Geographies*, Chapter 8, "It All Comes Together In Los Angeles" and Chapter 9, "Taking Los Angeles Apart."
20 See, for example, Julianne Burton (ed.), *Cinema and Social Change in Latin America* (Austin: University of Texas Press, 1986).
21 See Burton Pike, *The Image of the City in Modern Literature* (Princeton: Princeton University Press, 1981).
22 Manuel Castells and Peter Hall, "Technopoles: Mines and Foundries of the Informational Economy," in *Technopoles of the World: The Making of Twenty-First Century Industrial Complexes* (London: Routledge, 1994), excerpted in LeGates and Stout (eds.), *The City Reader*, p. 481.
23 As Miles, Hall, and Borden warn, in *The City Cultures Reader*, a balance must be achieved between the opposed tendency to exaggerate the future of the postmodern, post-industrial or electronic city, on the one hand, and the realities of massive global uneven development, on the other. See *The City Cultures Reader*, p. 4.
24 See David Chaney, *The Cultural Turn: Scene-Setting Essays on Contemporary Cultural History* (London and New York: Routledge, 1994), p. 27.
25 See Daniel Bell, *The Coming of a Post-Industrial Society* (New York: Basic Books, 1974); and *The End of Ideology* (New York, Free Press, 1962); Marshall McLuhan, *Understanding Media* (New York: McGraw-Hill, 1964); Jean Baudrillard, *Toward a Political Economy of the Sign* (St. Louis, MO.: Telos Press, 1981 (1972)); *The Mirror of Production* (St. Louis, MO: Telos Press, 1975); and *America* (London and New York: Verso, 1988).
26 On the emergence of global postmodernism in the early-1970s, see Harvey, *The Condition of Postmodernity* (Oxford: Blackwell, 1989), p. 40.
27 Nicos Poulantzas, *Political Power and Social Classes*, trans. Timothy O'Hagan (London: New Left Books, 1973), pp. 13–16; Williams, *Marxism and Literature*, pp. 115–23.
28 Williams, *Marxism and Literature*, p. 118.
29 Harvey, *The Condition of Postmodernity*, p. 84.
30 See, in addition to Wasko, *Movies and Money* and *Hollywood in the Information Age*, Tino Balio, *The American Film Industry* (Madison, WI: University of Wisconsin Press, 1985); Colin Hoskins, Stuart McFadyen, and Adam Finn, *Global Television and Film* (Oxford: Oxford University Press, 1997); and Jean-Pierre Jeancolas, "From the Blum-Byrnes Agreement to the GATT Affair," in Nowell-Smith and Ricci (eds.), *Hollywood and Europe*, pp. 47–60.
31 Fredric Jameson, "Notes on Globalization as a Philosophical Issue," in Fredric Jameson and Masao Miyashi (eds.), *Cultures of Globalization* (Durham, NC: Duke University Press, 1998), p. 63. With reference to contemporary Hollywood and consumerism, the reader is particularly referred to Justin Wyatt, *High Concept: Movies and Marketing in Hollywood* (Austin, TX: University of Texas Press, 1994).

Wyatt (p. 20) defines the "high concept" film, which he argues has been the dominant type in Hollywood over the past twenty years, as "a product differentiated through the emphasis on style in production and through the integration of the film with its marketing."

32   The most comprehensive study of the relationship of dominance and resistance between US (or Western) cinema and Third World filmmaking is undoubtedly Ella Shohat and Robert Stam, *Unthinking Eurocentrism: Multiculturalism and the Media* (London and New York: Routledge, 1994).

33   See Castells, "The Reconstruction of Social Meaning in the Space of Flows," in *The Informational City: Information Technology, Economic Restructuring and the Urban-Regional Process* (Oxford: Blackwell, 1989), pp. 348–53. See also Castells, *The Network Society* (Oxford: Blackwell, 1996).

34   On deterritorialization, see Mitchell, *Cultural Geography*, pp. 273–4; on the any-space-whatever, see Gilles Deleuze, *Cinema 2: The Time-Image*, trans. Hugh Tomlinson and Robert Galeta (Minneapolis: University of Minnesota Press, 1989), p. 272.

35   Miles, Hall, and Borden, *The City Cultures Reader* p. 4; Peter Marcuse and Ronald van Kempen, *Globalizing Cities: A New Spatial Order* (Oxford: Blackwell, 2000), p. 19; Alejandro Portes, Manuel Castells, and L. Benton (eds.), *The Informal Economy: Studies in Advanced and Less Developed Countries* (Baltimore: Johns Hopkins University Press, 1989).

36   On the nation-state in the present world system, see Mitchell, *Cultural Geography*, pp. 262–73. Of course, many commentators argue that globalization does not have to mean the end of the nation-state but may simply mean a new phase of challenge to and constant transgression of it. In this case, at the very least, the extent to which globalization "disrespects" and transgresses national boundaries and identities is keenly evident and popularly experienced in cinema, particularly fuelled by the hybridizing influences of international co-production as a standard procedure in (especially European) cinema and of offshore production (the production of Hollywood films outside the US) as a common practice in Hollywood cinema.

37   Jameson, "Notes on Globalization," p. 67.

38   Manthia Diawara, "Toward a Regional Imaginary in Africa," in Jameson and Miyashi (eds.), *Cultures of Globalization*, pp. 103–24.

39   Leslie Sklair, "Social Movements and Global Capitalism", in Jameson and Miyashi (eds.), *Cultures of Globalization*, p. 291.

40   Castells, *The Informational City*, p. 353. It must be admitted, however, that the hopes for democratic, even anti-systemic liberation through information technology held by Castells and others from the late 1980s to the late 1990s now seem somewhat dashed against the rocks of both the ascendancy of e-business on-line and the recent merger of AOL and Time-Warner, one of the largest corporate mergers in history, sealing the "incorporation" of the internet.

41   Castells, *The Informational City*, p. 350.

2

Film and Urban Societies in a Global Context

Tony Fitzmaurice

Emphasizing film as a fundamentally spatial rather than as a textual medium, one aim of this interdisciplinary volume in the Studies in Urban and Social Change series is to examine the many ways in which various international cinemas, in their exploration of the fabric of contemporary urban spaces, articulate the dynamics of contemporary power. In terms of case studies, the range is from prototypical postmodern cities (Los Angeles as the exemplary but not the only instance) to the colonial and the postcolonial (including examples of the postcolonial within the First World). Specific attention is devoted to the United States (Los Angeles, New York, Philadelphia, Houston, and Tampa), Canada (Montréal), Europe (Milan, Paris, London, and Dublin), Australia (Sydney), South Africa (Johannesburg/ Port Elizabeth), Nigeria (Lagos), the Philippines (Manila), and Vietnam (Saigon).

Both individually and collectively, and utilizing a range of methodologies, the chapters examine three forms of power (economic, political, and cultural) as these are mediated (or reinforced, or challenged) through the cinema, and as they impact on the social and the spatial in traditional, modern, and emergent urban landscapes in terms of a renegotiation of concepts of place, location, home, region, territory, nation, and, most particularly, city and suburb. The chapters also investigate the possibility or viability of cinema as a counter-discourse, with the potential to articulate resistance to power.

It is, of course, a truism to point out that film is *the* urban cultural form *par excellence* – that film is a highly capitalized and labor-intensive product, whose origins (in Lyon in 1895) and destination (the now ubiquitous multiplex) are tied in with the fortunes of the twentieth-century city. Correspondingly, the city is constructed as much by images and representations as by the built environment, demographic shifts, land speculation, and patterns of capital flight and investment. It is also the case that, more than ever before, cinema, world cinema, has become synonymous with Hollywood – a suburb of Los Angeles. Los Angeles itself is one of the great world cities, one of the major command centers of capital, regarded by Edward Soja as "a *prototopos*, a paradigmatic place . . . the world's largest 'technopolis' . . . the 'capital of capital' in the Pacific Rim."[1]

In *Postmodern Cartographies*, Brian Jarvis describes how Los Angeles and Southern California supposedly experienced a "bloodless revolution in socio-spatial relations" after World War Two, which, so the argument ran, resulted in "the eclipse of class" and what Daniel Bell called an "end to ideology."[2] In effect, what actually did happen was "the redeployment of manufacturing activities to developing host countries replete with enticing free trade zones and a non-unionized labor supply."[3] One result of the rise of the sunbelt economy was that Los Angeles became what Soja calls the site of "the largest homeless population in the United States."[4]

If "class" and the historical dialectic have all but disappeared from socio-cultural discourse in favor of a synchronic description conceptualized in terms of mapping and of spatial networks, it is well to heed Fredric Jameson's reminder that " 'cognitive mapping' was in reality nothing but a code word for 'class consciousness'," and that what he calls "Late Capitalism" (or third-stage, post-imperial, multinational capitalism), after Ernest Mandel, now penetrates every aspect of the life-world.[5] The total commodification of all culture is a process which went into high gear with the rise of Hollywood, which Adorno and Horkheimer famously dubbed the "Culture Industry as Mass Deception."[6] But class as a category has not been totally eclipsed, and Mike Davis, in his book *City of Quartz*, has shown how the development of a globalizing mall culture has been at the cost of racial and class segregation in "Fortress LA."[7]

The first part of this book, focusing on Los Angeles, opens with a chapter in which Davis illustrates how film – in this case, popular Hollywood genre cinema – as a spatial-imagistic medium, cannot but register class apartheid in Los Angeles even when it is not on its official agenda to do so. The fate of Bunker Hill (the privatization of public space by the free-market economy) as represented in a range of films from the 1940s to the 1980s emblematizes the colonization by capital of public and civic space, and with that the erosion – indeed, the forced relocation – of longstanding communities and the further disenfranchizing of the already disadvantaged. According to Davis, *They Live* (1988) is a film which speaks for those lost voices, but it is nevertheless a weak, because belated, form of cultural resistance. The Bonaventure Hotel, one of the most famous architectural icons of postmodern consumerism, now overlooks Bunker Hill, transforming downtown into the monumental visual emblem of finance capital.

In terms of the relationship between film and planning, John Walton's chapter on *Chinatown* (1974) and its role in the historical development of Los Angeles offers a more positive account of the impact of one film's representation of the city and surrounding counties on recent regional environmental politics. Though the jury may always be out on the question of the power of film to generate measurable effects of any or whatever kind in the real world, *Chinatown* is a case of one film's successful intervention in social and political processes.

Can the superstructure act upon the base? As a first part of a proposed trilogy (on LA's Department of Water and Power) relating the history of the physical development of the LA urban region since the turn of the last century, *Chinatown* is a strong example of a proven connection between a mainstream film and direct social effects, not only in terms of its impact when it was first released, but also in terms of the pressure it continues to exert over City Hall.

As always, however, the converse is also true, as Josh Stenger's chapter on the Hollywood Redevelopment Project shows. Whereas *Chinatown* may have appropriated and offered up a version of LA's history in the name of more than mere entertainment, LA is now appropriating images from Hollywood's past in the name of urban renewal, and in the process reshaping the physical fabric of the city itself into the simulation of a simulation. In this reversal of the co-optation of history by film, LA is becoming a postmodern simulation of itself or, at least, of Hollywood's image of it. In this instance of image preceding essence we can see the concrete role of the Hollywood studios' symbolic but nonetheless fully negotiable cultural currency in the reformation of LA's downtown, as real-estate developers and City Hall combine to appropriate and exploit the cultural iconography and mythic spaces of LA for their own ends. If *Chinatown* is a film which articulates, and around which has been mobilized, resistance to institutional power politics and financial machinations within one of capital's most powerful centers, LA, in a curious dialectical move, is now doubling back on its own history in an act of highly profitable self-cannibalization in order to re-project and re-image itself as a tourist destination: LA made over as a Hollywood theme park feeding on its own culture industry.

It is inevitable, of course, that cinema – in this case, Hollywood cinema – as institution and industry, and as an image-bank of representations, would impact more or less directly upon the material environment which generated it in the first place, upon LA itself as one of the capitals of the new world order in which consumption feeds production. If cinema has played an un-questionable part in the physical development of LA, film production, distribution, and exhibition have played their part in the formation of other cities and civic identities elsewhere.

The second part of the book looks closely at how present trends and new developments in the coordinated (if not fully integrated) system of film production, distribution, and exhibition are closely tied to demographic changes and to the economic and structural fabrics of particular cities – Houston, Philadelphia, Milan, New York, Tampa, Berlin, and others.

James Hay offers a historical narrative which shows how investment capital actually depends on cultural capital in order to valorize its expansionist drive: how the spectacularization of postwar Houston on the national stage was achieved by its association with the Western – and with Hollywood excess (not to say kitsch), attracting colossal investment by flaunting its conspicuous consumption in order to finance one of the most massive real-estate developments ever. The result was a transformation of Houston into a new national media center, which in turn created a new super-suburban geography of shopping malls and drive-ins: a then-new but now-familiar kind of social/cinematic space.

Taking Philadelphia as a case in point, Paul Swann describes how one rustbelt city has coped with the fall in employment due to its decline as a manufacturing base by accommodating itself to the post-industrial image culture. Exploiting cinema's double ontology, as both image and industry, Philadelphia has reversed its economic decline by marketing itself as a film location, offering visiting film crews production facilities and services which revitalize the local economy in the course of manufacturing a product which in turn displays Philadelphia as a place and a location worth visiting.

Geoffrey Nowell-Smith explores what might be termed the politics of location from a different perspective. Historically in Film Studies, the most powerful engagement with the relationship between cinema and the city has been staged on the level of representation. Italian neorealism, which privileged location shooting using available light on "found" sets, was about the specificity of time and place, about pro-filmic reality rather than a highly manufactured *mise-en-scène*, and the subsequent work of modernists like Antonioni, rooted in postwar realism, was animated by what Fredric Jameson describes as a conviction

> that the discovery or invention of a radically new form was at one with the discovery or invention of radically new social relations and ways of living in the world. It is those possibilities – filmic, formal, political, and social – that have disappeared as some more definite hegemony of the United States has seemed to emerge.[8]

What Jameson and Nowell-Smith both deplore is a growing homogenization of the image, the disappearance from representation of the spatial specificity of real cities and places and their replacement by, in Gilles Deleuze's formulation, the "any-space-whatevers" of the generic city.[9] The accelerating Hollywoodization of world cinema is a function of the logic of capital which dictates that, as Time-Warner, Inc. (now AOL-Time Warner), the world's largest media conglomerate, declared in its 1989 annual report, "no serious competitor can hope for any long-term success unless, building on a secure home base, it achieved a major presence in all of the world's important markets."[10]

The tendency of recent Hollywood cinema to abandon location shooting in favor of incorporating more computer-generated imagery (CGI) denies the arbitrariness and unpredictability – the specificity – of place (the urban location) by submitting every potentially chance element to the predestination of advance technological control. The increasing world domination by an expensive, highly-produced and technologically-sophisticated American cinema raises questions about the future viability of national cinemas. If one of the tasks of a national cinema is (or used to be) to reveal local social realities and to explore cultural tensions, then the increasing standardization of cinema internationally registers a crisis which confronts not only world cinema, but the world outside the cinema. The homogenization or universalization of cinema corresponds to, or is only a highly visible part of, the transnationalization of culture globally, of what Masao Miyoshi has called "universal consumerism . . . the total economicization of culture."[11]

Capitulation and resistance to that consumerism are the subjects of Mark Neumann's and Janna Jones's chapters. IMAX-3D is a production and exhibition format which is so expensive as to be viable only in large metropolitan centers. Neumann describes a visit to New York's Sony IMAX theater to watch a film, *Across the Sea of Time* (1996), one of whose purposes is to foreground the spectacular nature of the presentation itself: the viewer (wearing special headgear) is totally immersed in an audiovisual experience which eschews extended narrative or density of character and event in favor of spectacular display, and whose inflated format allegorizes its relationship to the scale of its production and technological capital.

At the other end of the exhibition spectrum, Jones's chapter on the cultural demographics of the patrons of a relatively small, independent arthouse theater in Tampa describes one mode of resistance to the cinema of the spectacle. This is based on a dual distinction. The Tampa theater patrons prefer the difficulty and complexity of art cinema (loosely defined as any recognizably non-mainstream film valorized for its difference from a Hollywood or quasi-Hollywood product) to the films programmed in the multiplexes of Tampa's suburban malls. They also prefer the experience of the theater itself, precisely because it is a historical building located downtown and not in the suburbs. In combination, the Tampa theater patrons create an identity for themselves when they make a distinction between the bland and packaged "any-space-whatever" of the mainstream cinema as consumed in the mall, and the intimacy and unpredictability of the art cinema and downtown. In making these choices they are resisting precisely those globalizing tendencies in social-cinematic space in 1990s Tampa, whose emergence James Hay traced in 1950s Houston.

One of the platforms for the international marketing of the kind of film favored by the Tampa theater patron is the film festival, whose principal function is usually understood as that of publicizing and launching less obviously "commercial" projects into the international distribution and exhibition system (itself now more and more in the hands of the Hollywood conglomerates).[12] Julian Stringer's chapter identifies a number of other priorities, and ultimately sees the film festival as less about promoting the heterogeneity of world cinema (by celebrating its difference from the uniform template of the hegemonic mainstream) than as about promoting the festival venue itself. Festivals are associated not with their host countries but with the cities in which they take place. The business of the festival is primarily that of spectacularizing those cities, identifying them as prestigious cultural centers, promoting them as glamorous tourist destinations, flagging them as potential sites for investment and development, and only secondarily of encouraging local or national film production.

In other words, the international film festival is increasingly less about the films themselves, or even film culture as such, than about the promotion of the cities in which the films are showcased. The paradox here is that the future development of these cities – many of them in what is still known as the Third World – is tied to their visible success in attracting attention to themselves as platforms for exactly that kind of cinema which is itself threatened by the same conditions of globalization in which the festival operates and to which it responds. In both the First World (as in the case of Philadelphia as described by Paul Swann) and in the developing world the fortunes of the city are meshed with and dependent upon those of the cinema: the international film festival is a conspicuous example of the active and integral role which film plays in the contemporary global economy.

The third part of the book contains chapters which explore the concrete relationships between cinema(s) and cities and regional and cultural identities in a number of colonial and post- or neo-colonial contexts. Almost all of the films discussed in this part are in one way or another antagonistic to the effects of the export to their countries of, in one guise or another, Western consumerism, the "expressive form" or ideology of one statistically small and mainly Euro-American population sector – what Fred Pfeil calls "the baby-boom PMC" (professional-managerial class) – which has been translated in large part through filmed entertainment and extended thereby to the rest of the world.[13]

Resistance to the hegemonic monoculture promoted by mainstream Western and especially Hollywood cinema and imposed economically, legally, and politically by transnational corporations (TNCs), the World Trade Organization (WTO), the International Monetary Fund (IMF) and the World Bank is a task of near-Sisyphean proportions. European and American interests have, from World War One onward, controlled the structures of distribution and exhibition throughout the colonial world, almost exclusively so in Africa, and most of these arrangements have persisted long beyond the moment of formal independence. As Roy Armes has pointed out, just two French companies enjoy a monopolistic hold over the market in Francophone West Africa, and the smaller regional distribution companies that serve the sub-Saharan market "are no more than outposts of the multinational interests that control the flow of [the same] films throughout the world."[14] Janet Wasko has pointed out that (as of 1994) "the historical strengths of the US entertainment industry still persist. Through worldwide film distribution cartels – United International, Warner and Columbia – the Hollywood-based companies not only market their own products but other countries' products as well."[15]

One result of this cartel power is that "80 per cent of European films never leave their own country."[16] The situation outside Europe is worse, where the financial and technological gap is even wider, making film production all the more difficult. Thus the question of parallel and uneven development is the main thread linking the chapters in this part of the book.

J. Paul Narkunas analyses how the recent history and political economy of Vietnam, with specific reference to the activities there of the IMF and TNCs, are articulated and critiqued by the film *Cyclo* (1995), whose art-house form allegorizes the erosion of national/state power which results from the recolonization of post-occupation space by transnational corporatism. *Cyclo*'s representational strategies attempt to visualize the relationship between the official and shadow economies and between what Manuel Castells has identified as "the space of places" and "the space of flows."[17] Turning to the Philippines, Rolando Tolentino describes how two films, *Manila in the Claws of Neon* (1975) and *City after Dark* (1980), perform a similar allegorical function as the (also location-shot) *Cyclo*, through their representation of spaces resonant with references, for Filipino audiences, to the city's colonial and postcolonial history and to the effects on Manila of the Marcos regime's lust for Western-style modernity, at whatever the cost.

Resistance to globalization takes a different formal inflection in a low-budget, independent Australian film. Justine Lloyd's chapter discusses *The Castle* (1997) in terms of its production, setting, and wider political-economic context. Though based on actual events, the film's treatment of these is far from documentary-like. If, in Fredric Jameson's words, "form is immanently and intrinsically an ideology in its own right," then it is no less true but at the opposite end of the production spectrum from, for example, IMAX, that *The Castle*'s telematic form and sitcom format also allegorize its antagonistic relation to the forces of global capitalism against which its comedy is directed.[18] The film's "voice" as articulated through its chosen form is that of the new white Anglo-Australian subaltern, living in the suburban outreach, whose medium of choice is not film but television. This is resistance in a popular, if not populist and utopian, mode.

The African films discussed by Gary Baines and Obododimma Oha are totally different in form and conception from the kinds of films discussed above, as might be expected, given the very different conditions of their making and intended reception. *The Urgent Queue* (1958) is a documentary which was commissioned by the South African Government Information Service in order to show the "progressive" side of the apartheid system. Even though as a documentary (a genre which, unlike the fiction film, makes a special claim to truth) *The Urgent Queue* is not historically accurate, the film's official agenda was negated precisely because the camera – film as a photographic medium – could not but register the pro-filmic as well as the artifice. The reality of apartheid stayed in view: the propagandist intent was cancelled by the film's effect.

The Nigerian video films discussed by Oha are a kind of low-budget *samizdat* production, centered in Lagos, whose informal video distribution system secures their financial viability even amidst widespread poverty and social deprivation and against a backdrop of organized crime and military dictatorship. Belonging to the genre of the "exploitation film" which tends to sensationalize its subject matter, these films offer representations of urban street life as it is actually lived in Lagos and its hinterland, images which run counter to the rhetoric of modernization articulated in the more prestigious 35 mm cinema productions shown in theaters. As truly opportunist popular-culture productions, they register the layers of contradiction embedded in official government discourse.[19]

Bill Marshall and Kevin Rockett direct their attention to the relationship between film and cultural identity in Montréal and Dublin, two postcolonial cities in the First World. The films discussed earlier in this part of the book all originate in cities, countries, and regions rushing toward modernity, but Dublin and Montréal belong to regions which have either resisted or were bypassed by such development. In the Irish case, as Rockett explains, this resistance took the form of a draconian censorship, by successive governments from the 1920s to the 1970s, of British and American cinema and their representations of urban modernity. In the Québecois case, as Marshall demonstrates, Montréal's dislocation from the general development and modernization of North America in the twentieth century eventually contributed to the development in Québec/Montréal of a distinctive and vibrant film culture and film industry from the 1960s.[20] In both cases, a historical suspicion of cinema was a product of the cultivation of an isolationist national identity predicated on an anti-modern, Catholic conservatism, in some measure a reaction against the perceived cosmopolitan liberalism and expansionism of their former rulers and their metropolitan capitals, London and Paris.

The last part of the book turns to those two cities as two post-imperial colonial centers, the century of cinema coinciding with the end of Empire, although, as Subramani points out, "it needs to be emphasized that in parts of the Pacific, formal colonialism, by Americans and the French, still continues, and . . . colonialism continues through global capitalism."[21] Indeed, the headquarters and offices of many transnational corporations, including film industries, are located in London and Paris. Issues and debates centering around planning, welfare, architecture, housing, street crime, and suburbanization are addressed in the four chapters in this part, as these are articulated in four films which directly explore relationships between identity and (dis)location. London is explored in terms of the progression from social idealism and the rise of the Welfare State after World War Two and during the collapse of the British Empire, as expressed by British documentary, to the realities of social exclusion and alienation in the Thatcher era. Paris is examined in terms of the development from modernism in architecture and urban planning during the Gaullist 1950s to its apparent failure in the deprivation and brutalization of French working-class youth enduring *la malaise de banlieue* in present-day Paris and its suburbs.

Leo Enticknap's essay on the documentary-feature *The Way We Live* (1946) focuses on the cinematic and extra-cinematic contours of a postwar utopian moment, in which the commercial British film industry briefly committed itself to supporting the democratization of the government town-planning system – an exercise in civic responsibility which was not repeated, since the finished film displeased the Rank Organization (which financed it) because of its generic uncategorizability, which they believed would damage its commercial potential.

Mike Mason locates the 1993 film *Naked* within the tradition of British social realist cinema (in turn loosely linked to the Italian neorealism discussed by Geoffrey Nowell-Smith) which is notable for its preference for location shooting and its analysis of class. One of *Naked*'s most trenchant ironies emerges from its location shooting: the film clearly takes place in much the same unreconstructed urban wasteland as did its forebears thirty years earlier. This is a negative visual critique of the failure of the Thatcherite free-market "revolution" whose ideology underpins globalization today. Uneven development blights even the post-imperial center, where unrestrained capitalism has left significant sectors of the population behind, and created a new and deeply alienated underclass infected with apathy, cynicism, and *anomie*, in urban environments where the homeless and financial high-rises coexist in contiguous spaces.

The same trajectory – from utopian resistance to defeat – characterizes the two Parisian city films *Play Time* (1967) and *La haine* (1995). Laurent Marie describes *Play Time* as a modernist art film whose polemic can be best understood by considering it in relation to Situationist theories on urbanism and by reference to Guy Debord's *Société du spectacle* (published in the same year as the film's release), all of which are critical of Gaullist modernization and especially of its impact on public space. *Play Time* attempts to combat the "society of the spectacle" by means of the cinematic spectacle, as a kind of homeopathic remedy of the image to be achieved by subverting the rules of mainstream film.

La haine could be described as an anti-art film whose fast cutting and *bricolage* soundtrack connote the frustrations of its disaffected main characters. In terms of genre, *La haine* borrows its template from the African-American "'hood" film, but in transposing it from an American to a French setting, transforms it. As Adrian Fielder points out, the film also creates from its raw urban materials a *mise-en-scène* which generates what is in effect an allegorical (as well as a geographically authentic) cartography in that the relationship between the space of the city (center) and *banlieue* (margin) metaphorizes that between France and its ex-colonies, and, ultimately, between the global and the local, the regional or the national.

If it seems that what has been described here is a closed binary, it should be recalled that *La haine* proposes a third kind of space and an activity named after it. The film's characters enjoy their free time "zoning," discovering and playing, and finding themselves briefly empowered in free spaces away from official surveillance. Theirs is a cultural resistance – these characters are not motivated politically – but the film's cartography politicizes their situation for the viewer, who can clearly see that their particular drama is a metonym for a more global one.

The world market is not, of course, a cultural concept, and globalization – world capitalism – is driven by an economic logic, supported by political institutions with legal empowerment. Resistance to this dynamic at the level of culture (in this instance, cinema) may not count for world revolution, but nothing is foreclosed in advance. In December 1999 38,000 people did protest at the WTO convention in Seattle. Globalization may on occasion bring benefit as a modernizing force, and economic homogenization ("harmonization") might not result in a cultural McWorld. Resistance is still possible, on occasion, whether within the mainstream (*Chinatown, They Live*), or outside of it: in art house (*Play Time, Cyclo*), independent (*Naked, The Castle, La haine*), artisanal (exploitation video) or, with regard to films as yet unmade, through the choice (financial and practical but ultimately political) between location shooting and the constructed space of the studio or the non-space of CGI. Say not the struggle nought availeth.

Notes

1 Edward Soja, "It All Comes Together In Los Angeles," in *Postmodern Geographies: The Reassertion of Space in Critical Social Theory* (London and New York: Verso, 1989), pp. 191–2.
2 Brian Jarvis, *Postmodern Cartographies* (London: Pluto Press, 1998), p. 16.
3 Ibid., p. 20.
4 Soja, *Postmodern Geographies*, p. 193.
5 Fredric Jameson, "Marxism and Postmodernism," in *The Cultural Turn: Selected Writings on the Postmodern, 1983–1998* (London: Verso, 1998), p. 49.
6 Theodor Adorno and Max Horkheimer, "The Culture Industry: Enlightenment as Mass Deception," in *Dialectic of Enlightenment*, trans. John Cumming (London: Verso, 1979), pp. 120–67.
7 Mike Davis, "Fortress LA," in *City of Quartz: Excavating the Future in Los Angeles* (London: Pimlico, 1998), pp. 221–63.
8 Fredric Jameson, "Notes on Globalization as a Philosophical Issue," in Fredric Jameson and Masao Miyoshi (eds.) *Cultures of Globalization* (Durham, NC and London: Duke University Press, 1998), pp. 54–77.
9 Gilles Deleuze, *Cinema 2: The Time-Image* (London: Athlone Press, 1989), p. 272.
10 Quoted in Tino Balio, "The Globalization of Hollywood in the 1990s," in Steve Neale and Murray Smith (eds.) *Contemporary Hollywood Cinema* (London and New York: Routledge, 1998), p. 58.
11 Masao Miyoshi, "Globalization and the University," in Jameson and Miyoshi (eds.) *Cultures of Globalization*, pp. 247–70.
12 For information on international film distribution, see Colin Hoskins, Stuart McFadyen, and Adam Finn, *Global Television and Film* (Oxford: Oxford University Press, 1997), pp. 51–67.
13 Fred Pfeil, *Another Tale to Tell: Politics and Narrative in Postmodern Culture* (London and New York: Verso, 1990), pp. 97–125.
14 Roy Armes, *Third World Filmmaking and the West* (Berkeley, Los Angeles, and London: University of California Press, 1987), p. 45. For a history of the US film industry's global activities, see Thomas H. Guback, *The International Film Industry: Western Europe and America since 1945* (Bloomington: Indiana University Press, 1969). See also Manthia Diawara, *African Cinema: Politics and Culture* (Bloomington: Indiana University Press, 1992), especially chapter 7, "Film Distribution and Exhibition in Francophone Africa," pp. 104–15; and Toby Miller, "Hollywood and the World," in John Hill and Pamela Church Gibson (eds.) *The Oxford Guide to Film Studies* (Oxford: Oxford University Press, 1998), pp. 371–81.
15 Janet Wasko, *Hollywood in the Information Age* (Oxford: Polity Press, 1994), p. 226.
16 Ibid.
17 Manuel Castells, "The Reconstruction of Social Meaning in The Space of Flows," in *The Informational City* (1989), reprinted in Richard T. LeGates and Frederic Stout (eds.) *The City Reader* (London and New York: Routledge, 1996), pp. 493–98.
18 Fredric Jameson, *The Political Unconscious: Narrative as a Socially Symbolic Act*

(London: Methuen, 1981), p. 141.

19 See Diawara, *African Cinema*, pp. 120–5, for information on Nigerian film pro-
    duction.

20 Roy Armes argues that state policy, incentives and assistance to indigenous film
    production, in the Third World context, are an essential first prerequisite for the
    fostering of a national cinema. See Armes, *Third World Filmmaking and the West*, p.
    40.

21 Subramani, "The End of the Free State: On the Transnationalization of Cul-
    ture," in Jameson and Miyoshi (eds.) *Cultures of Globalization*, pp. 146–63.

Part 1

Postmodern Mediations of the City: Los Angeles

Part 1 focuses on Los Angeles as the exemplary post-metropolis, a city-region which dynamically combines elements of both First and Third Worlds, and the center of global cinematic and media production. The three chapters in this part examine the intimate relationship between Hollywood (both as industry and product as well as place) and LA in terms of their historical development, environmental politics, and planning, particularly focusing on the ways in which cinema has intervened in the physical development of Los Angeles as a built environment from the 1940s to the present day.

In "Bunker Hill: Hollywood's Dark Shadow," Mike Davis addresses the incestuous and parasitical relationship between the city of Los Angeles and the Hollywood film industry through an analysis of the historical development of the district of Bunker Hill and its representation in film since the 1940s. John Walton, in "Film Mystery as Urban History: The Case of *Chinatown*," examines the role played by the film *Chinatown* in influencing public debate and official policy regarding land zoning, public utilities (water), and environmental control in Southern California in the 1980s and 1990s. Josh Stenger's essay, "Return to Oz: The Hollywood Redevelopment Project, or Film History as Urban Renewal," focuses on the reciprocal relationship between cinema and Los Angeles, and the influence of their relationship upon the city's local politics, architecture, and larger built environment in the 1980s and 1990s, with particular reference to the Hollywood Redevelopment Project.

3

Bunker Hill: Hollywood's Dark Shadow

Mike Davis

In the beginning, of course, Los Angeles was (in Orson Welles's words) simply a "bright, guilty place" without a murderous shadow or mean street in sight. Hollywood found its own Dark Place belatedly and only through a fortuitous amalgam of older, migrant sensibilities. Once discovered by hardboiled writers and exiled Weimar *auteurs*, however, Bunker Hill began to exert an occult power of place.[1] Here, overlooking LA's monotonous, Midwestern flatness (Reyner Banham's "plains of Id"), was a hilltop slum whose decaying mansions and sinister rooming houses might have been envisioned by Edgar Allan Poe.[2] Its residents, "women with the faces of stale beer . . . men with pulled-down hats" (Chandler), suggested Macheath's minions in Brecht and Weill's *The Threepenny Opera*. The Hill was broodingly urban and mysterious – everything that Los Angeles, suburban and banal from birth, was precisely not. With such star qualities, it is not surprising that it so quickly lodged itself in our nocturnal imagination. Disdaining to be mere location, Bunker Hill was soon stealing the best lines in *film noir*. Here are some fan notes on a brilliant career.

Five Points

Some cinematic mappings of the metropolis – *Berlin, Symphony of a City* (1927), *I, the Camera* (1955), *Rome, Open City* (1945) – were truly avant-garde in that they anticipated or paralleled similar conceptions in literature and painting.

But studio film has generally preferred to meet the city on the familiar terms of literature (and, later, of commercial photography and advertising). Thus 1940s *film noir*, with its trademark "city of night," was indelibly derivative of classic templates laid down a century before by Dickens, Eugène Sue, Poe, and Baudelaire. Indeed, the antipodal contrast of the city's divided soul – high and low, sunshine and shadow – was a ploy with roots in *The Beggar's Opera* and even ultimately Dante. Christian eschatology made it all the easier to interpret documentary images of urban polarization as spatialized allegories. The urban Lower Depths quickly became the romantic equivalent of Niagara Falls or the Wreck of the Medusa in the competition to satisfy the Victorian public's peculiar need to be simultaneously horrified, edified, and titillated.

An American appetite for the underworld was most memorably stimulated by Dickens's famous expedition to New York's notorious Five Points in the heart of the "Bloody Ould Sixth Ward" in 1842, published in his *American Notes*.[3] Protected by "two heads of the police" (as was his custom in London), the great writer "plunged into" the maze of reeking alleyways, decaying Georgian houses ("debauchery has made the very houses prematurely old"), and fetid cellars that housed New York's poorest people: a cosmopolitan mixture of seafarers, Irish immigrants, German widows, freedmen, and escaped slaves: "What place is this, to which the squalid street conducts us? A kind of square of leprous houses some of which are attainable only by crazy wooden stairs without. What lies beyond this tottering flight of steps, that creak beneath our tread?"

The contemporary reader may have shuddered in suspense, but Dickens knew exactly where he was. The description was already in the can: "hideous tenements, which take their name from robbery and murder: all that is loathsome, drooping, and decayed is here." He had written the same thing about London's Five Dials and, indeed, makes clear that the Five Points is the generic Victorian slum – "the coarse and bloated faces at the doors have counterparts at home, and all the wide world over" – with a few New World idiosyncrasies like the cheap prints of George Washington on the squalid walls and the "cramped hutches full of sleeping Negroes." Dickens was hardly aiming at documentary realism. If anything, he was trying to take his readers somewhere already subliminally familiar to them, a secret city visited in dreams. This archetypal place – slum, casbah, Chinatown – is a museum archiving vices and miseries of potential fascination to the middle class. "Ascend these pitch-dark stairs, heedful of a false footing on the trembling boards," he invited his fellow voyeurs, "and grope your way with me into this wolfish den, where neither ray of light nor breath of air, appears to come . . . ."

With his official bodyguards glowering over residents, the great writer was free to probe, question, and intone judgments. (An English biographer once wrote that his nocturnal slumming "seems indistinguishable from his trips to the London Zoological Garden.") He interrogated a feverish, possibly dying man, stirred exhausted black women from their sleep, and visited an interracial saloon (or was it a bawdyhouse?) where the proprietor – "with a thick gold ring upon his little finger, and round his neck a gleaming golden watch-guard" – forced two "shy" mulatto girls to dance for their celebrated visitor. Dickens's adventure made the Five Points as infamous as Whitechapel, and spawned an imitative industry of risqué urban travelogues, of which E. Z. C. Judson's *Mysteries and Miseries of New York* ("a perfect daguerreotype from above Bleeker to the horrors of Five Points") and Mathew Hale Smith's *Sunshine and Shadow in New York* became bestsellers.[4] There was now a full-fledged New World franchise for gothic cities and midnight tourism.

Angel's Flight

The early film industry in New York, as in London, Paris, or Berlin, interacted with an urban landscape comprehensively reconnoitered by naturalist writers, modernist poets, muckraking journalists, secessionist painters, and first-generation street photographers. Districts like Greenwich Village, the Lower East Side, Fifth Avenue, and Hell's Kitchen had become famous metonyms for classic aspects of city life (bohemia, immigrant poverty, the swank classes, delinquency) and were instantly recognizable to millions of people who had never actually visited Gotham. The city was too familiar, in an imagined sense, for film to wander very far from literary geography. Movies accordingly entrenched and magnified the hegemonic clichés of O. Henry's generation of writers, including the pathos of the nocturnal slum. Although Five Points was long gone, the Hell's Kitchen waterfront remained potent Dickensian terrain, especially when seen through Josef von Sternberg's monocle in the famous *The Docks of New York* (1928).

Los Angeles, on the other hand, had no compelling image in American letters. When the film industry suburbanized itself in Hollywood, as several historians have pointed out, it acquired a locational freedom from powerful and unavoidable urban referents. While turning a lens on itself and constructing "Hollywood" (the spectacle and pilgrimage site, not the workaday suburb), the industry otherwise had no need to acknowledge the specificity of place. LA was all (stage) set, which is to say, it was u-topia: literally, *no*-place (or thus *any* place). Indeed by the early 1920s, the set had rapidly become the architectural *Zeitgeist* of the region, and movies were, in a very real sense, redesigning the city in their own image. Historicized stucco-façade bungalows – for example, Zorro next door to Robin Hood in adjoining "Spanish Colonial" and "English Tudor" boxes – were the house rage of the 1920s, and the great Griffith and de Mille bible epics produced a small epidemic of "Egyptian revival" apartment houses and masonic temples. A decade later, Westerns gave birth to dude-ranch subdivisions (Rancho Palos Verdes, for example) and an infinity of John Ford-inspired "ranch-style" tracts.

Thanks to Hitler and the Depression, however, the studios were soon crowded with exiled Berliners and New Yorkers whose creative and affective universe was *Metropolis*, not the Frontier. A national obsession with gangsters and a new "hardboiled" style in popular fiction abetted Hollywood's return to gritty urban locales and classic slums, although this meant Manhattan or, sometimes, San Francisco and its mysterious Chinatown. It was not until the 1940s that breathless location scouts brought word to the writers' huts that the Land of Sunshine itself harbored a dark place of quasi-Weimarian grandeur. With its aging Victorian cliff-dwellings connected by a crazy quilt of stairways, narrow alleys, and two picturesque funicular railroads ("Angel's Flight" and "Court Flight"), Bunker Hill eventually bedazzled the exiles like an Expressionist mirage. If this neglected understudy for the Evil City seemingly called out for a film career, its big break – Robert Siodmak's *Criss Cross* (1949) – came only after it was already a literary icon.

Raymond Chandler, of course, created the *noir* street map of Los Angeles which Hollywood subsequently took as its guide. He choreographed the class conflict of locales – Pasadena mansions, Bunker Hill tenements, Central Avenue bars, and Malibu beach homes – that made Los Angeles recognizably a city after its long apprenticeship as a back lot. His stroke of genius was the *frisson* created by Marlowe's ceaseless commutes between equally sinister extremes of wealth and immiseration. Yet Chandler worked from prefabricated parts as well as his own perception, and the Bunker Hill ("lost town, shabby town, crook town") which he so famously enshrined in *The High Window* (1943) had already been "invented" by the writer John Fante and the painter Millard Sheets.

Fante was one of the tough-realist "regional" writers, like Louis Adamic and James M. Cain, whom H. L. Mencken cultivated in the pages of *American Mercury* in the late 1920s and early 1930s. In the early Depression, he worked as a busboy in a downtown restaurant and lived in a cheap hotel room in Bunker Hill, where he pounded out the stories that would become his 1939 novel, *Ask the Dust*. It was the first declension of Bunker Hill's human melodrama. Twenty-year-old Arturo Bandini – like Fante, a first-generation Italian-American and desperately aspiring screenwriter – falls into a doomed love triangle with Camilla Lopez, a pretty Chicana waitress, and Sammy, the consumptive who is his rival for Camilla's affection. In other short stories, Fante wrote with both poignancy and condescension about the melancholy Filipino bachelors – also busboys and waiters – who were a major ingredient in Bunker Hill's cosmopolitan ethnic mix.

The Bunker Hill that Fante evoked for Mencken's readers was Los Angeles's most crowded and urban neighborhood. According to the 1940 Census, its population increased almost twenty percent during the Depression as it provided the cheapest housing for downtown's casual workforce as well as for pensioners, disabled war veterans, Mexican and Filipino immigrants, and men whose identities were best kept in shadow. Its nearly two thousand dwellings ranged from oil prospectors' shacks and turn-of-the-century tourist hotels to the decayed but still magnificent Queen Anne and Westlake mansions of the city's circa-1880 elites. Successive Works Progress Administration and city housing commission reports chronicled its dilapidation (60 percent of structures were considered "dangerous"), arrest rates (eight times the city average), health problems (tuberculosis and syphilis), and drug culture (the epicenter of marijuana and cocaine use).[5] Yet grim social statistics failed to capture the district's *favela*-like community spirit, its multiracial tolerance, or its closed-mouth unity against the police.

As a local historian later conceded, its residents (perhaps like those of Five Points 100 years before) actually seem to like their aged but colorful perch above the city's bustle:

> The high-ceilinged rooms and low rents suited them. The streets might be steep, but they were remote from traffic rush, with trees along the sidewalks, and a profusion of the more vigorous garden flowers – nasturtiums, holly-hocks, tough-stemmed geraniums – still thriving behind the old carriage houses. At night, there were the lights to watch – office windows in the City Halls, cars lining endlessly . . .

Figure 3.1   Millard Sheets's *Angel's Flight,* 1931 (*Courtesy of the Los Angeles County Museum of Art, Gift of Mrs L. M. Maitland. Photograph © 2000 Museum Associates/LACMA. Museum number 32.17*)

Millard Sheets's "Angel's Flight" – virtually the only famous Southern California painting from the Depression era (1931) – portrays better than Fante's novel a defiant Bunker Hill attitude. Usually considered a Thomas Hart Benton regionalist, Sheets for a brief moment was a hard-eyed, unpuritanical Otto Dix. Two streetwise but attractive "courtesans of the tenements" in casual conversation look down on the city from the top of the stairway that paralleled the tracks of the little Angel's Flight cable car. Their relaxed insolence, the commanding view, the inference of erotic sanctuary – nothing suggests that they are anywhere other than exactly where they want to be, and probably where young Sheets – doomed to become a gray arts institution in the 1950s – yearned to be as well. It was as close to Montmartre as LA would ever get.

But the Hill, at least by the time that Siodmak got around to it, was living on borrowed time. It not only picturesquely overlooked downtown but brusquely interrupted real-estate values between the new City Hall and the great department stores on Seventh Street. "Bunker Hill," argued a civic leader in 1929, "has been a barrier to progress in the business district, preventing the natural expansion westward. If this Civic Center is to be a success, the removal or regrading of Bunker Hill is practically a necessity." World War Two only temporary postponed the crusade of downtown leaders to destroy the "blight" and relocate its 12,000 residents.

Criss Cross

Producer Mark Hellinger – a veteran newspaper reporter – had a clear vision of big cities as actors in their own right. In promoting *Criss Cross* (loosely based on a 1936 pulp by Don Tracy) to the studio, he boasted that it "would do for Los Angeles what [his film] *Naked City* had done [the year before] for New York."[6] Although Hellinger died before production began, director Robert Siodmak – fresh from shooting his Richard Conte *noir, Cry of the City* (1948), in the mean streets of Manhattan's Little Italy – preserved the central idea of shocking the public with a hardcore Los Angeles not usually seen on Grayline tours. However, he considerably "Weimarized" the project, scrapping the original screenplay and (with the help of Daniel Fuchs) importing major elements of his own *Sturme der Leidenschaft* – a pathological *Blue Angel*-like tale of male humiliation and jealousy – into the new scenario. The Universum Film AG (Ufa) veteran Franz Planer (Max Ophuls's favorite cinematographer) was brought in to ensure a "Berlin touch."

The story line is industrial-strength sexual obsession unraveling through complex duplicities to the final betrayal of the otherwise-decent protagonist by the *femme fatale*. Steve (Burt Lancaster) is clearly in need of some serious advice from Sam Spade on how to deal with his scheming ex-wife Anna

(Yvonne De Carlo) as she plays him off against her new beau, gangster Slim Dundee (Dan Duryea). After a year of cooling his libido elsewhere, Steve is back on the block with the tragic delusion that he has broken Anna's spell. It takes only a few rotations of the famous De Carlo hips, however, to sink Steve as hopelessly back in lust as if he were a clumsy mastodon trapped in the nearby La Brea Tar Pits. While Anna is convincing him that he is still the only one who can really ring her bell, she is also sighing "but Slim gives me diamonds." Police Lieutenant Pete Ramirez, a chum from the old neighborhood (and one of the rare Chicano characters this side of Zorro), accurately warns of what will follow next, but Steve lets his lower anatomy lead him ahead blindly. In a desperate gambit to satisfy Anna's greed, he helps Dundee and his gang plot the robbery of the armored car company where he and his stepfather work. The complicated heist, of course, is also an ambush designed to rid the jealous Dundee of his competition. Steve, although wounded, kills several of Slim's henchmen and is acclaimed as an innocent hero. Dundee tries to have him murdered in the hospital, but Steve bribes his way past the hit man and finally to a rendezvous with Anna, who, of course, has betrayed him comprehensively. He is still masticating the full extent of her duplicity when Slim barges in and plugs them both.

It is a fairly grim ending and apparently did not please contemporary audiences. Newspaper critics, with few exceptions, panned *Criss Cross*. Moreover, its release coincided with the beginning of the Cold War and intensified ideological surveillance of film. In England, France, and Germany, *Criss Cross* was heavily censored and even, in some instances, pulled from distribution. Its emphasis on predestination – "it's all in the cards," Steve tells Anna – struck guardians of public taste as subversively "amoral." Within a decade, however, *Cahiers du Cinéma* was singing its praises, and Borde and Chaumeton, in their influential *Panorama du film noir*, esteemed *Criss Cross* as one of the supreme *noirs* and "the summit of his [Siodmak's] American career."[7] Subsequent film histories have endorsed this judgment, and it is now generally recognized that *Criss Cross* was also one of Lancaster's finest performances. In my opinion, however, it was Bunker Hill that clearly deserved Parisian adulation.

Siodmak adopted a fascinating strategy for achieving Hellinger's goal of a revelatory, neorealist LA: he subsumed the city entirely into Bunker Hill and adjacent downtown streets. Apart from the opening aerial view of LA at night and the dénouement in a Palos Verdes beach house, *Criss Cross* is entirely located in Bunker Hill and its social space (Union Station and a Terminal Island factory count as the latter). The compression of the city is literally claustrophobic and perfectly matches Steve's jealous self-implosion. It is the first explicitly LA film, to my knowledge, that refuses any concession to canonical postcard landscape, except for the implacable, almost sinister sunshine that heightens the emotional tension. Otherwise, Siodmak has annihilated suburbia and drained the Pacific. This is emphatically Mahagonny, not Burbank.

Perhaps the most nostalgic Berlin touch – and undoubtedly Siodmak and Planer were still in crêpe over the *Götterdämmerung* of their hometown – is the "Rondo Club": the Isherwoodian cabaret at the base of Bunker Hill where the film's most unnerving scenes and violent erotic confrontations take place. Every modern critic of Siodmak has lingered in awe over the notorious rumba scene where Steve watches with both growing jealousy and voyeuristic excitement as Anna sways closer to the handsome young gigolo played by (the then still unknown) Tony Curtis. Equally, Planer (who obviously knew Sheets's 1931 painting) must have exulted over such fabulous shots as the visual conjugation through a window of the Angel's Flight cable car ascending the incline and Slim's gang discussing their heist in the drawing room of a ruined Bunker Hill mansion. Some have likened Planer's stunning compositions in *Criss Cross* to Rodchenko photographs; certainly their technical audacity rivals anything in his Ufa period.

But the depiction of the city stops short of pulp cliché. Siodmak (who had inactive left sympathies on the margins of the Hollywood Ten) refused the kind of Dickensian simplification that too many modern viewers mistake as the essence of *noir*. The *lumpen* mob led by Slim is counterbalanced by hard-working proletarians like Steve's family. Bunker Hill is portrayed not as the heart of darkness but, more realistically, as a vibrant, hard-working neighborhood under siege from Slim's fascist bullies. The Rondo Club is alternately a depraved fleshpot and the friendly neighborhood bar in *Cheers*. And – at least on the days when Anna isn't floorboarding his testosterone level – Steve is a sentimental sort of fellow, almost a working-class hero.

Kiss Me Deadly

Ralph Meeker's Mike Hammer in *Kiss Me Deadly* (Robert Aldrich, 1955), by contrast, is a serial killer with a detective's license: the clear anticipation of later Bronson and Eastwood films where the "hero" is as violently psychotic as any of the villains. He also has a formidable co-star. After walk-on roles in innumerable B-movies, Bunker Hill once again has top billing in Robert Aldrich's adaptation of the 1952 Mickey Spillane bestseller. An even more acclaimed *noir* than *Criss Cross*, *Kiss Me Deadly* almost defies genre description. Like the infamous "thing-inside-the-box," it is a small apocalypse, with no obvious precedent in film history.

The novel is set in New York. Mike Hammer is driving back from Albany to the city when a mysterious "Viking blonde" lurches in front of his headlights like a frightened deer. "Berga," wearing only an overcoat (whose contents are soon revealed in "a beautifully obscene gesture"), is a desperate

Figure 3.2 Mike Hammer (Ralph Meeker) and Velda (Maxine Cooper) in
Kiss Me Deadly (*Courtesy BFI Stills Library*)

dame on the run, and Hammer is sufficiently intrigued to lie their way past
a police roadblock. Soon after, their car is run off the road by a gang and
Hammer is sapped down. He awakes to the horror of Berga being slowly
tortured to death ("the hand with the pliers did something horrible to her")
in quest of some secret. Thinking he is still unconscious, the gang put him in
the driver's seat next to the dead Berga and push his car off a cliff. Hammer
manages to jump out the door as it begins to fall into "the incredible void."

He next awakes in a hospital in New Jersey where his luscious girl Friday
Velda and his cop friend Pat are keeping him out of reach of the angry
upstate New York police. Hammer cajoles Pat into revealing that the killers
were actually the Mafia and that some incredibly vast conspiracy is afoot.
After ritual warnings from Pat and later the FBI to "stay out of it," Hammer
returns to Manhattan to conduct a solo *jihad* against the Mafia – "the stink-
ing, slimy Mafia" – who have not only murdered Berga but, more importantly, wrecked his car. He proceeds to rub the Mafia's face in forensic gore.
Disarmed by police order, he discovers he enjoys ripping out eyeballs and
crushing thoraxes even more than shooting punks in the belly. A long trail of

corpses and blondes finally leads him to the Secret: a key in Berga's belly that opens a foot locker containing $4 million of narcotics stolen from the Mafia. Berga's former roommate, the seemingly sweet and terrified Lily Carver, is likewise unmasked in the last scene as a disfigured female monster. She considerably annoys Hammer by shooting him in the side and then demanding a kiss. As her lips approach his, he literally flips his Bic.

> The smile never left her mouth and before it was on me I thumbed the lighter and in the moment of the time before the scream blossoms into the wild cry of terror she was a mass of flame tumbling on the floor with the blue flames of alcohol turning the white of her hair into black char and her body convulsing under the agony of it.

Aldrich, we are told, despised the book, regarding Spillane's "cynical and fascistic" hero with "utter contempt and loathing." A much more serious fellow-traveler than Siodmak, he clearly understood that the Hammer series had become the popular pornography of McCarthyism. Although he later told François Truffaut that he should have refused the adaptation, his subversion of it was a much more powerful protest.[8] In collaboration with A. I. Bezzerides, the brilliant scenarist of *Thieves Highway* (1949), Aldrich transformed *Kiss Me Deadly* into a Cold War allegory that deliriously combines *grand guignol* hyperbole with subtle commentaries on the psychology of fascism. The Herculean machismo of Hammer in the novel is now exposed as the sadism of a small-time bully who routinely batters Velda and, in one chilling scene, wantonly destroys a precious phonograph record belonging to a harmless old opera fan. The Mafia, in turn, are replaced by an occult conspiracy led by the Himmler-like Dr. Soborin (Albert Dekker) and the ravenous Lily Carver (Gaby Rogers). Most masterfully, the sordid stash of street drugs becomes a mythic Pandora's box of stolen plutonium. In the incomparable final scene, the incautious Lily literally unleashes the fires of Hell. The wages of fascism and greed, it seems, are nuclear holocaust.

And what better location for ground zero than a Malibu beach-house? The film version is unmoored from the novel's hackneyed Manhattan settings and re-anchored in witchhunt-era Los Angeles. Although the action moves through an archipelago of sinister locales, the film is visually dominated by Hammer's repeated forays to Lily Carver's Bunker Hill tenement. Where Siodmak treated the Hill as a complex urban microcosm, Aldrich strips it down to the darkest layer of metaphor, removing all traces of vibrant normalcy. Its residents now cower behind their doors as killers (including Hammer) silently stalk their prey in the hallways. Whereas Siodmak filmed almost exclusively in full daylight, Aldrich prefers allegorical darkness, and uses the deep-focus "3-D" technique of *Citizen Kane* (1941) to accentuate the shadowy vertigo of interior stairwells and landings, creating the ambience of a single, vast haunted house.

The Hill's visual and architectural antipode is Hammer's fastidiously modern (Wilshire Boulevard?) apartment with its Eames chairs, telephone-answering machine, and middlebrow art. Here Aldrich is accurately mapping the polarized social geography (and real-estate values) of LA in the mid-1950s. Mike is emphatically a "westside" guy in a period when Downtown was generally presumed to be dying, and the cultural and business life of Los Angeles was migrating westward down Wilshire Boulevard toward Westwood and the future Century City. If Chandler's Marlowe (like his creator) incarnated an old-fashioned petit-bourgeois work ethic, Aldrich's version of Hammer is primordial material boy, a sleazy hustler interested only in Jaguars and expensive gimmicks, who has managed to shoot his way into a petite version of the Westside *nouveau-riche* lifestyle and obviously wants more. He is a human type nauseatingly familiar to Aldrich in a city and industry where greed and betrayal packaged as patriotism had recently made a hecatomb of the careers of his best friends.

They Live!

A few years after the release of *Kiss Me Deadly*, the wrecking balls and bulldozers began to systematically destroy the homes of 10,000 Bunker Hill residents. After a generation of corporate machination, including a successful 1953 campaign (directed by the *Los Angeles Times*) to prevent the construction of public housing on the Hill, there was finally a green light for urban renewal. A few Victorian landmarks, like Angel's Flight, were carted away as architectural nostalgia, but otherwise an extraordinary history was promptly razed to the dirt and the shell-shocked inhabitants, mostly old and indigent, pushed across the moat of the Harbor Freeway to die in the tenements of Crown Hill, Bunker Hill's threadbare twin sister. Irrigated by almost a billion dollars of diverted public taxes, bank towers, law offices, museums, and hotels eventually sprouted from its naked scars, and Bunker Hill was reincarnated as a glitzy command center of the booming Pacific Rim economy. Where hard men and their molls once plotted to rob banks, banks now plotted to rob the world. Yet history is sometimes like the last scene in *Carrie* (1976).

In John Carpenter's *They Live!* (1988), the old Bunker Hill suddenly rises from the grave to deal summary justice to the yuppie scum who have infested its flanks. Carpenter, of course, is notorious (and amongst some, well-loved) for his use of right-wing plot elements – like the Bronson revenge-massacre formula or the City-as-penal-colony – to advance his progressive sympathies. The only Hollywood liberal with a bigger gun collection (I am being metaphorical) than Charlton Heston, he had the chutzpah in

They Live! to suggest guerrilla warfare as a well-deserved response to Reaganomics and the Age of Me.

The opening of the film contains the bluntest imagery of class polarization since *Battleship Potemkin*. On now glamorous Bunker Hill, the *nouveaux riches* cavort in Armani splendor, while across the freeway, in the little valley (Beaudry Street) that separates it from Crown Hill, the Other America is camped out in homeless squalor. The Sears and Roebuck middle class has disappeared, and there are only yuppie princes and blue-collar paupers left. Still stunned by the enormity of their downfall, the workers (now racially integrated in catastrophe) sulk in their postmodern Hooverville under the watchful eye of the now openly fascist LAPD.

These scenes had authentic local poignancy since Carpenter's neighborhood – Temple-Beaudry – was deliberately turned into a wasteland in the late 1970s and early 1980s by corporate speculators based in Singapore, Dallas, and Toronto, who preferred to destroy the housing of an estimated 7,000 residents than face future resettlement costs. At the time the film was shot, the area was mainly occupied by fugitive gang members, older homeless black men, and young Mexican and Central American immigrants. Their homes were razed, but from the flanks of Crown Hill they could arrange old car seats and discarded sofas to enjoy the spectacle, every dusk, of the illumination of the great downtown office towers. In an ironic Dickensian reversal, the poor were now the voyeurs of the rich.

In the film, the passivity of the homeless workers explodes into resistance when John Nada (whom Carpenter himself has characterized as "an everyman/working class character") discovers that the Reagan voters, when viewed through special glasses, are actually alien invaders who have hijacked the city and immiserated its common people.[9] This is, of course, Spillane's McCarthyite paranoia turned back against itself, and once Nada (Nothing) convinces his fellow-workers that their class enemies are monstrous extra-terrestrials, there is no longer any moral scruple preventing a war of total extermination/ liberation. From then on, it is urban renewal in violent reverse, and the Rainbow Coalition puts a serious hurt on the grotesque insects masquerading as LA Law. The concept of a second Battle of Bunker Hill is, of course, idiotic and breathtaking at the same time. But the return of the repressed is always that way.

Notes

1   See the section "Sunshine or Noir" in my own *City of Quartz, Excavating the Future in Los Angeles* (New York: Vintage, 1992 (1990)).

2   Reyner Banham, *Los Angeles: The Architecture of the Four Ecologies* (London: Allen Lane, 1971).

3 Charles Dickens, *American Notes* (London: Chapman & Hall, 1842); with an introduction by Christopher Hitchens (New York: Modern Books, 1996).
4 E. Z. C. Judson, *Mysteries and Miseries of New York* (New York: Dick & Fitzgerald, ca.1848); Mathew Hale Smith, *Sunshine and Shadow in New York* (Hartford, CT: J. B. Burr, ca.1868).
5 See Pat Adler, *The Bunker Hill Story* (Glendale, CA: La Siesta Press, 1963).
6 See Deborah Lazaroff Alpi, *Robert Siodmak: A Biography, With Critical Analyses of his Films Noirs and a Filmography of all his Works* (Jefferson, NC: McFarland, 1998); Hervé Dumont, *Robert Siodmak: le maître du film noir* (Lausanne: Éditions l'Age d'homme, 1981).
7 Raymond Borde and Étienne Chaumeton, *Panorama du film noir américain, 1941–1953* (Paris: Éditions d'Aujourd'hui, 1975).
8 Edwin T. Arnold and Eugene L. Miller, *The Films and Career of Robert Aldrich* (Knoxville: University of Tennessee Press, 1986).
9 Carpenter quoted on *They Live!* website at http://www.toptown.com/dorms/creedstonegate/they/jcarp.htm, copyright Creed Stonegate and Stonegate Design, 1998.

4

Film Mystery as Urban History: The Case of *Chinatown*

John Walton

Introduction

Historians and students of film are familiar with movies based upon historical events and particularly with cinematic representations of those events which are said to distort, reinterpret, or otherwise alter history in popular memory. Seldom, however, do we find instances of the effect of film and popular culture on history. The reason, perhaps, is that the latter side of this dialectic is rare or inconsequential in the unfolding course of history. This chapter will argue, on the contrary, that sometimes life imitates art, that renditions of the past in popular culture can have a forceful impact on the making of history. This proposition is examined in the context of Los Angeles's historical, and often controversial, efforts to acquire water for development, the political movement to restrain the city's appropriation of natural resources mounted by citizens of the Owens Valley in the 1920s, the selective reinterpretation of these events in Roman Polanski's classic film *Chinatown* (1974), and the influence of the film on the subsequent and ongoing controversy over water rights and land development in the region since the mid-1970s.

These events began when the City of Los Angeles reached out 230 miles to the north-east along California's eastern Sierra Nevada Mountain chain and appropriated water from the Owens Valley in an aqueduct constructed from 1905 to 1912. Subsequently, drought and growing groundwater exploitation by the city in the 1920s resulted in the valley's steady desiccation.

Urged on by growing desperation and traditions of popular action, the valley rose in revolt in 1924, protesting politically and, when that failed, bombing the aqueduct. Although the community struggle of the 1920s ended in defeat, it left a growing residue of memory in accounts of the David-and-Goliath struggle produced in fiction, local history, and early films. Many of these distorted the facts of the conflict by attributing a conspiratorial design to the city's original effort to build the aqueduct and heroic motives to local resistance. In California parlance, these events came to be known histrionically as "the rape of the Owens Valley." *Chinatown* built on this myth and it too altered the facts of the case. The site of the conflict was moved 200 miles closer to the city, the events were advanced by thirty years to the depression-era LA of Raymond Chandler and the story was reconstructed as a murder mystery revolving around conspiratorial land speculation.

Meanwhile, the original controversy had evolved into a complicated legal struggle involving new environmental legislation, a strategic lawsuit mounted by Owens Valley officials, and a revitalized popular movement. By contrast to failed attempts in the 1920s, the local cause was now publicized widely, state political actors drawn into the process, and state courts persuaded that rural communities were entitled to some defense of their resources. In this new struggle of the 1980s and early 1990s, public opinion assumed that *Chinatown* represented the true history of the conflict – much to the advantage of a burgeoning environmental movement.[1]

In some respects, popular culture became political history and collective action proceeded from a new set of assumptions. Contemporary history unfolded with redressing results, some of which could be traced to the influence of film and popular culture.

The Story

Early on the Sunday morning of November 16, 1924, seventy men from Bishop, California, drove south in a caravan of Model T Fords through the eastern Sierra's Owens Valley and took possession of the Los Angeles Aqueduct at the Alabama Gates spillway. Technicians in the insurgent crowd soon accomplished their mission by opening the spill-gates that held back the man-made river. By mid-morning an assembly of several hundred valley residents had gathered at the site five miles north of Lone Pine to watch most of the Los Angeles water supply flow out of its concrete channel on to the dry bed of the Owens River. Within a day, a makeshift camp was created, neighbors brought picnic baskets, and Tom Mix's western movie crew joined the festivities, bringing their own Mariachi band. A rebellion was under way, a rebellion that would figure prominently in the unfolding history of California's political struggles, popular culture, and their reflexive connection.

The picnic at the Alabama Gates typified the struggle between rural communities and expanding cities. The 1924 aqueduct occupation came as the culmination of a local movement begun in 1905 as an effort to defend the small communities in the Owens Valley against the growing depredations of urbanization in Los Angeles. The city had extended its water-supply network to the eastern Sierra over local protest which flared and then cooled until the early 1920s, when a combination of drought and urbanization led to redoubled exploitation of the city's hinterland. On one front, the city exported increasing quantities of ground water, drying up local farms and communities, while on another front it bought up farms, town lots, and water rights in a master plan to depopulate the region and convert it into the city's own reservoir. Farmers and townspeople in four valley settlements (including, from north to south, Bishop, Big Pine, Independence, and Lone Pine) mobilized in the hope of ensuring that local development would rise on the tide of urban growth. Led by local business interests, the valley alliance attempted to negotiate with the city, guarantee local water supplies and continued irrigation, and establish the authority of a valley association to enter into agreements with the city. All this was denied by the city's highhanded methods of colonizing and exploiting its rustic neighbors. The rebellion in 1924 was a desperate move, a last resort by the valley to save its communities and way of life.

Although the aqueduct occupation succeeded as a *cause célèbre*, enjoying publicity around the country and even in Europe, it failed as a political action and brought about the end of the movement. The city ended the occupation by promising negotiations, but stood firm against any concessions to local interests. State authorities declined to intervene. Valley residents, still suffering the effects of drought and economic collapse, began to lose heart. Some sold out, others persevered (even selling and leasing back their own farm land from the city), and a few carried the struggle to the courts, winning small victories in the 1930s and 1940s.

With the collapse of rebellion, however, a legend began to grow, fed by depression-era sentiments centering on an underdog narrative in which the wholesome and ingenuous countryside bravely opposes the wicked and beguiling city. This narrative inevitably imposed gross simplifications on the historical record – local citizens were far from "rubes" and were never opposed to urbanization, only to their exclusion from its rewards. Yet the narrative did capture the plight of the Owens Valley in culturally accessible form which later became and provided a symbolic resource in renewed political struggles over water and, now, the "environment."

In the 1970s, the Owens Valley–Los Angeles controversy was revived as the result of a new local citizens' movement which was enabled by federal and California environmental legislation. It was in this context that Polanski's remarkable film *Chinatown* appeared to an enthusiastic commercial and critical reception. For Los Angeles and national audiences who knew little of the historical background, *Chinatown* became *the* LA water story – the political intrigue that made urbanization possible. With its apt power-politics imagery, the film became urban history in the effective realm of popular culture, though its story was largely false. The ironic effect was that the critical narrative underpinning the screenplay was appropriated by environmental activists and a new citizens' alliance in the 1970s and 1980s. That struggle ultimately succeeded in recovering an important share of Owens Valley natural resources, community control, and local dignity.

Symbols and Politics

Chinatown's narrative of conspiracy and intrigue did not appear in a vacuum. Critical accounts began circulating in popular culture from the earliest days of the Owens Valley–Los Angeles controversy and flourished in the 1920s rebellion. Paradoxically, as the Owens Valley economy and society revived in the 1930s, the legend of local destruction grew even faster. The publicity that rebels in the 1920s had hoped would save their communities was reinterpreted and reproduced as California folklore and commercial fiction over the next half-century – too late for some purposes, but not for others.

As the legend grew, historical fact, in the sense of consensus among contemporaries and experts, inevitably suffered. Interpretations never entertained by the rebels themselves – such as conspiratorial intrigue behind city actions – were advanced in romantic and muckraking accounts. Dispassionate observers have properly exposed these "distortions," but few have moved on to analyze the nature and uses of the legend. Historian Abraham Hoffman speaks for many, including Los Angeles partisans, when he laments that a popular film about water and corruption based on the Owens Valley experience takes liberties with the city's legitimate development efforts: "*Chinatown*, its excellent story supported by a distorted version of history, assures new misunderstandings . . . hopefully the cause of history may be spared yet another contrivance manipulating time and events."[2]

Hope for some impartial factual resolution of a highly charged political conflict now in its eighth decade seems not only quixotic, but neglects the opportunity to analyze the cultural politics of the controversy – the manner in which symbols, indeed distortions, have become part of the political struggle. A distinctive aspect of this legend, moreover, is that in partisan accounts and popular culture, "the Owens Valley controversy came to be one instance in which the history of a conflict was not written by the victors."[3] History became symbol, and symbolism played an essential part in California water politics from the 1930s onward.

The legend, elaborated over some sixty years, appears in two stages divided by the watershed years of the late 1920s. A critical shift occurs at that time when the folkloric master theme changes from rural romance to state intrigue.

Literary interpretations of Owens Valley society began appearing in the 1910s, using the struggle over water rights as a backdrop for Western morality plays. With the valley's future still an open question, authors could write their own resolution and make their chosen protagonists responsible for the result. Peter Kyne's 1914 novel *The Long Chance* is an engaging melodrama with overtones of Zane Grey's *Riders of the Purple Sage* which appeared two years earlier. Kyne's hero, Bob McGraw, an improbable combination of desert rat, clever lawyer, and social reformer, is committed to outmaneuvering corrupt officials in the state land office for the benefit of the toiling masses.

> I've cast my fortune in the desert of Owens river valley. I've cut out for myself a job that will last me all my life, and win or lose, I'll fight to a finish. I'm going to make thirty-two thousand acres of barren waste bloom and furnish clean unsullied wealth for a few thousand poor, crushed devils that have been slaughtered and maimed under the Juggernaut of our Christian civilization. I'm going to plant them on ten-acre farms up there under the shadow of Mt. Kearsarge, and convert them into Pagans. I'm going to create Eden out of an abandoned Hell. I'm going to lay out a town site and men will build me a town, so I can light it with my own electricity. It's a big utopian dream. A few thousand of the poor and lowly and hopeless brought out of the cities and given land and a chance for life, liberty, and the pursuit of happiness; to know that their toil will bring them some return, that they can have a home and a hope for the future.[4]

McGraw succeeds, of course, by detecting "powerful private interests at work in the state land office . . . aided by corrupt minor officials" who were trying to grab land which they had "suddenly withdrawn from entry and thrown into a Forest Reserve."[5] Kyne's plot uses familiar events, but substitutes, on the one hand, private speculators and dishonest bureaucrats for the City of Los Angeles and Forest Service chief Gifford Pinchot, and, on the other hand, the intrepid McGraw leading thousands of crushed devils in place of the historical citizens' movement. The conflict is presented in nineteenth-century cultural terms which juxtapose capitalist greed, public corruption, urban exploitation, and Christian hypocrisy against rural virtue, populist utopia, the return to honest toil, and philanthropy. Whatever distortions Kyne may commit, his drama resonates the cultural wellsprings of the 1905 protest movement. Rural probity, urban imperiousness, and all they entrain were the opposing symbols of the conflict and the meanings that fueled local action.

Mary Austin's more serious novel *The Ford* (1917) is similar to *The Long*

Chance in important respects, despite a shift of moral responsibility to the settlers themselves and a more jaundiced opinion of pioneer character. The story involves divisions within the valley between the strong and scheming land baron Timothy Rickart (after Owens Valley rancher Thomas Rickey) and the doleful farmers who, like Mary's own ineffectual husband, dream of one day "getting into something." The geographically repositioned valley of Tierra Longa is coveted by unsavory oil interests and city agents from San Francisco who are taking options on land and water rights amidst local confusion over whether they are "government men representin' the Irrigation Bureau." Young Kenneth Brent uncovers Rickart's connivance in a land-grabbing plan to export water and endeavors to unite valley farmers in "common resentment [and] tribal solidarity," but fails. "The solitary, rural habit which admitted them to a community of beguilement could not lift them to a community of enterprise." Austin is clearly evaluating the farmers' failure in 1905, attributing it to "their invincible rurality . . . how, by as much as they had given themselves to the soil, they were made defenseless against this attack on it." They lacked any vision of an alternative to life on the land.

> It isn't the Old Man's capital that the people of the valley are up against, so much as it is their *idea* of it, and their idea of the situation, or their lack of ideas . . . The greatest common factor of the Tierra Longans was their general inability to rise to the Old Man's stature; they were inferior stuff of the same pattern.[6]

Both novels cast the legend in terms of class struggle – the rich, urban, and powerful bent upon dispossessing the humble poor. Although Austin's moral is equally critical of rural parochialism, neither author moves beyond individual actors motivated by stereotypical vices. Institutional actors and state designs were not yet evocative cultural themes, but that would soon change.

A big step from sympathetic news coverage to legend-building occurred when the Watterson brothers, local bankers, began financing, from the reserves of their bank, the Los Angeles civic reformer and publicist Andrae Nordskog. A man of varied talents, Nordskog published the weekly newspaper *Gridiron* in Los Angeles. Looking for bigger stories than his usual exposés of excessive telephone rates and deficient city services, Nordskog traveled to the Owens Valley in June 1927 and immediately became an impassioned ally of the Watterson brothers. Before long the *Gridiron* was publishing denunciations of the city's water commissioners. Through his business connections, Nordskog carried the fight to a weekly radio broadcast and to civic groups – all of this subsidized by cash contributions from the Wattersons' bank, which Nordskog tried unsuccessfully to hide. When the Wattersons' bank failed and the brothers were tried for fraud, Nordskog only intensified his efforts to expose injustice. He traveled to Washington, DC to research Bureau of Reclamation records in connection with the events of 1905 and their parallels to the new Colorado River project that would bring additional water to Southern California. The results of his study were presented in a long and, by all accounts, chaotic manuscript which Nordskog tried to publish – hounding Mary Austin and Los Angeles attorney and writer Carey McWilliams to provide a foreword that would sway New York publishing houses. On the podium or in print, Nordskog's faults included prolixity, self-importance, histrionics, and a tendency to misrepresent his hard-won evidence by overstating conspiratorial aspects of the case. McWilliams was impressed with the revelations in his work, but found him tedious and "as a man, rather naive. N [sic] writes like a bond salesman with a yen to be a poet."[7] The manuscript, "Boulder Dam in Light of the Owens Valley Fraud," was never published.

Through an odd set of circumstances, however, Nordskog's brief had a greater effect on subsequent events than anything written up to that time. As a result of his investigations, seeming expertise, and public visibility as a champion of water-management reform, in 1930 Nordskog was elected chairman of the Southwest Water League, an organization of forty-eight Southern California cities. With this organizational base, "a new opportunity for Nordskog to alert the public to Los Angeles's water aggressions came in early 1931 when the state senate adopted a resolution creating a special committee to investigate the city's actions in the Owens Valley. Nordskog was asked to testify before the [Senate] committee."[8] With the state legislature increasingly hostile towards Los Angeles, this investigation eventually led to laws protecting county water resources. In preparation for the hearings, Nordskog condensed the Boulder Dam tome into twenty-eight pages which the committee, in an unusual act of assent, ordered published in the *Assembly Journal*. Under the official state seal, 1,500 reprints of Nordskog's *Communication to the California Legislature Relating to the Owens Valley Water Situation* were printed and mailed on request at public expense. According to Abraham Hoffman, "critics of the actions of Los Angeles had what appeared to be a state-sponsored document supporting the view that it had all been a giant conspiracy."[9]

The following year, the popular book *Los Angeles*, published by journalist Morrow Mayo, converted Nordskog's dense investigation into the stuff of popular legend. Mayo's breezy chronicle is best remembered for its chapter on "The Rape of the Owens Valley." Relying mainly on Nordskog and on Bishop newspaper sources, Mayo tells the story of "a rich agricultural valley" destroyed by the US government for Los Angeles developers. Mayo's distinct contribution to the legend comes in the combination of an inflammatory narrative and a sense of institutional action – a formula unknown in earlier writing on this history but resonant in the years of the Depression and the emerging welfare state.

Los Angeles gets its water by reason of one of the costliest, crookedest, most unscrupulous deals ever perpetrated, plus one of the greatest pieces of engineering folly ever heard of. Owens Valley is there for anybody to see. The City of the Angels moved through this valley like a devastating plague. It was ruthless, stupid, cruel, and crooked. It deliberately ruined Owens Valley. It stole the waters of Owens River. It drove the people from Owens Valley from their home, a home which they had built from the desert. It turned a rich, reclaimed agricultural section of a thousand square miles back into primitive desert. For no sound reason, for no sane reason, it destroyed a helpless agricultural section and a dozen towns. It was an obscene enterprise from beginning to end.

Today there is a saying in California about this funeral ground which may well remain as its epitaph:

"The Federal Government of the United States held Owens Valley while Los Angeles raped it."[10]

Mayo's sexual symbolism had a sharp impact in the 1930s and, indeed, still carried force forty years later when a new citizens' movement would rally to the slogan "the rape of the Owens Valley." The countryside became re-metaphorized as feminine and nurturing, and the city as masculine and brutal. The federal government was recast as sadistic and complicit, a long way from 1905, when homesteaders had turned to Uncle Sam's paternal justice on behalf of the common folk. In the emerging modern symbolism, violated citizens and rapacious institutions supplant wholesome pioneers building the West for the nation's benefit. Indeed, the masculine metaphor of conquering pioneer communities, their victory over nature and savages, is replaced by an agriculturally fertile land and feminine hearth. This symbolic shift transfigures the moral grammar. Mistreated pioneers deserve recognition, compensation, and fair play – the full rights of political citizenship. But violated innocents and homemakers demand vindication – restoration of their honor. Symbolically, the modern struggle has moved beyond politics to virtue.

It was a short step from Mayo's journalistic obloquy to novelistic social realism. *Los Angeles* supplied the plot for a series of books and films dealing with exploitation and the wages of avarice. Will Rogers helped advertise the Owens Valley story in his nationally syndicated column:

Ten years ago this was a wonderful valley with one quarter of a million acres of fruit and alfalfa. But Los Angeles needed more water for the Chamber of Commerce to drink more toasts to its growth, more water to dilute its orange juice, more water for its geraniums to delight the tourists, while the giant cottonwoods here died. So, now, this is a valley of desolation.[11]

Citing Mayo's inspiration, Cedric Belfarge published *Promised Land* in 1938, a novel about the downfall of a family divided between Hollywood demoralization and federal fraud in the Owens Valley. A John Wayne film of the following year entitled *New Frontier* (George Sherman, 1939) pits the homesteaders of New Hope Valley against the Irish construction engineer for Metropole City's water project. Not long after World War Two, which had temporarily "suppressed" the controversy, *Golden Valley: A Novel of California*, by Frances Gragg and George Palmer Putnam, appeared in 1950. Like the stories of Austin and Kyne, this one centers on the Owens Valley and its infiltration by facsimiles of agents working for the Los Angeles Department of Water and Power (LADWP). When a fraudulently represented reclamation project is revealed as a screen for the Los Angeles Aqueduct, local citizens organize and threaten to dynamite the construction. Violence by land speculators matches bureaucratic speculation but, in the end, city and valley reach an accord, malefactors are purged, and settlers compensated for land lost to reservoir and canal sites. As the repetition in these fictional works suggests, by mid-century the legend was firmly entrenched in popular culture – the Owens Valley had become a symbol of urban aggrandizement and bureaucratic malice.

Figure 4.1 A production still from the film *Chinatown* in which local farmers protest Los Angeles's water policy by herding sheep into the City Council Chamber, ca.1937 (*Courtesy BFI Stills Library*)

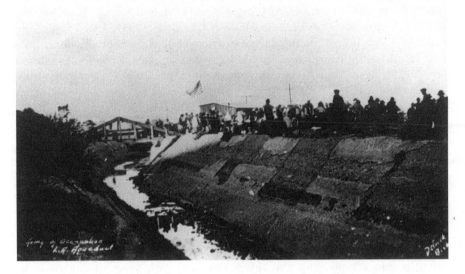

Figure 4.2   Owens Valley citizens take possession of the Los Angeles Aqueduct, November 16, 1924 (*Photo by courtesy of the Eastern California Museum*)

As adverse opinion mounted, Los Angeles followed the Wattersons' lead and recruited its own publicists. Beginning in 1924, the city had responded to newspaper accounts sympathetic to the rebels. In July of that year, the Municipal League of Los Angeles *Bulletin* explained that "The Owens Valley 'Revolt'" was prompted by "the Wattersons [and farmers] as land specula-tors" – an interpretation that continues in modern historical works, as we have seen.[12] In December, *Fire and Water Engineering* revealed "What Really Happened . . . No Justification for the Mob's Action."[13] Over the following years, the LADWP hired Don J. Kinsley to write a series of exculpating tracts and published some of his work under such beguiling titles as "The Romance of Water and Power: A brief narrative revealing how the magic touch of water and hydro-electric power transformed a sleepy, semi-arid Western village into the metropolis of the Pacific" and "The Water Trail: The story of Owens Valley and the controversy surrounding the efforts of a great city to secure the water required to meet the needs of an ever-growing population." Despite these efforts, Los Angeles was losing the propaganda war, in part because it lacked the sympathy of an underdog and in part because its contradictory policy for managing the valley generated new dis-putes readily interpreted by critical opinion.

Unchastened by growing opposition, the city retaliated against the valley with an announcement that its policy of negotiating land sales with extant leaseholders would be superseded by sale to the highest bidder. Local protest of the action was met with a rent hike at Christmas 1944. Once again, the California legislature responded by approving a bill by Senator Charles Brown that required the city to give leaseholders first option on properties offered for sale. A new controversy erupted in the US Congress over previously approved bills that gave Los Angeles a right of way to extend the aqueduct northward into Mono County. Although the extension was built in 1940, Congress now refused to grant the city control of additional acreage for power plants as the original bills provided. The controversy ultimately centered on distrust of Los Angeles, a mood that had overtaken the interpenetrating realms of popular culture and practical politics.

Film and History

The water wars between Los Angeles and the Owens Valley have inspired novelists, muckrakers, and filmmakers since the early years of the twentieth century. History and drama have combined in a set of accounts which has created a popular culture surrounding these events, particularly a conspiratorial interpretation of the city's deeds. *Chinatown* is the most celebrated in the genre. Robert Towne's brilliant screenplay takes great liberty with historical fact, yet forcefully portrays the Los Angeles power brokers in a manner consistent with the transformed legend. The whole story is moved to 1937 and the protagonists become unscrupulous city developers bent on acquiring the land of farmers in the San Fernando Valley immediately adjacent to the city. Officials of the LADWP collude with speculators by secretly dumping city water during a drought in order to win public support for a bond issue on dam and aqueduct construction. Meanwhile, the farmers are cut off from irrigation water, forced into ruin, their land acquired by syndicate dummy buyers for a pittance. The aqueduct will serve the ill-gotten land of the speculators and make fortunes for the cabal. Incest is an important subplot, extending the sexual symbolism of rape to the vile association of money and political power. Chinatown, the tarnished hero's police beat before he became a private eye, is a trope representing intrigue, deceptive appearances, and the futility of efforts to expose corruption. In one of the film's final lines a policeman comments, "You can't always tell what's going on in Chinatown." Attempts to reveal the scheme are discredited and one is left with the understanding that Los Angeles was built on exploitation in the face of a guileless public.

    In fact, of course, the decisive events occurred around 1905 and involved no conspiracy or contrived water shortage. City voters overwhelmingly approved repeated bond measures for aqueduct construction without the inducement of panic. A land syndicate of prominent business interests did purchase San Fernando Valley real estate for subsequent profit, but that was well known and little regarded by a public that shared in the spirit of boosterism. With the exception of covert actions to subvert the original plan for a federal reclamation project in Owens Valley, and some unsuccessful speculation by a former city mayor, officials of the LADWP pursued the aggrandizement of their own agency.

The significance of *Chinatown*, however, is that, despite factual inconsistencies, it captured the deeper truth of the rebellion. Metropolitan interests appropriated the Owens Valley for their own expansionist purposes through the use of blunt political power. The film refueled popular interpretation and energized protest that returned to the valley in the 1970s. Indeed, it contributed to the success of a new county–LADWP agreement limiting groundwater pumping and restoring some of the habitat. To this day, Los Angeles authorities are livid on the subject of *Chinatown*, knowing that the perceived "rape of the Owens Valley" is an albatross hung around continuing work to ensure the city water supply.

If, as Oscar Wilde suggested, life imitates art, one explanation is that art can become a force with which life must contend. Events surrounding the impact of *Chinatown* illustrate the proposition. In 1983, ABC Television and Titus Productions of New York produced a film for television based on the prizewinning screenplay *Ghost Dancing* by freelance writer Phillip Penningroth. Set in Paiute Valley, the teleplay begins with the elderly heroine, Sarah Bowman, dynamiting a reservoir in an effort to get arrested and call attention to the valley's destruction by appropriation of its water. Sarah is outmaneuvered by the chief engineer of the unnamed city's water department. By persuading friendly local authorities not to make an arrest, the city avoids a public trial and the effective defense planned by Sarah's adopted Indian daughter who works for the district attorney's office. Although Los Angeles was never mentioned in the script (after changes made on legal advice), the reference was so transparent and the public relations effect so worrisome in the wake of *Chinatown* that the LADWP refused to grant permission for filming on its Owens Valley property. As Robert Towne explained about the filming of *Chinatown*, "we just told them we were doing a detective story set many years ago, so they had no idea what was going on."[14] Los Angeles did not intend to be burned again. *Ghost Dancing* was filmed in Utah with much of its impact neutralized by censorship.

But life had not finished its imitation. The *Ghost Dancing* controversy erupted in the midst of negotiations over a permanent agreement to settle disputed water rights, and it strengthened the hand of local activists. Following reports on Bishop radio and cable television, 600 residents signed a petition condemning Los Angeles for intimidating ABC. The County Board of Supervisors agreed and unsuccessfully urged the filmmakers to reconsider shooting on privately owned property in the valley. Literally, the term "ghost dancing" referred to a nineteenth-century Paiute Indian ritual which would cause the disappearance of whites and the restoration of native land. If the teleplay endeavored to adapt the symbol for modern political purposes, Los Angeles hoped to quell the legend. The LADWP acknowledged its fear of copycat aqueduct bombings that might be inspired by the film, but local observers saw more to the censorship. Inyo County Administrator John K. Smith observed, "Most of what they're doing now has nothing to do with getting water to Los Angeles. From here on in, its all psychological damage to keep us down and make people forget what the valley used to look like."[15]

Yet the effects of the now-celebrated legend and each new controversy that recalled it worked in the opposite direction. The 1920s protest movement and subsequent urban domination became part of a living history. An oppositional culture developed around the controversy and helped mobilize subsequent movements on behalf of community survival and environmental protection. Popular culture not only depicts nostalgically the lost world of local society, but re-creates potent symbols for modern use.

Notes

1　John Walton, *Western Times and Water Wars: State, Culture, and Rebellion in California* (Berkeley: University of California Press, 1992).
2　Abraham Hoffman, "Fact and Fiction in the Owens Valley Water Controversy," Los Angeles Westerner's Corral, *Brand Books* (no. 15), pp. 179, 191.
3　William L. Kahrl, *Water and Power: The Conflict Over Los Angeles's Water Supply in the Owens Valley* (Berkeley: University of California Press, 1982), p. 319.
4　Peter B. Kyne, *The Long Chance* (New York: H. K. Fly, 1914), p. 115.
5　Ibid.
6　Mary Austin, *The Ford* (Boston: Houghton Mifflin, 1917; Berkeley: University of California Press, California Fiction Edition, 1997), pp. 403–4.
7　Letter from Carey McWilliams to Mary Austin, 27 January 1930; held at the Henry E. Huntington Library, San Marino, CA.
8　Abraham Hoffman, *Vision or Villainry: Origins of the Owens Valley–Los Angeles Water Controversy* (College Station, TX: Texas A&M University Press), p. 226.
9　Ibid., pp. 226–8.
10　Morrow Mayo, *Los Angeles* (New York: Alfred Knopf, 1932), pp. 245–6.
11　Quoted in ibid., p. 241.
12　"The Owens Valley Revolt," Municipal League of Los Angeles *Bulletin*, July 1924.
13　"What Really Happened . . . No Justification for the Mob's Action," *Fire and Water Engineering*, December 1924.
14　Walton, *Western Times and Water Wars* p. 232.
15　Ibid., p. 233.

5

Return to Oz: The Hollywood Redevelopment Project, or Film History as Urban Renewal

Josh Stenger

In 1986, the Los Angeles City Council decided to answer a question George Cukor had posed over fifty years before. The question: *What Price Hollywood?* The answer: $922 million. This was the amount allocated by the LA City Council to the Community Redevelopment Agency (CRA) to finance a thirty-year campaign in Hollywood, known simply as the Hollywood Redevelopment Project.[1] The Hollywood Redevelopment Project is currently one of twenty-nine redevelopment zones administered by the CRA, the agency which oversees city-funded renewal programs in Los Angeles. With one of the biggest budgets in LA's urban planning history, the Hollywood Redevelopment zone includes roughly 1,100 residential and commercial acres, making it second in size only to the CRA's fifty-year-old campaign to redevelop Bunker Hill and the Central Business District in LA's downtown. Alongside its formidable surface area and dizzying price-tag, one can add the statistic that within the zone reside 37,000 people who reportedly speak over eighty languages, making the Hollywood Redevelopment Project the most populated and heterogeneous redevelopment zone in LA history.[2] In this chapter, I will provide a brief account of how the CRA's approach to redevelopment in Hollywood contributes to LA's long history of aligning itself with the spectacle, glamour, and cultural purchase of the movies. Specifically, I am interested in calling attention to how the CRA is working to incorporate an idealized version of Hollywood's perceived "Golden Age" into the contemporary urban landscape, staging the recovery of film history as a viable form of urban renewal.

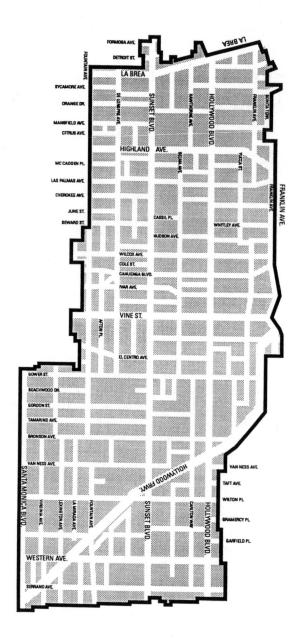

Figure 5.1 Area map of the Hollywood Redevelopment Project

The relationship between Los Angeles's cultural mythology, urban land-scape, and Hollywood film is hardly new, nor is the enlistment of cinematic representations of LA to obfuscate and elide real racial, cultural, and socio-economic tensions. As David Thomson remarks of the place in "Uneasy Street," "Los Angeles became a city through the act of seeing its industrial transmission all over the world . . . . Its great urban and civic problems may slip past if it plays well."[3] Indeed, both materially, at the level of the built environment, and symbolically, at the level of its cultural mythology, LA has for over a century promoted itself as a singular form of urban fantasia, a utopian space characterized by beauty, fame, leisure, and conspicuous con-sumption. As the film industry began to play a defining role in the produc-tion and distribution of LA's cultural mythology, it became increasingly difficult to distinguish the city's cultural geography from that of its cinematic doppelgänger, rendering Los Angeles and Hollywood as interchangeable spaces and interchangeable signs.

Attempting to solidify this bond, which has been strained of late, Los Angeles and the CRA intend to reclaim Hollywood's lost luster for their own, gambling nearly one billion dollars that an economic and cultural resurgence in Hollywood will, like the tide that lifts all boats, benefit the entire city. There is, of course, an irrefutable ideological project at work in Hollywood's (and now the CRA's) conflation of "city" with "fantasy" – hegemonic versions of city history and urban space exist at the obvious expense of other, marginal histories and less idyllic built environments. In the case of the Hollywood Redevelopment Project, this takes on at least three dimensions, all of which reify the dominant ideological myth of a paradisai-cal Los Angeles. First, there is the casting of film history in the role of urban renewal, a process wherein the CRA hopes to build a future by resurrecting Hollywood's imagined past. Second, there is the attempt to create a geogra-phy where before there was only a set of signs, invoking the fame, leisure, and lifestyle of conspicuous consumption associated with Hollywood as a way to cement at the broadest level the city's association with the whole historical map of Hollywood cinema; in doing so, the CRA can build a virtually instant, and instantly nostalgic commercial landscape. Third, there is the prioritization of projects that thematize urban histories and circum-scribe consumption, spectatorship, and tourism as the preferred forms of urban experience.

In *America,* Jean Baudrillard remarks of Los Angeles that it

> seems to have stepped right out of the movies. To grasp its secret, you should not, then, begin with the city and move inwards to the screen; you should begin with the screen and move outwards to the city. It is there that cinema does not assume an exceptional form, but simply invests the streets and the entire town with a mythical atmosphere.[4]

In order to begin with the screen and move outward to the city, then, I would like to briefly describe the beginning of two films, *Hollywood Hotel* (1938) and *Pretty Woman* (1990), for these films neatly illustrate the imbrication of the cinema, the city, and fantasy in LA, while establishing Hollywood Boulevard as the *locus classicus* of that imbrication. The opening scenes of each announce plainly that these are films of different genres, different eras, different industries, and, to be sure, different Hollywoods. Moreover, each in its own way documents a particular moment in time wherein lived experience in Hollywood and LA is definable by, indeed reducible to, the liminal space of Hollywood Boulevard.

Hollywood Hotel opens at St. Louis Airport with Benny Goodman and his orchestra serenading friend and saxophonist Ronny Bowers (Dick Powell) with "Hooray for Hollywood." Bowers has landed a ten-week contract in Hollywood and, though skeptical about finding fame and certain he'll rejoin his friends at the end of his term, receives a hero's send-off. After Bowers takes off, with "Hooray for Hollywood" still playing insistently, the film cuts to a montage of Hollywood's many famous place-names. "Hollywood", as the film depicts it in this sequence, is a utopian landscape – one that is made possible by the movies and offered exclusively for the spectator's consumption, for Bowers is still on the airplane and does not have diegetic access to this onslaught of images.

Beginning with an establishing shot of a Hollywood Boulevard street sign, the brief montage sequence guides the spectator through a tour of the city's most recognizable "Hollywood" landmarks, all of which appear to exist in the imaginary space of a seemingly boundless Hollywood Boulevard. Moving quickly from the Hollywood Bowl to the Brown Derby, the Café Trocadero, Sardi's, the Vendôme, the Ambassador Hotel and Cocoanut Grove, and the Hollywood Hotel, the montage vigorously asserts Hollywood Boulevard as the spatial epitome of film production, exhibition, and consumption. The final images of the sequence show maps to the stars' homes for sale, Grauman's Chinese Theater, film crews shooting on location, and an aerial view of the First National/Warner Bros. studios. During this montage, and throughout the film, *Hollywood Hotel* shows us Hollywood Boulevard in its heyday, a place where dreams come true and where stars are born. And yet, the film's version of Hollywood Boulevard is not simply expansive, it is downright fantastical: the Hollywood Bowl is several miles north on Highland Avenue, while the Ambassador and Cocoanut Grove are even further away in the mid-Wilshire district near Downtown. Still, the fact that half of the images featured in the montage are either historical anachronisms or geographical inaccuracies notwithstanding, Hollywood Boulevard as depicted here is the street LA's boosters had taken to promoting as "The Great White Way of the West."

In stark contrast to the Hollywood Boulevard depicted in *Hollywood Hotel*,

Pretty Woman goes some way to illuminating the need for redevelopment in Hollywood by 1990. No longer the "Great White Way," *Pretty Woman* shows us the "Boulevard of Broken Dreams," a place where teenage runaways peddle drugs, where prostitutes mark their turf by the stars on the Walk of Fame, and where the glamour of the klieg lights has surrendered to a garish neon reality. Whereas *Hollywood Hotel* reveals a thriving commercial and entertainment district that is inseparable from the movies, *Pretty Woman* represents a more nocturnal, predatory urban habitat in which the cultural purchase of Hollywood appears less as a unifying principle than as an occasion for satire. However, no matter how far into neglect it may have sunk, *Pretty Woman*'s Hollywood Boulevard remains a site of fantasy, for it is on this street that the film's lovers – Vivian, the titular Pretty Woman (Julia Roberts), and Edward, her knight-errant (Richard Gere) – will meet, crossing paths just as we are reminded that "everyone who comes to Hollywood's got a dream." As it turns out in this fairytale, the "Once-upon-a-time" of Hollywood Boulevard is quickly exchanged for the "and-they-lived-happily-ever-after" of Beverly Hills and Rodeo Drive. The moral of the story? Even when the community of Hollywood disappoints, Hollywood the culture industry reminds spectators – potential tourists and consumers all – that the LA landscape can be read most conveniently as a series of consumer-cultural metonymies.

I mention these films because they reveal rather nicely the dialogic relationship between LA's urban landscape and Hollywood film, the former always already mediated by the latter. Indeed, films like *Hollywood Hotel* and *Pretty Woman* provide a complex map of an imaginary and recombinant Los Angeles. Each in its own way contributes – whether through reinforcement or subversion – to what Mike Davis, in his seminal "excavation" of Los Angeles, *City of Quartz*, calls LA's "city-myth," which, according to him, "enters the material landscape as a design for speculation and domination."[5] Broadly, one might understand this myth as embodying the hegemonic sentiment that LA is essentially a simple equation of sunshine, beaches, palm trees, and a uniformly classless yet always upwardly mobile consumer society. Davis credits the city's early boosters with giving form and function to the city-myth, but even its originators could not promote the illusion as well as Hollywood could. To be sure, while LA has a long history of vigilant boosterism, the "fairy-tale" side of Los Angeles has never been given better, more persistent representation than in the flickering half-light of the movie theater.

Baudrillard and Davis approach the city with decidedly different agendas and from decidedly different perspectives, yet each reminds us in one way or another that to live in Los Angeles is in many ways to live according to the metaphors made available by the film industry. Inside this place of "pleasure domes decreed," Davis argues, the perspective of the LA resident is like the projected image, depthless and inauthentic: "To move to Lotusland is to sever connection with national reality, to lose historical and experiential footing, to surrender critical distance, and to submerge oneself in spectacle and fraud."[6] Perhaps the same might be said of the CRA's Hollywood Redevelopment Project, for it too asks us to surrender critical distance. It too is deeply submerged in and organized around the spatial and cultural logic of the spectacle.

Typically, the CRA's primary objective in a redevelopment zone is to act as the catalytic agent for the tangible and expeditious improvement of the quality of life for residents and commercial tenants within the neighborhood and/or community.[7] The aim in Hollywood, however, seems substantively different, with an increased emphasis given over to the cultivation of entertainment-related and entertainment-themed businesses whose goal is to generate greater profits for the area from tourists and local consumers. Given that over 37,000 people live within the 2 square miles of the Hollywood Redevelopment zone, one might reasonably conclude that improving living conditions and community services for these residents would constitute major goals of the project. While state law requires the CRA to spend at least 20 percent of the $922 million in redevelopment funds to construct new, and improve existing, housing for very low-, low-, and moderate-income families, the lion's share of the money has been earmarked for the subsidy and development of commercial projects designed to foreground the entertainment industry and intended to court tourists and their money back to Hollywood.

According to CRA reports, the agency anticipated spending $7 million on housing from 1994 to 1999, while almost $20 million was slated to underwrite entertainment-related business loans, the construction of the Hollywood Entertainment Museum and the improvement of parking lots and streetlights in commercial areas.[8] These numbers are lopsided enough by themselves, yet they fail to account for the $90 million the CRA has committed to the Hollywood-Highland project, the crown jewel of Hollywood's redevelopment, a subject I will return to shortly. While the disparity between these figures goes some way toward revealing the business-oriented approach to redevelopment favored by the CRA, the agency is more explicit in its 1998 "Progress Report" on its five-year implementation plan. Although this CRA report insists that the "preservation and expansion of housing and the meeting of community needs of area residents" constitute primary redevelopment objectives, the top three priorities listed – "(1) [to] encourage economic and commercial development; (2) [to] promote and retain the entertainment industry; and (3) [to] revitalize the historic core" – do little to address the "needs of area residents."[9]

Indeed, in order to accomplish these aims, the CRA has prioritized the stimulation of entertainment and retail businesses in order to attract tourists, consumers, and moviegoers – the distinction between these roles being blurred whenever possible. As I mentioned, the promotion of entertainment landmarks and of studio-era Hollywood's fabled past is central to the CRA's strategy for spurring redevelopment in Hollywood. In its attempts to recover the spirit of Hollywood's Golden Age, the CRA has approached urban renewal as a kind of film adaptation. Armed with a blockbuster-size budget, the CRA is planning to bring the world "Hollywood: The Sequel," wherein a kind of crude spatialization of Hollywood film history will act the part of genuine material revitalization. In 1996, *LA Times* writer Duke Helfland described the situation quite succinctly: "For the 1990s remake [of Hollywood Boulevard], investors and boosters are betting Hollywood's future on its storied past. They believe that preserving and capitalizing on a bygone elegance will satisfy hungry tourists who flock to the movie capital expecting to be dazzled . . .".[10] To be sure, the CRA's strategy for economic recovery in Hollywood hinges largely on its ability to successfully merchandise film history as a form of consumer nostalgia.

One important mechanism in this strategy is the reassertion of Hollywood Boulevard's status as a center of film exhibition or, more accurately, to reposition exhibition as the bridge between the Boulevard's halcyon past and the anticipated success of the area's future. In other words, in order to ensure the large-scale economic success the CRA has promised the city, the film industry, and the business community, Hollywood must foreground itself as a preferred site of movie*going* if not of movie*making*. In an early move to do just that, the Hollywood Chamber of Commerce jumped on the "redevelopment" bandwagon in June 1991, designating a new Cinema District along an eight-block stretch of Hollywood Boulevard. The new district, comprising six different theaters – the Ritz, the Vogue, Pacific's El Capitán, the Chinese, the Galaxy Theater, and the Egyptian – touted moviegoing as Hollywood's stock-in-trade.[11]

The announcement of the Cinema District was timed precipitously to coincide with the high-profile reopening of the newly renovated El Capitán Theater, which became the first major effort to exploit the purchase of Hollywood-past as a way to resuscitate the Boulevard's future when it reopened in June 1991. That the El Capitán was to be the new West Coast flagship for Disney releases was key to the CRA's goal of attracting other investors to the area. As the *LA Times* reported, "City officials saw the grinning mouse's squeaky-clean image as a boon to any urban renewal plans. If Disney was willing to set down amid sex shops and pizza parlors, the logic went, Hollywood must be good for the whole family."[12] Although it may be difficult to gauge at this point how directly Disney's presence affected other development projects within Hollywood, the El Capitán's successful restoration did little to discourage the CRA from pursuing its initial hunch – namely, that the recovery of Hollywood's "bygone elegance" would either fulfill or replace the mandate to redevelop the area. And although the El Capitán did not receive CRA funds, its successful reopening did help pave the way for the second major renovation effort along the Boulevard – the CRA-subsidized recovery of the Egyptian Theater.

The first movie palace in Hollywood, the Egyptian opened in 1922 on Hollywood Boulevard, several blocks east of the future sites for the El Capitán and the Chinese Theater. However, by the early 1990s the theater had become defunct and was finally shut down in 1992 in the face of dismal attendance and extensive structural deficiencies. Following the success of the El Capitán, the City of Los Angeles purchased the Egyptian Theater in that same year to ensure its preservation. But the Egyptian's fate was far from decided, for when the Northridge earthquake struck in January 1994, the theater suffered significant structural damage and was condemned.[13] In 1996, the CRA agreed to sell the Egyptian to the American Cinémathèque – a non-profit organization – for $1, and offered to help renovate the time-addled theater by contributing $5 million of the $13 million needed for the restoration. The remaining funds were raised through the contribution of public and private donors.[14]

When the Egyptian reopened on 4 December 1998, it not only provided a home for the American Cinémathèque – whose charter involves hosting retrospectives of classic Hollywood, *avant-garde* and foreign cinemas – it marked another strong connection to Hollywood's cinematic past with which the CRA was so enamored. Yet problems persist, for not only is the American Cinémathèque still heavily in debt following ballooning restoration costs, but the organization's agenda seems to have shifted in order to meet its financial obligations.[15] Hoping to draw more moviegoers, the Cinémathèque, which had formerly been a reliable place to escape the industry's stranglehold on movie culture in the area, is "now focused on bringing in mainstream Hollywood," going so far as to feature a James Cameron retrospective in order to "broaden its appeal."[16] Such a shift is indicative of the impact of place, for Hollywood Boulevard, as the alpha and omega of American film production and consumption, is not renowned for promoting cultural diversity, and one might reasonably conclude that the American Cinémathèque's victory in securing such palatial headquarters was at least in some respects a Pyrrhic one.

With the fanfare created by the announcement of the Cinema District, the El Capitán's grand reopening, and the promise of a restored Egyptian theater, the CRA's emphasis on laying claim to the movies as a way of reinvigorating commercial life appeared to be working. However, despite the movie theaters and the CRA's sponsorship of two film-related museums, even ardent supporters of the Hollywood Redevelopment Project could see that, as late as 1994 or 1995, the CRA had neither stimulated the commercial and cultural renaissance described in its charter nor attracted the kind of marquee investors it so desperately wanted.[17] The initial optimism was beginning to fade.

In 1995, however, David Malmouth, a former Disney executive who over-saw the renovation and relocation of Disney's New Amsterdam Theater in Times Square, pitched the CRA an idea on how to develop the corner of Hollywood Boulevard and Highland Avenue, the former site of the Holly-wood Hotel. Malmouth, representing development firm TrizecHahn, pro-posed a massive urban entertainment center to be called, simply, Hollywood-Highland, the "crown jewel" of the Hollywood Redevelopment Project, to which I alluded earlier. By virtually all accounts, the inception of the Hollywood-Highland project has finally stimulated interest from major commercial and entertainment-related investors within the designated Holly-wood Redevelopment zone.[18]

Situated immediately next to and behind the Chinese Theater, the Holly-wood-Highland project dwarfs virtually every other construction, renova-tion, or expansion project either planned or under way in the Hollywood Redevelopment zone. It is truly grandiose: spanning over eight acres, or nearly one and a half city blocks, the project will create over 650,000 square

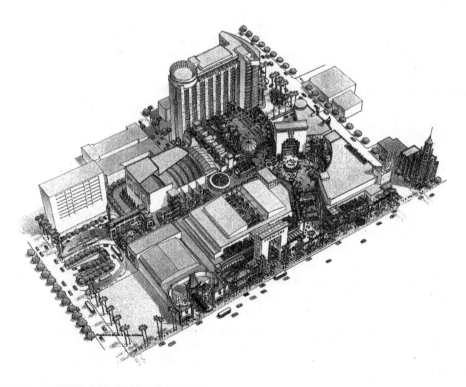

Figure 5.2 Artist's impression of an aerial view of the Hollywood & Highland site, looking north (*Courtesy of Ehrenkrantz Eckstut & Kuhn Architects*)

feet of commercial space that will include theme restaurants, studio showcase stores, retail shops, a 14-screen, 4,000–seat multiplex theater, a newly-remodeled 415–room hotel and a 3,300–seat live broadcast theater that will be home to the Academy Awards. The cost for the project is estimated at $385 million.

Hollywood-Highland offers a compelling example of how public adminis-tration, urban planning, and private investment have come together to forge an identity for Hollywood Boulevard. Although TrizecHahn's project will obviously provide business opportunities for a number of private entertain-ment-related interests, it nonetheless has the financial, legal, and political backing of the CRA, which has pledged $90 million (or 10 percent of its total operating budget) to Hollywood-Highland. This money will finance the struc-ture's underground parking lot and the Academy Theater, and has all but obliterated meaningful distinctions between "community redevelopment" and "commercial expansion." In addition to its financial contribution, the CRA helped secure such a marquee investor for the project site through its part-nership with the Metropolitan Transit Authority, whose $2-billion, seven-mile Red Line winds from the center of Downtown to Hollywood, and will eventually extend to Universal City and its own host of movie-themed attrac-tions. Along this planned entertainment corridor, the CRA and MTA were together able to provide TrizecHahn with the added incentive of a dedicated subway station at Hollywood-Highland, despite the fact that a few blocks away at Hollywood and Vine, a $56-million station opened on June 12, 1999, boasting its own replica of the Yellow Brick Road from *The Wizard of Oz* as if to remind commuters and tourists alike they weren't in Kansas anymore.[19]

Like the Cinema District, the Hollywood museums, and even the Holly-wood subway stations – all of which comply with the CRA's emphasis on marketing a fictionalized, or at the very least romanticized, Hollywood past – the Hollywood-Highland project is guided by a conceptually strategic pas-tiche which allows for the simulation of film industry history and urban history as commercial window-dressing. Conscious of how dear the past is to the CRA's grand illusion, Hollywood-Highland's historical sensibility and its willingness to play freely with that sensibility are made manifest in the fact that the project all but absorbs the Chinese Theater and features the first live-broadcast theater built specifically for the Academy Awards, thereby incorporating two of Hollywood's most globally recognizable icons under the roof of a single multi-use consumer space. Designed to collapse distinctions between the cinematic past of Hollywood and the hoped-for near-future of LA's consumer culture and tourist economy, Hollywood-Highland capital-izes on the signifying power of the former as a way of ensuring the latter. In addition to the Chinese and the new Academy Awards facility, one of the most prominently featured "sets" in this distinctly postmodern space is a

Figure 5.3 Artist's impression of the Babylon Court in the Hollywood & Highland development (*Courtesy of Ehrenkrantz Eckstut & Kuhn Architects*)

reproduction of the Babylon Court from D. W. Griffith's *Intolerance*, complete with Griffith's fabled white elephants. In its time, Griffith's set towered over the intersection of Sunset and Hollywood Boulevards for months after production was completed in 1916, at once a monument to the industry's prodigality and a metaphor for the city's collective investment in fusing architecture and cinema to create new forms of spectacle. In this sense, Hollywood-Highland's quotation of Griffith's set illustrates perfectly the complex spatial logic of cinematic, historical, and geographical recombination employed to conjure up "the Hollywood that exists foremost in the expectations of the tourists who wander the boulevard in search of it."[20]

Of course, even before Hollywood fell prey to urban neglect, tourists arrived on Hollywood Boulevard to the disappointing realization that, to paraphrase Gertrude Stein's famous remark about Oakland, "there was no there there." As Carey McWilliams described Hollywood over fifty years ago, "one of the most famous place-names in the world exists only as a state of mind, not as a geographical entity."[21] Indeed, where were all those magical places from the opening of *Hollywood Hotel?* Tourists looking for stars had to settle for a star map or, after 1960, the Walk of Fame, while those in search of the studios were directed to Universal City, Burbank, Century City, or Culver City. Hollywood itself seems to have always been an insubstantial, ethereal set of signs more than an inhabitable *topos*.

But the CRA is working hard to forge a built environment out of this collective memory. With the help of hyperbolic projects like the Hollywood-Highland spectacle, the CRA's work in Hollywood might be described most simply as a recuperative effort to put a "there" there. On a conceptual level this has meant working to erase the line between LA's material landscape and cinematic representations of it, a strategy that lays bare the historical importance of Hollywood film not only in articulating the city's cultural mythology, but also in shaping a material landscape in which that mythology can be inscribed, enacted, and consumed. On a practical level, the CRA's efforts to recreate an entertainment community out of a formerly dispersed geography has meant the aggressive recruitment of specific kinds of businesses – another reminder that this "LA story" is subject to the CRA's "final cut." In the CRA's Hollywood business information packet, for instance, investors are reminded that "there's no business like show business." The brochure courts interested parties with the CRA's "Entertainment Industry Attraction and Retention Program," offering no-interest loans of up to $250,000 simply for relocating to Hollywood, with complete loan forgiveness if the business remains in Hollywood for a decade, or, as described in the dictum of the packet's enthusiastic boosterism: "Stay here for 10 years and we'll make that loan disappear. Like Hollywood magic!"[22]

The more the Hollywood Redevelopment Project takes shape and continues to promote and recruit the entertainment industry as the *sine qua non* of the city, the more it is clear that projects like Hollywood-Highland will acquire spatial and representational hegemony in Los Angeles. Of course, it's easy to predict success for a project so thoroughly preconceived and so well-funded. As a chimerical shopping mall, theme park, movie theater, and general urban spectacle, it is likely to pique the curiosity of most LA locals as well as the millions of tourists who visit the region each year. Likely to become a fixture of the newly redeveloped Tinseltown, the Hollywood-Highland project epitomizes how a utopian consumer space can be forged out of an ebulliently eclectic architectural syntax. Celebrating the city, the film industry, and the consumption of both, the project's spatial logic makes concrete the triangular relationship between LA, Hollywood, and hegemonic consumerism.

The Hollywood-Highland project – and its unique ability to spatialize cultural history without historicizing cultural space – is at once exceptional and representative of the modes and sites of consumption being privileged within the Hollywood Redevelopment zone specifically, and in the emergent emphasis on themed urban environments more broadly. It is a space wherein the gaze of the moviegoer, the shopper, and the tourist become interchangeable, where the spectacular overwhelms the mundane and where Hollywood-the-place can be rendered in stucco façades of Hollywood-the-cultural-myth. Because it has been credited with drawing other investors and developers into the redevelopment area, the Hollywood-Highland project is an important point of consideration, for it speaks to the general strategies for renewal and revitalization employed by the CRA. Moreover, it invites us to consider whether or not these kinds of multimillion-dollar spatial fantasies can engender genuine urban reform and community redevelopment, as Los Angeles and the CRA overlook the city's history of deep racial and class divisions, re-creating LA in the image of *Oz* even as it future looks more and more like *Blade Runner*. The Yellow Brick Road at the Hollywood and Vine subway station reminds us of how clearly the CRA sees the Los Angeles of its dreams as being, while not exactly over the rainbow, at least on the other side of the screen.

Notes

1 The Hollywood Redevelopment Plan was adopted on 7 May 1986. For more details of the proposed redevelopment initiatives, see "Hollywood Redevelopment Plan: City Council Ordinance #161202 Project Guidelines."

2 David Ferrell, "Judge OKs Plan for Hollywood," *Los Angeles Times*, 21 January 1989, p. 31; Evelyn DeWolfe, "Developers Hope to Recapture Old Hollywood Glitter," *Los Angeles Times*, 8 March 1987, p. 1.

3 David Thomson, "Uneasy Street," in David Reid (ed.), *Sex, Death and God in LA*, (Los Angeles: University of California Press, 1994), pp. 325, 327.

4 Jean Baudrillard, *America*, trans. Chris Turner (London: Verso, 1989), p. 56.

5 Mike Davis, *City of Quartz: Excavating the Future in Los Angeles* (New York: Vintage, 1992), p. 23.

6 Ibid., p. 18.

7 The CRA's function in LA is to "eliminate slums and blight; revitalize older neighborhoods; build low- and moderate-income housing; encourage economic development; create new employment opportunities; support the best in urban design, architecture and the arts; and ensure broad citizen participation in Agency endeavors." Quoted from the Community Redevelopment Agency's website at http://www.cityofla.org/CRA/glance.htm

8 For information regarding CRA specifications regarding minimum percentages of funds to be spent on housing, see "Hollywood Redevelopment Plan: City Council Ordinance #161202," p. 19. For details on the allotment of funds to individual residential, commercial, and civic projects during the five-year period 1995–9, see the CRA/LA, Hollywood Redevelopment Project, "Hollywood 5 Year Implementation Plan: Health and Safety Code Section 334190" (4 May 1995), pp. 5–8.

9 The CRA/LA, Hollywood Redevelopment Project, "Hollywood Five-Year Im-

plementation Plan Progress Report", (28 January 1998), p. 1.

10   Duke Helfland, "Hollywood: Is It Ready for Its Close-up?," *Los Angeles Times*, 10 November 1996, p. A-32.

11   Dean Murphy, "Hollywood Remake: New Cinema District Aimed at Restoring Film's Capital," *Los Angeles Times*, 18 June 1991, p. B-1+.

12   Nicolai Ouroussoff, "Could It Be Magic – Again?," *Los Angeles Times*, 23 November 1997, p. F-6.

13   Sara Catania, ("Screen Test,") *LA Weekly*, 30 July–5 August 1999 (http://www.laweekly.com/ink/99/36/news-catania.shtml).

14   Carla Rivera, "Bringing Back the Past," *Los Angeles Times*, 10 April 1998, pp. B-1+.

15   Catania, "Screen Test."

16   Robert Welkos, "Ancient Egyptian's Reincarnation," *Los Angeles Times*, 3 December 1998, p. F-6.

17   For more information on the CRA's involvement with Hollywood museum construction, see Hollywood Redevelopment Project, "Hollywood Five-Year Implementation Plan Progress Report," p. 4, and Hollywood Chamber of Commerce, "Capital Investment in Hollywood" (March 1998), p. 2.

18   Since the LA City Council and the CRA approved construction of the Hollywood-Highland Project, an onslaught of projects has begun. For more information on specific project details, see Hollywood Chamber of Commerce, "Capital Investment in Hollywood."

19   Jeffrey Rabin, "Hollywood Subway Line Opens Today," *Los Angeles Times*, 12 June 1999, p. B-1; Hugo Martin, "MTA Raises Curtain on Movie Glitz," *Los Angeles Times*, 15 September 1998, pp. B-1+.

20   Greg Goldin, "MALL-YWOOD," *LA Weekly*, 18–24 December 1998, p. 30.

21   Carey McWilliams, *Southern California: An Island on the Land* (Salt Lake City: Gibbs Smith, 1995 (1946)), p. 330.

22   "Hollywood Redevelopment Project," Promotional Kit (Hollywood Chamber of Commerce, 1986), p. 4.

Part 2

Urban Identities, Production, and Exhibition

Part 2 deals with the reciprocal relationship between the formation of particular city identities, on the one hand, and the construction of those identities through film/media production and exhibition, on the other. Production is dealt with in terms of three case studies: Houston, Philadelphia, and Milan. Exhibition is investigated, first, in terms of the opposition of downtown and suburban space, and, secondly, in terms of distinctive forms of exhibition (the film festival, IMAX) as these relate to the formation of city identity.

James Hay's chapter, "Shamrock: Houston's Green Promise," interrogates the implication of cinema and broadcasting in the transformation of the built environment of Houston, Texas from the 1940s to the 1960s, with particular reference to the oil tycoon and real-estate developer Glenn McCarthy. Paul Swann, in his chapter "From Workshop to Backlot: The Greater Philadelphia Film Office," examines the role played by the cinema in constructing the civic identity (and contributing to the cultural economy) of the city of Philadelphia, particularly in the 1980s and 1990s, and the self-conscious promotion of the city as a film location by the Philadelphia Film Office. In "Cities: Real and Imagined," Geoffrey Nowell-Smith describes how, in the case of Italian cinema and location filming in the city of Milan, cinematic representation has shaped collective imaginings of (and day-to-day interaction with) urban space. Mark Neumann, in "Emigrating to New York in 3-D: Stereoscopic Vision in IMAX's Cinematic City," deals with the increasing corporatization and commodification of life in New York City from the beginning of the twentieth century to the beginning of the twenty-first, as articulated in the development of visual technology from early photography to IMAX. Janna Jones, in her chapter "Finding a Place at the Downtown Picture Palace: The Tampa Theater, Florida," provides an exemplary empirical case-study of the migration from city to suburban space, and from cinema to television, through the history of the Tampa Theater and its relationship to the changing demographics of South Florida. Julian Stringer, in "Global Cities and the International Film Festival Economy," assesses the role of the film festival in the development and self-promotion of global cities in the late twentieth century, with a particular focus on the cases of Berlin, Hong Kong, Bombay, Seoul, and Toronto.

6

Shamrock: Houston's Green Promise

James Hay

This chapter is both an allegory and an intervention. My allegory about Houston, Texas during the 1950s and early 1960s will be modest, or at least as modest as Texans are reputed to be with their allegories. I offer it as a means of addressing the tendency in cinema studies to understand the relation between cinema and the city as one of textually constructing identity – of seeing/reading the city *in* films rather than of locating cinema *and* the city. While some films do represent cities, those representations *matter* beyond cinema, in ways not often acknowledged by film criticism (reading the city in films) or a semiotics of the city (deciphering the city as text). In fact, cinema and its modes of representation matter only in relation to other sites and spheres of sociality. Understanding the "mattering" of film representations involves mapping their imbrication and circulation within changing social arrangements and environments. Figuring out how representations have mattered in/for urban environments involves considering how they have operated interdependently with other technologies of urban development. Locating cinema and the city (recognizing that cinema and the city are locations), therefore, does not presume that either has ever been a discrete or abstract entity (except for disciplinary knowledges such as Film Studies or Urban Studies). Cinema and the city are *assemblages,* not just of images and meanings but of interdependent sites and social spaces – and technologies and institutions for organizing and governing those sites, spaces, and interdependencies. As such, cinema and the city have relied upon and developed through one another.

In 1949 Houston's most flamboyant oil-millionaire, Glenn McCarthy, opened that city's newest, most lavish, and "ex-centric" hotel. "Lavish" is perhaps an understatement to describe its relation to that context. As a tribute to his Irish heritage and to the mythology surrounding his rags-to-riches success, he called it the Shamrock Hotel, christened it on St. Patrick's Day 1949, had its interior painted with sixty-three shades of green, its employees outfitted in twenty-five varieties of green and lemon-green uniforms and its entire exterior bathed at night in green light. The Shamrock's enormous ballroom, the Emerald Room, sparkled with green glass-veneered doors and large, luminous Lucite emeralds. That the hotel's décor celebrated – even jested about – the color of money bespoke McCarthy's extravagance at having financed it to the staggering sum of $21 million, nearly all of which had come from his personal fortune as an independent land speculator and oil-"wildcatter." It is not quite true that McCarthy built the Shamrock to make the Waldorf-Astoria in New York look like a lodging house – he built it to make every other hotel in the world look like a lodging house. Certainly the hotel's designers keenly recognized the value of spectacle – the hotel's 500 oil paintings, and its claims to have the largest towels of any hotel in the world and the largest liquor vault anywhere. Patrons of the Shamrock were complicit in its extravagant promise and pleasures, paying exorbitantly not only for rooms but also for meals (pricey "Sham-burgers"), drinks, performances, and other amenities sold at the clubs and the various shops attached to the hotel. One New York visitor was quoted as saying, "We've heard in Brooklyn that the Shamrock has an oil well in every room; there wasn't one in our room but we'd have needed it had we stayed very long." Its display value and prestige certainly did not rely upon having a distinctive façade: the ordinariness of the hotel's exterior moved Frank Lloyd Wright to remark that Houston should erect in front of it an enormous electric sign that spelled out the word "Why?" To answer Wright's question involves recognizing the Shamrock's relation to Houston's political and cultural economy in those years. The Shamrock became an important coordinate in a new map of Houston – a socio-spatial rearrangement that was bringing Houston into a new relation with the nation and a new relation with its own past.

The Shamrock seemed taller and more massive than it was because its identity was so closely linked with Glenn McCarthy. Even before it opened, the Shamrock was legendary in its connection to him and to the way he embodied myths of Texas that had been developing over the first part of the twentieth century. The myth of Texas as an "independent state" had been nurtured during the nineteenth century through numerous accounts of its formation and annexation. In the twentieth century, particularly after World War Two, its identity as an independent state (and a state of independence) became articulated to representations of Texas as a land of oil-rich eccentrics prone to flamboyant displays of kitsch. (About the Shamrock's interior, Frank

Lloyd Wright remarked that he had always wondered what the inside of a jukebox looked like.) Through figures such as McCarthy and his Shamrock, Texas came to represent the excesses of postwar America – not only excesses frequently associated with mass culture but excesses of freedom and power, the total obsession with and disregard for material value that were admired and condemned by intellectuals and popular culture.

This ambivalence is evident in the 1950 *Time* magazine cover story, wherein McCarthy personifies the quirkiness and eccentricity of freedom in "the land of the big rich" and wherein the Shamrock is said to be for Houston what Hollywood is for the world. It also runs through Hollywood films such as *Giant* (George Stevens, 1956), wherein Glenn McCarthy's identity is rearticulated through James Dean's Jett Rink, a character whose most extravagant gesture is building a hotel as extravagant as the Shamrock. The McCarthy–Jett–Dean identity was pivotal in a group of Hollywood films during the 1950s that install the Westerner/cowboy figure in a postwar Western landscape. As a Modern narrative and about American Modernity, the Western had been about the relation between history and geography, a practice of spatially defining the West (America as the West) through narratives of territorialization, settlement, and land development. *Giant* transposes these dimensions of the Western to a mid-twentieth-century Texas. As a representation of national identity, *Giant*'s Texas is a vast, often sublime space suited to the neoliberal practice of "freely" developing "states of independence" – an autonomous space of self-made men. In the state of excess, Jett Rink represents not so much the limits as the over-exuberance of excessively free development and (as his name suggests) a new regime of mobility that was particularly invested in new practices for transcending terrestrial impediments. The empire that Jett builds becomes over-extended and fragile, while the empire developed by his former boss (Bic Benedict) is made to seem more stable, if not in many ways even more expansive. (For instance, the film's closing scene of the white patriarch warming to having bloodlines that will now include a child of Mexican-American descent foreshadows the neoliberal political economy that supports practices of "free trade" embodied in the North American Free Trade Alliance forty years later.) Furthermore, both Bic and Jett's empires are the antithesis of planning, and in this way the film is consonant with the Cold War practice of differentiating between "failed" empires (European Modernist and Communist initiatives to plan environments) and the virtue of a "freely-developed" environment. Not surprisingly, Glenn McCarthy, when asked about the film *Giant*, continually brushed off comparison between Jett Rink and himself, insisting instead on his similarity to Bic Benedict.

It is fairly irrelevant whether *Giant* drew specific connections between McCarthy, Jett Rink, and their hotels or whether Jett more accurately depicts McCarthy than does Bic. It is also misleading to see McCarthy as the author of the Shamrock or the primary basis for its meaning, development, and worth. How and where these identities and representations circulated, how the Shamrock's construction and use involved many social institutions and organized many of the city's social spheres, are issues that I do want to pursue since they pertain to Houston's becoming paradigmatic of, and integral to, a new political and cultural economy that regulated a new sociospatial arrangement during the 1950s.[1]

Giant pertains to a national discourse about Texas, about the nation *as* the most easily recognized state of independence. But the process of articulating Texas to the nation through cinema was predicated upon a new national *diagram* (and new "mappings" of the nation) wherein Texas and Houston were coming to matter in new ways.[2] Understanding this diagram entails considering how cinema and the Shamrock were mechanisms for producing and maintaining a new relation between Houston and the nation. For Houston, the legacy of the "independent state" was vital to the city's becoming a vaguely defined territory of "free development" and a model for how to govern "at a distance." Arguably, Houston became the most vivid example of a "free-range city" whose political and cultural economies organized and disciplined the most rapid expansion of any US city following World War Two. Ada Louise Huxtable is one of many historians to describe Houston as all process and no plan, though Huxtable is referring to the city's lack of commitment to city planning rather than to its *program* for development which depended upon a cultural economy.

Although Houston's commercial and residential development had been remarkable since the 1920s, it outpaced the growth of every city in the US after the war. In 1949, when construction on the Shamrock Hotel was completed, Houston had become the fastest growing city per capita in the US, a trend that continued throughout the 1950s, as Houston grew seven times faster than the average US city and its construction value ranked the highest in the nation.[3] In 1948, the city annexed enough land to double its 76-square-mile area, and ten years later that 150-square-mile area had more than doubled again. Although the fastest increase in the percentage of Houston's population growth occurred during the 1920s amidst the boom created by coastal oil production, its population grew most dramatically in the aftermath of World War Two.[4] Between 1930 and 1945 Houston's population grew by 300,000 (for a population of about 650,000), but between 1945 and 1950 alone it gained almost another 200,000 inhabitants (for a population of roughly 807,000), another 250,000 between 1950 and 1954 when its population passed one million, and nearly another 250,000 by 1960 when its population reached roughly 1.24 million.[5] Most of this growth in population and land mass occurred through the development of suburbs, and one of its suburban developments, Sharpstown, begun in 1954, quickly became the largest residential development in the world. But the scale of its expansion and suburbanization is not the only reason for thinking of Houston as the most blatant example of free-range city and neoliberal governance. By the 1940s Houston was one of the largest US cities without zoning; by 1962 it became the only major US city without zoning, and it did not implement its first official zoning laws until the mid-1990s. Its rapid expansion and its easy conversion of land to real estate and then to planned community perpetuated the nineteenth-century myth of Manifest Destiny, while redefining the frontier as a predominant objective of postwar municipality and settlement.

The Shamrock was instrumental in making Houston an important point within the postwar political and cultural economy largely because it linked the distribution of material and cultural resources in and beyond Houston. The hotel's relation to Houston's political economy pertained to its establishing an alternative commercial zone outside the downtown and to its bringing together new and established Houston businesses. For its opening every major business in Houston bought an advertisement trumpeting the hotel's value to the city and calling attention to the city's commercial resources and promise. An exhibition hall was constructed next to the hotel, and nearly one hundred and fifty Houston businesses staged exhibits there in conjunction with the hotel's opening festivities. Precisely because of the hotel's value in *representing* Houston and its modernity, the hotel reconfigured Houston through a new *cultural economy*. The hotel's design did not only become a means of representing the building of Houston (with McCarthy as developer-celebrity) and a point of a discourse about disciplining culture (an expression of "mass culture" and kitsch for both Frank Lloyd Wright and Hollywood), it was designed to be a stage for celebrity and spectacle. *Time* magazine's statement that the Shamrock was to Houston what Hollywood was to the world alluded to all of these possibilities, and is one way of thinking about Houston's value in a postwar cultural economy as a free-range city. As an icon of Houston's identity in the early 1950s, the hotel represented a new technique for constructing the city's identity, and one that was dependent upon Hollywood.

The Shamrock's connection to Hollywood was crucial to its design and to promoting Houston as spectacle. Organizers of the hotel's opening festivities chartered a 14-car Santa Fe Super Chief and airplanes to transport 30 Hollywood actors, 200 of their partners and associates, other celebrities and numerous business associates of McCarthy from Texas, New York, and Washington, DC. Stars attending included Pat O'Brien (who had broken ground for the hotel in 1946), Dorothy Lamour, Peggy Cummins, Robert Ryan, Ward Bond, Walter Brennan, Kirk Douglas, Van Heflin, Stan Laurel, and Robert Stack. Tickets were sold to 2,500 plainer citizens who were joined by over two hundred newsmen, columnists, photographers and newsfilm crews – some from outside the United States. The celebration was the most spectacular and most nationally publicized in the city's history.

McCarthy used the hotel's opening to premier his first Hollywood production, *The Green Promise* (William D. Russell, 1949), and all of the film's actors attended the hotel's gala and participated in a torchlight parade to the Metropolitan Theater, the second oldest in Houston's downtown. The film was (and remained) a rather obscure production that McCarthy made through RKO – one of several Hollywood studios that he had considered purchasing. The film's title refers to the efforts of its characters to cultivate a plot of land, the "green promise" referring to their connection to the soil. The title also refers to a future (a "promise") embodied in a child whose role in revitalizing her family and its homestead occurs through her enrollment in the 4–H Club – a modern organization dedicated to training youth to become "developers" and custodians of land and livestock.

While 4-H may have been an unusual subject, it was quite consonant with the vein of Hollywood cinema in the 1950s about settlement and land management in a modern rural and Western environment. The 4-H Club, first organized in the early twentieth century, emphasized educating youth in modern techniques of farming, husbandry, and "homemaking". Houston had been the site of one of the first urban chapters of 4-H (in 1910), but urban chapters remained fairly rare until the 1950s when 4-H became widespread in US cities and particularly suburbs – integral to their economic, civic, and cultural formation.[6] Initially managed by state agricultural extension programs (as represented by the film), new chapters of 4-H were promoted and underwritten in the 1950s by urban business leaders – so it is not unusual that McCarthy produced a film about 4-H. Membership in the organization increased dramatically during the 1950s when 4-H became an institution integral to a modern urban economy which continued to value displays of nineteenth-century agrarianism – as much as a kind of nostalgia and a procedure for naturalizing the rationality/science of land development as a way of marking the natural/social improvements achieved through neoliberal forms of management (growing one's own garden, raising one's own livestock, and submitting them to state-sponsored competition). Training the youth of the country became an indispensable component of displaying this improvement. A film dramatizing the value of the 4-H Club for the cultivation of a modern environment, to the engineering of homesteads, and to scientific principles of connecting and managing home and property all made *The Green Promise* an important allegory *for* postwar Houston. That the organization's well-known emblem was a green shamrock (with the letter "H" emblazoned on each of the four leaves) made the film's representations strategic to the hotel's and Houston's identity. As the film's male hero, an enlightened technical advisor of land management (and the adult sponsor of the local 4-H Club), explains to the prospective club recruit, the clover is not about finding luck but about "making one's own luck." The film is unusually didactic, a set of instructions about how to make one's own luck through modern techniques of engineering and governing home and land.

Clearly the film performed an important role in promoting the hotel and Houston. The film's resonance with the hotel's representation of a new Houston – the film's role in constructing the hotel's identity – conjoined cinema and hotel as interdependent technologies of Houston's postwar development. The new political and cultural economy to which Houston was becoming integral was predicated upon forming links such as this between the Shamrock, local/national broadcasting and local/Hollywood cinema. The parade from the hotel to the Metropolitan Theater was one display and materialization of these links.

Through the 1950s, cinema became increasingly reliant in Houston upon radio and TV broadcasting. The appearance of so many Hollywood celebrities for the hotel's opening was not merely a publicity stunt, and its historical implications went far beyond the event itself. The party was broadcast coast-to-coast as part of the Dorothy Lamour NBC radio show, though the network cut the broadcast short because of the overwhelming noise and the guests' drunken behavior. Throughout the early 1950s, numerous other local and national broadcasts from the hotel's Emerald Room, and the hotel's contracting in of Hollywood celebrities, not only made it Houston's premier night spot for socialites but made Houston a new center (alongside New York, Chicago, and Los Angeles) in a burgeoning postwar cultural economy of mass media. Just how much this historical convergence of the Shamrock, Hollywood, and local broadcasting pertained to a new commercial *and* cultural economy is affirmed by the many Hollywood celebrities (including Edgar Bergen, Tony Martin, Dinah Shore, Frank Sinatra, and Harpo Marx) who, having been contracted with the Shamrock, became shareholders in one of McCarthy's oil fields.

By 1956, when *Giant* premiered in Houston, the Shamrock Hotel had been bought by Hilton Hotels, and the enormous oil painting of Glenn McCarthy in the hotel lobby had been replaced with an equally massive portrait of Conrad Hilton. The première, in the private Cork Room of the Shamrock-Hilton, was a relatively sedate affair compared to the hotel's opening gala and was attended by George Stevens but none of the film's stars. The film, however, did break the attendance record for one week at the Majestic Theater where it opened. In the film, Houston is not the location of the gala, and in many respects Houston was not a city that fell easily into Hollywood's extensive mythologizing of Texas. For Houston's boosters, however, the film's première was an occasion to resurrect – albeit in a more disciplined fashion – the Shamrock as city allegory – and for Warner Bros., another studio in which McCarthy was rumored to have considered investing, the Houston debut became a propitious backdrop for promoting the film through the McCarthy–Shamrock legacy.

Within a few weeks, Columbia Pictures released a short-lived feature called *The Houston Story* (William Castle, 1956) – virtually the only Hollywood film explicitly set in Houston, and one of only a small number about the city in twentieth-century Texas. Its plot, typical of the crime film sub-genre of the late-1940s and 1950s known as the "police procedural film" (*The Naked City*, *The Phenix City Story*, *Northside 777*), followed the crusade of a police detective to root out organized crime in the local oil industry.[7] The film's selection of Houston to represent modern efforts to regulate nefarious empire-builders intent on freely developing states of independence attests to just how much Houston's identity had become suited for such representations. As in many Hollywood films, however, *The Houston Story* was not filmed in Houston – its "Houston" could have been Chicago or New York – and in that respect, the film's Houston is a prewar city lacking the rampant suburbanization which was dramatically transfiguring the real Houston during the 1950s.

Films such as *Giant*, and to a lesser extent *The Houston Story*, which were preoccupied with the modernity of Texas and the West, must be understood not only in terms of their system of representation (cinema) but in terms of the dominant sociocultural distribution of the 1950s (suburbanization). *The Green Promise*, which begins as its central characters arrive to develop their modern homestead, represented postwar mobility and settlement (the myth of America as waiting-to-be-developed land) and (through its connection to the Shamrock, built on the edge of the prewar city center) was a local mechanism for Houston's own suburbanization, part of the city's redistribution of cultural sites and resources. In Houston, this was evident in the changing styles and location of movie theaters. Between 1940 and 1949, the number of Houston's movie theaters grew from twenty-four to thirty-three, with four of the nine theaters built during the late 1940s being drive-ins. Between 1949 and 1956, the number of indoor theaters increased by only one while the number of drive-ins grew by nine, for a total of forty-three theaters. These theaters were located entirely in the suburbs, benefiting from still undeveloped parcels of land and being built without the intention of permanence. They were, in this sense, truly a feature of Raymond Williams's concept of mobile and semi-privatized spaces. As in many parts of the country (though perhaps more so because of its semi-tropical climate), Houston's drive-ins and drive-in movie attendance rivaled that of older, indoor movie theaters during the 1950s. A drive-in was erected at the gateway to Sharpstown (the biggest suburb in Houston, and in the US, during the 1950s), offering a vivid example of Houston suburbia's dependence upon cultural technologies and spaces such as drive-ins as makeshift and mobile markers of "hometown." In this regard, drive-in movie theaters were linked to the Shamrock Hotel through Houston's cultural economy.

In addition to the high-profile theaters that I have just described there were seven theaters located in African-American enclaves of Houston, attended only by African-American patrons, and thus invisible to the rest of the city. Through the 1950s, African-American inhabitants of Houston were more concentrated into particular sections of the city than at *any* time in Houston's history (91–93 percent occupying city areas rather than the suburbs). And unlike the suburban settlements, with names like Oak Forest, the Black sections of Houston retained (and still largely retain) their nineteenth-century designation as "wards," long after that system of government had disappeared in Houston.[8] In the 1950s, the "ward" was an effect of a spatial politics of containment and the distribution of cultural resources for postwar frontier living. Even though the Metropolitan Theater, the site of the premiere of McCarthy's *The Green Promise*, had been one of two downtown Houston movie theaters that had allowed the city's African-American inhabitants to attend screenings after midnight on weekends, African-Americans were not admitted to *The Green Promise*.

I cite Houston's drive-ins and its ward-cinemas as examples of the city's new socio-spatial arrangement and cultural economy. But this arrangement's installation involved a process of conversion. One particularly significant feature of Houston's expansion and reconfiguration during the postwar years was its implication in a local, national, and global process of *(re-)mapping* the West. This was a process whereby Houston's reconfiguration and its simultaneously changing relations with Texas, the South, the Southwest, the National, and beyond was predicated upon emerging and residual modes of imaging and imagining the West – both in and outside of Houston. This process involved the changing place and the changing circulation of the Western – in civic life, in the formation or disappearance of certain local institutions, in the domestic sphere, in emerging spheres of sociality, in areas of industry and leisure, in Houston's rapid geographic expansion and rapidly transfigured landscape. Understanding the Western's link to late-Modern forms of settlement, to land development and real estate, is therefore not only a matter of representation, unless one is willing to recognize the relation of cultural technologies such as cinema and broadcasting to other instruments of territorialization. Or, put another way, in representing the American West, the Western has been a practice of mapping – not only as a re-presentation of History and Geography (the Old West as the articulation of generic elements and as chronotope), but as a procedure implicated in the broad and complex structuring and governing of places and environments (the Modern West).

During the 1950s, Houston's expansion relied upon contemporaneous productions of the Western. Houston and the Western became linked through cinema and its relation to other cultural technologies.[9] This is quite remarkable given that it occurred more intensely during the 1950s than before and its implications more profoundly affected Houston than arguably any other city of its size in the US. The 1950s was certainly a period when cinema, radio, and television converged to produce performers such as Gene Autry and Roy Rogers, whose cowboy identities and musical styles were always

Figure 6.1 Glenn McCarthy (third from left) and "the singing cowboy", Gene Autry (third from right) – riding the free-range city (*Courtesy Houston Metropolitan Research Center, Houston Public Library*)

tied ambiguously both to the Old West and a landscape marked by Modern (and occasionally futuristic) technologies. The popularity of these figures became important to rapidly expanding urban environments such as Houston through broadcasting and cinema. There are examples of this that are not unique to Houston, such as the popularity of Western motifs in the architecture and décor of 1950s suburban homes. But there are other particularly striking local examples: that between 1950 and 1956 roughly 50 percent of the movies exhibited at theaters for African-American inhabitants of Houston were Westerns, that one of the largest children's amusement parks in Houston's newest suburbs was named the Wee Wild West, that Houston's first professional baseball team was called the Colt 45s and that they played at a stadium whose bar was decorated after the TV series *Gunsmoke* and whose parking lot was organized into zones named after figures from 1950s TV Westerns. As in many Southwestern cities, the street-sides of some of

Houston's drive-in movie screens were adorned with images from the Western (a convergence of the Western mural, cinema, and billboard advertising). That drive-ins were an effect of Houston's rapid expansion, that they were a technology and space suited to the forms of sociality occurring in newly formed settlements, makes their connection to the Western noteworthy.

While all of these are instances of how the Western became imbricated in the landscape of Houston in the 1950s, of how it marked particular sites of local culture, of how it organized Houston as a socio-spatial arrangement, the most vivid example of its relevance to Houston is in the Houston rodeo. Although the Houston rodeo began just before World War Two, it became the largest in the nation during the decade, attracting contestants and spectators primarily from Texas. By 1956, the parade through downtown Houston involved over 4,000 horses. Ticket sales for the then two-day event exceeded 100,000. The rodeo began to use Hollywood celebrities to promote itself and its connection to other events and businesses in the city. The most frequent guest stars were Roy Rogers, Dale Evans, and Trigger, who appeared in five of the Houston rodeos, several times with the entire cast of *The Roy Rogers Show*. Other celebrities included adult/child duos such as Johnny Crawford and Chuck Conners from *The Rifleman*, Lorne Greene and Michael Landon from *Bonanza*, and James Arnes from *Gunsmoke*. In 1956, contests surrounding the rodeo offered local children a chance to win a trip to Hollywood to meet the stars of film and new TV Westerns.

Significantly, the Houston rodeo became one of the most preeminent events in the local production of early Houston television. KPRC promoted the rodeo in 1952 through the first reenactment of the Salt Grass Trail cattle drive. The Salt Grass Trail was one of the many routes in Texas across which cattle were driven to market during the nineteenth century, and it remained a residual feature of an early Modern Texas cartography when Houston was emerging as a commercial center connected to other regions in North America through the railway system. But the 1950s reenactment (like the rodeo) celebrated Houston's postwar place in new economies wherein television was quickly becoming an essential instrument. In fact, the reenactment was conceived by the local TV station and organized so that the first reenacted trail rides would culminate at the TV studio and then be broadcast the following day as a parade through the city's downtown. Even in the years after the station grew too big for that location, the reenactment (by that time having taken on an authenticity of its own) continued to terminate at roughly the same place. In 1956, Roy Rogers greeted the riders at the end of their journey, expanding the reenactment's role in promoting the rodeo. By 1959, the local press publicized James Arnes's accompaniment of the Trail Ride through photo-ops of the TV star at towns along the way, though Arnes actually made the journey to and from these publicity appearances each day by car. By the early 1960s, the Trail Ride's last leg brought it through the city's new suburbs, and the park where it culminated had become inundated by commercial and suburban development.

Beyond the significance of these occurrences for Houston's political and cultural economy, they were also a basis for Houston's implication in a new national formation. Television particularly became instrumental in converting Houston for the nation through the city's invention of its Western heritage and pedigree, though locally and nationally television was an intermediating technology for cinema and radio. Between 1955 and 1957, NBC television featured Houston several times in its "Wide, Wide World," a series documenting localities in the US. One of these features was about the Texas Prison Rodeo, advertised as "The Wildest Show on Earth." And in 1960, NBC featured live coverage of Roy Rogers at the Houston Rodeo. These developments are particularly significant because they facilitated Houston's becoming crucial to the political and cultural economy of what John Kennedy labeled "the New Frontier" in the early 1960s. Significantly, the myth of a New Frontier was dependent upon Houston, the city which became the site of NASA and of broadcasting space launches. By 1964, Houston was christened "Space City" – a term that was predicated upon postwar projections of an Old Frontier and new ways of engineering settlement, upon an emerging relation between the West, the suburban backyard and space exploration. Already by the mid-1950s, *Giant's* Jett personified this contradiction. While his name refers to the "color of crude" (as in oil and rich Texans), it increasingly gets associated – in, through, and around this text – with hypermobility, the rapid and free conversion of land for commercial use, a state of sublimity resting upon supersonic technologies for promoting free movement in vast, open spaces.

Towards the end of Wim Wenders's *Lightning Over Water* (1980), director Nicholas Ray explains to a group of Barnard College students that his 1952 film *The Lusty Men* is not a Western. According to Ray, the film "is really about people who want to own a home of their own." "That," he explains, "was the great American search at the time this film was made." Ray's film was one of many Hollywood films and television series produced during the 1950s and early 1960s that set many traditional elements of the Western in a twentieth-century setting. His comment about the film's representation of home seems a fitting way to conclude my description of how "settlement" was spatially defined in a free-range city – a deeply neoliberal model of free development – such as postwar Houston. The construction of the Shamrock Hotel may have been an effective technique of spatially defining "home-town," but its manner of doing so was instrumental to an emerging political and cultural economy reliant upon a new practice of settlement. Interestingly, soon after the Shamrock was completed, Glenn McCarthy briefly explored the possibility of developing a massive indoor sports stadium (a "Colostadium") on land not far from the hotel. A decade later, in keeping with the city's "rebirth" as Space City, Roy Hoffienz (another Houston developer, broadcast company owner, and former mayor) opened such a complex: the Houston Astrodome and Astrodomain (which evangelist Billy Graham described as the eighth wonder of the world, in part because it was claimed that the dome could cover the Shamrock Hotel). In that sense, the New Frontier is a concept that can be gleaned from the convergence that I am describing through the allegory of the Shamrock – Houston's "green promise."

Notes

1   While "political economy" refers to the procedures (the "science") for managing population, territory, and capital through distributions and networks, I use the term "cultural economy" (a term linked to but not interchangeable with political economy) to refer to distributions and networks of populations, territory, and cultural resources/capital. While both terms refer to a sociospatial arrangement (the distribution of social classes in particular urban spaces, for instance), the latter term refers specifically to the arrangement of cultural sites and access to them by particular peoples.

2   The term "diagram" is one that I borrow from Gilles Deleuze's discussion of Foucault. See Deleuze, *Foucault*, trans. Sean Hand (Minneapolis: University of Minnesota Press, 1988).

3   See James Buchanan (ed.), *Houston: A Chronological and Documentary History* (Dobbs Ferry, New York: Oceana, 1975).

4   See *Population, Land Use, Growth: Background for a Comprehensive Plan – 1C*, Houston City Planning Commission document, 1959, Houston Public Library.

5   Ibid.

6   By 1958, only 57 per cent of its enrolment came from farm families, a 9 percent decrease in just four years. For more on the history of the 4–H Club, see Thomas and Marilyn Wessel, *4–H: An American Idea, 1900–1980* (National 4–H Council, 1982).

7   *The Naked City* (Jules Dassin, 1948), *The Phenix City Story* (Phil Karlson, 1955), *Northside 777* (Henry Hathaway, 1948).

8   During the 1950s, most African-Americans in Houston resided in the Third Ward (just south-east of downtown) and the Fifth Ward (just north-east of downtown). For more on Houston's wards in the twentieth century, see Robert Bullard, *Invisible Houston* (College Station, TX: Texas A&M University Press, 1987); and Howard Beeth and Cary Wintz (eds.), *Black Dixie* (College Station, TX: Texas A&M University Press, 1992).

9   Houston had developed around agricultural and then oil and petrochemical industries. It had never been a center for livestock (particularly cattle) markets as other parts of Texas had been. I mention this to emphasize that Houston's rather intense investment in the Western during the 1950s became particularly pertinent to representing its place within an emerging political and cultural economy.

7

From Workshop to Backlot: The Greater Philadelphia Film Office

Paul Swann

A great many American cities are crumbling at the core, having spun their wealth, growth, and much of their population to the periphery.[1] This phenomenon is rare in European cities. I was reminded of this when reading Jean-François Lyotard's essay on "the zone," the penumbra of poverty which skirts modern Paris while its core remains vibrant.[2] European and American cities are fundamentally different in this respect. Most big US cities, at least those in the Northeast and Midwest, must plan for the future while assuming shrinking or static populations and tax revenues. Or, as Peter Wollen has apocalyptically characterized it, the prospects for "the post-Fordist city" are "de-industrialization, casual and freelance employment, large-scale immigration, the privatization of welfare, and social polarization."[3] Local economic development strategies must increase revenue stability, decrease vulnerability to external forces, provide good jobs to local citizens, and, hopefully, increase the overall satisfaction of city residents. America's mayors assume they must do all this with relatively little help from the federal government, and a lively engagement with the marketplace.[4] The phenomenon of the regional or city film office, charged with wooing filmmakers into the city, is part of this equation.

Fredric Jameson's classic essay "Class and Allegory in Contemporary Mass Culture: *Dog Day Afternoon* as a Political Film" was a pioneering attempt to tie close textual reading and urban political economy.[5] Jameson connected the narrative and style of *Dog Day Afternoon* (Sidney Lumet, 1975) to the tensions between city and federal government, and inner city and transnational banking corporations, but did not address the material impact of a transnational conglomerate presence in the inner city in the form of the film's production crew. The current scholarly interest in relationships between the city and cinema has until now largely focused on issues of representation rather than political economy.[6] But focusing on cities as discourse should not exclude timely study of the material consequences of city-based location filmmaking.

I want to appraise the work of the Greater Philadelphia Film Office as part of a more general discussion of many American cities' transformation into postmodern spectacle.[7] Philadelphia is the paradigmatic late nineteenth-century city, whose quintessential forms were the department store, the Taylorized factory, and the nickelodeon. The early twenty-first-century city is grounded in symbolism and imagery, and its paradigmatic forms include the plaza, the entertainment complex, the gallery, and the film shoot. All of these transitions are especially overt in Philadelphia.

Many US cities now literally live off their appearances, exploiting their visual rather than their physical or human resources. Cultural production has replaced manufacturing as a source of urban vitality. America's mayors have become strong advocates for the arts, culture, and regional and national heritage. Regional earnings and employment invariably figure prominently in their arguments. What some critics have called the "three C's" (coliseums, casinos, and convention centers) are often the focus of their plans. Attracting cultural workers and cultural tourists vies with riverboat gambling, building aquariums, and hosting national political conventions as a way of reviving national standing and local economies of post-industrial cities. Nowhere is this truer than in Philadelphia, whose population has shrunk by a third since 1950 and by 9 percent since 1990 alone. During the same time frame, the city's stock of manufacturing jobs has declined from over 300,000 to fewer than 70,000.

The post-industrial city is increasingly based on what has recently been christened the "experience economy" in which, as B. Joseph Pine and others have explained, "those businesses that relegate themselves to the diminishing world of goods and services will be rendered irrelevant. To avoid this fate, you must learn to stage a rich, compelling experience."[8] Municipal authorities and cultural organizations increasingly think of their own activities in the same way. Cultural advocacy organizations such as the American Arts Alliance justify their efforts as central to urban revitalization as well as the tax rolls.[9] Philadelphia's Avenue of the Arts, for example, is at the core of the city's rejuvenation plans. Pennsylvania's governors and mayors woo filmmakers to come to make their next feature or TV commercial in the Keystone State. Metropolitan art galleries, aquariums, and museums are packaged and marketed like theme parks. Major exhibits – whether dinosaurs or fine art – are advertised with all the fanfare of a major movie opening. Perform-

ing arts centers are springing up in lapsed manufacturing cities like Philadelphia and Newark. The process of transformation and revitalization extends
in many directions. Cities strive to become brand names while they court
national conventions, sports events, and film shoots, generally framed in
terms of their contribution to employment and regional economies. Both the
Greater Philadelphia Film Office and the Philadelphia Art Museum emphasize the dollars and jobs they bring to the area in their promotional materials. The Film Office has attracted several major film shoots, and its own
website announces that it generated $22 million of regional "economic im-
pact" in 1999 alone. Likewise, just to cite one example, the Philadelphia
Museum of Art claims that the 1996 Cézanne show brought a "remarkable
fiscal boon" to Philadelphia, injecting, by one estimate, $86.5 million into
the city's economy.[10]

     This is not a complete break with the past. Georg Simmel, Walter Benjamin,
and others who examined modernity and its consequences prophesied many
of these developments. The modern shopping mall's ambience is reminiscent
of the department store. The urban entertainment complex is a descendant
of the World's Fair. However, there are differences in degree and kind in
how twenty-first-century cities put themselves on display, and their increasing commitment to what Buzz Bissinger recently characterized as "the audience economy."[11] Or as James Hay succinctly puts it:

> The historical overlay between the cinematic and the televisual in US cities is
> thus part of a process whereby the early commercial center of the city, which
> may have residually functioned in the manner of the medieval city center,
> multiplied and spread around the city as part of land development, only to be
> redeveloped for attracting consumers both from the outlying developments
> and from outside the city.[12]

The Museum

Museums across the United States, following the lead of the Philadelphia
Museum of Art's 1996 Cézanne show, aim at attendance maximization and
largely judge success or failure by numbers of visitors, hotel rooms filled, and
dollars spent. The Cézanne show pioneered a now standard imbrication of
hotel accommodation and museum admission packages.

     Modern exhibition techniques, often labeled "the new museology," strive
to make collections and special exhibits interactive and participatory.[13] Modeled
on the mall, the museum experience is increasingly one of strolling, min-
gling, and shopping. A factoid currently circulating within non-profit circles
in the US is that museums and art galleries currently have higher cumulative
attendance figures than professional sports.[14] Cultural districts are increas-

ingly regarded as an important way to revive flagging downtowns. An early indicator of this blurring of the line between the museum and entertainment occurred in 1989, when the Museum Trustees Association held their annual meeting in Disneyworld.

The Entertainment Center

Another major initiative is the urban entertainment complex. Many cities are taking their lead from Las Vegas, and are increasingly committed to structuring themselves around experience and amusement.[15] The fanfare surrounding plans for Jump Street, a leisure and shopping complex in North Philadelphia, and DisneyQuest, a Disney theme park to be housed in a five-story interactive theme park on Philadelphia's main thoroughfare, is as much about the renewal of moribund culture as jobs and dollars spent. In 1999, Philadelphia's former mayor, Ed Rendall, was photographed shaking hands with Goofy and Mickey, or as he put it himself, "All right, I'll do the fucking mouse." In return, the city got 200 jobs, and a venture which promised to lure visitors where Independence Park, the Art Museum, and other attractions capitalizing on Philadelphia's history had failed.[16] Independence Park, inaugurated at the Bicentennial, was an example of failed spectacle, and the crowds of visitors it was expected to generate never materialized. Twenty-five years later, it is being rethought by the city and the National Park Service.

Urban entertainment centers are to the first years of the twenty-first century what the department store was 100 years ago. Immersing oneself in an exotic virtual reality, purchasing a Disney-logoed sweater while watching a Disney movie on large-screen video in the Disney store, or buying a Cézanne-autographed baseball at the Art Museum's store, are increasingly interchangeable experiences.[17]

The Shoot

American cities compete frantically with each other to attract media production companies on location. The common wisdom is that film shoots generate no toxic byproducts, and represent a brief, yet dynamic injection of capital in their need for freelance workers, hotel rooms, and other services. Most location film shoots take place on public property. Granting access to these spaces and greasing the wheels of municipal and union bureaucracy are the strongest cards local film offices have to play when making a pitch to filmmakers. The Greater Philadelphia Film Office, for example, has attracted $150 million of expenditure to the Philadelphia region since 1992. Recently, for example, *The Age of Innocence* (Martin Scorsese, 1993), *Philadelphia* (Jonathan Demme, 1993), *Twelve Monkeys* (Terry Gilliam, 1997), *Beloved* (Jonathan Demme, 1998), and *The Sixth Sense* (M. Night Shyalaman, 1999) were shot entirely or in part in Philadelphia.[18] In addition to this interesting cultural shift, the claims regarding the benefits of transforming major cities into sound stages and backlots warrant close scrutiny. Such an audit would reveal whether the tax rebates and free or heavily discounted municipal services that are now standard packages for film shoots are justified. In the short term, they offer temporary employment for taxpaying citizens as well as some longer-term benefits, including the prospect of many more jobs being created over a longer time frame, and more nebulous gains such as promoting and advertising the city itself.

In the US, the infrastructure for wooing location shoots has been in place since the mid-1970s. Film officers and commissions now have their own annual conventions and trade journal, as well as established ground rules for their activities. At state and city level, film offices maintain databases, photo archives, and websites that provide ready access to location information, local talent, and other selling points.[19] Film officers constantly scan the film trade press for information about upcoming projects. Low-budget filmmak-

Figure 7.1 Philadelphia remade as nineteenth-century Cincinnati during the production of *Beloved* (*Photograph: Leon Sanginiti, Jr. Courtesy Greater Philadelphia Film Office*)

ers often complain that this courtship is directed primarily at large budget productions or commercial spot-makers.

At city level, film offices have the same public profile as convention and tourism promotion offices, although they often must struggle for funding. Philadelphia's last film officer, in fact, made the transition to head the city's convention agency. For some cities this activity is on a very large scale. To give the most extreme instance, 213 feature films were shot in New York City in 1997.[20]

The Value of Production

There are several formulae for calculating the economic benefits of a film shoot coming to town. Unsurprisingly, given the boosterist rhetoric that tends to be associated with this process, state and city film commissioners are generally optimists. Film offices depend on the media producers themselves to provide budget figures to generate production revenue figures. If a production company does not supply the numbers or applies creative accounting principles, in order perhaps to mask cost overruns, then the figures are not accurate from the outset. Underreporting is also a possibility, since film offices typically only report money expended on location shoots, not whatever may have been spent within the confines of a studio sound stage.

Film officers generally compute income to the state or city by using revenue figures and production day tallies. Their goal is to satisfy the film trade's and consumer press's information needs, while also justifying their own funding. Many film offices simply report the total of actual production expenditures, while others use economic multipliers, such as the Federal Reserve multiplier (currently running at 3.57), to determine economic impact. This is a somewhat arbitrary formula that multiplies the actual amount spent on production several-fold. The rationale is that out-of-pocket on-location expenditures have a ripple effect, and stimulate other spending within a local economy. Using one such formula, an Arthur Andersen study of a single film with a $14 million local production budget found that the project generated $21 million in local economic impact, created the equivalent of 183 full-time jobs, and generated nearly $800,000 in state, county, and city taxes. However, in a reaction to the multiplier method's subjective and arbitrary quality, the latest trend in reporting economic impact is to not officially calculate it at all.[21]

The Greater Philadelphia Film Office, for example, only reports hard numbers such as total production days and reported $21 million in actual production expenditure in the city during 1998.[22] Productions, of course, range from the big-budget to the modestly financed film. For example, at the high end, *Beloved* was on location in Philadelphia for eight months. This represented eight months of steady employment for between fifty and seventy-five skilled production workers. A medium-budget film, such as the surprise hit *The Sixth Sense*, provided employment for about thirty people for three months. A low-budget feature, such as Eugene Martin's *Edge City* (1998), provided comparable employment for perhaps ten people. These numbers indicate how much of a multiplier effect we need to have to make this into a major trend. *The Sixth Sense*, for example, was one of the top five box-office films in the United States in 1999, yet employed fewer people than, for example, a medium-sized restaurant.

What is not taken into account in these figures is any production that is not on location. Philadelphia is the Hollywood of the "infomercial" and is home to a number of home shopping networks, including QVC, yet none of the wages and taxes generated by this activity figures in the Film Office's calculations.

The *Hawaii Five-O* Effect

State film commissioners believe that entertainment and commercial production have promotional value and the potential to attract other investments or tourism. For example, the television series *Hawaii Five-O* ceased production more than twenty-five years ago but, according to that state's film office, international syndication of the late 1960s cop show continues to promote Hawaii around the world. Recent studies have shown that films can promote tourism. Currently, the two most visited tourist destinations in the state of Iowa, for example, are those featured in *Field of Dreams* (Phil Alden Robinson, 1989) and *Bridges of Madison County* (Clint Eastwood, 1995). And tourists show up in Savannah, Georgia, looking for Forrest Gump's park bench. A similar effect was felt from the filming of *Witness* (Peter Weir, 1987) in Pennsylvania's Lancaster County area. Currently, Philadelphia is bracing for tourists lured to the city shown in such a positive light in *The Sixth Sense* or, as the head of the Illinois Film Office put it, "I always thought Philadelphia was a crime-ridden, rat-infested, mayor-torching neighborhood hellhole. But when you see a movie like *The Sixth Sense* with its cosmopolitan settings, your image of Philadelphia changes."[23]

Many films are not explicit about precisely where they are set, so it is hard to see how they can directly promote a specific locale. Some filmmakers, such as Baltimore's Barry Levinson or Manhattan's Woody Allen, go to great pains to frame stories around their hometowns, but most filmmakers are less concerned about this issue.[24] Often cities are obliged to dissemble. "License plating," or changing vehicle license plates but little else, is a common way of disguising one city as another. Philadelphia has become Cincinnati (*Beloved*) and New York (*Age of Innocence*), and cities like Toronto and Prague have stood in for just about anywhere.

There are also bleak works such as *Twelve Monkeys* or *Eraserhead*, both made in Philadelphia, which seem a thoroughly dysfunctional way of promoting a city.[25] One might also speculate that *Taxi Driver*, for example, may well have discouraged tourists from visiting New York City. The *Hawaii Five-O* effect may also well be moot or, at best, subliminal if a location is not acknowledged or if the featured city is not a "brand name."

Contested Public Space

There are two commonly heard fables about location shooting. One is about the troublesome film shoot, how inconvenient and disruptive it was to the day-to-day lives of the local community. The other is about the helpful film crew, buying all their needs from the local hardware store and, incidentally, painting a lot of trim while they were in residence.[26] Newspaper reports often veer between these two disparate accounts of location shoots.

Like the tourist attraction or the convention center, the film shoot often subordinates permanent residents' needs to those of transient visitors. Reconfiguring public space to accommodate a location manager, such as dressing Third Street in Philadelphia's Old City section as nineteenth-century Cincinnati for the making of *Beloved*, generally entails battles over parking, rights of way, licenses, and permits, which are almost always won by the production company.

On more than one instance, residents have been told that they have forfeited basic civil rights and that they and their property have been mandated to cooperate with a production company. In New York, a film crew recently incensed a community by placing signs warning passersby that entering the street where they lived meant they were "irrevocably" consenting to having their image used "worldwide, for any purpose whatsoever in perpetuity." Clearly such warnings have little legal standing, but they draw attention to the contested nature of the location shoot.[27] As a crew member in another, far less contentious shoot in Maryland described on-location shooting's disruptions, "it's like having the circus coming to town and staying."[28]

Reality Check

The economic advantage of transforming cities like Philadelphia into theme-park backlots is of a much smaller order of magnitude than, for example, the loss of a major manufacturing plant or the closure of a military base. When the Philadelphia Naval Shipyard was closed, 35,000 jobs went with it. These were relatively well-paid, skilled blue-collar positions which are very hard to replace.[29] In contrast, most films bring in their own expertise, and do not make sustained use of highly skilled local talent. Nevertheless, replacing manufacturing with spectacle is an approach gathering momentum on both sides of the Atlantic. In New York, Mayor Rudi Giuliani and New York's film office are currently celebrating tripling the quantity of location shooting in the city during the last five years. Glasgow, a city with many similarities to Philadelphia, recently opened a film office and proclaimed a film charter promising benefits to filmmakers and citizens similar to those proffered by American film offices.[30] These are good developments, but they need to be kept in perspective. The motion picture industry is indeed providing large numbers of positions in the Philadelphia area, but the vast majority are minimum wage jobs working at video rental stores.[31]

There is a postmodern inexorability in valuing cities as images rather than as sites of production. There is also something profoundly troubling about the arithmetic of turning citizens into stagehands, extras, and concierges. It is easy to see the appeal for cities of marketing themselves without a major investment in physical plant. Yet there is already within the location film business a fear that cities themselves will eventually be replaced by digitally based virtual locations. This prospect has film officers worried. There have already been cases of film offices sending location photographs to prospective clients who then take these images, digitize them, use them, and essentially bypass the cities altogether.[32]

In the interim, the film office is part of the same agenda as the "malling" of the museum and the leveling of obsolete industrial plant to make way for the next urban theme park.

Notes

1   Robert A. Beauregard, *Voices of Decline: The Postwar Fate of US Cities* (Oxford and New York: Blackwell, 1993); Fred Siegel, *The Future Once Happened Here: New York, DC, LA and the Fate of America's Big Cities* (New York: The Free Press, 1998).
2   Jean-François Lyotard, *Postmodern Fables* (Minneapolis: University of Minnesota Press, 1997).
3   Peter Wollen, "Delirious Projections," *Sight and Sound*, August 1992, pp. 24–7.
4   See Chapter 3, "The Era of Entrepreneurial Cities," in Susan E. Clarke and Gary L. Gaile, *The Work of Cities* (Minneapolis, University of Minnesota Press, 1998).
5   Fredric Jameson, "Class and Allegory in Contemporary Mass Culture: *Dog Day Afternoon* as a Political Film," in Bill Nichols (ed.), *Movies and Methods II* (Berkeley: University of California Press, 1985), pp. 715–33.
6   David B. Clarke (ed.), *The Cinematic City* (London: Routledge, 1997).
7   Greater Philadelphia Film Office website, at http://www.film.org
8   B. Joseph Pine, James H. Gilmore, and B. Joseph Pine II, *The Experience Economy* (Boston: Harvard Business School, 1999).
9   Pennsylvania Economy League, "Greater Philadelphia's Competitive Edge: The

Nonprofit Culture Industry and Its Economic Value to the Region," September 1998; Kevin Mulcahy, "The Arts and Their Economic Impact: The Values of Utility," in Charles Dorn (ed.), *Developing Communities Through Culture, Heritage and Ecological Tourism* (Tallahassee, FL: Florida State University Center for Arts Administration, 1995).

10   "Cézanne Exhibition Has $86.5 Million Economic Impact: Museum Generated $122.5 Million for Philadelphia This Summer," undated Philadelphia Art Museum press release.

11   Buzz Bissinger, *A Prayer for the City* (New York: Random House, 1997).

12   James Hay, "Piecing Together What Remains of the Cinematic City," in Clarke (ed.), *The Cinematic City*, p. 225.

13   Peter Vergo (ed.), *The New Museology* (London: Reaktion Books,1997); Lisa C. Roberts, *From Knowledge to Narrative: Educators and the Changing Museum* (Washington, DC and London: Smithsonian Institute Press, 1997).

14   According to the 1997 Survey of Public Participation in the Arts, Summary Report, Executive Summary, "During a 12–month period, half the US adult population, or 97 million people, attended at least one of seven arts activities – jazz, classical music concerts, opera, musical plays, plays, ballet, or art museums." See the National Endowment for the Arts website, at http:// arts.endow.gov/pub/Researcharts/Summary39.html and *The American Canvas*, http://arts.endow.gov/pub/AmCan/Chapter5.html

15   John Hannigan, *Fantasy City: Pleasure and Profit in the Postmodern Metropolis* (London and New York: Routledge, 1998).

16   David McKenna, "Hardly Mickey Mouse," *Philadelphia Weekly*, 17 February 1999.

17   Lianne McTavish, "Shopping in the Museum? Consumer Spaces and the Redefinition of the Louvre," *Cultural Studies* 12, no. 2 (1998): 168–92.

18   Sabrina Rubin, "Armageddon in our Backyard," *Philadelphia* magazine, January 1996, pp. 72–5.

19   *Greater Philadelphia Film Office: 1999 Film and Video Guide* (Philadelphia, PA: Greater Philadelphia Film Office, 1999).

20   Clyde Haberman, "New York City, Celluloid City: Godfather of Locations," *New York Times*, 23 June 1998.

21   D. Martin, "Do the mathematics: Western States film commissions' revenues from film and television production companies," *Shoot*, 7 August 1998; Chris Guy, "States and the film industry. Lures and enticements," *The Economist*, 14 March 1998, pp. 28–9.

22   Sharon Pinkersen, Greater Philadelphia Film Office, telephone interview with the author, 11 January 1999.

23   Carrie Rickey, "Will Tourists Follow 'Sixth Sense'? Philadelphia's image polished by hit movie," *Philadelphia Inquirer*, 26 September 1999.

24   Graham McCann, *Woody Allen: New Yorker* (Cambridge: Polity Press, 1990).

25   Rubin, "Armageddon in our backyard," pp. 72–5.

26   Chris Guy, "Lights, Camera, Action in Berlin; Town Shines in Role as Location Shoot for Gere, Roberts film," *Baltimore Sun*, 6 November 1998.

27   Edward Levine, "Neighborhood Report: Morningside Heights, On Tiemann Place, Image-Conscious Is Redefined," *New York Times*, 16 November 1997.

28 Ibid.

29 Pennsylvania Economy League, "Economic Impact of the Philadelphia Naval Base and Shipyard on the Philadelphia Metropolitan Area," October 1990.

30 Chris Ayres, "Hollywood comes to the Clyde," *The Times*, 7 August 1998.

31 Arsen J. Darnay (ed.), *Service Industries USA* (Detroit: Gale Research, 1999, 4th ed.), p. 249.

32 J. Daniels, "Virtual location, going places: Hollywood substituting on-location filming with digital technology," *Hollywood Reporter*, 16 June 1997.

8

Cities: Real and Imagined

Geoffrey Nowell-Smith

Some years ago, when driving toward Rome along the via Tuscolana, I caught a glimpse of what seemed to be a Gothic cathedral standing in an empty field. Stopping for a closer look, I discovered it to be a model, considerably less than actual size, and, although more than just a façade, not completely three-dimensional either. I then realized that I was – as I should have guessed – only a few miles from the Cinecittà studios, headquarters of the Italian film industry since their inauguration by Mussolini in 1937, and that this therefore must be a film set. It didn't have to be perfectly three-dimensional because only the front and a bit of the side would be needed for the film, and it didn't have to be full-size because the shot in which it was going to be used would be a "process shot" – that is to say, one which mixes direct-to-camera action with other more or less synthetic elements.

The most likely use of that cathedral, I suspected, would be as part of the so-called Schüfftan process, in which a miniaturized set is located at the side of the action to be filmed while a partially scraped mirror is placed in front of the camera at an angle of 45 degrees. The action would be shot through the scraped part of the mirror while the little cathedral would be visible through the unscraped part. The process got its name from the great German cinematographer Eugen Schüfftan, who devised it in response to the problems highlighted in 1915 by the extreme cost of building full-size sets for the re-creation of ancient Babylon in D. W. Griffith's *Intolerance*.[1] Working for the major German film company, Ufa (Universum Film AG), he put his invention to work in Fritz Lang's *Metropolis* in 1927 and it became standard practice in the studio film thereafter. It can be see as part of a generalized move, which gained momentum from about 1905 and was complete by the mid-1920s, to control the cinema – not just to control costs (always a problem), but to control the whole filmmaking process, including the selection of materials necessary for there to be a film in the first place. If everything could be simulated in the studio there was no need to depend on the vagaries of the outside world – bad weather, out-of-period architecture, pilots who refuse to fly between tall buildings. If the filmmakers had a concept, they could enact it.

But not depending on the outside world also meant not learning from it. Filmmaking ceased to be an encounter with reality from which the filmmaker emerged – as the case might be – chastened or inspired. Concept became everything.

The first casualty when the cinema retreated into the studio was nature. The second was the built environment. We have probably all seen films in which machine-made snowflakes fall gently down onto plastic flowers, but probably not too often, because the artifice is too blatant and increasingly filmmakers avoid it. It looks wrong, and it is wrong. With built environments the situation is more ambiguous. Studio sets of buildings can imitate them almost perfectly, even if it does sometimes involve making miniature models if the original is too big, and many components of a set are arguably not imitations at all. A shot in a film of a man sitting at a desk, looking out of a window toward what we have been told is a garden, shows us a real man sitting at a real desk, looking out of a glazed opening in a real, if flimsy, wall. The only unreal thing is what he is presumed to be looking at. Ontologically as well as perceptually, the offence against built things is lesser than against natural things, so it is not surprising if it is more frequent.

The fact that it is easy, in a photographic medium, to simulate built environments has had important consequences, particularly for the relationship between cinema and the city. It has opened up a number of choices for filmmakers, beginning with a basic one: to confine oneself to what already exists or to create different things in accordance with the dictates of the imagination. Different answers to this dilemma have been offered at different times. Thus in 1927, the year when Lang, Schüfftan, and their collaborators created the imaginary dystopian city of Metropolis, another German filmmaker, Walter Ruttmann, went out onto the streets of Berlin to film what he saw (or some of the things he saw) under the title *Berlin: Symphony of a City*. In 1945 we can note a sharp divide between, on the one hand, the Italian neorealists, eager to remake contact with perceived reality by shooting in almost documentary fashion their country's war-ravaged cityscapes (for example, Roberto Rossellini's *Rome Open City*, 1945) and, on the other hand, filmmakers like Michael Powell and Emeric Pressburger in Britain, who ostentatiously turned their backs on the city streets to concentrate on lavishly recreated interiors and exteriors with painted backdrops (for example, *Black Narcissus*, 1947).

In relation specifically to the representation of built environments I propose to start with a broad-brush distinction (which we shall refine later) between two types of city film. On the one hand, there is the kind of film which is mostly studio-shot (perhaps with the additional enhancement of special effects) and often offers a generally dystopian vision of an undifferentiated "city" which is either unidentifiable with any actual place or only loosely so. This is the type to which *Metropolis* belongs, as do a number of science-fiction films, a lot of *films noirs*, and some films which mix the two genres such as Ridley Scott's *Blade Runner* (1982), but also some less easily categorized films such as F. W. Murnau's silent classic *Sunrise* (1927). Then, at the other extreme, there are films which are mostly location-shot and happen in a place which is identifiable, very often named, and where the name may even form part of the title. Thus *Hell Is a City* (Val Guest, 1959) takes place in a city recognizable as Manchester but not (to my recollection) named as such, whereas Tony Richardson's *A Taste of Honey* (1961) is not only clearly located in Manchester and nearby Salford but draws attention to the specifics of its setting by sending the characters off to an even more recognizable (and named) Blackpool for the day. A decade earlier the Boulting brothers' *Brighton Rock* (1947) not only shows its resort setting but names it in the title. The attraction of films in this second category can be touristic, as personal dramas are played out against attractive backdrops – San Francisco in Hitchcock's *Vertigo* (1958) or Venice in Joseph Losey's *Eva* (1962). But films in this category can also show aspects of cities which do not correspond to audiences' pre-existing expectations, as for example in Ermanno Olmi's *Legend of the Holy Drinker* (1988), set in a suburban Paris far from the tourist trail or that of filmmakers who follow it.[2]

The dystopian city vision does not always need special effects. *Film noir* is a case in point. The cinematic antecedents of 1940s American *film noir* are to be found in studio-based German films of the Weimar period and in the French *réalisme poétique* (also studio based) of the late 1930s – films such as Marcel Carné and Jacques Prévert's atmospheric thriller *Le Jour se lève* (1939). But its literary origins are the hard-boiled detective novels of Dashiell Hammett, James M. Cain, and Raymond Chandler, all of them, but especially Chandler, poets of urban *anomie*. Chandler's Los Angeles, while undoubtedly a very subjectively conceived literary creation, is also a very specific sociogeography. Marlowe's drives around the city are minutely described as he moves from neighborhood to neighborhood, each with its distinctive styles of architecture and its distinctive inhabitants, from old-money Pasadena to new-money Westside, passing through pockets of poverty and degradation on the edges of downtown and elsewhere. The screen adaptations of Chandler's novels made in the 1940s and 1950s make only the most perfunctory attempt to capture either the sociology or the geography of the novels. It is enough for them that "the city" is a place of crime, corruption, and darkness. They are mostly shot in the style from which *film noir* gets its name, with high-contrast lighting and lots of night scenes. A few lyrical daytime shots, set in the country and shot on location, may be inserted to make the contrast explicit – for example, *The Killers* (1946), *Out of the Past* (1947), and *On Dangerous Ground* (1952). The most celebrated of the Chandler adaptations, Howard Hawks's 1946 film of *The Big Sleep*, contains not a single shot which looks as if it was taken elsewhere than on the Warner Bros. lot in Burbank, though others, such as Robert Montgomery's rendering of *The Lady in the Lake* (also 1946), do contain actual daytime exteriors. It is not until the 1970s that you get a Chandler adaptation which takes a real interest in Southern California as a peopled environment, and that is Robert Altman's *The Long Goodbye*, made in 1973. But Altman's film is anachronistic: rightly enough, he makes no attempt to re-create Chandler's Los Angeles of a quarter-century earlier, but he does offer a plausible representation of Los Angeles in the 1970s. (Altman is, incidentally, one of the few American directors who actually takes the trouble to make films about Southern California which look authentic.[3])

Of course, the division is not absolute. There are a number of studio films which name the city in which they are set and throw in a few location shots to prove their authenticity. Hitchcock does this, quite aggressively, in *Psycho* (1960), which opens in Phoenix, Arizona, before proceeding to the spooky motel preserved, to this day, at Universal studios. Even in *film noir* the city may be named, though you may not see much of it except at night. Generic cities can, at a pinch, be created on location (this is the case with Godard's *Alphaville* (1965), set in an imaginary future but entirely location-shot in Paris), and cities can stand in for other cities. This procedure is called "license-plating" because what happens is that you shoot a film, say, in Canada but all the cars are decked out with American license plates. In his novel *Girlfriend in a Coma*, Canadian writer Douglas Coupland has one of his characters describe the use of Vancouver as an all-purpose location: "They film everything here because Vancouver's unique: You can morph it into any North American city or green space with little effort and even less expense, but at the same time the city has its own distinct feel. See that motel over there? That was 'Pittsburgh' in a Movie of the Week."[4] (In passing I'd note here a slight hint of Canadianism – a resentment that although Vancouver *is* different it manages not to seem so, and can be so comfortably subsumed into the United States.)

Shooting on location is sometimes an aesthetic choice, sometimes an economic one, often probably a mixture. In cases of marginal choice, well-equipped but high-salary businesses such as the American film industry will often go for the studio option, while in a country with poor facilities and low labor costs it may be cheaper to shoot the same scene on location. Italian neorealism was famous for its use of location shooting, but as soon as he could afford to, Federico Fellini broke with it and shot most of *La dolce vita* (1960) in studio sets. By re-creating Rome's fashionable via Veneto in the studio he could make far more things happen as he wished them than if he had been in a real street with real traffic and real passersby to contend with. And many – indeed most – location-shot films involve a lot of tampering with their locations to make it possible to shoot them. The shepherd's hut on the island where the characters take refuge in Michelangelo Antonioni's *L'avventura* (1960) was built by the art director, there being no huts (or shepherds) on the island itself. Furthermore, despite advances in microphone technology, the presence of alien sounds on locations (a passing airplane, a child screaming), or just too much sound (the lovely but noisy waterfall where the lovers swear undying love), means that location-shot films will also often have studio-dubbed dialogue.

In spite of all this compromise, however, there remains a core of films, one of whose characteristics is that they yield up a sense of place that would have been impossible without the ontological link between nominal setting and actual location. For the reason already mentioned, many such films are set in the countryside, which, whether represented as harsh and unfriendly to man or as fertile and yielding, is hard to simulate in the studio. But there are also films whose representation of the city plays heavily on authenticity or where the decision to shoot on location radically alters the character of the film.

In the latter category, I would cite in particular François Truffaut's *Tirez sur le pianiste* (1960). This is a *film noir* story, taken from a novel by David Goodis who, as a writer, is even more a poet of urban *anomie* than Chandler.[5] But it is also a Paris film, as are so many films by Truffaut and his French New Wave contemporaries.[6] The decision to set and shoot the story in Paris contributes to giving the film a very different and generally more domestic atmosphere than the novel. It is not that Paris is somehow a more cozy place than Philadelphia (where the novel is set) – though it undoubtedly is the case that Truffaut is a cozier director than Goodis was a novelist. A more substantial and more generalizable reason is that consistency of atmosphere is more easily realized in the studio, where every detail can be constructed to fit a purpose. Goodis's mean streets, every bit as mean as those of Chandler or Scorsese, would be hard to find in any actual American city. Locations, however carefully researched, are impure. Whatever idea the filmmakers may have, the location cannot be guaranteed to enact it. Indeed, it can almost be guaranteed not to enact it. To make it fit a preconceived idea the filmmakers have to rough it up a bit, force it to conform. That is why there will always be an art direction credit even on a 100 percent location-shot film, since at the very least someone is going to rearrange the furniture, put different pictures on the wall, and generally redesign a place around the characters whose lives are being portrayed.[7] This is also what makes Godard's *Alphaville* such an amazing *tour de force*. Everything in it has been pressed into service to stand in for something relevant to the action. An extraordinary bureaucracy, ruled by a monster computer, lurks behind the doors of a simple hotel corridor, while the computer itself, Alpha 60, is represented by what proves on closer inspection to be the control panel of a building's air-conditioning system. More frequently, however, the location is wanted to represent itself: if a film is set in a particular city, it (or parts of it) will be shot in that city in order to guarantee authenticity; but differences can always emerge between what the location is and what it is supposed to be for the purposes of the story, thus undermining the original concept, weakening it, or extending it, depending on your point of view.

There are plenty of films which start with an idea and then go out and find locations to fit. One of the best Los Angeles films, in my opinion, is Roman Polanski's 1974 film *Chinatown*, which succeeds brilliantly, with the aid of some period costumes and automobiles and the odd lick of paint, in creating the atmosphere of the city as it was before the war, using surviving clusters of suburban houses.[8] The resultant effect is – probably deliberately – quite disconcerting. The story of political and sexual corruption is all the more disturbing for taking place in such an Ideal Home environment, representative of the innocent California dream of the first half of the twentieth century. The fact that the world Polanski depicts can be physically brought before the audience in the form of photographic testimony unsettles its temporality and distinguishes the film from those set more comfortably in the past.

Most interesting, however, from my point of view, are the films in which the city as it is acts as a conditioning factor on the fiction precisely by its recalcitrance and its inability to be subordinated to the demands of the narrative. The city becomes a protagonist, but unlike the human characters, it is not a fictional one. The idea of the city as protagonist is quite an old one in cinema. A number of so-called "city films" were made in the silent period, art-film documentaries with a limited admixture of staged or quasi-fictional elements, which generally portray the city and urban life in a more or less celebratory mode.[9] But the idea that the city might infiltrate itself to become protagonist of an otherwise fictional film was slower to emerge, perhaps impeded by the move to studio filming in the 1910s and 1920s. If fiction filmmakers fled the studio in the years before World War Two, it was more often to immerse themselves in nature than to explore the relation between character and built environment.

The big change comes with Italian neorealism at the end of World War Two. Roberto Rossellini's three immediately postwar films – *Rome Open City* (1945), *Paisà* (1946), and *Germany Year Zero* (1948) – each in a different way homes in on war-devastated urban environments which provide the conditions of life for the films' characters and which are effective because absolutely authentic.[10] Rossellini pushes this same concern with environment even further in a later film, *Journey to Italy* (1954), in which a character played by (and to a certain extent based on) Ingrid Bergman enters a personal crisis brought on by her experience of Naples. This film was to have an enormous influence on the young French critics – François Truffaut, Eric Rohmer, Jacques Rivette, Jean-Luc Godard – who were to form the core of the *nouvelle vague* at the end of the decade and all of whom, in their different ways, were to make street filming a part of their style.

The neorealist city, particularly in Rossellini, is more complex than it appears. At first sight the neorealist film seems only to declare: this is how things are. In fact it is saying: this is how things were. For by the time the audience sees the film, what is being shown is a testimony to what the filmmaker (in this respect similar to the still photographer) saw at a particular time. Not only that: the city is often a ruin, and the film's testimony is to the prior existence of an integral city, prior to war, destruction, and decay, which demands to be restored.[11] Neorealism is above all a cinema of reconstruction, and its aesthetic in this respect follows its politics.

A very different conception of location filming is found in Italy a few years later in the work of Michelangelo Antonioni, a more pictorialist director than Rossellini, who had different reasons for preferring location shooting. Antonioni is a landscape artist, for whom physical settings of all kinds are important – deserts, seascapes, townscapes. It is the physicality of the setting, as much as the life within it, that provides him with his initial inspiration; or more accurately it is the possibility of integrating into a composition physical setting and some human fact which outside that setting would not appear significant.[12] It is, therefore, essential for Antonioni that the setting preexists the act of filming by which an image is crystallized. It is very rare for him to use constructed sets, and when he does so it is always in a location rather than in a studio.[13]

As an urban filmmaker, Antonioni reaches a high point with *La notte* (1960), set in Milan. The late 1950s and early 1960s were the years of Italy's "economic miracle," which was concentrated in the North and in Milan in particular. Antonioni's modernist concrete and glass city differs radically not only from the immediately postwar neorealist version but also from that portrayed by Luchino Visconti in *Rocco and His Brothers* a year earlier. Visconti's Milan, although it has modern bits, is historic, and the filmmaker dramatizes the city, using its landmarks – the Central Station, the spiky Gothic cathedral – as settings for dramatic action. For Antonioni it is more a matter of textures and surfaces, aural as well as visual, checkered patterns of rough concrete and smooth glass, the cacophony of motor horns translated into quasi-musical harmony. Although *La notte* is routinely described by critics as pessimistic, in its approach to the city it celebrates the here and now. In

Figure 8.1 Michelangelo Antonioni filming *La notte* on the streets of Milan, 1960 (*Courtesy BFI Stills Library*)

Antonioni's approach the city lives in a different way both from the expressionist cities of *Metropolis* or *Blade Runner* and from the popular cities of neorealism. But Antonioni's cities share with neorealism one fundamental thing. They are there before they signify, and they signify because they are there; they are not there merely in order to be bearers of signification. The fact of being able to work with real materials, which retain their original quality however much they are artistically transformed, is a privilege which filmmakers neglect at their peril.

Notes

1 Born in Breslau (now Wroclaw) in 1893, he later emigrated first to France (where he became Eugène) and then to the United States (becoming Eugene Shuftan) before eventually returning to Europe. Although best known for his studio work, he also shot the documentary feature *Menschen am Sonntag* in 1929 before escaping from Germany. In France before the war he shot *Quai des brumes* (1938) for Marcel Carné, and after the war was Georges Franju's cameraman on *Les Yeux sans visage* and *La Tête contre les murs* (both 1959). The process described here is sometimes referred to in its American spelling as the Shuftan process and is still in use, although it has increasingly been superseded – first, by advances in the technique of making matte shots and, more recently, by computer imaging.
2 It should be added that Olmi's source – the novel by Joseph Roth – also obliges him to have scenes set in a mining village in Silesia, for which he uses a stand-in location which looks to me suspiciously like eastern France.
3 There is an undoubted oddity in the fact that although the American film industry is based in Hollywood, California, a suburb of Los Angeles, it has yielded up few films that represent its home turf. New York and San Francisco have both been more memorable sites for films than has Los Angeles. I am never too happy with this kind of speculation, but it's almost as if Hollywood didn't want it to seem as if its products came from a real place for fear that this would destroy the mystique. There have not been all that many Hollywood-on-Hollywood films and, of those there have been, very few are city films. The great exception is *Sunset Boulevard* (1950), but were I to be asked to name my favorite film about Hollywood (Hollywood the business, not Hollywood the suburb), I think I would name a film that takes place, as its title implies, somewhere else: Vincente Minnelli's *Two Weeks in Another Town* (1962).
4 Douglas Coupland, *Girlfriend in a Coma* (London: Flamingo, 1998), p. 87.
5 The original title of Goodis's novel – a neglected masterpiece – was *Down There*. It was retitled *Shoot the Piano Player* after the success of the film drew attention to it.
6 The New Wave directors can perhaps be divided into those who often set their films in Paris – Jean-Luc Godard, Jacques Rivette (see *Paris nous appartient* (1960) or *Céline et Julie vont en bateau* (1974)), and, less consistently, François Truffaut, and those who prefer provincial settings – most of all Jacques Demy, but also Claude Chabrol and Eric Rohmer.

7 *L'avventura* again can serve as an example. For the film Antonioni "borrowed" a flat from a wealthy acquaintance to shoot a small scene. When he and the art department had finished with it, according to a diary included with the published script, it was left "like a battleground" (*L'avventura*, Bologna: Cappelli, 1960, pp. 29–30).

8 Some of the best LA films have been made by émigrés or visitors from Europe. Besides Polanski I would cite Billy Wilder's *Double Indemnity* (1944) and *Sunset Boulevard* (1950), Antonioni's *Zabriskie Point* (1969), and Wim Wenders's *The State of Things* (1981) and *Paris Texas* (1984).

9 Besides Ruttmann's *Berlin*, already mentioned, the genre includes Alberto Cavalcanti's *Rien que les heures* (Paris, 1926) and Dziga Vertov's *Man with the Movie Camera* (Moscow and Kiev, 1928).

10 Not every location in these films is precisely what it claims to be, and some of the scenes in *Germany Year Zero* have action filmed in a Rome studio in front of back-projections of Berlin locations, but almost all the exteriors are places unchanged since the moment described in the fiction.

11 This idea was suggested to me by James Donald in conversation after the *Cinema and the City* conference in Dublin in March 1999.

12 In an article written in 1959, Antonioni gives a vivid description of arriving in a small town and being served a coffee in a bar overlooking a windswept central square. He describes the very ordinary-looking woman serving the coffee and the only oddity in the scene, which is her unusual name, Delitta (feminine of *delitto*, the Italian word for crime – because, she explains, "my father thought it a crime to bring children into the world"). Capturing a scene like this, Antonioni says, is his idea of the real *cinéma vérité* (Antonioni, "Making a Film is My Way of Life," reprinted in Marga Cottino-Jones (ed.), *The Architecture of Vision*, New York: Marsilio, 1996, pp. 14–17).

13 There is an exception to this rule in the form of *La signora senza camelie* (1953), part of whose action set is set in a studio and which therefore uses the studio as a location.

9

Emigrating to New York in 3-D: Stereoscopic Vision in IMAX's Cinematic City

Mark Neumann

At the Sony IMAX Theater on Broadway and 68th Street in New York City, I sit in my high-back, stadium seat, put on my headgear, and lean back to watch *Across the Sea of Time* (Stephen Low, 1996). The usher calls the headset a "PSE," which stands for "Personal Sound Environment." It's a plastic helmet with a colored visor for enhancing 3-D vision. It has two micro-speakers mounted near my ears to simulate 360-degree audio; an infrared signal synchronizes the soundtrack and film. I glimpse at the rest of the audience as the film begins. Everyone is wearing a PSE, facing the screen. We look like a crowd of welders ready for work.

On the multistory IMAX screen, we follow the fictional story of Tomas, an eleven-year-old Russian stowaway on a freighter arriving in New York Harbor. Tomas is retracing the route his great-uncle Leopold took when he immigrated to the United States from Russia in 1904. Leopold's journey is the basis for the story and is told by a voice-over narrator who reads Leopold's letters to his family in Russia. Now, some ninety years later, his descendent Tomas jumps from the Russian freighter with his knapsack and swims to Ellis Island – the same port his uncle entered at the turn of the century. Tomas's pack carries a pile of Leopold's yellowed letters, a stereoscope, and a box of stereographs depicting the New York City his uncle once inhabited. The stereographs are important because Leopold made them. Upon arriving in New York, he found work as a photographer for a stereograph manufacturer and wandered Manhattan with a double-lens camera, making three-dimensional images of city scenes. For Tomas, these old letters and stereographs become a compass and map as he roams two New York Cities – separated by nearly a century – searching for evidence of Leopold's life in America.

Across the Sea of Time is more than a sentimental film of the immigrant experience (past and present) in New York City. It is an experience conflating a popular fascination for visual technologies with the observational modes of a mobile, urban observer. *Across the Sea of Time* is a text and a site where the representation of the city and visual technologies converge. The film illuminates contemporary relationships among urban geography, mobility, and a tradition of popular ocular amusements aimed at simulating the real. As IMAX technology imagines the immigrant experience, it also creates a cinematic environment showing continuity between turn of the century images of urban life and their magnified reincarnation in IMAX vision and sound. Watching Tomas search for his past, we follow a path that recovers a popular and historically concrete pursuit for a city of images and sensations manufactured for us and consumed from our stationary position in comfortable theater seats. In some ways, *Across the Sea of Time* becomes a technologically enhanced simulation of a journey that might more aptly be titled "Across a Time of Seeing." The film offers a vicarious excursion through urban space. Through Tomas (and Leopold) we encounter a city where images map the coordinates of private quests through public space, and where modern discontinuities find a temporary coherence in a narrative built on a promise of enhanced vision.

Mobility and Memory in the City of Progress

Across The Sea of Time tells a traditionally optimistic story of America as a modern spectacle. Much of the film relies on Leopold's narration, heard in a voice-over as Tomas reads the letters he sent to his family in Russia between 1904 and 1920. As Tomas explores the city, Leopold describes the immigrant's experience as one of bewilderment and excitement, fear and hope. While Tomas follows his great-uncle's trail, we follow him, seeing Leopold's New York through 3-D stereographs. Early in the film, after Tomas swims to Ellis Island, we find him exploring an abandoned immigrant processing building, rereading the letters and looking through his stereoscope. In a letter to his parents, Leopold narrates his arrival and tells of surviving the journey:

> After weeks on the open seas with hundreds of seasick strangers speaking languages I've never heard before, I finally arrived in America. I thought the ordeal was over. No. We disembarked at the place called Ellis Island where uniformed guards decided who could stay. You mean I could be sent back? My stomach twisted in fear as I was pushed up the steps to be judged. I heard my first words in English. "Hey, stupid, get in line . . . "

Watching the film with our PSEs, archival photographs of arriving immigrants appear before us in 3-D; we see through Tomas's eyes as he studies the scenes through his stereoscope. We witness what he sees and hears. We dwell inside his head, with his nostalgia and yearning for his American ancestry.

Historical images of immigrants standing in lines and crowded in waiting rooms while doctors examine them give detail to Leopold's description. "America is afraid . . . of disease," Leopold continues.

> If you carry disease or infection, the health inspectors put chalk on you, put you in a quarantine, or worse, send you back. . . . A little boy with tuberculosis was taken from his mother. Thank God I was healthy. But the inspectors said my name was too difficult. They typed out a new name. Minton. Leopold Minton. "I am now an American?" They said yes, and stamped the papers.

For Leopold, New York represents all of America. His story echoes some of the contempt faced by immigrants coming to the United States a century ago as well as today. Despite the poor reception he receives, Leopold welcomes his new American status, an identity emerging from the routinized surveillance of government processing, stamped papers, and a family name recast by the slapping keys of a clerk's typewriter. "I will not soon forget those faces at Ellis Island," he says. "Now, I wait for the ferry that will take me to New York City, and never have I felt so free."

Leopold soon forgets his bitterness toward the harsh immigration processing. Instead, America exceeds his wildest dreams. "It is a miraculous place like nothing I could've imagined," he writes.

> The grand avenues go on as far as the eyes can see and are lined with buildings that seem to touch the sky. You can think of me as I walk the city streets looking for work and looking. Yesterday, I explored the financial district – Wall Street. Here those in charge of American industry invest money in the future of the entire country.

While Leopold seems to recite the "America-as-melting pot" lesson from an elementary social studies textbook, his words project an enthusiasm for an ideology of American Progress that finds tangibility in the landscape of office buildings and avenues appearing on our screen. Following Leopold's "exploration" of the Financial District, we cut to the present, where Tomas stands on Wall Street asking for directions.

Leopold and Tomas are our anchors as we drift through two New York Cities. They cinematically incarnate Baudelaire's *flâneur*, the strolling subject whose gaze moves through the modern city as a contradictory expression of individualism and anonymity. "[T]he *flâneur* is a figure of excess: an incarnation of a new urban form of masculine passion manifest as connoisseurship and couched in scopophilia," notes Rob Shields.[1] "It is a spatial practice of specific sites: the interior and exterior public spaces of the city. These include parks, sidewalks, squares, and shopping arcades or malls."[2] Neither Leopold nor Tomas share the bourgeois status or class characteristic of the *flâneur*. Yet both function in this narrative as *flâneurs* because their strolling aims toward intriguing sights and places, and they become surrogates for our own fascination with the city as spectacle, as Shields explains:

> In a city "made strange", the *flâneur* wanders the streets, habituating himself to the urban décor. . . . [His movement is a] metaphorical exploration of the extra-local and extra-ordinary in the name of rendering them into the sphere of everyday life . . . the *flâneur* attempts to wallow in the rush of sensate information, taking pleasure in the diversity of stimuli of the urban environment . . . . This derives not merely from the scope or scale of urban stimulation but from its *simultaneity* in time and space.[3]

The *flâneur* is nothing less than an urban character of heroic proportion who "excels under the stress of coming to terms with a changing 'social spatialization' of everyday social and economic relations which in the nineteenth century increasingly *extended* the world of the average person."[4] This extension of the world as a visual marvel is central to Leopold's sense of New York's (and America's) *freedom*. He embraces the city's compressed segmentation of social and cultural life as if he were wandering the globe.[5] In a scene where Tomas walks along Canal Street, gazing back and forth between the sidewalk markets and restaurants of Chinatown and Little Italy, Leopold's narration tells of living in a tenement on the Lower East Side among other émigrés. "There are many Russians here, but also Italians and Germans and Irish and Scandinavians," he says, beginning another letter home.

> The neighborhoods sometimes seem like small countries bordered by the city streets. But even with our different tongues and customs, we can still become friends because we are all Americans. . . . Eating here is like traveling around the world, and you can smell where you are before you get there.

New York appears as a microcosm of Europe and the city takes on a utopian aura. Cultural differences are subsumed by a larger sense of the immigrant's identity as American. According to Leopold, "If you have skills you will find no shortage of jobs here. . . . If you don't, there are Germans who will teach you to pour bronze. Italians will show you how to make shoes. There are machines that manufacture things you never dreamed existed." We see images of factory and foundry workers, people on production lines, and Leopold's narration recasts these laborers with a communal spirit that overlooks the grim realities of unemployment, low wages, and cultural conflict inherently part of immigrant life. Instead, we are presented with a portrait of New York

immigrant experience in which class antagonisms are glossed over for a
sheen of social equality and a faith in a cooperative vision of industrial
progress. This is profoundly illustrated in a scene in which Tomas rides the
subway while we listen to Leopold describe the rapid transformations taking
place in the city:

> Now is a time of great adventure .... New York is changing so fast. You
> should see what they are doing under the city streets. Men come from all parts
> of the world to dig subway tunnels for two dollars a day. Shoulder to shoulder
> they risk their lives to make the city a better place for all of us.

Here we see workers digging subway tunnels that become a source of amusement for Tomas as he stands at the front of a subway car as it races along the
tracks. His point of view becomes our point of view and the 3-D simulation
is exciting. But the larger implications of this narrative and these images
suggest another facet of history not nearly as explicit as Leopold's story.

   This IMAX film is, to some extent, equivalent to the expositions of progress
first appearing in Europe and the United States during the late nineteenth
century. As the Russian Marxist George Plekhanov wrote, describing the
1889 Paris expositions, the "world exposition gave [the proletariat] an excellent idea of the previously unheard of levels of development of the means of
production that have been attained by all civilized countries."[6] The exposition offered a dreamy landscape of progress. But as unemployment, worker
dissatisfaction, and the rise of labor unions widened the gap between industry and anarchy, the more expositions were required "to perpetrate the myth
of automatic historical progress," argues Susan Buck-Morss:

> Not only did they provide a utopian fairyland that evoked the wonder of the
> masses. Each successive exposition was called up to give visible "proof" of
> historical progress towards the realization of these utopian goals by being more
> monumental, more spectacular than the last.[7]

Leopold's description is more innocent. He conjures New York City – and
America itself – as an industrial utopia. Following his ancestor's trail, Tomas,
too, comes to understand the city as an outgrowth of such allegiances. In this
way, the spectacle of this IMAX film holds a kinship with those early expositions that encouraged observers to recognize themselves as participants in a
great panorama of history, progress, and the future – all welded together
through each person's contribution. As *Across The Sea of Time* magnifies an
image of the city, its simulation also amplifies an ideology of progress and
prosperity.

   Leopold may sentimentalize the immigrant's optimism for American freedom and opportunity, but he is also an individual faced with a society which
is in a process of rapid institutional, economic, and military–governmental

growth. In 1938, sociologist Louis Wirth suggested that the American city gave rise "to the spatial segregation of individuals according to color, ethnic heritage, economic and social status, tastes and preferences."[8] For Wirth, this segmentation and segregation was likely to be stressful and to weaken bonds of "kinship," "neighborliness," and tradition. "Under such circumstances competition and formal control mechanisms furnish the substitutes for the bonds of solidarity that would hold people together," he wrote, describing how people confronting "urbanism as a way of life" would inherently come to live under a structure which leveled, standardized, and massified their distinctive differences.[9] Leopold saw the face of such power in the faces of the Ellis Island immigration inspectors guarding the gate to his freedom. As an American, he could freely wander as if in a museum where everything and everyone became an exhibit, and his eyes aimed always towards the future.

Belonging to the City Through Vision

To a large extent, Leopold and Tomas search for clues that tell them how to belong to the city. If Leopold's narration resembles the interiorized voice of a *flâneur*, it is only because the *flâneur* prefigures what he eventually becomes after arriving in America. "I have a good job now," he tells his family. "I am working for a company that makes these stereo pictures I am sending you. They are actually paying me to photograph New York City. They will ship the best pictures to people all over the world." As a professional observer, Leopold's new occupation extends the city beyond its physical geography, carrying it to others who can witness its scenes in commodified stereograph images, and allowing sightseers to travel without physically moving. (Ironically, Tomas inverts this relationship by transporting Leopold's stereograph images back to their place of origin.) Employed with an image-making company, Leopold's *raison d'être* for observation has a rationale that is an inherent part of all professional observers – journalists, photographers, novelists, sociologists, anthropologists, and filmmakers. But his insatiable gaze is also fueled by personal desire: his awestruck eyes aim continually towards assimilation. "My job takes me in and around the city on train tracks that run high in the sky," he writes. "I look into windows to see how Americans live. I listen so I will learn how Americans speak. I speed by the latest wonders of the world that spring up everyday."

Leopold describes his new profession as we look at historical images of factories and assembly lines. Suddenly the scene shifts to a stereograph factory which resembles other manufacturing plants. This juxtaposition merely underscores how all of these commodities – dresses, shoes, stereograph views – are part of an economy where anything can become a source of exchange and signification. Leopold's job is an occasion for explicating how mobility, observation, and opportunity thrive in the city. He takes us to Coney Island where we see beachgoers and arcades. In another scene, Tomas walks through the theater district while Leopold narrates: "At night, the city is lit up so brightly it looks like daytime." We see a city of amusements and spectacles centered on the IMAX screen. New opportunities for consumption open up with the installation of electric light. We experience the Coney Island roller coaster through the point-of-view IMAX camera mounted on the first car.

Documenting Manhattan, Leopold reports how its transforming landscape engendered new opportunities for visualizing the city. In one scene, Tomas climbs a fire escape to a rooftop, loads his stereoscope, and pans across the city as if looking through a telescope. It is as if panning the stereoscope might allow him to take in a view greater than the scene on the card mounted inches from his eyes. "From the roof of our new apartment, we have a wonderful view of the city," narrates Leopold. "They built the first sky-scraper in 1901. Twenty stories tall . . . . The skyline changes everyday as these monuments to American business rise higher and higher." With images of skyscrapers filling the screen, we can imagine Leopold and his Italian immigrant wife Julia feeling the power of this view from their rooftop. In the next scene, however, their vantage-point shifts. "For a nickel, Julia and I ride an elevator to the top of the Woolworth building, sixty stories above the street," he continues.

> It is the tallest building in the world. From here, *we can see where we live!* As I look out across the city, I am reminded of the countless immigrants who came through Ellis Island, who brought their courage and their skill from around the world to build this great city. I can only imagine what it might be like to look down on New York from the Heavens.

More than any other in the film, these scenes merge the relationships be-tween observation and experience in a visual society. Clearly, Leopold's mobile gaze places observation at the core of urban life. Viewing the city from their apartment building and, conversely, going to the highest place in the city *so they can see their apartment*, he and Julia grasp for a view of the city as a knowable totality. While much of *Across the Sea of Time* depicts New York's *differentiated segments*, this scene depicts the city as a spectacular *monu-mental totality* in the magnitude of which they can see their place. It is befitting that Leopold and Julia ride the elevator in the Woolworth building. They signify an emergent middle class increasingly defined as markets by the en-terprises and businesses housed in the buildings below them. Their nickel elevator ride acknowledges how any experience might become a leisure com-modity. Yet Leopold's fascination with this grand view of the city is also our own. Seated before IMAX's spectacle, Leopold and Julia seem our ancestors as we too seek a powerful viewpoint to claim the whole city, locate ourselves in its swells of concrete, steel, glass, noise, and people.[10] As Leopold imagines a "view of the city from Heaven," the camera glides over Manhattan's sky-scrapers. This is the view from Heaven that he fantasized. But there is more to this scene than a manufactured view, whether it is delivered by elevator or IMAX. Looking over Manhattan, Leopold sees his journey from Ellis Island, and all those who built the city. Like Tomas, Leopold's vision is not confined by the present. Perhaps this is the meaning behind Tomas panning the stereoscope from the roof. He gestures toward the panoramic vision of time he shares with Leopold, recognizing the subjective dimension of seeing that is integral to the stereoscope as well as to the ways we grasp the city and move through its spectacular landscape.

Jonathan Crary argues that by 1840 modern forms of institutional and discursive power had redefined the status of the observing subject.[11] While modern transportation collapsed space and time, visual technologies – from the stereoscope of the 1850s to early forms of cinema in the 1890s – relocated vision from a material site of observation which depended on the bodily presence of a viewer, to the subjectivity of an observer that "depended on the abstraction and formalization of vision."[12] Nineteenth-century technologies dislocated, extended, and reassembled images and knowledge, and aimed to affirm "the sovereignty and autonomy of vision."[13] Simultaneously, the autonomous viewing subject engendered by this shift became inseparable from "the increasing standardization and regulation of the observer."[14] Commodifying, regulating, and standardizing urban experience is an inevitable feature of the city Leopold describes and the city Tomas wanders through today. Crary's emphasis on the observer's subjective disposition as the locus of vision only underscores Tomas's strategy for seeing. His stereoscope is a retreat into an interior space where narrative and image converge, and the 3-D view manufactures a fiction of realism. Tomas does not need a guidebook or map to find his way around New York. Instead, he becomes lodged in a subjective drama in which his geographic location is circumscribed and mediated by Leopold's letters, images, and the stereoscopic device.

Were Tomas to have bought a stereoscope manufactured by the company that employed Leopold, it might have come with instructions such as those accompanying the 1904 Underwood stereoscope:

> Hold the hood of the stereoscope close against the forehead, shutting out all sight of your immediate surroundings. Move the sliding rack, with the stereograph, along the shaft until you find the distance best suited to your own eyes .... Read what is said of each place in this book. Refer to the map and know exactly where you are in each case. Read the explanatory comments printed on the back of each stereograph mount. Go slowly. Do not hurry. Go again – and yet again. Think it over. Read all the first-class books and magazines you can on the subject.[15]

Essentially, such instructions asked stereoscope users to enter into a contemplative, solitary space and study the scenes before their eyes. Information captions on stereograph cards, and from books and magazines, furnished narratives that made the scenes meaningful. This is what Crary means when he describes the relocation of vision to the subjectivity of the observer. The observer is literally the site on which space is mapped through texts and image. "The stereoscope signals an eradication of "the point of view" around which, for centuries, meanings had been assigned reciprocally to an observer and the object of his or her vision," argues Crary.[16] Since the 1850s, parlor stereoscopes engaged their users in a tangible production of

forms of verisimilitude . . . . What the observer produced, again and again, was the effortless transformation of the dreary parallel images of flat stereocards into a tantalizing apparition of depth. . . . And each time, the mass-produced and monotonous cards are transubstantiated into a compulsory and seductive vision of the "real."[17]

Instead of following a manual, Tomas retreats behind the stereoscope, listens to Leopold's voice, and "transubstantiates" his ancestor's journey with his own search for American "roots." Along the way, he resurrects the "roots" of the city as a spectacle made for consumers, a landscape of visions that simultaneously speak to everyone and no one in particular. He is living in an interior drama which becomes the basis for our entertainment in the IMAX theater. With PSEs fastened around our heads, it is not such a leap to think of the stereoscope's hood snuggled around Tomas's eyes and the sound of his great-uncle's voice echoing through his ears. In this capacity we too are kin to Leopold and Tomas.

The 3-D City

Ironically, what is missing from Leopold's account of New York between 1904 and 1920 is the movie theater. By 1905, nickelodeons populated Manhattan's tenement districts. In 1907, Manhattan had more than two hundred nickelodeons, a third of them located in the immigrant neighborhoods below 14th Street. Over the next five years, movie audiences grew and, by 1910, working-class men and women composed nearly 75 percent of all audiences.[18] By 1914, the motion picture business was booming and the audience shifted from one heavily comprising immigrants to an audience of an emerging middle class – a market which would soon extend itself into all quarters of twentieth-century American life.[19] A Russian immigrant like Leopold Minton would have been among those who sat in storefront nickelodeons and, later, the grand picture palaces that began to spring up in Manhattan. Yet his

Figure 9.1   Exterior of the Sony IMAX Theater, Lincoln Square, 68th St. and Broadway, New York City (*Courtesy Loews Cineplex, United States*)

letters say nothing about this growing industry which would soon overwhelm the amusement parks, roller coasters, and Broadway shows he describes. Historians of American leisure and cinema note the years between 1905 and the 1920s as a period during which the democratization of leisure led to an increasing standardization and privatization of experience through mass consumption.[20] Tomas Minton may be a fictional descendant of a fictional immigrant but, in some ways, so are we. Here in the theater, watching young

Tomas search for a New York and an ancestral past with his stereoscope, we occupy a privatized 3-D space. Like him, we benefit from the stereoscopic vision and are drawn toward a technological novelty simulation of a New York full of thrills. The chaos and naive wonder once encountered by the new immigrant is now our leisure pursuit.

When *Across the Sea of Time* ends, we file out across the rows of seats knowing others wait outside ready to fill them at the next screening. An usher takes my PSE and places it on a rack alongside hundreds more hanging on movable carts. Turning the corner, the Upper West Side appears through a huge plate-glass window. I glimpse my own reflection superimposed over the buildings outside. Riding down the escalator, I pass enormous murals of picture palaces, movie stars, and Hollywood scenes. All of it is homage to a golden age of movies, a dreamy geography of nowhere and everywhere. Out on the streets, making my way down Broadway towards Times Square, I can only wonder what became of Leopold Minton. His letters capture well the enthusiasm of many who find cities not merely places of technological wonder, but technologies in themselves. They are a reminder of how, as James Donald suggests, the city itself might be "better understood as a historically specific mode of seeing, a structure of visibility" that incorporates the fantasies that appear in the "fantastic cities" fashioned by cinema.[21] In many cases, the cinema does provide a sense of urban geography sought by those who come to places like New York. A colleague tells me that when he goes to New York, he spends most of his time looking for the city he's seen in Woody Allen's films. In his own way, he is describing a stereoscopic vision, a reconciliation of scenes from the cinema and the city.

On my way, I pass the Ed Sullivan Theater, home of television's "Late Night with David Letterman" show, and stop at the Hello Deli and the Rock America souvenir shop I've seen in Letterman's street skits. I pass Comedy Nation and MTV Headquarters. I see Planet Hollywood and the Fashion Café. This is a geography composed of commodities and lifestyles. Walter Benjamin would have seen this display as merely a continuation of the forces that "re-enchanted" the modern world for the consumer. The cities of cinema screens are an elaborate vehicle of such re-enchantment. They provide full-fledged dramas, exciting lives and events for viewers who – sooner or later – make it out of the theater and discover a labyrinthine maze of images and stories mapping the geography they tread over.

By the time I get to Times Square, the sky is growing dim with the oncoming night, and corporate neon lights up the street. I see the glowing red FUJI FILM sign and recall that Tomas lingered here as he wandered Broadway. Across the street, a facsimile of a Concorde jet hangs below the SONY Trinitron screen on the old Times Building – built in 1904, the year Leopold arrived. Behind me, a huge coffee cup spills out the last drop in a 3-D billboard for Maxwell House. A huge Coke bottle hangs from a building uptown, and another 3-D sign sells JELL-O. At 42nd Street, a sign reads "New Times Square," marking Disney's claim on a whole block of once-seedy porno theaters now remade into an urban theme-park. The refurbished Amsterdam Theater hosts a production of *The Lion King*, a play based on an animated film. A 3-D sign promoting American Express rises above the theater – it's a huge credit card and there's a set of black mouse ears hanging off the edge. The city has become three-dimensional, but it seems as flat as ever. Turning up the volume on my Sony Walkman, I drown out the traffic and let my private soundtrack carry me out of Times Square.

Notes

1   Rob Shields, "Fancy footwork: Walter Benjamin's notes on *flânerie*," in Keith Tester (ed.), *The Flâneur* (New York: Routledge, 1994), pp. 64–5.
2   Ibid.
3   Ibid., pp. 72–3.
4   Ibid.
5   Mark Neumann, "Wandering Through the Museum: Experience and Identity in a Spectator Culture," *Border/Lines* 12 (Summer 1988): 27.
6   George Plekhanov (1891) as cited in Susan Buck-Morss, *The Dialectics of Seeing: Walter Benjamin and the Arcades Project* (Cambridge, MA: MIT Press, 1991), p. 87.
7   Ibid., p. 97.
8   Louis Wirth, "Urbanism as a Way of Life," *American Journal of Sociology* (1938), excerpted and reprinted in Richard T. LeGates and Frederic Stout (eds.), *The City Reader* (New York: Routledge, 1996), p. 191.
9   Ibid.
10 Tony Bennett, "The Exhibitionary Complex," *New Formations* 4 (Spring 1988): 73–6.
11 Jonathan Crary, *Techniques of the Observer: On Vision and Modernity in the Nineteenth Century* (Cambridge, MA: MIT, 1990), p. 150.
12 Ibid.
13 Ibid.
14 Ibid.
15 These instructions appear in a 1904 stereoscope manual, *The Grand Canyon of Arizona: Through the Stereoscope* (New York: Underwood & Underwood, 1904), p. 7. I am assuming that the instructions published by the Underwood Co. would be found in manuals for other stereograph collections.
16 Crary, *Techniques of the Observer*, p. 128.
17 Ibid., p. 132.
18 Kathy Peiss, *Cheap Amusements: Working Women and Leisure in Turn-of-the-Century New York* (Philadelphia: Temple University Press, 1986), p. 146.
19 David Nasaw, *Going Out: The Rise and Fall of Public Amusements* (New York: Basic Books, 1993), pp. 205–6.

20   See ibid.; Peiss, *Cheap Amusements*; and Lary May, *Screening Out the Past: The Birth of Mass Culture and the Motion Picture Industry* (Chicago: University of Chicago Press, 1983).

21   James Donald, "The City, The Cinema: Modern Spaces," in Chris Jenks (ed.), *Visual Culture* (New York: Routledge, 1995), p. 92.

10

Finding a Place at the Downtown Picture Palace: The Tampa Theater, Florida

Janna Jones

Introduction

The Tampa Theater is a historically preserved picture palace in downtown Tampa, Florida. The film house exhibits foreign, classic, and independent films to a small but loyal following of patrons. Built in 1926, the Tampa Theater's architectural *bricolage* of Venetian façades, French colonnades, Persian balconies, Greek and Roman statues, and a simulated twilight sky brimming with stars and circulating clouds created for its early twentieth-century patrons a feeling of modern mobility. Such impressions mirrored the fluidity that spectators experienced as they watched the cinematic technology on the picture palace's screen. The auditorium of the Tampa Theater and the films shown there recalled the city outside the theater's door, for the downtown area was bursting with a proliferation of images and commodities during the early decades of the twentieth century. Strolling, dining, shopping, consuming the images in department store windows, and riding the city's streetcars sustained and reinforced the commonplace logic of an increasingly visual society.

The Tampa Theater managed to keep its 1,500 seats filled with patrons until the suburbanization of Tampa that began in the 1960s. As the city stretched away from its center, commercial enterprises such as stores, movie theaters, and restaurants migrated to the suburbs. Today, Tampa's downtown is primarily a central business district that is inhabited during the hours of the work week. Its streets and sidewalks are populated at the lunch hour,

Figure 10.1   Interior of the Tampa Theater, Tampa, Florida (*Copyright George Cott/Chroma Inc.*)

but they are practically abandoned in the evenings and on the weekends. The Tampa Theater remains a functioning film house, as it has since 1926, but its auditorium is rarely filled, for the theater, like the downtown area, has lost its position at the vital center of the city.

However, there is a brigade of faithful Tampa Theater patrons who are loyal to it. From interviews that I conducted during 1997, I have concluded that these patrons are faithful to the theater for the same reasons that many Tampa citizens stay away. They prefer the downtown area because it is geographically and ideologically distanced from Tampa's suburban shopping malls. Many of the theater's patrons relish the *idea* of the city and like to imagine that their trips to the theater are an urban experience. Tampa Theater patrons also explain that the films shown at the theater are complex and intellectually challenging. They describe the theater's films and their own tastes as distinctive, and they believe that the independent, foreign, and classic films they view are superior to the blockbuster films that are exhibited at the suburban cineplexes.

This chapter is about the contemporary perceptions and practices of audience members at the Tampa Theater. Beginning in the 1960s, the Tampa

Theater, its films, and the downtown became less familiar and accessible, and the theater lost its popular standing with the majority of Tampa's citizens. However, with the loss of its popularity, the theater was transformed into a treasure for some of Tampa's residents who perceive themselves as members of a high(er) culture. Many of the patrons who go to the picture palace imagine the Tampa Theater to be a place of *distinction* and they envisage themselves as part of a community of discriminating patrons. While the Tampa Theater's distinctive films help to define the picture palace as a site of high culture, its location in Tampa's downtown also helps to construct its highbrow category, for like the films that it exhibits, downtown Tampa is more complicated to navigate and less accessible to the masses than the mall movie theaters scattered across Tampa's suburbs. The perceived inaccessibilities that help shape the Tampa Theater experience are precisely what also helps to define the perception that the Tampa Theater is a place of high culture.

Members of Distinction

During the summer of 1991, the Tampa Theater Film Society was initiated. In part, the Society was formed to increase private participation in support of program growth and restoration projects. But, for many of the members of the Tampa Theater Film Society, membership means more than helping the theater stay afloat. It is a way to belong to a community where there is a perception that the members have important traits in common. Probably the most distinguishing characteristic Society members believe that they share is an appreciation of complex cinema and a general dislike of cineplexes and their movies.

"Well, I like foreign films over Hollywood films because they're so rich; there's so much more to them. There's no comparison," Ann Vernon, an accountant, explained; "Even when I've gone to a regular theater and I watch the coming attractions – I feel assaulted a lot of times." Carolyn Clark, a public affairs specialist, agreed. She joined the Society to assure year-round stimulation. "If I go to a regular theater, it's pretty much cut and dry. I don't think there's a lot of thought-provoking issues that come up," Clark explained; "I think we always need to be stimulated like that – or I need to be stimulated like that, intellectually." Vernon added that there is no reason to talk about a blockbuster movie after it is finished: "There's no reason to discuss it. I mean 'I get the picture.' You know, it's like, OK, I got it. I recently saw *Volcano* and I just kept saying to myself, 'Why don't you walk out?,'" Vernon said laughing. "I just laughed at myself. I mean it was typical Hollywood."

"It's good to see that at least the Tampa Theater is playing films that you're not going to get elsewhere, and they have so much more meaning,"

Mita Bahn, another Film Society member explained. Bahn, who has a ten-year-old son, finds that she regularly does have to go to the cineplex to escort her child to movies that he wants to see. She finds the experience so displeasing that she has adopted a survival strategy to cope with it. "I take turns with my best friend, so I don't get stuck with all of them because there's a tremendous amount of films that come out, and I can't imagine anybody sitting there and watching them all for two hours."

Dagmar Loman, a research statistician, explains that she is "completely left-brained" and has a hard time understanding the films at the Tampa Theater, but she prefers them to Hollywood movies. "I just don't care for American movies – I mean Arnold Schwarzenegger and those. There's no meaning behind those movies. Just violence," Loman complains; "Half the time I don't get the point of the movies that play at the Tampa Theater, but I'm trying. There's more to it than just killing everybody and rescuing everybody."

Loman's confession that the films at the Tampa Theater are often too difficult for her to understand may at first be puzzling. Why would someone use their leisure time to see films that require so much work to appreciate? Other Film Society members also expressed pride in their confusion. The French film *A Single Girl* (Jacquot Benoit, 1995), for example, created quite a stir with Film Society members because the film ended without any conventions signaling its conclusion. "I got deluged Monday morning with all these comments. We called the distributor and as it turns out, that's the way the film ends. There are no credits, she's walking and . . . ," John Bell, the Tampa Theater's director explained. Clark remarked that she thought it was an intermission, while Vernon explained, laughing: "Then they said, 'It's over,' and I said, 'It is?' Somebody said, 'What was it about?' I said, 'I can't even tell you,' but it was thought-provoking. I certainly enjoyed it. I mean I'm glad I saw it."

The willingness of film society members to be confused and their desire to be challenged rather than indulged by cinema provides a context for understanding why some people identify with the high-culture cinema at the Tampa Theater. At the same time, their taste in cinema reflects the social space of the theater. The cultural practices at the movie palace distinguish those who regularly go there as well as those who don't. As film society member Peter Buchanan explained, the films at the Tampa Theater are not everyone's "cup of tea." "We had a Florida State University student staying at our house for fifteen weeks, and of course we brought her here right away," Buchanan said. "We tried to invite her a second time, and she said that it was too 'artsy-fartsy' for her."

The film society members make clear distinctions between popular movies and the films that they prefer. It is nearly impossible for them to explain why they like the films at the movie palace without contrasting them with blockbuster movies. Their distaste of popular cinema helps them to define the kind of film that they prefer. In other words, their choice in cinema is defined by what is *not* played at the cineplex. As Pierre Bourdieu contends:

> Distinction and pretension, high culture and middlebrow culture – like, else-where, high fashion and fashion, *haute coiffure* and *coiffure*, and so on – only exist through each other and it is the relation, or rather, the objective collaboration of respective production apparatuses and clients which produces the value of culture and the need to possess it.[1]

For the highbrow social space of the Tampa Theater to function properly it is imperative that the cineplexes around Tampa continue to splash block-busters on their screens. In fact, the films at the Tampa Theater are hardly the pinnacles of the *avant garde*, but in relation to the films exhibited in other theaters, they seem highbrow. Lance Goldenberg, the film critic for a weekly newspaper, explained to me that the average American independent film exhibited at the Tampa Theater is more conservative and less interesting than the typical art-house film of thirty years ago: "Independent film has become – certainly over the last five or six years – less and less different from conventional studio products. As Hollywood films have become stupider and stupider, it becomes easier to pass off anything as an independent film – anything that doesn't entail non-stop explosions." But the (relatively) high-brow film preferences of the Tampa Theater patrons are more complex than choosing what is not a blockbuster. Their preferred taste in cinema portrays an aesthetic disposition toward that which requires them to distance them-selves from what they see on the screen. Preferring to be confronted with form over function, the mode of representation over the object represented, and experimental technique over themes, they distinguish their preferences in cinema from more popular films in much the same way that Immanuel Kant defined aesthetic judgment, for they prefer the act of contemplation of cinematic form over identification with the people or things represented in popular movies. As Kant explained in *The Critique of Judgment*, "disinterested-ness" is the sole guarantor of aesthetic contemplation:

> Everyone must allow that a judgment on the beautiful which is tinged with the slightest interest is very partial and not a pure judgment of taste. One must not be in the least prepossessed in favor of the real existence of the thing, but must preserve complete indifference in this respect, in order to play the part of judge in matters of taste.[2]

Bourdieu similarly explains that the difference between high and popular art is the distance that the spectator is expected to sustain from the art object.[3] When Vernon laughingly denounced the movie *Volcano*, saying that she "got the picture," she conveyed that her preference is not to get the picture, at least not immediately. Her taste demands that she wrestle with the cinematic form on the screen rather than be swept away by the sensations intended by blockbuster directors. Many of the film society members explained that they would rather not understand a film than be assaulted by the instant gratification offered by popular films. In this way they not only distinguish the films that they prefer, but they also distinguish themselves from cineplex spectators. Bourdieu explains: "Social subjects, classified by their classifications, distinguish themselves by the distinctions they make between the beautiful and the ugly, the distinguished and the vulgar, in which their position in the objective classifications is expressed and conveyed."[4] The films that the Tampa Theater exhibits, along with the distinctions that the film society members make about themselves and the films that they most enjoy, help to identify the movie palace as a highbrow social space.

One of the social functions of the Tampa Theater is the construction of a community that not only appreciates the sacred sphere of culture, but attests to its superiority over other cinematic domains. But the act of watching films is a solitary one, and film society members cannot construct a community by simply slipping into their theater seats. Conversations with one another about the complexities of the films that they watch is a crucial element of helping to create identity and build community – and, not surprisingly, film society members express their desires to talk to other film society members about the films. As Bourdieu argues, part of the symbolic profit of art cinema is the discourse that follows in which spectators attempt to appropriate part of its distinctive value.[5]

The Tampa Theater Film Society members explained that the pleasure that they find with the films at the theater doesn't end with the credits. Part of the satisfaction of watching the films is the discussions that follow. Clark explained that because the films at the Tampa Theater generally depict multiple perspectives, she and a friend who is also a Film Society member have plenty to talk about after the films that they see together: "I think the films here are more thought-provoking. My friend will have a slightly different slant on a film or her perception is a little different from mine. I find it very interesting that we both view the same movie, yet our perspective on it can be somewhat different." Clark was one of many Film Society members who voiced her desire to have organized exchanges between Film Society members about the films shown at the theater. "After a film I always like to talk about it. I would like to have discussion groups about films. That would be very interesting to me," Film Society member Sandra Sumner said. Loman agreed. "I would like someone to explain the films to me. I think, like a picnic in the park would be good. I mean, if you don't want to talk to anybody you don't have to, but you could talk about movies." Bahn expressed a similar interest: "I'm not an expert on film, and what I would love to see is an adult education program. You know, I sit and look at all the credits and I don't know what half of those positions do. There's a science to films and I would love to understand it better."

While Film Society members explained that they felt that they would like to become better acquainted with other Tampa Theater Film Society members because they felt that they were people with whom they would have much in common, several people felt that they already belonged to a community at the Tampa Theater. Though the community that they describe is not a particularly intimate one, it is based on the recognition that people who come to the theater share an appreciation of film. "There's a sense of community where I see a number of the same people all the time going to the films," contended Kevin Bordwell; "You know, you may just sort of nod your head and that's the extent of the interaction with a person, but there's that sense of community that begins to develop. It's like a connection that we like the same things."

The film society members that I talked to had fairly clear perceptions and descriptions of the film society profile. "Film society members – well, I just look at the people who come here and they certainly look different from the people that go to the multiplex," Loman explained; "They just look different. They dress different. They act different. They probably have a higher education level than average people on the street." Sumner added, "They're conscious. My best friends, who I see the movies with at the Tampa Theater, travel a lot. They have interests outside of their home. Other people that I know that are members travel a lot too, come to think of it. They have a lot of interests. They are not couch potatoes." "They're more aware. They're not just into their own little worlds. They're interested in other things," Loman continued; "People who come here are more open-minded. They are people who might actually know something outside of Florida. You know they might actually be able to find another state or country on the map. Not that there's anything wrong with rednecks." Vernon remembered a time when she came to the Tampa Theater and realized that she was not among regular Tampa Theater audience members. "*It Came from Outer Space* drew a lot of people that weren't typical Tampa Theater people. They were just rude," Vernon complained. "They threw their feet over the seats, and I was thinking, 'they don't belong here.' They didn't appreciate the theater. Usually I feel like I'm among people who appreciate the same kind of films. But they were just kind of rowdy."

The Downtown Experience

The benefits of membership and the film programming are not the only elements of the Tampa Theater to which the film society members are drawn. The building attracts patrons, and the location of the theater in downtown Tampa also draws people, as it did during the first half of the twentieth century. While downtown has nearly disintegrated, as Tampa has grown into a suburban city, the ghost of Tampa's downtown continues to captivate people, despite the perceived criminal dangers and, perhaps, because of them.

The Film Society members explained that the experience of seeing a film at the Tampa Theater is dramatically different from the cineplex experience. Columbus, an advertising executive, tried to explain the difference between leaving a modern movie theater after a movie is over and walking out of the Tampa Theater: "All of a sudden you're back out in the fluorescent lights and you're just sort of blinking, and that's about it," Columbus said scornfully; "But, here at the Tampa Theater, I know a lot of people, and I can usually talk to people outside and out front. We have just seen the same movie and we are all spilling out onto the street." Art Keeble, the director of the Tampa Arts Council, described a similar feeling about departing the Tampa Theater. "Well, here at the Tampa Theater it's not as if you're facing 300 more people standing in line to come in. You don't feel pushed out," Keeble said; "Or the guys are there with their garbage cans ready to clean up before the next group comes in."

Another film society member, Shelly Lind, finds *going* to the modern movie house to be an ordeal that she would rather bypass. "I'm not going to stand in line to see movies. If I don't come here I have to go to the Regency 20 – a nightmare. Or the University Square Mall – another nightmare," Lind said as she rolled her eyes; "You have to go through the *food court* to wait in line." In contrast, Keeble mentioned that coming to the Tampa Theater creates a sense of occasion, in part because of the urban plaza located across the street from the theater. "I think one of the luckiest things that we have going for us is the fact that TECO (Tampa Electric Company) is across the street and they always keep their plaza well groomed, twinkling lights in the trees," Keeble reflected; "You feel like you're *arriving* when you come here."

"I like it [Tampa Theater] being downtown. I actually think that a theater like this almost by definition has to be downtown," Buchanan explained. "That's where they were created. They were built in areas like this where the center of commerce and life was." Buchanan can't imagine the Tampa Theater being in a suburban area, for even though downtown is no longer the center of commercial activity, the Tampa Theater remains standing as a tribute to the area's past successes. "I love the idea that it is downtown. I think there is some magic about being downtown that has been lost in our society, and a lot of cities are trying to get that back. I know that Tampa is trying and maybe someday – ten, fifteen years from now – it will happen," Bachman said. "But I just think that there is a magic about the streets around here. You know, the cobblestone streets and the antique shops and the little restaurants." The idea of an "urban experience" is also part of what attracts

Keeble to the theater: "I think it's very urban to go downtown to a movie and not to the suburbs. You know, there's just something about being downtown at night, with all of its good and bad qualities." Keeble believes that the problems of downtown are intrinsic to an urban setting. "There's just on-the-street parking; we don't have good sanitation immediately after work, so a lot of times you'll find garbage in the street, and the street people you see," Keeble declared, "but that is just part of the urban experience."

While film society members prefer the cinematic selections of the Tampa Theater over blockbusters exhibited at the cineplex, some of them also favor the experience of seeing movies in the downtown movie palace over the multiplex at the mall. To be sure, part of their inclination towards the Tampa Theater is the building itself. Yet part of the pleasure for some of the patrons is the picture palace's place in downtown Tampa. Lind, who expressed her disgust at having to walk through a food court to arrive at a mall theater, is typical of the film society members who find the mall to be as base as the movies that are shown there. The Tampa Theater film society members make clear distinctions between the mall and its cineplex and downtown and the Tampa Theater. In fact, they frequently lament the ordinary and vapid spaces that comprise the shopping mall experience. With one mall indistinguishable from the next, and the stores inside barely distinct from one another, the shopping mall transports its occupants into a placeless, yet familiar galaxy.

On the other hand, like the films shown at the Tampa Theater that are pleasurable to film society members because they are a challenge to understand, the location of downtown Tampa provides a similar pleasure, for downtown's lack of hospitality renders it fairly inaccessible. Some of the Tampa Theater patrons feel the same kind of gratification in traversing downtown as they do from working to understand the films they see at the theater. Street parking can be difficult; there are few places to shop or eat; and the city's desolation at night and on the weekends seems dangerous. Going downtown to see a movie at the Tampa Theater requires much more effort and exposure to danger than going to a mall, where everything – parking, shopping, eating, and moviegoing – is nearly effortless and fairly safe.

Downtown Tampa is decidedly less legible than the city's malls. Pedestrians are not able to decipher the semiotics of the downtown streets, sidewalks, and independently owned shops sprouted here and there as easily as they can at the mall. While the space of the mall is democratic because nearly everyone is able to traverse its space adroitly, the boarded-up department stores, the unfamiliar store names, the dangerous areas, and the scarcity of conventional fast-food restaurants, clothing shops, and department stores make the rhythms and patterns of downtown less legible. Without the familiar department stores and fast-food restaurants serving as coordinates, the pedestrian experience downtown is less certain and more difficult to navigate. Downtown Tampa is not for everyone, and this is precisely part of its attraction for film society members.

While downtown Tampa was, during the first half of the twentieth century, *the* domain of Tampa's popular culture, at the end of the century, the city's dozen or so malls reign as the regions of consumer culture. Where once residents of Tampa arrived downtown by streetcar and then spent the day strolling, shopping, dining, and going to movies, today they now have virtually the same experience arriving by car or bus to the climate-controlled shopping malls. The nearly seamless, fluid consumer experience of the once-thriving downtown has been transported to Tampa's suburbs.

What was once a proliferation of images, commodities, and consumer choices is now a static, archaic, and nearly silent downtown. Today, Tampa's city center is left to those who work there during weekdays. At night and on the weekends, the phantom city lingers for the explorers who make their way to their lighthouse. They encounter only the hushed tones of the homeless and the apparitions of the once voluptuous city, as they navigate their way in the darkness toward the hundreds of tiny electric full moons that comprise the marquee. Finally, they arrive at their destination, *a place called the Tampa Theater*.

Conclusion

The Tampa Theater's apparent inhospitality further explains the film society members' attraction to it. As Lawrence Levine convincingly argues in *Highbrow/Lowbrow: The Emergence of a Cultural Hierarchy in America*, accessibility is a key to cultural categories. He writes that

> exoteric or popular art is transformed into esoteric or high art at precisely that time when it in fact becomes esoteric, that is, when it becomes or is rendered inaccessible to the types of people who appreciated it earlier. Thus a film like D. W. Griffith's *Birth of a Nation*, which was released in 1915, is transformed into high culture when time renders its "language" – its acting styles, technology, kinetics – archaic and thus less familiar and accessible to the masses.[6]

The Tampa Theater was a seat of popular culture from 1926 until the beginning of the 1960s – and while the theater is located in the same place, looks practically the same, and exhibits films in the same manner, its cultural category has been transformed, for it is now a site of high culture. According to Martin Jay, "So-called high culture has been and will continue to be renewed from below, just as popular or even mass culture derives much of its energies from above. The boundaries shift and dissolve, the categories harden and soften."[7]

As I have argued, the picture palace's relative inaccessibility has helped to reconstruct its cultural position. Its independent and foreign films are esoteric compared to Hollywood blockbuster films; its location downtown is complicated in its navigation in contrast to the city's malls. These relationships help to frame the theater as a site of high culture, at least for now. Such a category inevitably keeps many Tampa residents away from the theater, and for that very reason, it also draws some people, such as the Film Society members, toward it. "In matters of taste, more than anywhere else, all determination is negation," Bourdieu explains, "and tastes are perhaps first and foremost distastes, disgust provoked by horror or visceral intolerance of the tastes of others."[8] The Tampa Theater is a site of high culture precisely because it does *not* show blockbusters and it is *not* located in or near a mall.

The Tampa Theater, at least in relationship to other cinematic spaces in the city, is, first and foremost, a place. It is a place of distinction for the film society members. It is a place downtown, for it is isolated and distinct from the consumer mobility of shopping malls and the cineplex, and its one-screen/one-film format offers spectators fewer choices and less fluidity than other contemporary media. To be sure, the historical and architectural space of the Tampa Theater may help transport patrons to their own particular and personal pasts. The antiquated European architectural design still references other countries and epochs, and the films that the theater exhibits routinely transport patrons to exotic lands and time periods. But as Columbus, a film society member, explained, the difference between the Tampa Theater and the cineplex is the difference between traveling by train and traveling by plane: "You know, you just get on a plane and when you get off – the end is the same as the beginning. But when you take a train ride you know what's happening. You feel the land." While both methods of travel transport voyagers to their destinations, the difference, of course, is that passengers are more conscious of their transformation while traveling on a train. Similarly, while both the picture palace and the cineplex offer spectator mobility to ticket buyers, spectators are more cognizant of their travels at the Tampa Theater. Undoubtedly, the Tampa Theater is a less convenient way for the spectator to travel, but its pleasures remain *in place*, nonetheless.

Notes

1   Pierre Bourdieu, *Distinction: A Social Critique of the Judgment of Taste*, trans. Richard Nice (Cambridge, MA: Harvard University Press, 1984), p. 250.
2   Immanuel Kant, *The Critique of Judgment*, trans. James Meredith (Oxford: Clarendon Press, 1952) p. 43.
3   Bourdieu, *Distinction*, p. 4.
4   Ibid., p. 6.

5   Ibid., p. 282.
6   Lawrence Levine, *Highbrow/Lowbrow: The Emergence of a Cultural Hierarchy in America* (Cambridge, MA: Harvard University Press, 1988), p. 234.
7   Martin Jay, "A Hierarchy and the Humanities: The Radical Implications of a Conservative Idea," *Telos* 62 (1984–5): 144.
8   Bourdieu, *Distinction*, p. 56.

11

Global Cities and the International Film Festival Economy

Julian Stringer

A week doesn't go by these days without some city somewhere in the world staging its own international film festival. Events in Berlin, Honolulu, Hong Kong, London, Moscow, Toronto, and Venice provide just a few of the most visible pinpoints on a vast, sprawling map of transcultural film exhibition and consumption. Leaving its mark on select corners of the globe, this caravan of images flows from location to location, national border to national border, so as to connect exciting and emergent film industries with the international traffic in cinema. Festivals are significant on regional, national, and pan-national levels; they bring visitors to cities, revenue to national film industries, and national film cultures into the world cinema system. And their importance has increased significantly over the past two decades. As theatrical markets for movies have shrunk around the world, festivals now constitute the sole formal exhibition site for many new titles.

For these reasons, considering the power dynamics of the international film festival circuit is important to any understanding of contemporary world cinema. Festivals function as a space of mediation, a cultural matrix within which the aims and activities of specific interest groups are negotiated, as well as a place for the establishment and maintenance of cross-cultural-looking relations. Moreover, they play a key, if often underacknowledged, role in the writing of film history. Festival screenings determine which movies are distributed in distinct cultural arenas, and hence which movies critics and academics are likely to gain access to.

This last point is hardly negligible. As so many of the non-Western films that Western audiences are likely to be familiar with emerged as festival entries, scholars tend to approach them through the nostalgic invocation of those moments when non-Western industries were "discovered" – that is, discovered by Westerners – at major international competitions. A recent example of this can be found in Kristin Thompson and David Bordwell's popular textbook, *Film History: An Introduction*. Assigning a mere sentence to the history of Korean cinema, they assert that "South Korea, site of a flourishing industry in the late 1960s, eventually attracted festival notice with such meditative films as *Why Has Bodhi-Dharma Left for the East?* (1989)."[1] This sentence has the unfortunate effect of implying that Korean film production is a mere adjunct to the primary historical importance of international film festivals, and it underpins a critical position which consigns virtually the entire history of a divided national film industry to oblivion. Aside from illustrating how what are ostensibly *distribution* histories of world cinema too often masquerade as *production* histories, this example assumes that non-Western cinemas do not count historically until they have been recognized by the apex of international media power, the center of which is located, by implication, at Western film festivals.

Similarly, Yingjin Zhang has discussed how the importance assigned to film festivals carries implications for the histories of both film production and film studies. Zhang explores the consequences of the recent global unspooling of a number of so-called Chinese "ethnographic" films, such as *Red Sorghum* (Yimou Zhang, 1987), *Raise the Red Lantern* (Yimou Zhang, 1990), and *Ju Dou* (Yang Fengliang, Yiman Zhang, 1991). As he puts it, "favorable reviews at international film festivals lead to the production of more ethnographic films, and the wide distribution of such films facilitates their availability for classroom use and therefore influences the agenda of film studies, which in turn reinforces the status of ethnographic films as a dominant genre."[2]

In addition, film festivals provide a focus for the convergence of issues concerning the relation of cultural production to cultural policy. As just one manifestation of this convergence, scholars are beginning to take note of how closely film festivals relate to issues of national identity, how intimately their histories are tied up with the politics of cultural nationalism. Marla Susan Stone, for example, has shown how the first such event, held at Venice in 1932, was organized as an explicit act of propaganda aimed at legitimizing and promoting Mussolini's fascist state on the world's stage.[3] Similarly, Heidi Fehrenbach's research on the ascendancy of the Berlin Film Festival in the 1950s demonstrates how that particular event was tied to the spectacle of German reconstruction and democratization after the fall of Hitler.[4] Indeed, one might say that all the major festivals established in the immediate postwar period (Berlin, Cannes, Edinburgh, Moscow, London, Venice) were closely aligned with the activities and aims of particular national governments. This kind of historical work suggests that such events worked to promote official state narratives and hence perpetuate the continuation of the nation-state system itself.

In Britain, the popular newspaper critic Dilys Powell wrote as early as 1947 of how film festivals provide a unique opportunity to contemplate other national ways of life. In her article, "The Importance of International Film Festivals," published in the *Penguin Film Review*, she wrote that "The value to critic and creator alike of detaching himself from his normal surroundings and looking at the cinema against a neutral background will remain. And here, I fancy, in this temporary escape from the national projection room, is the lasting value of the film festival."[5] But Dilys Powell got it wrong. Film festivals have not offered an escape from the national projection room, so much as one of its major showcases: they have not provided a neutral background for the pure gaze of aesthetic contemplation so much as a location for the implantation of nationalist agendas. In Thomas Elsaesser's telling phrase, the international film festival circuit has constituted "a kind of parliament of national cinemas," a network of official diplomacy implicated in the institutional policies of host and participant nations.[6] Certainly, this remains a key way of conceptualizing film festivals, despite the fact that with the rise of the international co-production in the 1970s, many festivals (including Cannes and Venice) dispensed with national classifications altogether, in recognition of their increasingly problematic and redundant nature.

While the question of national politics continues to be crucial to the idea and practical organization of film festivals, the reasons for their growing importance have changed and become more complex over time. What matters now is not just the showing of films within a context of national display and objectification, together with the "opportunities for comparison, for the renewing of serious standards of judgment" that Dilys Powell talked about in 1947, but also the symbolic qualities of a festival's connection with a sense of extra-national place and identity.[7] At the same time as we need more work on the historical link between film festivals and concepts of national cinema, we also need to move the discussion on to considerations of the exhibition site itself as a new kind of counter public sphere. While the establishment of events like Berlin, Cannes, and Venice in the postwar period signaled that the balance of power was shifting in the new world order, the rise of film festivals on a global scale since the 1980s is implicated, too, in the restructuring of an alternative social object, namely the modern city.

Mapping the Circuit

As David Morley and Kevin Robins have pointed out, the reorganization in recent years of transnational finance and speculative capital, as well as of electronic delivery systems and other communications networks, has changed the role of cities around the world, bringing about new confrontations between city administrators and transnational corporations, and stimulating global competition between cities so as to attract ever more mobile investments.[8] Within this worldwide marketplace, film distribution has taken on some of the same characteristics as other indicators of deep social and economic change. Major cities now find themselves in competition with each other for the cultural resources of global financing, just as they do for the money generated by tourism and the heritage and leisure industries.

Once upon a time, festivalgoers could contemplate other national cinemas at the small number of major events held throughout the year, and the films on display were clearly labeled as the products of specific countries. In the immediate postwar period, the festival circuit constituted less than a dozen events, all of which could be attended by a jet-setting elite of filmmakers, cultural attachés, distributors, royalty, and journalists – that charmed circle of the great and the good described by Peter Baker in his 1962 novel, *To Win a Prize on Sunday* (published while Baker was editor of *Films and Filming* magazine).[9] As local film festivals began to proliferate in the 1980s and 1990s, however, this aura of exclusivity evaporated – with over five hundred events now being held in all four corners of the world, is there really anything special about any of them? Consequently, cities have sought to establish a distinct sense of identity and community – an aura of specialness and uniqueness – through promoting their film festivals within the terms of a highly competitive global economy. Cities and towns all around the world have found it necessary to set up their own events so as not to be left out of the game.

It is worth pausing for a moment to consider the key metaphor used by media discourses to describe the organization of international film festivals – namely, the "festival circuit." What exactly does this term mean? In order to answer this question, let us consider three possible usages. First, our common-sense understanding of the term, gleaned from journalistic and trade sources, suggests, simply, a closely linked network of interrelated, interdependent events. Second, for more discriminating or politically-oriented commentators, as well as for such festival participants as traveling filmmakers and visiting programmers, it may represent a closed system impossible to keep up with. Simply put, some festivals within the circuit are more dispensable then others, some worth the decision to attend, others not worth investing time and money in, particularly if they are deemed politically objectionable, opportunistic, or ineffectual. Practical financial decisions determine which events are most important for hard-pressed media workers unable to participate in all the festivals that make up the system.

Yet it is also possible to read the festival circuit in a third way, namely as a metaphor for the geographically uneven development that characterizes the world of international film culture. By this I mean that the development of trade and information links between nations and regions through film festivals has necessitated the establishment of new core–periphery relations; there is a positive need for a dominant center (big festivals) and its subordinate or dependent peripheries (little festivals). The film festival "map" that one could draw up at any given time, showing the proliferation and distribution of such events around the world, does not just chart their existence on a mass spatial scale, it also provides a temporal dimension to the circuit's organization. In other words, the point is not just that some festivals are bigger than others, but that the timetabling, or scheduling, or temporal management of the festival season determines the activities of distinct cities in relation to one another. Events are measured and compared, high spots differentiated from low spots, glamorous and sexy locations separated out from the not-so-glamorous and not-so-sexy. Inequality is thus built into the very structure of the international film festival circuit. In part, the astonishing growth of such events in the 1980s and beyond may be viewed as the logical result of the global economy's need to produce a large reservoir of other locations in other cities so as to continually rejuvenate the festival circuit through competition and cooperation.

Just as cities seek to imitate and reproduce each others' success through spatial and city planning, the proliferation of film festivals has been characterized by a similar modular quality. Events are established on the basis of other, prior, and successful events, and a new category of individual, "the international film festival consultant," has played an important behind-the-scenes role in mediating and solidifying the links between disparate cities and their film festivals.

I wish to use the term "the international film festival circuit," then, to suggest the existence of a socially produced space unto itself, a unique cultural arena that acts as a contact zone for the working-through of unevenly differentiated power relationships – not so much a parliament of national film industries as a series of diverse, sometimes competing, sometimes cooperating, public spheres. My argument is that it is cities which now act as the nodal points on this circuit, not national film industries. In short, I am asking that we pay as much attention to the spatial logics of the historical and contemporary festival circuit as we do to the films it exhibits. The circuit exists as an allegorization of space and its power relationships; it operates through the transfer of value between and within distinct geographic localities.

Festival Image

Any individual film festival strives to remain competitive on two fronts. On the one hand, a sense of stability is crucial to the promotion of events on the circuit – such and such a festival is worth attending because it is established, a regular fixture in the diaries of the great and the good, and so on. On the other hand, expansion is also necessary if the individual festival is not to be left behind by its rivals; festivals are advertised as Bigger Than Ever, Better Than Ever, Comprising More Films Than Ever. Yet one of the peculiarities of the whole phenomenon is that just because a festival in a particular city is internationally established and growing more successful by the minute, it does not necessarily follow that this will lead to growth in the film industry of the respective nation that city belongs to. For example, Manthia Diawara has pointed out that the success of African film festivals has not led to many benefits for distinct national African industries.[10] Furthermore, this kind of observation backs up the work of Saskia Sassen, who has illustrated how major financial centers such as London, New York, and Tokyo constitute a system of world cities whose success rates run independent of current economic situations in, respectively, Britain, the USA, and Japan.[11]

Consequently, the ambition of many festivals – regardless of their actual size and the catchment area they draw participants and audiences from – is to aspire to the status of a global event, both through the implementation of their programming strategies and through the establishment of an international reach and reputation. Their ambition is to use the existing big festivals as models so as to bring the world to the city in question, while simultaneously spreading the reputation of the city in question around the world.

Such ambitions indicate that intercity rivalry and cooperation through film festivals has occurred at a variety of different levels on the basis of a range of differing administrative, governmental, and cultural and political activist concerns. In the case of what I call (following art historians Carol Duncan and Alan Wallach) the "universal survey festivals" – that is, those major events that aspire to show movies from all four corners of the globe and attract a good deal of international media exposure – such events constitute attempts by a coalition of the state, local government officials, corporate sponsors, and intellectuals equipped with film expertise to make their own intervention into the festival scene by competing in the bidding wars for audiences and titles.[12] In order to compete within the terms of this global space economy, such events must operate in two directions at once. As local differences are being erased through globalization, festivals need to be similar to one another, but as novelty is also at a premium, the local and particular also becomes very valuable. Film festivals market both conceptual similarity and cultural difference.

Another way of putting this is to say that as local festivals are forced actively to conceptualize themselves so as to compete for global financing, they have to create their own sense of community, and hence their own marketable trademark or brand image. It is important to analyze the specific marketing strategies cities utilize as they attempt to secure what may be called a "festival image" for themselves. Elsaesser points out that "Festivals are the Olympics of the show-business economy, even though not all are as market-oriented as the Cannes Festival. What competes at festivals are less individual films than film concepts, film ideas, sales angles, or what Stephen Heath called a film's 'narrative image.'[13] Elsaesser's perceptive comments are written in the context of the international circulation of New British Cinema in the 1980s, but my argument is that this kind of thinking needs to be extended more to the extratextual and extranational levels as well. What many festivals actually now market and project are not just "narrative images," but a city's own "festival image," its own self-perceptions of the place it occupies within the global space economy, especially in relation to other cities and other festivals.

Treating film festivals as a constituent feature of today's global city – something it is necessary for every major city to have – and taking the rise of the global city as a metaphor for the simultaneous allegiance and rivalry between events on the international film festival circuit, may be taken in either of two ways. Positively, events that establish festival images that fully engage with global/local dynamics, that fully suggest the international dimensions of local film cultures, may produce a genuine local city identity based around a shared sense of cinephilia and an engagement with dynamic processes of cultural exchange. Such is the case, for example, with the Hong Kong International Film Festival which, since its establishment in 1977, has grown to the point where it now attracts 100,000 visitors a year. Hong Kong has a cultural remit to provide both an international forum for the exhibition and evaluation of pan-Asian cinemas, and a repository for archival knowledge about local film cultures.[14]

On the other hand, of course, all of this may simply lead to the establishment of a touristic and commodified aesthetic. This latter tendency has been a vital, if underexplored, aspect of the festival circuit since the beginning (Venice, 1932, did not just promote fascism, it also brought visitors to the city's hotels during the off-season). This process was articulated very directly by the Mayor of Berlin when introducing visitors to the 1998 Berlin Festival held in February of that year:

> For the 48th time the Berlin International Film Festival is brightening Berlin's often dreary, gray February skies. And just when it seems as if winter will never end, inside the movie theaters everyone can catch a glimpse of star glamour. Along with the great variety of films presented during the festival, the line-up of international film stars adds yet another highlight to the already rich cultural agenda of the Berlin winter season . . . . while you are enjoying encounters with exciting new worlds of cinema from all the five continents, don't forget the real world outside, off the silver screen, and take a little time to discover the streets and squares of Berlin: there is much to be seen in the city's many museums, theaters and exhibitions.[15]

The fact that film festivals provide opportunities for tourism and the boosting of a city's economy is obvious enough, but it is worth highlighting the felt need for the constant reiteration of touristic rhetoric – festivals need to keep plugging subsidiary attractions because cities need to keep in the public eye. During the weeks immediately before and after it is being held, for example, Berlin has to attract programmers, filmmakers, and other visitors from similar events in Rotterdam, Miami, Bombay, Gothenburg, Hiroshima, Portland, Texas, Victoria, and St Petersburg, cities which will all seek to build on their attractions, festival images, and sense of unique local culture with each passing festival season.

Planning the Festival Spectacle

As the example of the highly visible Berlin Film Festival suggests, one feature of the uneven geographical development that characterizes the global film festival economy is the two-tiered system it now embodies. Little festivals handle specialized audiences and create new opportunities, while big festivals, specifically the universal survey festivals, attract tried and tested talent and appeal to a much wider market. The two-tier system represents the consolidation of power amongst a handful of mega-events, or global festivals in global cities, together with the bustling activity among a veritable throng of niche operations, or smaller events catering to particular tastes and particular constituencies.

What unites these tiers is the necessity of determining the key locational criteria used in deciding when and where new film festivals will be established and older ones maintained. Processes of city planning and spatial planning are clearly important in this regard. Fixing the regional characteristics of festivals through their identification with particular cities requires a consideration of the links they forge between local councils, businesses, governments, and communities, as well as some discussion of how all of these relate to global networks of power and influence. On one level, film festivals are being used to tap local alliances that may well blossom in the future, encouraging in the process forms of urban movie spectatorship that promote place and community-bound affiliations. As with comparable phenomena such as sports meetings, beauty contests, museum exhibitions, and the rise of the conference circuit, film festivals are planned and marketed around a clear sense of visibility. More and more these days the festival crowd does not appear to be there primarily to enjoy the show so much as to provide evidence of its existence for worldwide observers (for example, through spectacular open-air screenings.) Whereas at Venice in 1932 the glamour of the festival audience was used to promote and legitimate the politics of the fascist state, it is now used for a variety of different reasons as well, including as a prop in a grander show staged for the festival circuit and the rival cities that participate within it. While there has been a shift in the understanding of how spectacle can be deployed at film festivals, the proliferation of the virtual festival experience (for example, through websites) has similarly taken festival and city identities into cyberspace – into wholly new notions of spectacle and wholly new (electronic) space economies. In this regard, the establishment of the FILM-FEST project in the USA (a series of commercial DVDs based around individual festivals like Sundance and Cannes, comprising clips from featured movies, *cinéma vérité* tours of key locations, interviews with visitors and organizers, and so on) is highly significant.

The planning of spectacle around a city's distinct festival image has a further function: it helps develop initiatives related to real-estate activity within cities, thus helping to rejuvenate the value of urban space through the mobilization of global interests. Just as the long-term value of local real estate is determined by the recognizable and marketable differences between places, festivals within any one specific nation-state may end up in competition with each other in terms of potential land prices as much as in terms of which festival will gain access to which films and filmmakers. Take the example of the Pusan International Film Festival, held in postcolonial Korea. Pusan provides an interesting case study in that it has been self-consciously modeled (as a showcase for Asian cinema in the region) along the lines of the existing, highly successful Hong Kong annual event. As Soyoung Kim has pointed out, Pusan is attempting to mobilize a sense of local identity around its festival as part of a wider initiative, on the part of Korea's newly inaugurated local governments, to challenge the legacy of the "Seoul Republic," or the heavy industrialization of Seoul which proceeded on the whim of the authoritarian, centralized government regime of the 1980s.[16] As such, the festival has sought to attract financial investments to the city, its beaches, and the Pusan Yachting Center in Haundae, and away from the national capital, Seoul.

As this example suggests, a particularly important question concerns the status of international film festivals in postcolonial societies, and particularly in postcolonial global cities. How do festivals in these locations position themselves within the uneven power differentiations of the global economy? How do they interact with other cultural and non-cultural institutions so as to build up a sense of a postcolonial, local film culture? More than that, what role do international film festival consultants play in the conceptualization of postcolonial urban identities? The case of India is particularly intriguing here, as it holds its national festival in a different city each year, thus stimulating intense rivalry and competition among a range of key locations.

In sum, a quick scan of the hundreds of events with their own web pages on the internet testifies to the ubiquity of the boom in local film festivals today. Such events open up new and counter public spheres within a circuit of globalized media distribution, cutting across concepts of the national in complex but instructive ways. An average of over forty towns and cities now hold such events during each and every month of the year. As such events can be found splattered around the world, it is worth raising the question of whether or not it is still possible to pinpoint exactly where the core of the festival circuit resides – where its center is. For example, some Western journalists have complained that there are now "too many" film festivals in the world. This is a statement which seems to betray an anxiety over journalists' own inability to attend – or police – all the major events, and hence an implicit recognition of the impossibility of making too grand or sweeping statements about the state of contemporary world cinema. The complaint, "There are too many film festivals in the world today," also raises the specter of the *situated* nature of the different and contingent positions from which the spatial logics of the contemporary international film festival circuit can be observed and understood.

Notes

1   Kristin Thompson and David Bordwell, *Film History: An Introduction* (New York: McGraw-Hill, 1994), p. 774.
2   Yingjin Zhang, "Chinese Cinema and Transnational Cultural Politics: Reflections on Film Festivals, Film Productions, and Film Studies," *Journal of Modern Literature in Chinese* 2, no. 1 (1998): 121.
3   Marla Susan Stone, *The Patron State: Culture and Politics in Fascist Italy* (Princeton, NJ: Princeton University Press, 1998), pp. 100–10.
4   Heidi Fehrenbach, *Cinema in Democratizing Germany: Reconstructing National Identity After Hitler* (Chapel Hill: University of North Carolina Press, 1995), pp. 234–53.
5   Dilys Powell, "The Importance of International Film Festivals," *Penguin Film Review* 3 (1947): 60.
6   Thomas Elsaesser, *Fassbinder's Germany: History, Identity, Subject* (Amsterdam, Amsterdam University Press, 1996), p. 16.
7   Powell, "International Film Festivals," p. 61.
8   David Morley and Kevin Robins, *Spaces of Identity: Global Media, Electronic Landscapes and Cultural Boundaries* (London and New York: Routledge, 1995), p. 119.
9   Peter Baker, *To Win a Prize on Sunday* (London, Souvenir Press, 1966).
10 Manthia Diawara, "On Tracking World Cinema: African Cinema at Film Festivals," *Public Culture* 6, no. 2 (1994): 385–96.
11 Saskia Sassen, *The Global City: New York, London, Tokyo* (Princeton, NJ: Princeton University Press, 1991).
12 Carol Duncan and Alan Wallach, "The Universal Survey Museum," *Art History* 3, no. 4 (1980): 448–69.
13 Thomas Elsaesser, "Images for Sale: The 'New British Cinema,'" in Lester Friedman (ed.), *Fires Were Started: British Cinema and Thatcherism* (London: UCL Press, 1993), pp. 52–69.

14   Hong Kong International Film Festival (HKIFF), *20th Anniversary of the Hong Kong International Film Festival 1977–1996*, (Hong Kong: Urban Council, 1996).
15   "Welcome: Governing Mayor of Berlin," *Moving Picture Berlinale Extra*, 11–12 February 1998, p. 3.
16   Soyoung Kim, "'Cine-Mania' or Cinephilia: Film Festivals and the Identity Question," *UTS Review*, forthcoming.

Part 3

Cinema and the Postcolonial Metropolis

Part 3 interrogates the relationship between urban identity and urban development, on the one hand, and the cinematically articulated identities of a range of postcolonial nations and cities, on the other. Moving beyond the Western European and US centers, this section foregrounds the shared conditions of cities such as Hanoi, Manila, Port Elizabeth, Lagos, Sydney, Montréal, and Dublin, all of which have experienced economic and cultural peripheralization, subordination, and/or exploitation; a legacy of cultural division between various ethnic/national/linguistic populations; and often traumatic adaptations to the realities of transnational capital and economic development in the late twentieth century. These common conditions are examined in terms of their articulation through appropriately (and often necessarily) non-industrial cinemas, including low-budget production, civic documentary, local video, and art-house film. The section considers the possibility and practice of cinematic resistance by "subordinate" or "marginal" cities and film cultures, to economic, political, and cultural crises, particularly as these are precipitated by globalization.

In "Streetwalking in the Cinema of the City: Capital Flows Through Saigon," J. Paul Narkunas analyses the articulation in the film *Cyclo* of recent market liberalization and capitalization in Vietnam, through a focus on the traumatic history of Saigon from French colonialism, through American occupation, to bankruptcy in the aftermath of the Vietnam War. Rolando B. Tolentino, in "Cityscape: The Capital Infrastructuring and Technologization of Manila," describes the contentious roles played by a number of Filipino films about the urban poor in the development of Manila, from the Marcos regime to the present day, as part of the increasing incorporation of the Philippines into the global economic system. Justine Lloyd, in "The Politics of Dislocation: Airport Tales, *The Castle*," examines the film *The Castle* as an articulation of Australian domesticity and suburban social organization in the 1990s, relating these to Australian public discourse and official policy on land use in the aftermath of the Mabo decision, and within the context of Australia's incorporation into the economy and transport networks of the Pacific Rim. In his chapter, "Representing the Apartheid City: South African Cinema in the 1950s and Jamie Uys's *The Urgent Queue*," Gary Baines demonstrates the official use of ethnographic documentary and public education films in 1950s South Africa as a problematic means of endorsing the social organization of the apartheid regime, with particular reference to slum clearance and housing projects in Port Elizabeth. In "The Visual Rhetoric of the Ambivalent City in Nigerian Video Films," Obododimma Oha examines the neglected role played by video film in public discourse on the city and social organization in present-day Lagos, arguing that recent Nigerian video film has both countermanded the official projection of Lagos as a civilizing center by the country's military dictatorship and influenced official policy with regard to planning, welfare, urban crime, and gang violence. In "Montréal Between Strangeness, Home, and Flow," Bill Marshall explores the cinematic construction of Québecois identity, and its self-definition in opposition to modernization and post-modernization in North America at large, through a focus on the film industry of, and cinematic representation of, the city of Montréal. Kevin Rockett, in "(Mis-)Representing the Irish Urban Landscape," focuses on official censorship in Ireland of imported (primarily Hollywood) cinematic representations of modernity and metropolitan space as part of the conservative postcolonial state policy of successive Irish governments in the 1940s and 1950s, arguing that the official agenda conspired to promote a resolutely rural national ideology in opposition to modernization, particularly in relation to the capital city, Dublin.

12

Streetwalking in the Cinema of the City: Capital Flows Through Saigon

J. Paul Narkunas

Tran Anh Hung's 1995 film *Cyclo* (*Xich Lo*) traces the movements of an eighteen-year-old cyclo (pedicab) driver through the streets of Ho Chi Minh City/Saigon, Vietnam. *Cyclo* focuses on spaces in transition after Vietnam's 1986 market liberalization "reforms," called *doi moi* (renovation). The film's camerawork emphasizes spaces of exchange, diagramming not only the mobile cyclo's travels through spaces in economic transition, but also the flow of money and bodies. By highlighting signs of exchange, *Cyclo* underscores an increasingly important social issue that is often overlooked in discourses of economic development: money and capital can exercise more agency and power than human beings. In *Cyclo*, capital has more freedom to move in post-*doi moi* Ho Chi Minh City than do people. While the film's critique of economic development discourses is far from novel, its techniques for thinking time as an image of exchange warrant further speculation. *Cyclo* does not follow a linear storyline; rather, it puts various disconnected events into resonance. The film disrupts chronological narration, whereby events follow a linear unfolding of past–present–future. Instead, the film thinks time as simultaneity and bifurcation to bring into focus various stages of capital production that coexist in the urban fabric.

Cyclo uses cinematic technique to interrogate time as measured and rational and, consequently, provides tactics for thinking the multiple signs of capital. As such, I propose in this chapter that cinema is a form of thinking, helpful for critics to formulate strategies for struggling with capital's fluid and, at times, immaterial extension and the hyper-commodification of every facet of life.

Cyclo begins with the main character, the eponymous "Cyclo," pedaling through the streets of Ho Chi Minh City. We hear in voiceover the Cyclo's dead father (who was himself killed while driving a pedicab) explaining that he died in poverty and left nothing to his son except this backbreaking work and a recommendation to seek another living. Accordingly, the Cyclo, seemingly heeding his father's advice, meets a patriarchal state official in order to apply for a government loan. (None of the characters in the film has a name. Rather, they are identified by their function, their profession or their position in society.) State Official meticulously records the Cyclo's information while scarcely bothering to look at him, and informs him that he will be contacted in due course on the status of his application. A long shot of the bureaucrat's decrepit space reveals a growing pile of applications. The Cyclo's application joins the others, suggesting that relief of his plight will not be forthcoming from the state. Too overburdened by the sheer magnitude of requests from those left by the wayside during *doi moi*, the film draws attention to the reality of a virtually bankrupt state apparatus in Vietnam, offering loans to sectors of the population outside the circuits of money, influence, and power.

Since *doi moi*, Vietnam's government has shifted its economic focus from national self-sufficiency – its mantra during wars with France (1945–54) and the US (1964–73) – to a market-driven economy. It has privatized its eco-

Figure 12.1 Sectors of the population outside the circuits of money, influence, and power (*Cyclo*) (*Copyright Les Films Lazennec*)

nomic, educational, and health systems, rapidly sold state-owned enterprises to foreign investors, or forced them virtually overnight to compete in the global market. As if in recognition of this shrinking of the state, its official representatives disappear for the rest of *Cyclo*, with the exception of traffic police who regulate the Cyclo's movement through the city.

Despite *doi moi*, international investors and political agencies, including the US State Department, routinely castigate Vietnam as a repressive communist regime whose economic vitality is undermined by state centralization, thereby preventing it from becoming another of East Asia's "tiger" economies. Rather than add to the Cold War-inflected discourses of communism's failures, however, *Cyclo* focuses on the "working poor" who are caught in the maelstrom of rampant economic expansion. The film challenges the conception of the strong Vietnamese state by foregrounding spaces and practices which avoid and challenge state control, while nonetheless exercising considerable power in the everyday life of Ho Chi Minh City.

Vietnam was colonized, invaded, or at war with France, China, Japan, Cambodia, and the US for much of the twentieth century. Although the country's strong nationalist tradition helped to repel every invading military force, virtually non-stop warfare between 1945 and 1989 left Vietnam one of the poorest countries in the world. After reunification of North and South in 1976, Vietnam's entire economy remained mobilized for war, particularly given its occupation of Cambodia (1978–89), which prompted China's invasion of Vietnam in 1979. Outfitting a standing army of one million troops drained the economy of much-needed liquidity and resources. Forty percent of GNP routinely went to defense.[1] As a result of war, drought, and an infrastructure still devastated from the "American war" (1964–73), Vietnam's "informal" or "shadow" economy provided a livelihood for large sectors of the population otherwise unable to find work in the government's agencies, factories, farms, or institutions.

The informal or shadow economy, in the eyes of the government, comprises areas of economic activity which do not adhere to government labor, licensing, and taxation laws. These include the self-employed, and small-scale labor-intensive workers, such as clothes-makers and sidewalk vendors, who do not register their earnings with the state. The criminal economy meanwhile encompasses small-scale currency changers, smugglers of electronic goods, bicycles, cars, and mopeds, drug dealers, pimps, and prostitutes. Throughout the shadow economy, the primary mechanism of exchange is the US dollar.

That American money is the currency of choice is an unwitting effect of the Vietnamese government's banking policies after unification. In 1976, the government implemented procedures which required all citizens of the former South Vietnamese regime to deposit savings into state-run banks, and to convert all earnings into the currency introduced from the North, the *dong*.

As a result, there was little incentive to register savings, and money was converted instead into American dollars. Massive inflation, due to the prolonged directing of resources to military production, coupled with severe droughts and a world embargo because of Vietnam's invasion of Cambodia, destabilized the *dong*. The dollar became "the store of value" and, in effect, a shadow economy of "dollarization" operated simultaneously with the state's financial regime.[2]

According to economist Michel Chossudovsky, the move to *doi moi* exacerbated this dual system.[3] In 1984/5, at the suggestion of the International Monetary Fund (IMF), the Vietnamese government repeatedly devalued the *dong* against the dollar in an effort to curb inflation and generate liquidity for the government's industries. The results were disastrous. Poverty intensified, and the government was forced to seek extensive loans from the IMF and World Bank. These loans were conditional on severe macroeconomic reforms, producing traumatic effects throughout Vietnamese society. From the introduction of *doi moi*, over one million workers and 200,000 public employees (including thousands of teachers and health workers) had been laid off by 1992, while 5,000 (out of a total of 12,000) state enterprises had gone bankrupt by 1994.[4]

In 1993, the Paris Agreement was reached between the donor countries of the IMF, the World Bank, and Vietnam. This agreement ended the world embargo of Vietnam but, in order to receive further loans and aid from the World Bank, Hanoi was forced to recognize "bad debts" which had been accrued with the IMF by the defunct South Vietnamese government and which had been arranged by the US during its withdrawal in 1973. To repay the debt, Vietnam had to take out further loans with Japan and France – both previous colonizers of Vietnam. Although North Vietnam had defeated the South Vietnamese regime, unified Vietnam was forced to pay off a debt to the IMF for a regime it had fought so long to oust. In effect, this reversed the role of victors and losers of the war, as debt imposed a structure of domination seemingly more powerful than military control.

Although Vietnam has experienced tremendous statistical growth in its GDP, wealth is not evenly distributed, nor does it benefit Vietnamese-owned companies. Rather, industrial growth in Vietnam – supposedly the sign of an Asian "tiger" economy to come – is fueled by massive debt. Indeed, the World Bank has guaranteed over $1.8 billion in loans and aid to Vietnam since 1993.[5] Again, these loans require structural adjustment programs which undermine the autonomy of the state. The state's supervision of many business and infrastructure projects is, in effect, constrained by the imperatives and loan agreements of the World Bank.

Cyclo provides a concrete analysis of the pitfalls of statist institutions. Specifically, it challenges the valorization of the state as the best agency with which to cope with and regulate the chaos and flow of capitalist forces, while avoiding any suggestion that the state's inability to regulate the shadow economy represents the triumph of market capitalism. Instead, *Cyclo* focuses on the violence immanent to capitalism itself. As Marx indicates, capital

> must on one side strive to tear down every spatial barrier to intercourse, i.e. to exchange, and annihilate this space with time, i.e. to reduce to a minimum the time spent in motion from one place to another . . . . There appears the universalizing tendency of capital . . . . [Indeed], the free, unobstructed, progressive and universal development of the forces of reproduction is itself the presupposition of society and hence of its reproduction.[6]

Marx describes how capital's endless drive for efficiency annihilates space through time by circulating the production process throughout the social field. In other words, capital produces and standardizes spaces, cultures, communities, and production processes in different geographies in order to expedite the circulation of goods, people, and forms of knowledge. Capital is a "social hieroglyphic" for Marx, a set of fluctuating sign-values and images that must be organized.[7] Capital accumulation depends on the repetition and systematization of practices that are perceived as natural and transparent. Modes of identification such as the national subject and culture can be organized into generalized concepts and applied in numerous contexts that can, in turn, be transformed into a type of "thing-ness." Consequently, identities and forms of culture can be commodified and then circulated in a host of arenas, regardless of their specific geographical locations, or "imagined communities."[8] In short, identities can facilitate commodification. The global tourist industry, for example, isolates specific practices, places, and handicrafts as artifacts of "authentic" culture that can be experienced or purchased within the global market. In this system, forms of identity, cultural practices and objects, and historical sites can become *loci* of capital accumulation. Consequently, identity and modes of identification such as the "imagined community" cannot provide "oppositional" critical tools in the light of the dynamic, creative, and amorphous transnational forces of commodification.

Cyclo describes the inability of the "imagined community" – the symbolic representation of national culture and historical lineage – to challenge the belief that "authentic" national culture can operate as a site of resistance in the face of capital. The Cyclo's means of production (his pedicab) is stolen by the "Boss Lady" from whom he rents it, and, in the process, he is deprived of the one connection he has to his father, his lineage, and his utilitarian identity. The Boss Lady forces the Cyclo to take part in various criminal enterprises, including drug-trafficking, the sabotage of competitors' stores of rice, and setting rival cyclo garages on fire. It is only in such activities that he begins to make "real" money, when he is paid in American dollars. Indeed, most of *Cyclo*'s characters share a fascination with American money more than any common history, ancestry, or ethnicity. In one incident, police are checking the Cyclo's cargo of pig carcasses for illegal drugs when looters distract them. A military truck hits another pedicab driver, who collides with the Cyclo and comes to rest in a pool of blood on the pig carcasses, mimicking, in the Cyclo's mind, his father's violent death. We cut to the Cyclo waking startled from sleep, and thanking his father for helping him to avoid the police. The Cyclo ascribes his lucky escape to his father's intervention from beyond rather than to chance or contingency.

Reflecting on the history that he has inherited from his father, the Cyclo recognizes a stronger tie with him than mere work: they are connected by blood. Next, in a series of disjointed shots, the film maps the Cyclo's body through a series of close-ups of his hands, ears, arms, and lips. The Cyclo announces "to his father": "These veins – the paths of life you called them. Now I understand." From these fragments of the human body, we move to a mapping of an American $10 bill: a close-up of Alexander Hamilton's face, the emblem of the Department of the Treasury and of the Federal Reserve, the signatures of the Secretary of the Treasury and the Treasurer, and the serial number of the bank note. This mapping of money leads to the famous phrase – perhaps incomprehensible to the Cyclo, but already felt and understood: "This note is legal tender for all debts, public and private." These disconnected images effect a shift in focus from historical lineage and family heritage to capital as the embodiment of connection and equivalence. In other words, it is not blood as lineage that flows through the Cyclo's "paths of life," but capital. Instead, the montage implies a simultaneity of registers between capital and human cultural practices and lineage, one of which has a more definite and lasting impact upon the Cyclo's daily existence. The images of American money highlight the continued American presence in Vietnam through capital and money, more than the cultural legacy of his father's "imagined community," the Vietnamese language, and the state apparatus. The scene highlights commerce as a form of war, a struggle for control between local, regional, national, and global systems of exchange. Moreover, the scene suggests a transformation from forms of power premised on military and sovereign state control of violence to that of capital and exchange as ubiquitous yet imperceptible forms of power. There is no way out of the structure of debt when capital subsumes society. Debt provides a kinder, gentler form of control which is sensed before it is perceived or understood.

Cyclo reflects on the modification of Ho Chi Minh City/Saigon, a site of conflicting networks of historical, neocolonial, cultural, and economic forces. Ho Chi Minh City has functioned historically as a location of commerce, a port city, and a node of trade distinct from the seat of government and education in Hanoi. Governments have historically plotted and partitioned its space to maintain power over a demarcated territory and make it ever more defensible for the state's monopoly of violence. As urban theorist Henri Lefebvre describes in *The Production of Space*, "sovereignty implies 'space', and, what is more, it implies a space against which violence, whether latent or overt, is directed – a space established and constituted by violence . . . every state is born of violence, and that state power endures only by virtue of violence directed towards a space."[9] Nation-states use institutions to determine and police the epistemological limits of the possible by creating material spaces through urbanization. They incorporate separate geographical entities into a larger urban conglomeration. For example, contemporary Ho Chi Minh City comprises the historical areas of Saigon and Cholon – a primarily ethnic Chinese industrial area. These were separate urban entities first conjoined conceptually by the chief architect for the French colonial regime, Ernest Hébrard, in his master plan of 1925, and then legally ratified by the colonial government in 1931.[10] The colonial regime did not consider the indigenous population when enacting this policy. Distinct zones were created between the European districts and "the natives" to preclude the mixing of races and ethnicities – articulated not with walls and garrisons but through zoning laws.[11] In this manner, the state controlled the distribution of people in space; it ultimately decided the location of streets, commercial districts, industrial centers, parks, and public spaces, monumentalizing its own power and history.

Here, the distinction made by Gilles Deleuze and Félix Guattari between "striated" space (linear, hierarchically organized) and "smooth" space (non-linear, flowing) is of value.[12] Striated space, as they describe it, is made up of lines and points, demarcating and organizing fixed physical territory. Smooth space – which Deleuze and Guattari describe by reference to a mathematical model of space which takes multiplicity as its point of departure – postulates neither points nor lines, nor a fixed and stable territory. This smooth space allows multiple transitory itineraries – it is not measurable because it undulates and it is consistently affected by connections to other lines and points, which formulate plan(e)s and *milieus*. These planes only indicate rather than represent the network of possible connections. Smooth space is in continuous variation, and may not enter into representation. It is conceptual and physical but can avoid human perception. According to Deleuze and Guattari, "a smooth, amorphous space of this kind is constituted by an accumulation of proximities, and each accumulation defines a *zone of indiscernibility* proper to 'becoming' (more than a line and less than a surface; less than a volume and more than a surface)."[13]

Transnational companies work *in between* striated/organized and smooth/flowing spaces.[14] They use state institutions to their advantage – for example, to pay for the roads on which they transport goods – and always threaten immediate departure unless their needs are gratified. It is dangerous for *this* reason to view smooth space as *de facto* a space of resistance. Capital is creative and promotes paradoxical forces of consolidation (localization) and fragmentation (globalization). Nevertheless, Deleuze and Guattari suggest that the fluidity of capital, its working in the interstices of smooth and striated space, requires techniques of thinking power other than the juridical mode of sovereignty in the determination of space. Rather, they indicate that it is important to think the *relationship* of striated/organized and smooth/flowing spaces in order to formulate strategies for reversing power.

Cyclo highlights the incapacity of sovereign forms of government – the Vietnamese state, in this instance – to produce space and determine the urban fabric. The city does not function in the film as a choreographed spectacle celebrating the scientific, cultural, intellectual, political, and economic grandeur of the Vietnamese nation-state. Rather, the film's representation of the city registers the *traces* of power, the decaying colonial infrastructure and the increased role of capital in the production of space. Multiple historical layers come together in the space of the city, which is emphasized as a "smooth space" of exchange and flow. The city fabric is simultaneously historical palimpsest and space of indeterminacy.

Deleuze, in *Cinema 2: The Time-Image*, points to a need to rethink cinema as a proliferation of images of thought – a dynamic "practice of images and signs" – rather than as a technologically dependent cultural form which is structured like a language and affected by time.[15] Deleuze confronts what he proposes as the key "internal presupposition" of cinema, namely that "time is money":

> The cinema as art itself lives in a direct relation with a permanent plot [*complot*], an international conspiracy which conditions it from within, as the most intimate and most indispensable enemy. This conspiracy is that of money: what defines industrial art is not mechanical reproduction but the internalized relation with money . . . . Money is the obverse of all the images that cinema shows and sets in place, so that films about money are already, if implicitly, films within the film or about film.[16]

Money structures the form and content of the field of representation. For Deleuze, cinema helps us to think time "differently," not only as movement and equivalence, but also as indeterminacy. Deleuze makes a distinction between two semiotic structures of time: the *movement-image* and the *time-image*.[17] The movement-image characterizes a film as a series of moments and images in which time is subordinated to narrative action. In short, narrative organizes the events of the film, and characters relate to each other in terms of an overarching "story" – as, for example, in classical Hollywood cinema. The movement-image creates equivalencies between forms of time, and ironically follows the same structure of organization that creates equivalencies between money and value. Money is the form of appearance of value and labor for Deleuze; in other words, it is an image. The time-image, on the other hand, characterizes a film in terms of a priority of time over movement (narrative action). Coming to prominence with Italian neorealism, the time-image exceeds the equivalencies of managed time and, instead, bifurcates and proliferates endlessly. The time-image draws our attention to what Deleuze calls the "forking of time," the indeterminacy of images and concepts which precede and structure representation. With the rise to prominence of the time-image in cinema, narrative structure shifts its temporal focus from coherence and chronology to the chaos and indeterminacy of simultaneous events. In the process, the time-image challenges the linear management of time so imperative to capital's control of people and institutions, and the "truth" claims of empirical representation.

Deleuze's notion of the time-image also foregrounds the related crises of the individual in global capitalism and of the protagonist in contemporary cinema. In *Cyclo*, numerous characters find themselves unable to respond to situations or events which exceed their limits of understanding and imagination. Two of the main characters, the Cyclo and the Poet, exemplify this. They desperately try to assert agency in response to the transformation of their lives by capital. However, their only strategy of escape from capital is to kill themselves. They cannot "think" alternatives. The Cyclo, ordered by Boss Lady to carry out a murder, instead tries to kill himself but passes out before he can do so. The Poet sets fire to his apartment, to himself and to his cache of American dollars. Death and destruction seem to be the only way out of the networks of exchange and the domination by money.

If the film cannot locate a utopian space beyond the reach of capital, its cinematography – the movement of the camera – suggests an alternative other than death through which to struggle with capital. *Cyclo* juxtaposes several narrative strands which coexist in the city and which coincide through the logic of capital. The circular narrative ends by returning the Cyclo to the streets, caught in an eternal network of exchange relations. Throughout the film, the moving camera emulates a free-floating *flâneur*, consuming disjointed fragments of experience which fall within its view as it explores space. Shots change rapidly, seem disconnected, and limited in perspective, as if the camera occupies the points of view of several observers simultaneously. *Cyclo* rarely uses a fixed camera, preferring panning shots to encompass or suggest what exceeds the frame. The cuts between shots are not "rational," nor do they facilitate narrative coherence. The film forces us to think about the smooth space of capital flow by focusing on minutiae, highlighting the historical "layers" of the city, but disarticulating coherent or rational space. The space of Ho Chi Minh City becomes what Deleuze calls an indeterminate space, an "any-space-whatever" which could be virtually anywhere in the world, not because cities and people are everywhere the same but because of capital flow.

The cinematography accentuates the fluid movement of human circulation and traffic both inside and outside of architectural spaces. The camera moves continuously and repeatedly, crossing thresholds of interiority and exteriority. Through this simultaneity of registers, events are shown to coexist in a determinate space – they are connected but separate. For example, one of the Boss Lady's crew, the Lullaby Man, slits the throat of a rival gang member while directly outside his window flow traffic and crowds. The event is entirely shielded from view of, and from the chaos of, the street, though geographically adjacent to it. This juxtaposition emphasizes the incongruity of the everyday and the bizarre, the inherent limitations of fields of visibility and of fields of thought.

The end of the film underscores this with a disorienting panning-shot of the city in one continuous long take: an office tower crowned by the ubiquitous satellite dish; a building crane reflected in its mirrored windows; a colonial statue pointing to some indeterminate space; apartments for the wealthy; a barren lot; the ruins of jerry-built shacks; a luxury condominium with a swimming pool and tennis courts. Alongside it, we see the Cyclo bringing his family through the streets on his pedicab. The condominium and the street occupy different social spaces which only we as spectators – the art-house audience of international film – can see and grasp simultaneously. We are privileged to see this critical image. We are in an "any-space-whatever." Capital has flowed through us, and we, the viewers, participate in the production of capital.

Cyclo repeatedly throws us into nonrepresentational space, forcing us to think about how capital operates, not in terms of personal or cultural identity, but in terms of fluctuating matrices of dynamic relations. As capital flows through Ho Chi Minh City, specific places and localities unhinge from the nation-state's self-historicization as the central mediator of people and culture. Indeed, the film portrays space, place, and locale indeterminately, disconnecting historical, cultural, or national narratives from territory and space. Space loses its geographic and cultural specificity – its sense of being a "place." This could be Los Angeles as readily as Ho Chi Minh City.

To recall Deleuze, the key "internal presupposition" of cinema as a network of images is money. Cinema is a form of thought which focuses on the forking of time, of time as flow, not only as conditioned or managed value. It can provide a means of conceptualizing the indeterminacy of capital flow. Through its imagery, *Cyclo* provides a map which helps us to think fluidly about prerepresentational relations and spatial flow without the baggage of such age-old concepts, structures, and transcendental theories of the nation or state apparatus (even where these have historically provided "strategies of resistance"). As the critique of patriarchal or sovereign forms of power in *Cyclo* suggests, global capitalism requires tactics of resistance as fluid as global capitalism itself. The film unravels celebrations of free-market capitalism without evoking a nostalgia or pathos for the state.

Cinema and the time-image offer tactics through which to consider the smooth space of capital. *Cyclo* invites reflection on the indeterminacy of what is seen and not seen and forces us to consider the wisdom of Walter Benjamin's warning that structures of power, like capital, are simultaneously homogenizing and differentiating: the state of emergency is the rule.

Notes

1   See Nigel Thrift and Dean Forbes, *The Price of War: Urbanization in Vietnam, 1954–1985* (London: Allen & Unwin, 1986), p. 60.

2   This entire section owes a debt to Donald Freeman's "*Doi Moi* Policy and the Small-Enterprise Boom in Ho Chi Minh City, Vietnam," *Geographical Review* 86, no. 2: 178–97.

3   Michel Chossudovsky, *The Globalization of Poverty: Impacts of IMF and World Bank Reforms* (London: Zed Books, 1997).

4   Ibid., p. 147.

5   Ibid.

6   Karl Marx, *Gründrisse*, trans. Martin Nicolaus (New York: Penguin Books, 1973), pp. 539–40.

7   For Marx's discussion of the social hieroglyphic of value, see "The Fetishism of the Commodity and Its Secret," in *Capital, Volume 1*, trans. Ben Fowkes (New York: Vintage, 1977), pp. 163–77.

8   Benedict Anderson, *Imagined Communities: Reflections on the Origin and Spread of Nationalism* (New York: Verso, rev. ed., 1991).

9   Henri Lefebvre, *The Production of Space*, trans. David Nicholson-Smith (Oxford: Blackwell, 1991), p. 280.

10   Hébrard, "L'Urbanisme en Indochine," *L'Urbanisme aux colonies*, 1, p. 279.

11   Gwendolyn Wright, in *The Politics of Design in French Colonial Architecture* (Chicago: University of Chicago Press, 1991), analyzes the effects of France's colonial regime on the organization of knowledge, education, and the spatial fabric in Vietnam.

12   Gilles Deleuze and Félix Guattari, *Capitalism and Schizophrenia: The Thousand Plateaus*, trans. Brian Massumi (Minneapolis: University of Minnesota Press, 1987), p. 469 (chapter 14).

13   Ibid., p. 488.

14   Ibid., p. 492.

15   Gilles Deleuze, *Cinema 2: The Time-Image*, trans. Hugh Tomlinson and Robert Galatea (Minneapolis: University of Minnesota Press, 1989), p. 280.

16   Ibid., p. 77.

17   Deleuze explains his distinction between the movement-image and the time-image in terms of the historical development of classical Hollywood cinema, apotheosizing the movement-image, and its subversion by various forms of post-war European art cinema such as Italian neorealism and the French *nouvelle vague* (New Wave), apotheosizing the time-image. See ibid., pp. xi–xiii.

13

Cityscape: The Capital Infrastructuring and Technologization of Manila

Rolando B. Tolentino

Introduction

In a 1991 survey of the "ten best Filipino films up to 1990" by film critic Joel David, the top two films took the city of Manila as their central focus: Lino Brocka's *Manila in the Claws of Neon* (*Maynila Sa Mga Kuko ng Liwanag*, 1975) and Ishmael Bernal's *Manila After Dark* (also generically titled as *City After Dark*, 1980).[1] As such, the two films attested to the dual significance of the city: its historically-rooted importance to the hegemony of the Philippines as a national project, as a "showcase" city; and as also a semi-autonomous sphere which has historically moved, and which continues to move, on a somewhat different trajectory to the rest of the nation.

Manila, having "a life of its own," is a site for conflicting representations of the nation as a whole in Philippines cinema. The two films I will discuss in this chapter can be used as nodes in a discussion of the mapping of the city – a mapping which encompasses the multinationally-motivated national development of the Philippines and the translation or impact of that development in the margins of life in the Philippines and its capital city. I will explore the city both as a site and as a component of the narrative of national development: as *the* hub of the nation's developmental strategies, and as the site in which its developmental contradictions are most clearly manifested. *Manila in the Claws of Neon* and *Manila After Dark* can be deciphered as historical documents as well as social commentaries.

A population of ten million residents, reaching twelve million during the daytime when outside travelers also enter the city, makes Metro Manila the eighteenth largest metropolitan area in the world.[2] Thirteen percent of the country's population is accounted for by Metro Manila although the city accounts for only 0.5 percent of the nation's aggregate land area. The metropolis accounts for 32 percent of gross national product. Its 1991 labor force of 5.4 million accounted for 62 percent of the employable population. 43 percent of households in the city are squatters. In 1993, of Metro Manila's population of 10 million, 3.4 million were squatters, a figure which grew to 5.48 million in 1997, accounting for 7.5 per cent of the nation's population of 72.72 million.[3] With a housing backlog of 2.9 million units in 1992, the government could only provide 60,000 of this housing need for some half a million people, one-tenth of the 1997 squatter population. Furthermore, "among the urban households, 29 per cent have no electricity, 50 per cent have no running water and 56 per cent have no adequate sanitary facilities."[4] Some 50,000 scavengers make their living in the seven dumpsites in Manila; the figures reach 90,000 when "all types of scavengers" are considered.[5]

This mapping of Manila in terms of embodiment and contradiction is best structured according to the three historical layers of the city's development: the era of Spanish colonization; the era of US neocolonialism; and the Marcos era, in which the competing realities of Manila – as a would-be center of global capitalism, on the one hand, and as a "dying city" of poverty and disenfranchisement, on the other – come to the fore.

In writing the history of the present, *Manila in the Claws of Neon* and *Manila After Dark* reveal fundamental contradictions in the nation and the city and, in their representation of these colonial and imperial pasts of the Philippines, engage in a dialogue with the maneuvers of the Marcos regime in the 1970s to modernize the nation in the name of a teleological, transnational future. If the national project of the Marcos regime negated the nation's colonial and imperial histories to construct a modern state which would be attuned to multinational operations, which would be "transnational-ready," *Manila in the Claws of Neon* and *Manila After Dark* quote these histories to historicize the nation's present predicament.

In this chapter, therefore, my argument will be guided by recent theorizations of the city in terms of spatial discourse which have privileged the city as the locus of transnational operations. For Edward Soja, urban restructuring and mutation provides the focal point of the analysis of postmodern geography.[6] For David Harvey, the construction of the city as spectacle in order to attract capital intensifies competition and displacement in society.[7] For Fredric Jameson, film as a cultural form provides the perfect site for investigation and representation of notions of the urban in terms of the historical development from nation and modernity to transnationalism and postmodernity.[8]

Capital Infrastructuring and the Flatness of Manila

Of course, the preparation of the city for transnational national development
by the Marcos regime required the development of a national transport
infrastructure – to speak metaphorically, a network of developmental grids
which might foster the flow and mobility of capital in and through the
nation. But in Manila, such construction efforts – to build and maintain
elevated roadways through and around the city, to build and maintain de-
sired directional and relational flows – have been prone to real difficulties as
a result of the physical flatness of the city, as noted by Filipina critic Neferti
Xina Tadiar in her essay "New Metropolitan Form."[9]

This flatness has compromised efforts to raise a transport infrastructure
above and out of reach of the city's problems: flooding, slum colonies, poverty, traffic, and congestion. The city also notoriously suffers from an endless
cycle of road, telephone, water, and sewer diggings. Although capital desires
the safeguarding of channels within the nation which circumvent the city's
problem-prone surfaces, in Manila everything is surface, everything is exposed. The narrative of capital involves a paradox: it desires mobility, but to
achieve it must morph into a material form which is vulnerable to bogging-
down on the surface of Manila.

Capital's infrastructuring of Manila has been realized through what Manuel
Caoili has described as a "chain of surplus extraction."[10] Historically, the
city's prosperity was largely due to the extraction of agricultural surplus from
the countryside and involved the immigration of people from poverty-stricken
rural areas, depressing wages, maximizing exploitation, and leading to an
exacerbating income gap and patterns of dominance and subordination.
This inequality in society is aggravated by transnationalism which has, on
the one hand, resulted in extraordinary improvements and services for some
individuals and groups in the city, but not for most. This infrastructuring is
maintained by what Caoili describes as "[the] tendency for middle-class
living standards to be pushed up to international levels by increasing linkages
between Manila and other metropolitan areas in the world."[11] But while
living standards are pushed up for some, greater impoverishment and disenfranchisement are the reality for many others.

If film and the city are often conspicuously entangled, in Manila this
entangling takes a distinctive form. The literal mobility of the city – the
development of its infrastructure – is partially funded by a "flood tax" which
is imposed on cinema ticket sales. This tax is used to fund flood prevention
and city management projects in Metro Manila. The Metro Manila Development Authority, composed of the metropolitan area's seventeen cities and
municipalities, is host to an annual local film festival during the ten-day
Christmas holidays, when the city is dressed up with yuletide décor and

lighting, and a parade, an awards ceremony, and a showcase of "quality films" are held. The festival functions as a key source of funding and publicity for the Metro Manila Development Authority and its constituent municipalities and cities. Films, therefore, pave the way for the figurative mobility of the governing of Metro Manila.

Manila in the Claws of Neon and the Three Historical Phases of the City

Lino Brocka's *Manila in the Claws of Neon* condenses signifiers of three modes of production as the placements of the present national predicament: feudalism through its quotation of Spanish colonialism; monopoly capitalism through its quotation of American imperialism; and transnational global capitalism in its representation of the Marcos era.

In the film, Julio, a young migrant from the countryside, searches Manila for his sweetheart, Ligaya, who has been deceived into coming to the city to work as a prostitute and who has been taken in as a kept woman by the Chinese Ah-tek. While searching, Julio takes various jobs in construction and prostitution to survive, living among the marginalized peoples of Manila's slums. He finds the oppressive reality of the country replaced by the oppressive reality of the city. When he does find Ligaya, discovering her fate – trapped in the "white slave" trade – they plot to escape and return to the country. But, in the event, Ligaya is killed mysteriously before they can leave. After her funeral, Julio stabs Ah-tek with an ice pick and, as he tries to escape, is chased and cornered in a dead-end alley by a mob. In the final scene, Julio desperately raises the ice pick in a futile attempt to hold off his attackers who pick up wooden bats and steel pipes as they confront him.

Spanish Colonialism

Much of *Manila in the Claws of Neon* takes place in settings which are the architectural "remnants" of Manila's Spanish past – the plaza, church, elite homes, and so on. Through these, the film invokes the conditions of colonial oppression. Though Ferdinand Magellan's earliest contact with the Philippines dates back to 1521, Spanish colonization began with Miguel López de Legaspi's expedition in 1571 to conquer the islands under the seal of the Spanish monarch. Manila was established as a base for the expected growth of trade between East and West.

The first structure to be built was a fortified settlement, later enclosed in stone walls. This inaugurated the building and demarcation of a solely Spanish enclave which would become known as Intramuros, completed in 1594, a fortified area of 1.2 square kilometres. As well as providing a workforce for the municipal administration and retail trade, local, Chinese, and Japanese workers maintained the settlement during the day but departed at night when drawbridges were closed. The enclosure of Intramuros sealed the colonizer's space, secure from the rest of the colony. Everything outside the walls was designated as Extramuros. The Spanish colonizers constructed the "outside" national space along racial and occupational lines. If Intramuros was the base for Spain's transpacific trade, its unblemished racial and structural position had to be secure at all times.

Intramuros was the showcase of colonial power in all its glory as the "military stronghold, the seat of government, the womb of the Catholic faith, and the exclusive residential quarter of the Spaniards."[12] Its architecture and planning emphasized majestic structures and indigenized baroque designs. However, as the Augustinian historian Juan de Medina explains, even the Spanish would often leave the city, travelling to their summerhouses on the Pasig river, where they "enjoyed a coolness and freedom which the city does not possess."[13] The city was constructed not so much to be livable as to be a projection of colonial power.

The spatial organization of the town is analogous to its social structure. In *Manila in the Claws of Neon*, we see the Luneta, the national plaza established by the Spanish as the center of the nation's power structure, being taken over at night by the people – particularly the city's gay community – and being transformed into a space of play and sex. The plaza was originally designed as the hub of a grid system of pueblos and *cabeceras* (subordinate centers).[14] The Luneta was surrounded by the two major colonial infrastructures: the church (and its accompanying school); and the municipal buildings (and the nearby marketplace). The town elite lived nearby, their large houses flanking the plaza, while most lived further away in more modest dwellings, and others chose not to inhabit the Spanish settlement at all, living instead in mountains and farmland. As such, the spatialization of the town articulated hierarchies of knowledge and power and taste.

The control of the countryside was left primarily in the hands of the religious orders, who owned and managed the lands through religious conversion, resettlement (*reducción*), forced labor (*polo*), and an agricultural production quota system (*bandala*). In the town plaza, the church belfry imposed its symbolic order visually and aurally. The sound of the church bells (*bajo de los campañas*) imposed pedagogical time on the *reducciónes*, as Robert Reed has explained: "Through a regularized system of tolling, Christian converts were gradually accustomed to the fixed routines of prayers and other parish activities."[15] Spanish rule imposed its own temporal and spatial structures on the people. The *encomienda*, a system of giving royal land to *conquistadores* for their participation in colonization, was followed by the more economically efficient *hacienda* system, which in turn produced a feudal national economy, and formalized social relations between landlords and tenants, priests and worshippers, civilian authority and religious order, government and the community, *alcalde mayores*, *gobernadorcillos* and their constituents.

In *Manila in the Claws of Neon*, the legacy of the superiority of Intramuros in the Spanish colonial period is quoted as a powerful contributor to Filipino self-loathing in the present day, as a continuing reminder for the Filipino or Filipina of the historical failure of his or her people to achieve self-determination. Meanwhile, the imposition of rigid feudal authority and social structure is allegorized in *Manila in the Claws of Neon* in the continuing feudal relations between Ligaya and Ah-tek, and in Julio's subordination to his foreman on the construction site and to the gay clients in the sex-house (*casa*). Finally, the film also foregrounds the historic migration of able-bodied people to the city: in the Spanish colonial period, to escape the *polo* system of labor or to escape sporadic agrarian unrest.

US Neocolonialism

The condensation of Spanish colonial signifiers in *Manila in the Claws of Neon* emblematizes the country's belated and uneven development and particularly its delayed industrialization and technologization. It articulates the nation's ambivalence on the subject of modernization in terms of an unresolved racial dilemma. The film's narrative acknowledges two contradictory impulses: to return to traditional native ways or to modernize and thereby to aspire to the Enlightenment ideals of the developed West. Although the film contains a critique of American urbanization, it also valorizes the American myths of self-reliance and self-determination in the notion of "getting one's act together." Filipino identity becomes projected onto America, as elsewhere. America becomes present in the national space through signifiers of modernity (the English language, telecommunications, modern government), although most people's access to it is limited to the popular culture which has saturated the Philippines since the turn of the century.

On May 1, 1898, Admiral George Dewey's fleet defeated an ill-matched Spanish armada in Manila Bay. As Filipino revolutionaries besieged Spanish troops in Intramuros, the Spanish negotiated with the Americans for their surrender. The Treaty of Paris ceded the Philippines to the US for $20 million. Three years later and at a cost of $170 million, the conquest was formalized with the capture of nationalist leader Emilio Aguinaldo, and President William McKinley's establishment of a civil government in the islands.[16] The Philippine–American War cost 600,000 Filipino lives in "ten years of bayonet treatment."[17] With the departure of the Spanish, their regime was replaced by an American system of enforced resettlement (hamleting), forced labor, and counter-insurgency measures. This new authority also brought its own ambitious spatial organization.

The city-beautiful aspirations for Manila developed by planners in the post-World War Two period as part of America's imperial project are also critiqued in *Manila in the Claws of Neon* in the film's proliferation of images of a ruthless and menacing city. Daniel Burnham, who had designed the Chicago World's Fair (1893), was commissioned by William Howard Taft, the Secretary of War, to provide for Manila a city design which would incorporate both a modernistic interest in the future and appropriate representations of the "power and dignity of [the American] nation."[18] Burnham's motto was "to make no little plans, for they have no magic to stir men's blood."[19] A follower of Haussman, he urged students to plan cities by viewing the possibilities from the highest vantage-point.[20]

Ironically, that the only high vantage-point from which to view the city Burnham and co-designer Peirce Anderson could find was the prison tower in Bilibid, Muntinlupa, brings into sharp focus their design's propensity for discipline, and for demarcations of inside and outside. Their plan called for a civic center as the focus of the city, for the building of a promenade boulevard around Manila Bay, and for parks as architectural accessories or breathing spaces for the people: "The plan envisioned colonial comfort in a grand style."[21] In choosing to apply an intricate network of city sections in a radial street pattern connected by parks, the American vision, like the Intramuros of the Spanish, was designed to invoke difference, where imperial power was racially positioned as benevolent in its efficient delivery of public services. However, Burnham and Anderson's design was prone to failure.[22] The plan was never fully implemented by William E. Parsons, who chose to modify the implementation to meet "developed real estate and other controlling conditions."[23]

The Modern Period

What Manila ended up showcasing, then, like *Manila in the Claws of Neon* itself, was both the failure and success of American city planning in particular, and imperialism in general, to structure and control the space of the capital city (and the country). *Manila in the Claws of Neon* presents fundamental contradictions between the past idealization of the city and its antithetical realities in the present day.

In the film's final sequences, Julio, a native Filipino, is unable to orient himself in relation to the layout of the city streets in which he finds himself trapped. He tries to flee the scene of Ah-tek's murder but is corralled in an enclosed *esquinita* (narrow alley). In a close-up and slow-motion shot, his contorted face evokes alienation from familiar places and bodies. The final scene represents the natives' own distance from their bodies and spaces.

The realities of Manila in the era of transnational capital are foregrounded in three related issues in Julio's urban experience: immigration, labor, and the body.[24] Spurred in turn by the Spanish colonial *polo* system, by American pacification drives, and by modern economic necessity, immigration to the city has been a historical march of a rural reserve army of inexhaustible cheap labor. The immigrant, while important to the economy, is also considered as urban refuse. The poor, like refuse, exist everywhere in the fringes. Without education or skills, even their bodies become currency. Julio's physical size gains him employment in construction work. With the building nearing half-completion, most of the *peons* (manual laborers) are laid off. A wealthy gay client advises him to learn to "sing and dance" (perform oral and anal sex) to earn more in prostitution. A dead worker's body, unclaimed by relatives, is sold to a medical school (most of whose graduates will work abroad). Transnational capital, driving the construction industry, pervades the exploitative practice of arbitrary wage cuts, suspiciously called "taiwan."

In *Manila in the Claws of Neon*, then, immigration, skilling, and bodies are "low-tech" issues which foreground the "high-tech," massive transformation of the city. Their lack of skills contrasts with the valorization of education, diligence, patience, and knowledge of English by colonial and imperial systems and the Marcos regime alike. It also contrasts with or contradicts the prioritization in the Marcos era of the tourism and catering industries. While this priority fuelled the proliferation of beauty contests and the aestheticization of the "body beautiful," on the periphery, the bodies of children and young adults were circulated in the sex-trade underbelly of the new tourism. In *Manila in the Claws of Neon*, as Julio walks the street at night, gays take pleasure in their performance at a Miss International beauty pageant. Foregrounding "lifestyles of the rich and famous," the beauty contest is one of the city's pervasive cultural events and provided a platform for propagating both the image and values of the Philippines' First Couple, and their plans and development of Manila abroad (the 1974 Miss Universe pageant and the 1978 Mr. Universe contest).

Manila's incorporation into the larger sphere of Metropolitan Manila in 1975 was supported by the World Bank. Enlarging the demarcation of the premier city, Marcos reorganized the seventeen municipalities under the Metropolitan Manila Commission (MMC) and appointed his spouse Imelda as its governor, thus "effectively transforming metropolitan governance into a national government concern."[25] *Manila in the Claws of Neon* engages in a dialogue with the First Couple and their machinations. Like the city in the film's representation of the ideals of Spanish colonialism and American imperialism, the Marcos' city is an entity in which such ideals have not so much materialized as wrought havoc on the majority of the people. Imelda's role as MMC governor entailed transforming what was often described as a "dying city" into an ideal "City of Man."

So tight was her rein on the capital that Imelda even intervened in cinema. Unhappy with the negative image of Manila which it would ostensibly project internationally, she delayed the release of Ishmael Bernal's *Manila After Dark* which was due to compete in the Berlin Film Festival, and which presented a harshly realistic portrait of life in the city revolving around a contingently related ensemble of marginal city characters and representing *inter alia* a rampant drug subculture and the transgression of normative sexual boundaries. Imelda demanded that all footage showing the dying city or any direct mention of Manila be deleted. Though the film was generically retitled *City After Dark*, it still did not make it to the festival on time.

The Dying City

From the Marcos to the Ramos administrations, Manila has been projected as dying and in need of resuscitation. The project of wholesale transformation of Manila envisaged by the Marcos regime and initiated in the form of the MMC was predicated upon a desire to clean the city of its literal proliferation of refuse and to cleanse it of its "scum" – that is, prostitution, pornography, graft, and crime. *Manila in the Claws of Neon* produces this antithetical image of the city, but there has never been any possibility of completing the city's slum clearing.

Even in the 1990s, the "dying city" is the dominant paradigm in the rhetoric of metropolitan administration. A headline in 1995 asked, "Can Manila be saved from choking to death?"[26] There has long been a tendency to explain away the city's problems by reference to excessive rural migration and its detrimental effects on the quality of urban life and the metropolitan infrastructure. The critical position is to question this reactive response of "city cleaning" to the rural premise – as, for example, implemented from 1988 by the mayor of Manila, retired police-general Alfredo Lim. For Lim's declaration – "we will clear up the streets and unclog the thoroughfares to allow the city to breathe again, and let the lifeblood of its commerce flow freely once more to give life to our city" – is not so much an expression of a real desire as a pretext for the authorities' "necessary" actions of surveillance and enforcement in the city.[27]

The use of the Luneta as a setting in both *Manila in the Claws of Neon* and *Manila After Dark*, therefore, calls into question the place of such official discourse. For if the city is pedagogically decipherable in the light of day, then the Luneta as a site of subversive anarchy comes alive only after dark.

Squatter Colonies and Cities

Manila in the Claws of Neon locates resistance to the hegemonic ideals of the city within the everyday, not only in the case of the Luneta but in the image of the squatter colony, one of the most disturbing social developments in Manila, and one of the most persistent and disruptive images in Philippine cinema, since World War Two. The squatter colony was tackled in film as early as Lamberto Avellana's *Anak-Dalita* (1955), which dealt with squatters' lives in Intramuros. Lino Brocka proliferated the image in the 1970s not only in *Manila in the Claws of Neon*, but also in *Insiang* (1976), *Jaguar* (1979), and *Bona* (1980). In these films, the squatter colony appears as a site of disruption in the ideal space of the transnational economy – a transnational economy which seeks both to erase poverty in the name of utopian ideals while simultaneously ensuring the continuance of poverty through its insistence on a steady supply of cheap labor in the city.

Self-sustaining communities in their own right, the squatter colonies of Manila comprise low-income shanty houses or semi-permanent structures laid out in networks of alleys (*esquinitas*), with communal sanitary facilities and services including *sari-sari* stores, beauty parlors, barber shops, tailors, dress shops, eateries (*karinderya*) and street markets (*talipapa*), and are typically located on the city's fringes and unused spaces (under bridges, along railroad tracks).

The economic hype which accompanied the entry of Manila into the transnational global economy, prompting a mushrooming of malls and condominiums in the city, was devastating for the squatter colonies and for the squatter, who became demonized and positioned as the city's "abject" in the hegemonic culture's popular constructions, depicting the figure as refuse and a public menace. Squatter colonies were simply demolished rather than relocated. The implementation of Executive Order 129 in 1993 sanctioned "clearing operations" in forty identified *esteros*, threatening some 70,000 families.[28] Such "clearing" actions articulate the desire not only to decongest the city but to erase the "squatter experience," to negate all signifiers of poverty and underdevelopment which might impede the transnational project. Such is the reasoning behind Ramos's intent to erase "Smokey Mountain," the garbage dump which has long been an icon of poverty in the local and international media. In the case of Smokey Mountain, not only is the city sitting on a gold mine of undeveloped real estate, but the project of transnational development requires the mountain's eradication.

Squatter colonies also represent alternative spaces for profit-oriented consumerism alongside transnational culture. *Manila in the Claws of Neon* foregrounds the squatters' patronage of such businesses as local beer houses and local markets, which operate as part of a different economy which positions even squatters as a viable market for conquest. A cottage industry known as "repacking" is based on repackaging standard commodities such as oil, salt, and sugar in affordable volumes and packaging to suit the low-income buyer's purchasing power.

As such, self-reliance is an emblematic feature of the squatter community

– making sense of the literal and figurative garbage dumped on top of them. Scavenging in the refuse heap and collecting recyclable materials with "pushcarts" constitutes the dominant source of livelihood of people residing in the dumps. As noted at the beginning of this chapter, some 50,000 scavengers make their living in the seven dumpsites in Manila, while the figures reach 90,000 when "all types of scavengers" are considered.[29] While Smokey Mountain accounts for a third of garbage collection, with 20,000 individuals or 3,000 families "harvesting" (as scavenging is more popularly known in the site), even it does not accommodate the volume of refuse generated by Metro Manila. What remains is disposed of in the sewers which flood during the monsoon season.

In a further twist connecting squatters with transnational garbage, the country has also begun accepting other nations' toxic waste.[30] Scavenging and recycling may be considered menial work, but they are necessary to Manila's multinational operations. Amidst these oppressive conditions, the continuing visibility of the squatter figure is a testament, at the very least, to the survival instincts of the individual and the community.

Conclusion

The aim of any cartography of location must be the daily reiteration of the power play which produces the contradictions which generate sites of resistance. The presence of squatter communities in Metro Manila in sites that impede urban flow and mobility is antithetical to the post-World War Two drive to produce the quintessentially sterile, rational, and productive city.

What the kind of cityscaping attempted in this chapter literally and graphically foregrounds is the need for a culturally and historically specific remapping of the urban, national, and global experiences. If cartography has always played a key role in the production of the hegemonic grid, then one must maneuver for breathing spaces in the urban, national, and transnational geoscapes against this hegemony. As one relates one's experience to that of others, one also comes to understand local subversive acts – such as the making of a film – as potential templates for new sets of social relations.

Notes

1   Joel David, "Ten Best Filipino Films up to 1990," *Fields of Vision Critical Applications in Recent Philippine Cinema* (Manila: Ateneo de Manila University Press, 1995), pp. 125–36.
2   I am culling this information from MMA's *Metropolitan Manila Situationer*, n.d.
3   Erlie U. Lizardo, ". . . Meanwhile in Metro Manila: More Squatters," *Ibon Facts and Figures* 16, no. 2 (31 January 1993): 8.

4   Pamela Asprer et al., "Real Estate: Not a Bargain Sale," *Ibon Facts and Figures* 13, no. 24 (31 December 1990): 10; see also Emi Navalta, "Poverty in the City," *Ibon Facts and Figures* 18, no. 6 (31 March 1995).

5   Vangie Villena, "Picking at the Waste Problem," *Ibon Facts and Figures* 17, no. 3 (15 February 1994): 5.

6   Edward Soja, *Postmodern Geographies: The Reassertion of Space in Critical Social Theory* (New York and London: Verso, 1989).

7   David Harvey, *The Condition of Postmodernity* (London: Verso, 1989).

8   Fredric Jameson, "Remapping Taipei," in *The Geopolitical Aesthetic: Cinema and Space in the World System* (Bloomington and London: Indiana University Press and BFI, 1992).

9   Neferti Xina M. Tadiar, "New Metropolitan Form," *differences* 5, no. 5 (1993): 159.

10   Manuel Caoili, "Reflections on Metropolitan Manila Reorganization and Social Change," *Philippine Journal of Public Administration* 29, no. 1 (1985): 1–26; and "Manila and Philippine Development," *Philippine Social Sciences and Humanities Review* 47, nos. 1–4 (January–December 1993): 113–30. Other useful sources on Manila's urban development include: Luzviminda B. Encarnación et al., "Manila Urban Development Project: A Case Study in Public Borrowings and Project Development, "*Philippine Journal of Public Administration* 22, no. 1 (January 1978): 45–78; Romeo Ocampo, "Planning and Development of Prewar Manila: Historical Glimpses of Philippine City Planning," *Philippine Journal of Public Administration* 36, no. 4 (October 1992): 305–27; Ernesto M. Serote, "Socio-Spatial Structure of the Colonial Third World City: The Case of Manila, Philippines," *Philippine Planning Journal* 22 (1 October 1991): 1–14.

11   Caoili, "Reflections," p. 12.

12   Robert R. Reed, *Colonial Manila* (Berkeley: University of California, 1978), p. 50.

13   Quoted in ibid., p. 49.

14   Setha M. Low, "Cultural Meaning of the Plaza: The History of the Spanish-American Grid-Plan-Plaza Urban Design," in Robert Rotenberg and Gary MacDonogh (eds.), *The Cultural Meaning of Urban Space* (Westport, CT and London: Bergin & Garvey, 1993), pp. 75–94.

15   Reed, *Colonial Manila*, pp. 103–4.

16   Felice P. Sta. Maria, "Brown Man's Burden," in Gilda Cordero-Fernando and Nik Ricio, *Turn of the Century* (Quezon City: GCF, 1978), p. 149.

17   This quote is from General Arthur MacArthur. For a comprehensive view of the casualties of the war, see Luzviminda Francisco, "The Philippine-American War," in Daniel B. Schirmer and Stephen Rosskam Shalom (eds.), *The Philippines Reader* (Quezon City: Ken, 1987), pp. 8–19.

18   Daniel Burnham and Edward Bennett, *Plan of Chicago* (New York: da Capo Press, 1970), p. 29.

19   Ibid., p. 29.

20   Christine E. Moe, "Daniel Hudson Burnham, Architect and Planner," *Architecture Series* A-358.

21   Ocampo, "Planning and Development of Prewar Manila," p. 315.

22   Moe, "Daniel Hudson Bushham." As Moe remarks of Burnham's kind of city

planning, "Without princely powers, stringent controls, and heavy capital investments, baroque plans were not successful."

23   William E. Parsons, "Burnham as Pioneer in City Planning," *Architectural Record* 38, no. 1 (July 1915); quoted in Ocampo, "Planning and Development of Prewar Manila," p. 316.

24   If "the politics of immigration is closely tied to the politics of cities," then the history of internal migration can be analyzed as the history of the city. See James Holston and Arjun Appadurai, "Cities and Citizenship," *Public Culture*, 19 (1996): 196.

25   Jurgen Ruland, "Metropolitan Government under Martial Law: The Metro Manila Commission Experiment," *Philippine Journal of Public Administration* 29, no. 1 (January 1985): 30. Other assessments of the Metro Manila governance include Manuel A. Caoili, "Notes on Metropolitan Manila Reorganization," *Philippine Journal of Public Administration* 22, nos. 3–4 (July–October 1978): 328–49; Manuel Caoili, "Recent Developments in Metropolitan Manila Commission Government," *Philippine Journal of Public Administration* 21, nos. 3–4 (July–October 1977): 374–86; Ileana Maramag (ed.), *Metropolitan Manila and The Magnitude of Its Problems* (Manila: NMPC, 1976); Asteya M. Santiago, "Urban Development and Administration in the Philippines: An Institutional Response," *Philippine Planning Journal* 23, no. 1 (October 1991): 42–56.

26   "Can Manila be saved from choking to death?," *Philippine Daily Inquirer*, 28 July 1995, p. 20.

27   Alfredo Lim, "A Vision of Manila," *Panorama*, 20 June 1993; quoted in Tadiar, "New Metropolitan Form," p. 163.

28   Navalta, "Poverty in the City," p. 6.

29   Villena, "Picking at the Waste Problem," p. 5.

30   In 1991, some 50 shipments or 1,858 tons of toxic wastes were brought into the country. Villena further writes, "In 1992, 164 tons came from the United Kingdom and 58 shipments amounting to 538,902 lbs. of plastic and 7 million kilos of toxic plastic wastes from the US firms Alligator Trading, Ever General, Astro Property, and Ever Green. It is further estimated that waste imports could increase by as much as six times in [1993]." Ibid., pp. 5–6.

14

The Politics of Dislocation: Airport Tales, *The Castle*

Justine Lloyd

It's every Australian Family's dream – a quarter acre block, a barbie, a pool room . . . and an airport over the back fence.[1]

In a year of Hollywood blockbusters such as *Men in Black*, *The Lost World: Jurassic Park*, and *Titanic*, *The Castle* (Rob Sitch, 1997) was the thirteenth most popular release in Australia in 1997, and was the most popular Australian production of the year.[2] Even more remarkable was *The Castle*'s financial success. It was more profitable than *Shine* (Scott Hicks, 1996), the most successful Australian film of the previous year. *Shine* had performed well as a distinctly Australian production in the global media market after Geoffrey Rush received the Best Actor award at the Academy Awards in 1997. Following this, *The Castle* was bought by Miramax for an American rerelease in 1999, with Australian terms such as "barbie" redubbed and with a more highly produced soundtrack.[3] This was a puzzling outcome for a low-budget film with no international star and an ensemble of local actors who were more familiar to Australian audiences from the daily routines of domestic television soaps than the global market of feature films.

Part of the success of *The Castle* could be attributed to the producers' promise to the audience to "bring the Aussie Backyard onto the Big Movie Screen where it belongs."[4] The features of this cinematic backyard include the kind of architectural castoffs only visible at the very margins of suburbia, where the city meets a wasteland or a "non-residential" zone such as an airport. Such unimpressive locations have been ignored by filmmakers and planners alike perhaps because, as American artist and writer Martha Rosler has observed, airports are part of the transport infrastructure of a globalizing society and so remain "in the realm of the technocrat" and "do

Figure 14.1 Flyer for *The Castle*, 1997 (*Copyright Roadshow Film Distributors, reproduced by kind permission of Working Dog Pty. Ltd.*)

not encode capital in the way large urban structures do."[5] In *The Castle*, this spatial juxtaposition of the everydayness of the backyard with the international vectors of travel, tourism, and trade is mirrored by a narrative that creates a connection between the domestic and the distant. The inherently funny storytelling strategy of the film is to show up, and eventually transcend, this separation of the space between the suburbanite and the technocrat.

While this juxtaposition of the "extraordinary" and "ordinary" in the family's story is centered on the struggle of an "average" suburban family to remain in their home, it expands from their struggle for location, to examine dislocation more broadly. The film really begins when the family's quarter-acre block, and in fact their whole street, is rezoned to expand their city's airport facilities. The tragicomic adventure to save the family house continues as they try, unsuccessfully, to use the civic spaces of a modern democracy (courts, local councils, neighborhood meetings) to defend the "castle" of the film's title. This process creates the house as a locale through which to assess and explore the meaning of home and the political effects of spatial change and dislocations in late twentieth-century Australia.

The ways in which this particular story about "home" imagines and represents the suburban house proposes some unusual relationships between suburban and urban desires for mobility. As the story of the "castle" develops in the narrative – as the family's right to property and their house is placed in question – the notion of home as a transparent attachment to place is also unsettled and drawn from invisibility into a discourse on homeliness in a postcolonial world. While working toward an ending that sees the family reunited and relocated in their home, the film also offers a representation of the suburban landscape that could be described as an articulation of the suburb to its "others." An acknowledgment of the complexity of this relationship has far-reaching implications that *The Castle* only starts in train: that the suburb itself in settler society might be somehow contingent on displacing others; that colonial history might be mixed up with the present; and that the Australian dream is predicated on a set of social exclusions and inclusions. Seeing these spaces as socially related is only possible at this moment in Australian history, after the long and continued struggles for recognition of native title in the Australian legal system from the 1930s through to the 1990s. This chapter seeks to focus these on implications by examining the ways in which *The Castle* perceives and creates these relationships through a narrative of "ordinariness."

Looking Over the Back Fence

The Castle is the first feature written by the television comedians Rob Sitch, Santo Cilauro, Jane Kennedy, and Tom Gleisner, and produced by their company, Working Dog Pty Ltd. The team's reputation for comedy and satire had been established by their breakfast radio programs and their television comedy series *The Late Show*, as well as by the very popular current affairs parody, *Frontline*, which had been screened on the government-funded Australian Broadcasting Corporation (ABC) television network. *Frontline*'s scripts were characterized by their immediate linking of topical news events to a critique of news-gathering practices. The on-location setting of the episodes and guest appearances by politicians and celebrities brought what Roland Barthes has described as a "reality effect" to the weekly show that highlighted the rhetorical pretensions of television news and current affairs.[6]

The team's approach to filmmaking in *The Castle*, directly translated from this television experience in both process and product, makes for a deliberately "small-screen," home-video aesthetic. That shooting was completed in ten days also attests to their emphasis on story rather than filmmaking craft. In the release publicity, the filmmakers explain their approach by firmly establishing *The Castle* against the tradition of the Australian big-screen heroic epics of the early 1980s such as *Gallipoli* (Bruce Beresford, 1981) and *The Man from Snowy River* (George Miller, 1982). The aesthetic of fast shooting and low production values signifies their attempt to diverge from the grandiose bush-mythology of such films.

Strategies such as these deliberately and humorously undermine the "AFC genre" identified by Australian film critics Susan Dermody and Liz Jacka in the 1980s, so named as the films identified with it were funded via the Commonwealth Government's Australian Film Commission (AFC).[7] Established in 1975, the AFC gave directors such as Gillian Armstrong and Peter Weir unprecedentedly large budgets during the 1980s to produce a series of character-based "quality" films such as *Picnic at Hanging Rock* (Peter Weir, 1975), *My Brilliant Career* (Armstrong, 1979), and *Breaker Morant* (Beresford, 1980). The distinguishing features of the genre were the films' ubiquitous historical settings and realist aesthetic. The wide-screen mythologizing of the Australian rural landscape in these films paralleled their exploration of questions of national and personal identity, creating a sense that cinematic explorations of struggles over identity and place in Australia were held firmly in the past or the bush, and preferably both.

Indeed, when *The Castle*'s advance publicity promised to "bring the Aussie Backyard onto the Big Movie Screen where it belongs!" it also signaled a displacement of a kind of national culturalist cinematic imaginary of Australia. This description of the protagonist from the film's synopsis clearly places the story and setting within and against an established "quality" Australian filmmaking tradition:

> If you thought Burke and Wills [colonial explorers who crossed the continent from south to north for the first time in 1860, although most of their party didn't make it and they themselves perished under a tree in midsummer] were the worst equipped people in Australian history, you're in for a surprise.
>
> "The Castle" is a sweeping saga that takes the harsh Australian outback, the rugged characters of the ANZAC legend, the spirit of Banjo Patterson and ignores them in favor of a greyhound racing, tow-truck driver who never meant to be a hero.

The Castle instead can be placed in a generic trajectory which runs in 1990s Australian cinema from *Sweetie* (Jane Campion, 1989), *Muriel's Wedding* (P. J. Hogan, 1994), and *Strictly Ballroom* (Baz Luhrmann, 1992) through to *Floating Life* (Clara Law, 1996): all films which tell stories of contemporary suburbia rather than the bush, although the themes of national and personal identity articulated through a coming-of-age narrative remain no less present.[8] Similarly, *Priscilla, Queen of the Desert* (Stephan Elliot, 1994) questions the relationship of the outback to the city, with its road-movie scenario of drag queens on tour in the country renegotiating Australian male identity in many ways that would not have been possible in the 1980s.

The Castle, however, maintains a deep affection for and creates an overwhelmingly positive portrayal of the characters and their location. In other "suburban camp" films such as those mentioned above, the main characters seek to transcend their past and cast aside the signs of suburban "dagdom."[9] Typically, the main character is transformed by passage from the suburb to the city. This is represented by a shift in setting from the wide, silent, and lonely spaces of the suburban street, with their gauche inhabitants and kitsch houses, to the exciting, dynamic cosmopolitanism of the urban center. The characters similarly shed their ugly duckling status with a change of clothes, and the film ends with some kind of return or acknowledgment of the changed status of the main character by those who have been left behind.

The Castle works in a different territory to other Australian suburban films of the 1990s. The landscape of the suburb depicted in the film bypasses the "city center" itself, as it is not only unnecessary to the story, but it also seems superfluous to the daily lives of the characters. *The Castle* locates itself in the home and the suburb by constructing a hybrid form of televisual and videomatic codes extended into a feature-film plot structure. The film opens with a teenage boy speaking directly to camera, saying "My name is Dale Kerrigan and this is my story." His character continues by voice-over to narrate the family's story and take the audience on a tour of his home, as if this was a school project or a home video sent to overseas relatives. The film's director, Rob Sitch, has explained that the voice-over device was used to introduce the characters as quickly as possible because the catering budget would only last ten days.[10] But interestingly, in this regard, the film also echoes the docudrama form of the infamous BBC "real-life" soap opera *Sylvania Waters* (1992). Further, the film uses actors not known for quality feature-film acting or stage roles. The lead actor, Michael Caton, played "Uncle Harry" in the long-running 1970s historical soap *The Sullivans* and Anne Tenney, cast as "Sal Kerrigan," played "Molly" until her character died of cancer and caused national mourning in the 1980s medical soap *A Country Practice*.

These divergences from the AFC genre are not to say that the film does not address the issues of identity championed by the national cultural project

of the 1980s. The setting of the film in contemporary suburbia and its intertwined imaginary of the home and the televisual mediascape, do, however,
suggest a radical and subversive gesture that sets a contemporaneous minor
cinema of the family backyard against an established major cinema of the
heroic outback.

We've Got to Stop Taking Other People's Land Away . . .

While the film takes a broadly comic approach by enumerating and portray-
ing the family's quirks and everyday habits, it also employs a dramatic structure to motivate the story and address some ethical and moral themes. The
drama begins when a faceless entity, "Airlink" (a business consortium) and
the Federal Airports Corporation conspire to compulsorily acquire the
Kerrigan's house, "Number 3 Highview Crescent, Coolaroo." The house is
situated on an (unfinished) suburban street, so close to the airport that the
runway is at the end of the street and the family can walk home from the
international terminal when they go to meet their daughter and her new
husband returning from their honeymoon.

The comedy here works through a tension that is raised when parodying
the middle-Australian suburban dream, and a tension that reflects a modernist ambivalence about the pleasures of suburbia. The Kerrigan family pas-
sionately participate in an ordinary Australian-ness which is signified by everyday
pursuits such as greyhound racing, fishing, an enthusiasm for fast cars and
boats, watching reruns of highlights of television variety shows and themselves
appearing on game shows, and home renovating and decorating. The house
remains a "work-in-progress" as it undergoes endless renovations until the
end of the film. It is a fine example of the kind of house that Australian
architect Robin Boyd would have called "featurist" in his 1960 book *The
Australian Ugliness*, with its scrupulously fake Victorian lacework and brick-
faced chimney.[11] Boyd's text expressed his frustration with Australians' an-
tipathy to and ignorance of modernist architectural style, signified in the
suburban urge to incorporate "useless" ornamentation and kitsch detail in
postwar Australian domestic architecture: "To hide the truth of man-made
objects the Featurist can adopt one of two techniques: cloak or camouflage."[12]

These signs of an excessive and exaggerated suburbia work by addressing
an audience who will be familiar with, but separate from, the characters and
setting portrayed. This conflictual and negotiated relationship to suburbia
can be summed up in a quote from Stephen Curry who plays the character
of Dale, the film's narrator: "Australians are all going to 'get' *The Castle*
because they know or have met every single one of the characters in the
film."[13] So although the intended audience is expected to "know" the characters, they are not expected to "be" the characters. This parallels the kind of

exaggerated and "camp" suburban setting that has appeared in other Australian films such as *Muriel's Wedding*. Unlike *Muriel's Wedding* and *Sweetie*, however, as films which feature heroines who have to transcend their suburban backgrounds by leaving home for the city, the ground for action of the *Castle* remains entirely in the space of the suburban home. The characters traverse the suburban main street and travel to the nation's High Court, but they never visit a recognizable "downtown" or urban center.

When a crisis of authority over space is triggered by a threat to their home, the centrality of the Anglo family as national subjects in Australia is challenged. The right to property that underlies Western notions of political subjectivity is exposed as fragile and mythic, creating a turning-point for the taken-for-granted constructions of race, gender, and class. As this overlap between the house and the home starts to slide apart, the family's experiences of loss and displacement start to resonate with those of other migrants and eccentric suburbanites.

Throughout the story, Darryl Kerrigan's inability to defend the family's home signals a crisis of patriarchal power constituted in the structure of the nuclear family. Darryl had previously been an enthusiastic modernist, admiring the high-voltage pylons at the end of his street as a "sign of man's ability to produce electricity." He also considered the proximity of his house to the airport an asset (public transport lies just at the end of the road, if the family ever to needs to fly).

Generally participating in and finding pleasure in narratives of progress, the Kerrigans exhibit an ordinary passion for domestic and suburban technologies: Walkmans, cars, boats, lawnmowers, television – reflected in the description of the house in the film's synopsis as having "more driveway than lawn."[14] But the limits of their participation in a technologized urbanism is exposed by the intrusion of the global economy into their lives in the shape of the ever-expanding airport freight facility. The family's exclusion from suburbia that follows this "tragic" development illuminates the heterogeneity of modernity itself. That the family's world is a "world apart" from the benefits of global cosmopolitanism stands in sharp contrast to their participation in a culture of privatized mobility in speedboats, cars, and trucks. Their case is a poignant example of the urban problematics of the 1990s, which continue to be bound within this stretch between the promises of technological solutions to technological problems and the problems themselves. The scenes in which the family members express feelings of loss and betrayal at the idea of losing their home are plainly not just expressions of loss of the house itself. The sense of tragedy here is also linked to the negation of a vision of humanist relations to machines. This suburban home-world is so thoroughly mixed with technology on an ontological level that the idea that the airport, as a marker of place and connection to the global beyond, could itself be a threat to their sense of place creates a critical turning-point in their sense of location.

In the face of this displacement of the domestic, the option of defending
the house in a "shoot-em-up" last stand is offered by the eldest son when he
aims a secondhand air rifle at the police who come to the house, but refused
by Darryl in his position as father of the household. The characters instead
move from defending their very own private houses to a collective action to
defend their whole neighborhood. The other houses on the street represent
socially and economically marginal suburbanites: a divorced woman, a recently migrated Lebanese family, and a pensioner. The film's co-writer explains how this shift from the house as "castle" to the street as an arena for
visualizing the collective came about: "It's an accidental byproduct . . . we
didn't set out to make a comment about the fabric of Australian society. We
set out to tell the story of a family and their house . . . as simple as that. You
hear stories and you create a bit of a neighborhood in your own mind."[15] In
an anecdote about neighborliness, the film's director expresses a notion of
cultural difference that comes down to eating or not eating a certain food:

> It's really looking at the landscape of Australia, and really Australians get on
> pretty well no matter who is the next door neighbor, and Australia is dysfunc-
> tional, but I don't think it's a nasty form of dysfunction. Different ethnicities
> will look over the back fence and say "I don't know how you can eat that
> radicchio or whatever it is", and someone else will look over, "I don't know
> how you can eat a meat pie", you know I think it's pretty harmless.[16]

This notion of a backyard multiculturalism turns the Anglo family from
ground to figure, but it also makes invisible a set of differences that cannot be
reduced to food. The reduction of difference to a purely aesthetic dimension
is an appealing but problematic move that points to a more global blurring
of identities that occurs within the film. The potential threat to friendly
banter over a meat pie that brings the street together in Highview Crescent
is founded on a sense of community that forms a continuum between migration during war, colonization, and urban development, posing them as equal
causes of dislocation. On one level, this could be seen in Meaghan Morris's
terms as "a refusal to make difference 'nuclear', claustrophobic."[17] Neighborly
differences are portrayed as cohesive, they create a dialogue over the back
fence. But in this process the distinctions and limits of alterity must be closely
examined.

In particular, the family's loss of authority over domestic space in the film
creates an intersection between a myth of suburban locality and other struggles over rights to define place. Most strikingly, *The Castle* places the Kerrigans'
fight to save their house on the same plane as aboriginal struggles for land
rights. The film explicitly creates a relationship between the family's claim to
the suburban house as a kind of sacred site (invested with memories, stories,
and connections to place) and the High Court of Australia's 1994 "Mabo"

judgment rejecting the colonial notion of *terra nullius*. The parallel between the Kerrigan's claim to stay in their house and aboriginal rights to land is underpinned by an architectonics of democracy and justice which – in the words of suburban solicitor Dennis Denuto as he tries to defend the Kerrigan's case in the Federal Court – can be summed up as the all-around "vibe" of the Australian constitution.

Thus the film poses the process of globalization as metonymic for the process of colonization. The very ordinariness of this move illuminates many of the complexities of home as a "lived" time/space which in the film (and outside it) remains indeterminately public and private, constructed spatially somewhere between local, national, and global, and temporally between past and present. The Kerrigan's "castle" is *imaged* and *imagined* in such a postcolonial Australian cinema as a site that is contingent and relational. Doreen Massey has argued that only a relativist, extroverted "global sense of place" can adequately describe these social and spatial trans-locations of modernity.[18] However, I think it important here to examine some of the ethical limits that a sense of place might meet, and how the particular strategies adopted by the characters in this film might explain some of them. How far can this global sense of place stretch? Is it possible that such a sense of place might ensure survival for some and annihilation for others?

In answering these questions I would raise as critically important some of the slippages between global and local senses of place that occur in *The Castle*. The solution to the disjuncture between the representations of dispossession in the film and the phenomenon itself lies in maintaining a sense of the unequal measures of belonging that operate for all citizens in a globalizing world. Both the suburban home and the filmic representations of it are sites of cultural production of belonging-ness, but it is crucial to understand how these are themselves formed. As Peter Stallybrass and Allon White explain, any home is a place of belonging and not-belonging, and equally suburbia, as the homeland of ordinariness, rests on an identity, already and "always a boundary phenomenon [whose] order is always constructed around the figures on its territorial edge."[19]

This edginess of spatial identity characterizes discourses of displacement and dislocation. Suvendrini Perera has described the ways in which stories of migration and loss of home constitute their objects. Through such stories, the longed-for "lost" origin of the exile is actually performed and given shape: "For many of us, "homeland" is also a *product* of migration: it is recreated and reclaimed in loss; its cultures and people are not invariably lost and dead, but live in difference."[20] Thus the family's discovery of their community is only possible because of the tragic structure of feeling that the narrative contains and describes as it works to its conclusion. When suddenly this structure shifts in the last stages of the film, and the family triumphs over the threat from outside, the home and community is finalized. This finalization takes place literally in the film when in the final sequence the seemingly interminable extensions and patio are finally finished and the family reunited. The family is only able to be "at home" when their "castle" is reclaimed successfully from a threatening situation.

Ideally, such an imaginary "home" might operate as a meeting place from which to question the rhetorics of globalization, while avoiding either a retreat to a reactionary and closed sense of self and place, or an all-out embracing of the heady potentialities of global capitalism. As suggested by Arjun Appadurai, cultural forms such as cinema and television offer an "elsewhere" to the real. In this mediascape the notion of the local as "dead space" in globalization can be contested and critically reconstituted in practice.[21] This elsewhere is always perhaps an extraordinary/ordinary place, and the intertwining of the cultural forms of cinema and the built environment can be seen as "goods to think with." An example of this production of meaning through materiality and spatiality, the suburban house in *The Castle* poses an alternative to the development hypermarket which has arisen in most Australian cities and boomtowns since the 1980s.

As Australia's economy proceeds from a resource-based to a service-based one, the mobility of people and goods has created pressure on an outdated and badly managed tourism and transport infrastructure, as evidenced in contestations over sites at the local/global interface: the debate over the location of Sydney's airport, on which this film is clearly based, is just one symptom of the problem, but one with its own specific dynamics. In debates about the location of the airport and its meaning for people living near it, the character of Darryl Kerrigan has been used to explain the situation of residents such as Anthony Fias-Ayon, a Filipino immigrant who lives within a kilometer of Sydney airport. The mention of the fictional character of Darryl Kerrigan in a "hard" news story on the front page of a national newspaper discussing the effect of airport noise issues in an upcoming federal election demonstrates how real a figure he has become:

> The deafening drone of jets is unbearable and they sometimes dip so low you can read the writing on their underbellies as they fly over Anthony Fias-Ayon's backyard . . . . Just like his celluloid counterpart, Darryl Kerrigan . . . Mr Fias-Ayon has turned down government offers of nearly $200,000 to buy his home . . . . He says he was proud to be paying off his home and embracing the great Australian dream after emigrating from the Philippines 11 years ago.[22]

The only way to "see" this place, so close to the airport that it is zoned unfit for housing, is to use a photographic technique adopted from film: montage. A staff photographer from the newspaper made a series of photographs over three hours that recorded sixty-four planes passing over the house. A digital imaging artist then overlaid each exposure so that there

Figure 14.2 "On a clear day he can see planes forever," *The Australian,* June 27, 1998, front page (*Photographer Brett Faulkner. Digital manipulation by Peter Muhlbock. Copyright News Limited*)

appears to be a continuous stream of planes above the house. It seems increasingly difficult to distinguish between Barthes's "reality effect" of local mediascapes (such as the digitally altered photograph of Sydenham) and the "fiction effect" of the cityscape, such that each seems explicable only in relation to the other in the intertwined televisual and located world of narratives such as *The Castle.*

One of the co-writers, Santo Cilauro, has used the metaphor of the film as a home-cooked meal to describe how the filmmakers wanted to leave the audience – you went to someone's house and left saying to yourself, "Geez, I feel good, really good, the chicken was good, I had some good dessert. I hope they come out satisfied as if they've had a really good meal."[23] The sweetness of the ending remains somewhat at odds with the stabilized urban dysfunction still in place at the end of the film.

The appeal of the ending of *The Castle* lies in its sublimation of the local into the national: the democratic right to representation in the legal system and justice is upheld when the High Court overturns the acquisition order. Although complex questions of identity and place cannot be resolved so neatly into a nationalist politics, in achieving this satisfying closure the "place" of the suburban home as a homogeneous and unified entity against the "space" of the global has been ever so slightly destabilized. The film's "coalition" between suburban homeowners and indigenous peoples is practically impossible given the concerns outlined above, but in the film it does imaginatively facilitate a *magical* perceiving and fixing of a "tear" in the fabric of the urban. Certainly as processes of globalization fragment the local, the tenuous claims to territory that a colonialist Australia still maintains in the 1990s are exposed. This shifting of the very ground upon which the suburb is constructed creates the potential space for a new politics of home which the film articulates.

By the end of the film, because the dislocation or rupture of the identity of the family as "homeowners" has been temporarily resolved, the liminal moment is over and the ethical analogy of globalization versus suburbanity and colonization versus aboriginality remains hanging in the balance. The film stops short of an ending that would see the Kerrigans welcome a native title claim on their backyard or their holiday house next to a hydroelectric dam. This kind of narrative would be a step slightly too far, unthinkable given the intense disputes over aboriginal reconciliation and self-determination that have taken place in post-Mabo Australia. Ultimately, a sharp lack of equivalence exists between enforced removal of aboriginal peoples from their land since 1788 and the kinds of displacements "ordinary" Australians have felt in the expansion of global economic space into the urban environment. Perhaps once this story has been told, a very small but productive fracture remains in the imaginary of the suburban home as self-contained and grounded on a natural right to land that white Australians enjoy. Still a place most intrinsic to Australian "ordinariness," it now might exist as a visible site of the production of that ordinariness.

The moment of physical displacement and relocation in the film is a twofold process: first, national identity and belonging is rethought; secondly, local struggles over space reflect and rethink the relationship between locality and globalization. In this, *The Castle* diverts the relationship between ordinariness and extraordinariness from an essentializing of the place of both, and transforms homemaking into an event with unpredictable consequences. Such a notion of place should not be embraced without making clear its limits and potentialities. The film's longing for narrative coherence is an attempt to understand rather than overcome the radical heterogeneity of a global sense of place. The challenge here is that this narrative of identity *in* difference should never be reduced to an easily digestible "otherness." The undermining of a national project of "serious" cinematic grandeur in favor of the risks of humor, rather than the solution of a final pronouncement on "ownership," is a story that might be more long-lasting than the safe return of the family to their home.

Perhaps the renegotiated happy home still standing alongside the airport might serve as an after-image with which to grasp some ethical questions posed to communities in the global world: how can we relate the here and now to the there and future?

Notes

I would like to acknowledge the School of Cultural Histories and Futures, University of West Sydney Nepean, for a conference grant to attend the *Cinema and the City* conference, and to give especial thanks to Ien Ang for her generous and practical support of postgraduate research in the School. Zoe Sofoulis suggested the subject of the paper in the first place, and has provided useful comments on various drafts.

1 "*The Castle* Press Kit," Melbourne: Working Dog/Village Roadshow, 1997.
2 Claudia Eller, "Indie *Castle* Prospers on Shanty Budget," *Los Angeles Times*, 20 January 1998, p. 3.
3 Joanne Gray, "Homely comedy pitted against US big guns," *Australian Financial Review*, 24 April 1999, p. 4; David Hay, "This guy's home is his castle," *Sydney Morning Herald*, 22 March 1999, p. 3.
4 "*The Castle* Press Kit."
5 Martha Rosler, "In the Place of the Public: Observations of a Frequent Flyer," *Assemblage* 25 (1995): 68. The visual and narrative possibilities of the airport as a filmic chronotope remain underexplored in film since Chris Marker's *La Jetée* (France 1963), with the exception of *Tombe du Ciel* (*Lost in Transit*), directed by Philippe Loiret (France 1992).
6 Roland Barthes, "The Reality Effect," in Tzvetan Todorov (ed.), *French Literary Theory Today*, trans. R. Carter (Cambridge and New York: Cambridge University Press, 1982), pp. 11–17.
7 Susan Dermody and Liz Jacka, *The Screening of Australia: Volume 1: Anatomy of a Film Industry* (Sydney: Currency Press, 1987) and *The Screening of Australia: Volume 2: Anatomy of a National Cinema* (Sydney: Currency Press, 1988); Liz Jacka, "Film," in Stuart Cunningham and Graeme Turner, *The Media in Australia: Industries, Texts, Audiences*, Allen & Unwin, Sydney, 1993, pp. 180–91.
8 Like *The Castle*, *Muriel's Wedding* and *Strictly Ballroom* were also internationally distributed by Miramax.
9 According to the Macquarie dictionary, a "dag" is "a person who, while neat in appearance and conservative in manners, lacks style and panache." See *Macquarie Dictionary* (Sydney: Macquarie University, 1987), p. 460.
10 "*The Castle* Press Kit."
11 Robin Boyd, *The Australian Ugliness* (Penguin: Sydney, 1960).
12 Ibid., p. 24.
13 "*The Castle* Press Kit."
14 Ibid.
15 Ibid.
16 Ibid.
17 Meaghan Morris, "Tooth and Claw: Tales of Survival, and *Crocodile Dundee*," *Art*

and Text 25 (1988): 52.

18 Doreen Massey, "A Global Sense of Place," *Marxism Today*, June 1991, pp. 24–
    9; Doreen Massey, "A Place Called Home?," *New Formations* 17 (Summer 1992):
    3–15.

19 Peter Stallybrass and Allon White, *The Politics and Poetics of Transgression*, (Ithaca:
    Cornell University Press, 1986), p. 200.

20 Suvendrini Perera, "Falling Out of Place," *Meridian* (1997): 70.

21 Arjun Appadurai, "Disjuncture and Difference in the Global Cultural Economy,"
    Public Culture 2, no. 2 (Spring 1990): 1–24.

22 Stefanie Balogh, *The Australian*, 27–8 June 1998, p. 1.

23 "*The Castle* Press Kit."

15

Representing the Apartheid City: South African Cinema in the 1950s and Jamie Uys's *The Urgent Queue*

Gary Baines

There is a fairly extensive historiography of the apartheid city in South Africa which shows it to have been highly regulated and spatially segregated.[1] However, nothing much has been written about how the apartheid city has been imagined in film.[2] Yet the imagined landscape of the South African city is, at least partly, a cinematic one, for certain films (from *Jim Comes to Jo'burg* (1949) to *Mapantsula* (1988)) have created indelible images of the apartheid city and warrant further examination.

By way of a start to this project, this chapter examines a relatively unknown docudrama, *The Urgent Queue* – made in 1958 by South Africa's most commercially successful filmmaker Jamie Uys – in order to ask whether or not it was apartheid propaganda.[3] Uys is perhaps best known as the director of *The Gods Must Be Crazy* (1980) – one of South Africa's biggest critical and box-office successes at home and abroad – which recounted the adventures of a Coca-Cola bottle which drops out of the sky into the path of an unsuspecting Kalahari bushman, and which occasioned considerable debate over whether it should be viewed as a political statement or pure entertainment.[4]

The Urgent Queue is best approached by relating it to prevailing discourse in the 1950s about the place of Africans in the city. A sequence of feature films which treated the theme of African urban life appeared in the late 1940s and early 1950s. This sequence commenced with *Jim Comes to Jo'burg* (Eric Rutherford, 1949) which, although the film's producers claimed it was a realistic "true reflection of the African Native in a Modern City," was actually a celebration of Johannesburg, the "Golden City" (*Egoli*).[5] This and a string of other films – which included *Zonk* (Hyman Kirstein, 1950), *The Magic Garden* (Donald Swanson, 1951), and *Song of Africa* (Emil Nofal, 1952) – constituted a genre which depicted township life in a highly romanticized fashion and indirectly addressed the issue of how rural Africans sought to come to terms with the urban environment. The storylines of these films are usually thin and most of the action consists of singing and dancing on stage, in night-clubs, or in the streets. The films are essentially musicals which suggest that the townships are cultural melting pots in which residents are spellbound by Hollywood films, Broadway musicals, and African-American jazz record-ings.[6] Black characters in the films seldom encounter whites as officials or employers, and the impression is created that life revolves around leisure rather than labor. Poverty can be overcome by good luck, crime is an aber-ration and not pervasive, and the city is simply a setting for the story. This cycle of films did little to define a historically specific imagery of the apart-heid city.

Much literature and film of the period had a decidedly anti-urban bias. For instance, Alan Paton's novel *Cry the Beloved Country* (1948) was adapted for the screen by Zoltan Korda in 1951, retaining the book's country/city anti-nomy: the country is a pastoral idyll while the city is a metaphor for the decay of modern society. The country is a safe haven while the city harbors criminals, prostitutes, and political "troublemakers." Criminality is ascribed to weakness of character (a country boy who is easily led astray by streetwise gangsters (*tsotsis*)) and to the breakdown of the fabric of traditional African society in urban areas. No blame is put on the sociopolitical system of apart-heid. The fiction is maintained that African migration did not stem from dire economic need but was voluntary and, consequently, that there was no need for Africans to remain in the city.[7] This was in line with apartheid doctrine which maintained that Africans were temporary sojourners in the "white man's cities."[8]

But urban apartheid policy was beset by contradictions. The policies of urban segregation/apartheid were informed by the *Report of the Transvaal Local Government Commission* of 1921, which posited that "The native should only be allowed to enter the urban areas, which are essentially the white man's creation, when he is willing to enter and to minister to the needs of the white man, and should depart therefrom when he ceases so to minister."[9] This line of thinking became known as "Stallardism" after the chairman of the Commission. Although it achieved the status of a hegemonic discourse in white political circles between the 1920s and the 1950s, "Stallardism" was not fully implemented in practice. Urban segregation/apartheid effectively admitted the permanence of Africans in the cities because they provided essential labor for industry and white households. The Nationalist Govern-ment even embarked on projects during the 1950s which provided large numbers of dwellings in segregated townships on the peripheries of South

African cities. This reflected the contradiction between the inclusionary and exclusionary imperatives of urban apartheid: to have labor without the presence of the laborers. In fact, the real distinction was between "tribal" and "detribalized Natives," or "outsiders" (migrants) and "insiders" (permanent residents) in these cities.

The first feature film to challenge the official definition of Africans as migrants who were out of place in the city was Lionel Rogosin's clandestinely made *Come Back Africa* (1959). In this film, the main character migrates to the city out of economic necessity and is later joined by his wife and children. The township in the film does not operate simply as a backdrop to provide the audience with entertainment. Instead, it is a place to which people return after a day's work and drown their sorrows in the *shebeens* (or taverns). In short, it is "home." Rogosin's use of non-actors in natural settings, especially the *Drum* magazine journalists in the *shebeen* scene in the Johannesburg township of Sophiatown, shows his concern to be "true to life." The influence of the neorealist tradition of Italian filmmaking is evident in Rogosin's attempt to deal with social and political issues affecting everyday life. As a narrative feature film attempting realism, *Come Back Africa* blurs the distinction between fiction and non-fiction.[10] *The Urgent Queue* also does this in its own way – but that is not the film's only ambiguity.

Made in black and white on 16mm film, *The Urgent Queue* runs for twenty-eight minutes and was commissioned by the South African Government's Information Service as a government-sponsored project which, according to Peter Davis, would extol the virtues of the state's low-cost housing schemes for Africans who had migrated to the city in search of employment.[11] Initially released as *The Condemned are Happy*, the film was subsequently retitled *The Urgent Queue*, probably because of the negative implications of the original title which referred to scenes of residents in an unnamed slum falling over one another in order to have their houses "condemned" so that they might qualify for a plot in a new housing scheme. As such, the film represented a departure from conventional depictions of African life in the city. Like *Come Back Africa* – albeit somewhat differently – it subverted prevailing apartheid discourse that the countryside was "the natural environment of the native."

The setting of the film, Port Elizabeth, is actually mentioned by name and, as such, is a specific place rather than a generic apartheid city. This in itself is important, for Port Elizabeth was a city with a distinctive "discursive" presence in 1950s South Africa – a presence shaped by official statements, newspaper reports, traveler's accounts, tourist brochures, photographs, art, song, and even anecdotes.[12] Despite certain repressive political measures taken in the wake of riots in the city in 1952, the hegemonic narrative of Port Elizabeth was that it was a "progressive" city and that it enjoyed a deservedly "liberal" reputation on account of the City Council's reluctance to enforce urban apartheid legislation such as the Group Areas Act.[13] Uys's *The Urgent Queue* was influenced by this discourse of a "progressive Port Elizabeth."

The plot of *The Urgent Queue* is very simple and straightforward. It depicts the struggle of a stereotypical "tribal" man and his extended family to find a new home in the "white man's city." Using a first-person voice-over narration, it tells the story of the family leaving Port Elizabeth's drought-stricken hinterland and trekking to the city in search of work. Manual labor in a factory proves easy enough to find but a suitable place of abode more difficult. The family has to make do with a wooden shack in a slum, exploited by a greedy African landlord. Their cheek-by-jowl existence with people of different ethnic groups brings them into contact with the "evils" of the city. The eldest child turns to a life of petty crime and is arbitrarily jailed. Further distress follows the outbreak of the "sickness" (bubonic plague) which kills one of the protagonist's wives as well as his youngest son. Fortunately, a savior appears in the person of the city's mayor who offers to rehouse the slum residents in a new township on the city's edge. The elderly head of the family is eager to have his dwelling condemned by the municipal health authorities in order to qualify for a plot of ground in the new township, and eventually obtains a cement-block house with basic facilities and services. Here he and his (by now nuclear) family may live happily ever after, providing labor in the "white man's city."

In this way, *The Urgent Queue* displays some of the qualities of what Bill Nichols has described as "expository" documentary, and has definite didactic functions.[14] The film depicts urbanization as part of a natural and necessary developmental process for rural Africans. Uys represents the city as a site in which the rites of passage from "tribalism" to modernity are negotiated. The film depicts how modernity is mediated as the protagonist – finding work, finding a place to live, gaining an education – is forced to come to terms with the urban environment and make the city his new home. This he does, though slowly – shown up by the relative ease with which his children adapt. His children will have a better future by being educated to do "clever work," while he is unable to read and write. He must break symbolic ties of community and tradition and aspire to emulate the new ideal of the Western nuclear family. The city is a state of mind, both the location and embodiment of modernity.[15]

In spite of being government-funded, it would appear that Uys had complete creative control over *The Urgent Queue*. The film's credits show him to have been responsible not only for production and direction, but also for the script, screenplay, and editing. Uys was a well-enough established filmmaker to have his own production company by the late 1950s. He already had the making of an *auteur*.[16] His stylistic "signature" is apparent in certain comic touches in the visuals. Yet there is evidence that his project in *The Urgent Queue* coincided with that of former Port Elizabeth mayor Adolph Schauder, who appears in the film as himself. Schauder, who earned himself the hon-

orific title of *Sonceba* ("man of mercy") in recognition of his achievements in
getting Port Elizabeth's housing projects off the ground, regarded himself as
the city's PRO *extraordinaire*.[17] The film portrays Schauder as the visionary
driving force behind the City Council's efforts at rehousing African laborers
in better living conditions. As such, Uys and Schauder's Port Elizabeth in
The Urgent Queue did not altogether conform to the government's model apartheid city. But to leave the discussion here is to miss the key tension in the
film between realism and manipulation which constitutes the film as
"docudrama."

There is much in *The Urgent Queue* that is "realistic." The film tells a story
based in fact, using non-actors (in addition to actors) to enhance its realism.
It incorporates much actuality footage with its staged events and deploys
much local detail of language, music, and custom. Its story is told in the
broken English of a Xhosa-speaking African, while the soundtrack includes
the *kwela* (pennywhistle jive) music popularized in the 1950s by the film *The
Magic Garden* and artists such as Spokes Mashiyane.

Moreover, the film was shot entirely on location in and around Port
Elizabeth – in the slum of Korsten, which had been dubbed the "worst slum
in the world" in the 1930s by the Minister of Health in the United Party
Government.[18] The narrator of *The Urgent Queue* describes the residents as
"living together like ants in a heap." This is vividly shown in footage of
shacks erected without thought to building restrictions or the constraints of
space, in which poor living conditions were accompanied by high infant
mortality rates, alcohol abuse, criminal activity, and prostitution.[19]

In all of this, to use Bill Nichols's words, *The Urgent Queue* "provides an
impression of authenticity based on the reality of representation more than the
representation of reality."[20] Its realism is not the realism of fiction which,
according to Nichols, "serves to make a plausible world seem real." It is,
instead, as Nichols holds of all documentary, a realism which "serves to
make an argument about the historical world persuasive."[21]

So when Uys employs the conventions of realism it is to construct an
imaginary world that is credible but not primarily historically accurate. *The
Urgent Queue* is not a reliable historical account. Two events in particular are
mentioned by the narrator which allow the viewer to situate the story within
a rough time frame. The most obvious historical reference is to World War
Two, which is blamed for causing shortages of building materials and, as a
result, exacerbating Port Elizabeth's housing backlog. The other reference is
to "the sickness," a euphemism for the bubonic plague which conveniently
reduces the protagonist's extended family to a nuclear one. The story incor-
rectly situates the outbreak of the disease after World War Two rather than
before it. Thus Uys *re*-creates the historical context in such a way as to make
it dovetail with the plot of the film. History is rewritten for the convenience
of the film's storyline. The primary aim of this rewriting of history is to justify

the efforts of the Port Elizabeth authorities to clear slums such as Korsten and remove their populations to new housing projects.

For if Korsten was "the worst slum in the world," one of its greatest evils – disease – is foregrounded in the film as contagious. Korsten is suggested as a breeding ground of disease which threatens to infect other (particularly white) areas or suburbs of the city. The bubonic plague actually exacted a heavy death toll in Port Elizabeth's black townships in 1937 and the fear of the spread of disease, captured in the discourse of the "sanitation syndrome," was frequently invoked by the authorities to justify the eradication of slums.[22] As such, *The Urgent Queue* depicts slum clearance as an altruistic act on the part of the authorities. Uys claimed in an interview that "there was a genuine effort there to alleviate the [slum] conditions by creating living areas for [blacks], and even helping them to build their own houses and so on. I believed implicitly in what I was saying at the time."[23] Notwithstanding Uys's idealism, the film reinforced the myth of slums in the public imagination and prepared it to accept the necessity of their removal on account of the health threat posed to other residents of Port Elizabeth, especially the white population.

Uys's film underscores Port Elizabeth's reputation as a "progressive" city concerned to provide houses for its African population. In one sequence of *The Urgent Queue*, Schauder approaches a foreman at the Ford Motor Company assembly plant – where the film's protagonist is employed – to requisition the large wooden crates in which knockdown car assembly kits are imported into the country. This sequence amounts to a reenactment of a historical event: Schauder did, indeed, approach Ford for permission to use packing cases for the construction of wooden shacks in the aptly named Kwaford, which was an extension of Port Elizabeth's New Brighton township.[24] These makeshift dwellings eased the acute housing crisis in the city in the 1950s and were probably being erected even as *The Urgent Queue* was being shot. Indeed, in one scene in the film, the slogan "There's a Ford in your future" is actually visible on one of the slum houses made of crates. This suggests that the source of Schauder's idea to use the packing cases for a housing scheme in the first place might have been inspired by the ingenuity of squatters who had been erecting their own shacks from crates disposed of by the Ford factory. In any event, Schauder appropriated the idea as his own and gained publicity for finding inventive solutions to the city's housing problems. Such publicity redounded to the credit of the city fathers and bolstered Port Elizabeth's image as a place concerned for the welfare of its African population.

The Urgent Queue also reinforced Port Elizabeth's reputation as a "progressive" city through acts of omission rather than commission. Unlike *Come Back Africa*, where workers are asked to produce a pass at every turn, in *The Urgent Queue* passes and curfews are conspicuously absent. Pass laws enforcing the carrying of identity documents by African workseekers entering urban areas had been applied widely by the local authorities throughout the country by the late 1950s. But because the legislation was enabling, the pass laws had to be enacted in accordance with Section 10 of the Urban Areas Act by the local authority, and Port Elizabeth did not implement them until 1953, when the city came under pressure from central government.[25] The story line of *The Urgent Queue* shows the protagonist entering the city prior to World War Two. He obtains employment in the Ford motor-vehicle assembly plant without any form of identification being required. This is historically inaccurate: even if employers had not insisted on identification, officials would have done so. As Jennifer Robinson has shown, the residents of Port Elizabeth's townships were subjected to surveillance and control exercised by township managers through what she has termed the "location strategy."[26] In any event, by the time the film was made pass laws were enforced in the city. Not only did Uys ignore a very real form of repression but also the reality of post-liberal Port Elizabeth.

Is *The Urgent Queue* a piece of South African propaganda extolling the benevolence of apartheid in general and the government's housing policies in particular? The film historian Keyan Tomaselli has shown that Uys never considered himself a propagandist.[27] In fact, he rather disingenuously claimed that his films never sought to convey a message. Like D. W. Griffith, who created the epic *Birth of a Nation* (1915), Uys held that he was unaware of the racist sentiments of his films, although when he distanced himself from the Department of Information because it tried to set the agenda for films which it commissioned in the 1970s, he implicitly acknowledged the power of film to propagate ideas – whether subliminally or not.[28] Uys may have had a rather naive grasp of the function of ideology in cinema and society at large but his films were not apolitical on account of it.

Finally, then, we must ask whether, if the film *is* propagandistic, this necessarily implies that Uys was an apologist for apartheid? It has been contended that propaganda films tell the viewer as much about the filmmaker's as the subject's culture and ideology.[29] If so, what do we learn from an analysis of the text of *The Urgent Queue*? There is undoubtedly a crude and unsophisticated ethnographic representation of the values and the mindset of the "tribal" African in the film. The discourse of racism shapes this cultural stereotyping of "the other," and the voice of the African protagonist is clearly circumscribed by the patronizing tone of the scriptwriter. Yet the urbanizing African is shown to be adept in adapting to new and changing circumstances. Uys does not portray blacks as temporary sojourners in the cities whose natural home is in the rural areas or so-called "homelands." The main character in *The Urgent Queue* not only sets up home in the city but appears to break all ties with his previous rural existence. The (extended) family moves lock, stock, and barrel to Port Elizabeth, even with the elderly father in tow. Apartheid ideologues would have insisted that the male breadwinner be an unaccompanied migrant laborer rather than a family man who sets up home in the "white man's city." Despite the use of this term in the film, *The Urgent Queue* defines the city as a welcoming environment for African workseekers, as a place of opportunities and new beginnings. Uys's own idealism was probably colored by the rhetoric of apartheid and its apparent capacity to address the problems faced by South African cities. But his embrace of apartheid ideology was tempered by the paternalism implicit in the discourse of "progressive Port Elizabeth" and, as a result of this tension, *The Urgent Queue* emerged not only as an ambiguous but as an incoherent text. Effective propaganda solicits a stereotyped response, and any hesitation or ambivalence complicates that response. This ambivalence alone would have rendered the film problematic as a persuasive piece of pro-apartheid propaganda.

Finally, there remains the question of to whom it was intended to exhibit this commissioned film. Geoffrey Mangin (1998) holds that in 1950s South Africa, 16mm black-and-white "non-theatrical" films were earmarked for special target audiences and were never screened on the commercial circuit.[30] It is known that many Information Services-sponsored films were shown as "educational" films to black audiences, and it seems plausible that *The Urgent Queue* was intended for exhibition, and might have been exhibited, in this context – particularly given its specific mandate to convince audiences (or more specifically, potential residents) of the merits of Port Elizabeth's housing schemes. However, there is no evidence that *The Urgent Queue* was ever shown to local audiences. One source suggests that it was "obviously meant for overseas distribution."[31] The South African government certainly considered film to be a useful means of projecting a benign image of its settlement policies abroad, and the State Information Services had signed a contract with Twentieth Century-Fox in 1957 for the worldwide distribution of its propaganda films.[32] If this was the case, it would account for some of the liberties taken in terms of local and historical accuracy. The use of the incongruous term "hashish" for *dagga* or marijuana by the narrator suggests that the filmmakers did not have local audiences in mind, while the *kwela* (pennywhistle jive) soundtrack, referred to above, would have been instantly recognizable as *South African* music by overseas audiences. These "modifications" would have enhanced the film's appeal outside South Africa. It is, then, possible that the film's failure to promote the government's policies unequivocally in itself explains its seeming "disappearance" from view and continuing obscurity today.

Notes

I would like to acknowledge the financial assistance of the Rhodes University Joint Research Committee in funding this research and the trip to Dublin to give a paper at the *Cinema and the City* conference, March 10–12 1999, on which this chapter is based. Thanks, too, to Jenny Robinson and an anonymous referee for comments on an earlier draft.

1   For a useful survey of this literature, see Paul Maylam, "Explaining the Apartheid City: 20 Years of South African Urban Historiography," *Journal of Southern African Studies* 21, no. 1 (1995): 19–39.

2   Whilst Peter Davis makes a few passing comments on the representation of the city in South African cinema in his book *In Darkest Hollywood*, he provides no systematic analysis thereof. Peter Davis, *In Darkest Hollywood: Exploring the Jungles of Cinema's South Africa* (Johannesburg: Ravan Press, 1996).

3   Davis, *In Darkest Hollywood*, p. 61, calls the Uys of the 1950s a "fervent acolyte of apartheid."

4   Keyan Tomaselli, *The Cinema of Apartheid: Race and Class in South African Film* (London: Routledge, 1988), p. 10.

5   Text which follows title credits of *Jim Comes to Jo'burg* (aka *African Jim*) (1949). Cited in Davis, *In Darkest Hollywood*, p. 27.

6   Rob Nixon, *Homelands, Harlem and Hollywood: South African Culture and the World Beyond* (New York: Routledge, 1994).

7   Davis, *In Darkest Hollywood*, p. 37.

8   Rodney Davenport, "African Townsmen? South African Natives (Urban Areas) Legislation through the Years," *African Affairs* 68 (1969).

9   Cited in ibid., p. 95.

10 Davis, *In Darkest Hollywood*, p. 47. On reality and imagination in film, see James Donald, *Imagining the Modern City* (London: Athlone Press, 1999). p. xii.

11 Davis, *In Darkest Hollywood*, p. 61. On the commissioning of the film, see Cape Provincial Library Service, Accession Record 6180qR for *The Condemned are Happy*.

12 My thinking on the city as discourse and yet also as a physical place here is informed by Colin McArthur, "Chinese Boxes and Russian Dolls: Tracking the Elusive Cinematic City," and Rob Lapsley, "Mainly in Cities and at Night: Some Notes on Cities and Film," in David Clarke (ed.), *The Cinematic City* (London: Routledge, 1997), pp. pp. 19–45 and 186–208, respectively; and Neil Campbell and Alasdair Kean, "The American City: The Old Knot of Contrarierty," in *American Cultural Studies: An Introduction to American Culture* (London: Routledge, 1997), p. 163.

13 Gary Baines, "Community resistance and collective violence: the Port Elizabeth Defiance Campaign and the 1952 New Brighton Riots," *The South African Historical Journal* 34 (1996): 39–76.

14 For an analysis of the expository mode of representation in documentaries, see Bill Nichols, *Representing Reality: Issues and Concepts in Documentary* (Bloomington: Indiana University Press, 1991) pp. 34–8.

15 Donald, *Imagining the Modern City*, p. 10.

16 See Keyan Tomaselli, "The Cinema of Jamie Uys," in Johan Blignault and Martin Botha (eds.), *Movies – Moguls – Mavericks: South African Cinema, 1979–1991* (Bellville: Anthropos Publishers, 1986).

17 Gary Baines, "New Brighton, Port Elizabeth, *c.*1903–1953: A History of an Urban African Community," Ph.D. thesis, University of Cape Town, 1994, p. 255.

18 Janet Cherry, "Blot on the Landscape and Center of Resistance: A Social and

Economic History of Korsten," BA Hons. Essay, University of Cape Town, 1988, p. 10.

19 Ibid., *passim.*

20 Nichols, *Representing Reality*, p. 185.

21 Ibid., p. 165.

22 Maynard Swanson, "The Sanitation Syndrome: Bubonic Plague and Urban Native Policy in the Cape Colony, 1900–1909," *Journal of African History* 16, no. 3 (1977): 387–410.

23 Cited in Davis, *In Darkest Hollywood*, p. 61.

24 See Baines, "New Brighton," pp. 39–76.

25 Jennifer Robinson, *The Power of Apartheid: State, Power and Space in South African Cities* (Oxford: Butterworth-Heinemann, 1996), p. 186.

26 Ibid.

27 Tomaselli, "The Cinema of Jamie Uys," p. 203.

28 On Uys and the Department of Information, see Davis, *In Darkest Hollywood*, p. 67.

29 Keyan Tomaselli, *Myth, Race and Power: South Africans Imaged on Film and TV* (Bellville: Anthropos Publishers, 1986), p. 35.

30 See Geoffrey Mangin, *Filming Emerging Africa* (Rondebosch: The Wordsmith, 1988).

31 Cape Provincial Library Service Record, Accession 6180qR.

32 Davis, *In Darkest Hollywood*, p. 152.

16

The Visual Rhetoric of the Ambivalent City in Nigerian Video Films

Obododimma Oha

Introduction

This chapter examines the ambivalent representations of the city of Lagos in a selection of Nigerian video films as rhetorical means of undermining the interpretation of the city as a civilizing center in postcolonial Nigeria, and of drawing attention to the "signs" (symptoms) of the "sickness" of the postcolonial city – in fact, to the sickness that *is* the postcolonial city. In a sense, video films are products of the city and generate a rhetoric which, following Roland Barthes's notion of the "rhetoric of the image," can be seen in the Althusserian sense as a process of "interpellating" the reading/viewing subject.[1] Cities (re-) construct themselves to be *seen*, in contrast to the imagined obscurity of rural/"non-civilized" environments. In Nigeria, Lagos has played a prominent role in the production of video films as visual/izing products, and thus, in a very interesting way, has generated discourses about itself and about rural space as "Other."

There are, of course, many films set in Lagos, but those selected for analysis here – namely, *Lagos Na Wah!!* (Parts I, II, and III), *Lagos Alaye Boys* (Parts I and II), *Living in Bondage* (Parts I and II), *Onome* (Parts I and II), and *Scores to Settle* – appear particularly committed to a critique of the city.[2] They deal with issues which are crucial to the engineering of life in the city: poverty, homelessness, lack of accommodation and amenities, disease, inadequate welfare and health provision, poor family planning, single parenthood, domestic violence, and the collapse of the concept of "family." These present Lagos as a place wrestling with contradictions, as a place which invites and as a place from which to run away.

As such, although they may be viewed as exploitation entertainment, these films – as part of a larger video culture in Nigeria – do articulate the fears, hopes, and dreams of city dwellers in Nigeria and are even held by their audience to be of educative value. Aimed primarily at the urban youth market, these films are made for profit by small-scale video production companies and individuals and currently comprise an essential part of modern Nigerian popular culture which dwarfs any 35mm *film* culture as such. The films are made in English, pidgin (the language of the cities), or indigenous Nigerian languages, and are produced in color on VHS on very low budgets. The films are distributed through a widespread and thriving network of video rental shops and communal viewing centers in Nigerian cities. While the video industry even has its own star system, most of its actors (and indeed its filmmakers) are not professionals and do not work in the business full-time. The films are exported successfully to neighboring West African countries such as Cameroon, Benin, Togo, and Ghana and have received some attention of late at West African film festivals. The latest films are eagerly awaited by the public, and are often reviewed in Nigerian magazines and newspapers, as well as being heavily advertised in posters around Lagos and other cities and on Lagos's twenty-four-hour television station, African Independent Television (AIT).

The *Milieu*

In all of these films, Lagos is significant in many ways. The capital of Lagos State (and until recently the capital of Nigeria as a whole), it presents itself as a center to which many Nigerians are drawn in their political, social, and economic aspirations. Though no longer the capital of Nigeria by policy, it remains the center of commerce and industry and occupies a pivotal position nationally as a modernizing force. Like many other cities in the postcolonial world, it is tremendously overpopulated, and appears to confirm the claim made by David Hecht and Abdou Maliqalim Simone, in their book *Invisible Governance*, that

> The African city cannot absorb and maintain its expanding rural population. Still they continue to come, permanently unsettling any ready solution. Governments may declare that they are in control of the situation but they cannot even assess population numbers or precisely describe the modes of living. There are neighborhoods that governments do not even know exist.[3]

Lagos, in fact, is one of the cities that give validity to Jose Ortega y Gasset's notion of "the crowd phenomenon" – cities which are perpetually "Full."[4]

The city has more than its fair share of crime, especially armed banditry, street gangs (referred to as "Alaye"), and what is known as "advance fee fraud" (referred to as "419" in Nigeria).[5]

To control crime and violence in the city, the former military administrator of Lagos State, Colonel Muhammed Marwa, created an anti-crime squad called "Operation Sweep" (now renamed "Rapid Response Squad").[6] In spite of its many successes, the squad itself fell prey to corruption, and was not only directly accused of criminal activity by the public and the media in Lagos, but was on occasion even physically confronted by the people.

One of the problems that Operation Sweep set out to control was the violent and criminal "Alaye" culture in which street gangs (or "Alaye Boys") appeared to be ruling the streets (and indeed the whole state at a micro-level). The Alaye Boys not only robbed individuals of their possessions, but made themselves available for hire as hit squads throughout the city. Jinmi Adisa observes that "Those who did not have patrons tried to find their own feet on the street, harassing traders and passersby for "protection" money. Whatever the case, "area boys" as they were now popularly known, had become veritable apostles of street violence."[7] Marwa applied a multidimensional approach in combating this culture of violence in Lagos: he used a dual strategy of counter-violence (Operation Sweep), on the one hand, which is expected of a military ruler; and of ethical reformation, involving the rehabilitation, or transformation, of the Alaye Boys into what became known as "Flower Boys." Instead of being committed to violence and crime, these "Flower Boys" are taught by the government to do such things as plant flowers for the good of the city, learn trades, and benefit from soft loans from the government to set themselves up in their new lives. Although the policy was not entirely successful in Lagos, much of the street violence subsided, only to intensify later with the return to democratic rule.

Such social conditions of crime, violence, and overcrowding as those described above provide useful material for the culture industry – especially the video film industry, which is in search of "sellable" stories. These "raw materials" from social experience undergo processes of ideological reproduction and transformation, as suggested by Stuart Hall et al. in their study of crime and the state, *Policing the Crisis*: "Not every statement by a relevant primary definer in respect of a particular topic is likely to be reproduced in the media; nor is every part of each statement. By exercising selectivity the media begin to impose their own criteria on the structured "raw materials" – and thus actively appropriate and transform them."[8]

Hall et al., working from a Marxist perspective which proposes that mental production is controlled by the ruling class, draw our attention to the existence of "professional, technical and commercial constraints" on the production and reproduction of ideology. They particularly call attention to how coding (or "mode of address") is used by the media to express ideological positions and to target audiences.[9] In this, their position recalls the argument by V. N. Volosinov, in *Marxism and the Philosophy of Language*, that "The domain of ideology coincides with the domain of signs. They equate with one another. Wherever a sign is present, ideology is present too."[10]

In sum, therefore, we may understand many Nigerian video films as creative "translations" of Lagos City life, agreeing with Hall et al. that

> Such translations depend on the story's potential-for-translation (its newsworthiness) and on its anchorage in familiar and long-standing topics of concern – hooliganism, crowd violence, "aggro" gang behavior. This process is neither totally free and unconstrained, nor is it a simple, direct reproduction. It is a transformation; and such transformations require active "work" on the part of the media.[11]

Between the "Jungle" and the Jingle of Excellence

Number plates of vehicles registered in Lagos carry the inscription "Center of Excellence," and this jingle indeed is an expression of the imagined paradise of Lagos for which many leave their villages and other (Nigerian) cities to search for salvation. This is the case with the layabout Solomon, protagonist of *Lagos Na Wah!!*, who leaves his village for Lagos, about which he has heard so much, especially on the radio and television. Solomon follows the media "jingle" about Lagos, but what he finds there is a crowded, chaotic, and violent "jungle." In this jungle, he soon learns, there is only heartlessness, craftiness, and smartness.[12] In fact, as he is told by the character Klarus, and as we find written on the bus which takes him to the city center, there is "No Paddy for Jungle" ("No friendship in a jungle"). Semiotizing Lagos as a "jungle" conjures up images of barbarity, which contrast sharply with the city's self-projection as a "paradise."

One aspect of this jungle life that shocks Solomon is the callousness people show toward each other. In Lagos, everybody is potentially a criminal. One is always afraid to trust or help anybody out – particularly strangers. Many city dwellers prefer to mind their own business. Many of the people Solomon approaches to ask for assistance in some way do not actually want to help him but only to take advantage of him in some way: as, for example, in the case of the layabout Solomon asks to look after his luggage at the bus station at Ojota; or the hostile and unhelpful police officers on night duty who make him pay with the little remaining money he has for the protection of a night in the police station. Any idea that the police are the friends of the people is dismissed. Later, even Solomon's companions Giringori and Klarus allow him to stay with them temporarily only because they will be able to take his money to buy breakfast.

Thus in the city nobody is another person's keeper. Several times in *Lagos Na Wah!!* Solomon is cautioned for not minding his own business ("Make you no dey put your mouth for something wey no concern you"). On one occasion he narrowly survives being lynched for intervening to catch a pickpocket when the pickpocket and his gang turn on him, attacking him and calling him a thief. This is a world in which everybody is on their own. Humanism and hospitality are seen as signs of idiocy and the preference, as noted by Hyginus Ekwuazi, is for individualism.[13] Only fools go out of their way to help other people and so the much-fabled "traditional African hospitality" is shown up as a myth in the contemporary postcolonial context.

Lagos Na Wah!! challenges this new condition of rampant individualism by showing that, in spite of the risks involved, hospitality can be a source of salvation for the Lagosian. In Part II of the series, Solomon resists the "new" city culture of indifference by offering his seat to a lady on a bus, despite Klarus's abuse of him as a *mumu* (fool). But this single act of courtesy – which contradicts the motto "No Paddy for Jungle" – turns out to be the key to the door to affluence and the good life for Solomon. Before leaving the bus, the lady gives Solomon her business card, asking him to pay her a visit. When he does, she offers him a well-paid job in her company. By Solomon's doing what appears foolish according to the doctrine of the jungle city, his fortune changes. As the lady tells him, "One good turn deserves another." In turn, this enables Solomon to come to the rescue of Giringori and Klarus, who have been evicted by their heartless landlord for owing rent. Solomon thus "progresses" from the position of "stranger" to that of "brother."

Part I of *Lagos Na Wah!!* draws upon the motif of the stranger – and the stranger-as-victim – in Nigerian culture. In the early stages of the film, Giringori and Klarus pray to God to spare them from the "Area Boys" and their cruel landlord, and to let Solomon be killed as a sacrificial lamb to this end. As interestingly dramatized by Wole Soyinka in *The Strong Breed*, the stranger in Nigeria has always been a victim in the country's frequent political and religious riots – a victimization facilitated, in some Nigerian cities, by the existence of *sabon garis* (strangers' quarters), which make it easier for ethnic strangers in the cities to be identified and victimized during national crises.[14] On the other hand, when Solomon becomes wealthy in Part II, Klarus begins to sing his praises, even referring to him as his "brother" where he had earlier denied even knowing him. But the term "brother" is used in Nigerian English to refer to somebody who is not even a near-relative but who might, for example, be from the same ethnic group. While Solomon's development from "stranger" to "brother" is a marker of his acceptance in the city, even this is qualified by the looseness of the term "brother" and the ease with which its loose social semantics lends itself to a politics of duplicity and discrimination, and operates as an important shibboleth in discourse on relationships in the Nigerian city.

The film, therefore, dramatizes two conflicting ways of dealing with the city: hospitality and kindness to strangers, or individualism and exploitation. These compete for "control" of the Lagos city dweller who, though recognizing the reality that there is "No Paddy for Jungle," nevertheless worries that resignation to that motto might deprive him of opportunities for wealth and the good life. Because the two "doctrines" contradict each other, the city dweller lives in a state of suspended ambivalence. He is divided between two sets of values which cancel each other out, complicating life, precluding any real sense of community, and leading to confusion and indirection.

Given this confusion and lack of "community," a culture of the survival of the fittest reigns, which is of course typical of the jungle. In *Lagos Na Wah!!*, Klarus, who operates in the film as an ideologue, frequently explains animatedly to Solomon: "This na Lagos. Anything you wan do, you must doam well well" (This is Lagos. Anything you want to do, you must do it firmly). And, indeed, Solomon learns to shout at people, feigning courage and aggressiveness in order to find his space in this urban jungle where there is no space for weaklings. Soon after arriving in Lagos, Solomon discovers that one has to struggle and fight to eat, to take a bath, to board a bus, or even to enter or leave one's home. This sense of life as struggle is compounded by the presence and violent activities of street gangs (the "Alaye Boys"), often employed by persons of privilege in society to protect themselves and their interests, to boost their prestige, or to oppress others. In a very disturbing sense, the use of the "Alaye Boys" by landlords and caretakers in *Lagos Na Wah!!* appears to relate to and mirror the reign of terror and dictatorship in Nigeria, especially in the era of Sanni Abacha. Just as the military dictator used his squads to terrorize his citizens, so do the landlords and caretakers use the "Alaye Boys" to terrorize their tenants.

The "Alaye Boys" do, however, roam the streets on their own, either demanding money (not begging it) from individuals or looking for an opportunity to steal their belongings. They also feature as parking-lot touts, most of the time posing as members of the National Union of Road Transport Workers. In a curious way, they indeed do *work on the road*, and especially on travelers, who hardly suspect their dubious motives. As pointed out earlier, the "Alaye" problem creates much insecurity in Lagos, especially for travelers and businesspeople. Video films which feature them can thus be seen as capitalizing on this crime wave, and treating it from a popular but realistic perspective.

In *Lagos Alaye Boys* we find a different but interesting dimension of the "Alaye" problem: the "Alaye Boys" not only operate in the streets, but in homes and business areas, this time making individuals steal or sell their possessions to *buy* their freedom from them. The consequence of not being able to buy this freedom is that domestic life becomes disrupted: people abandon their homes and go into hiding, as we find in the case of members of Amuta's family abandoning their home so as to escape from the "Alaye Boys" from whom Emeka (Amuta's son) cannot buy his freedom.

One problem leads to another. After escaping from their unsafe home, members of Amuta's family become destitute and are sexually exploited. As we often find in such cases, the women (Kate and her mother) are the greatest victims: the "Alaye Boys" threaten to rape them unless they produce Emeka, who has gone into hiding, and to escape rape they abandon their unprotected home, only to fall into the traps of men who are looking for women to deceive and exploit sexually. Once deprived of the comfort of home, people are emptied into the streets as destitute, where they fall further into the hands of criminals, as shown in the expulsion of Sade from her home by her son in the film *Scores to Settle*. Sade makes her home at the foot of a bridge, turns to begging, and eventually commits suicide.

The problem of destitution in the city of Lagos is truly disturbing. Not only does one have to deal with survival and the "crowd phenomenon," a destitute is also totally exposed and has nowhere to go, as the character Emeka reveals in *Lagos Alaye Boys*: "Ah, Madam, me I no dey go anywhere. I no know where I dey go. I just dey waka . . . dey waka about like dat . . . " (Ah Madam, I am not going anywhere particularly. I do not know where I am going. I am just walking . . . walking about like that. . . .).

This aimless street culture reflects a total sense of loss – just as one could indeed get lost in a jungle. But, generally, people's taking to the streets in Lagos, as noted by Jinmi Adisa, is occasioned by the sheer fight for survival, and may involve all the members of a family – including young children and their parents together – leading to the emergence of the phenomenon of "families on the street."[15]

Of course, this "disorganization of the family" which pushes more and more people onto the already crowded streets may result from the reverse impact of the street on the family. In *Onome* I and II, Tamuno has an illegitimate son, Tega, by Onome, who has lived on the streets herself. Tega makes the street his home at an early age because Tamuno's wife, Princess, will not accept him into the family home. Street culture is presented as an incurable blight: as Tamuno's rich father-in-law, Dafe Fregene, explains of Onome, each time she is "pulled out of the pit" she later returns. But it is also an issue of class, as noted by Okome: life on the streets is generally associated with poverty, and, to the wealthy, being "pulled out of the pit" means Onome being "saved" from her class.[16]

Therefore, *Onome* I and II, like other films of the type, present the parallel existence of extreme poverty and affluence in Lagos – the two sometimes intruding dramatically into each other's domain and ratifying the description of the city by urban sociologist Jinmi Adisa as a "city of sharp contrasts."[17]

But the display of affluence in the city remains an ever-present source of temptation, both for the poor and the not-too-poor. Many find no other better way to achieve wealth than through crime, sometimes with disastrous consequences. The quest for wealth – as we find in *Living in Bondage* (Parts I and II) – also creates a problem of insecurity: Andy Okeke comes under the influence of a secret cult and is persuaded in return for financial reward to provide his wife, Merit, for "use" in a cult ritual sacrifice. Though he becomes wealthy, he is ostracized by his parents, his sister, and other relatives in his village who can see through his sudden affluence. Though the village had always held the city in admiration as a source of civilization and as a place worth going to, it now dreads the city. The narrative repositions the city, with its occult/spiritual terrorist gangs, as de-civilized, and the village as a model of civility.

Of course, Andy's display of his newfound wealth does have the visual power which people in the city desire. The position put forward by Andy's friends in the cult – that "money speaks" – is the rhetoric which the city itself requires to distinguish itself from the village. Along this line, Jonathan Haynes and Onookome Okome have argued, in respect of *Living in Bondage*, that "The representation of the city is subsumed by a logic of acquisitive desire and magic because this same vast floating desperate mass of the population needs figures for the social processes of post-oil boom Nigeria which seem occult because they have so little to do with work or productive social processes."[18] It is interesting, however, that this wealth which asks to be admired – just as the city constructs itself as spectacle – is eventually undercut by Andy's collapse into madness and destitution. Feeding from refuse dumps and sleeping at street corners, the visual world Andy dreads is the world he now joins. This might lead us to disagree with Jonathan Haynes and Onookome Okome, whose reading of the film concludes that "It is very easy for the video dramas aimed at this audience (the city dwellers) to "misrecognize" the real social and political issues facing the urban masses, representing them in a way that falsifies the problems and makes solutions unimaginable."[19] Haynes and Okome perhaps underestimate the degree to which Andy's case in *Living in Bondage* serves as a warning against the seduction of the spectacle of wealth in the city.

Indeed, the film compels us to reconsider the privileging of the physical visuality of life in the city, and to make what appears to be an absence important to the meaning of the observable *city-presence*. The real social life of the city obscures secret practices like the cult Andy joins to become rich. Such occult practices and the supernatural absent-presence which they invoke are characteristic of postcolonial magic realism – they constitute the *hidden* worlds of the city. This opposition of various worlds in the city, which we find in many films, derives from traditional African beliefs in the presence of spiritual forces in the human world, or rather the interaction of the natural and supernatural. As such, conditions in the physical world are explained as having supernatural causes.

At another level, the drama of sacrifice-for-money in *Living in Bondage* – as a narrative of extreme "decadence" – correlates with actual recent cases in Nigeria: for example, the Otokoto case of ritual murder in Owerri, which led to violence in the city in 1997. As such, it and other films like it may be seen as restagings, or fictional variations, of actual events which have attracted great popular interest in Nigeria. At any rate, in their various representations of the decadence and corruption of life in the city, these films demonstrate the terms of Lagos's achievement of membership of the community of world cities.

Conclusion

The video films explored in this chapter present images of Lagos life which are not totally desirable. Exploring the urban condition, they present themselves as useful means toward the observation and understanding of the city, while also appealing to our desire for the spectacular. They try to play on our attitudes to the city, *making us believe* that they have seen and thus omnisciently know it (more than we ever could as individuals in a city crowd). Moreover, as *home* videos, they enable us to visualize the city as if we were outside it, safely at home watching the "crazies" outside.

Secondly, the postcolonial city, as articulated in the films examined here, appears as a world of disturbing contrasts. Not only does it display conspicuous affluence and no less conspicuous poverty, its visible glamor is a cover for both physical and spiritual decay. The city appears to resist any stable visual form or representation, lending itself instead only to ambivalence, difference, and a plurality of images. Its accession to the global community of world cities has gained it much and lost it more.

Thirdly, those films which rely on a sense of the absurd – especially *Lagos Na Wah!!* and *Lagos Alaye Boys* – laugh at life in the city. The postcolonial strategy of laughing at oneself (as a way of neutralizing the impact of others laughing at oneself) appears where the city, as an inherited "civilized" space, always already undermines its own difference, creates a sense of loss, and leaves the postcolonial subject stranded in a quest for "appropriate" space. The city laughs at itself, with itself (its *selves*), so as to reuse itself, even as a commodity.

Of course, there is a danger that films like those examined here may exaggerate and distort the real life of the city. But beneath their absurdity seems to be a serious commentary on the capacity of the city to *distort* the idea of civilized living – indeed, an interrogation of the city and its modes of existence. As such, all of these films raise two important questions: first, as to whether the city in our sight(s) – Lagos – is indeed a site of survival which we want to keep; and, secondly, whether the films discussed above might provide a means to that end.

Notes

1 Roland Barthes, "Rhetoric of the Image," in *Image – Music – Text*, trans. Stephen Heath (Glasgow: Fontana/Collins, 1979, 2nd ed.), p. 49.

2 "Lagos Na Wah" is an expression in Nigerian pidgin which could mean: (a) "Lagos is strange," or (b) "Lagos is confusing." The word *wah* does not have a stable meaning but could be used in expressing both positive and negative surprises, which correlates with the ambivalent imaging of the city of Lagos in the video films under study.

3 David Hecht and Abdou Maliqalim Simone, *Invisible Governance: the Art of African Micro-Politics* (New York: Autonomedia, 1994).

4 Jose Ortega y Gasset, "The Crowd Phenomenon," in Lawrence Cahoone, *From Modernism to Postmodernism: An Anthology* (Oxford: Blackwell, 1996), p. 220.

5 "Advance fee fraud" (AFF) is a now internationally recognized serious crime problem and a national scandal in Nigeria, which involves attempts by Nigerian criminal groups to defraud European, US, and other firms and/or private individuals through involving them in bogus business ventures in supposed cooperation with the Nigerian government and Nigerian corporations. AFF is known to feed directly into other forms of crime in Nigeria, particularly drug-trafficking.

6 The word "sweep" in the name "Operation Sweep" implies the presence of a *dirty* environment, which includes psychological and social dirtiness. Crime, in this sense, is read as a kind of social pollution, which "Operation Sweep" is assigned *to clean up.*

7 Jinmi Adisa, "Lagos: Street Culture and Families in the Street," in Georges Hérault and Pius Adesanmi (eds.), *Youth, Street Culture and Urban Violence in Africa* (Ibadan: IFRA, 1997), p. 110.

8 Stuart Hall, Chas Critcher, Tony Jefferson, John Clarke, and Brian Roberts, *Policing the Crisis: Mugging, the State, and Law and Order* (London: Macmillan, 1978), p. 60.

9 Ibid., p. 61.

10 V. N. Volosinov, "Marxism and the Philosophy of Language," in Charles Harrison and Paul Wood (eds.), *Art in Theory, 1900–1990: An Anthology of Changing Ideas* (Oxford: Blackwell, 1996), p. 468.

11 Hall et al., *Policing the Crisis*, p. 62.

12 Adisa, "Lagos," p. 110, corroborates this by saying that: "The secret is that in Lagos you must be smart. Habitual residents relay this to the new comer in three words – "Eko o gbagbere". To survive in Lagos you must constantly have your wits about you. You must learn not to place a high value on scruples. Lagos, in the Nigerian parlance, is "no man's land". The implication is that the city does not respond to the ethics of the average local community. No one is his brother's keeper. The rhythm of the street is every man for himself."

13 Hyginus Ekwuazi, "The Igbo Video Film: A Glimpse into the Cult of the Individual," in Jonathan Haynes (ed.), *Nigerian Video Films* (Ibadan: Nigerian Film Institute/Kraft; 1997), p. 74.

14 Wole Soyinka, *The Strong Breed: Three Plays* (Ibadan: Mbari Publications, 1963), pp. 81–117. On the persecution of the ethnic stranger, see Obododimma Oha,

"Cross-cultural conversation and the semiotics of ethno-cultural domination in Nigeria," *Journal of the African Anthropological Association* 6, no. 1 (forthcoming).

15 Adisa, "Lagos," p. 98.

16 Onookome Okome, "Onome: ethnicity, class, gender," in Haynes (ed.), *Nigerian Video Films*, pp. 83–92.

17 Adisa, "Lagos."

18 Jonathan Haynes and Onookome Okome, "Evolving Population Media: Nigerian Video Films," in *Nigerian Video Films*, p. 39. See also Jonathan Haynes, "Nigerian Cinema: Structural Adjustments," in Onookone Okome and Jonathan Haynes (eds.), *Cinema and Social Change in West Africa* (Jos: Nigerian Film Corporation, 1997), pp. 1–25.

19 Haynes and Okome, "Evolving Population Media," p. 39.

17

Montréal Between Strangeness, Home, and Flow

Bill Marshall

There is a well-established corpus of cultural criticism that places the relationships between city, modernity, and cinema at the center of its analysis. As David B. Clarke points out,

> the spectacle of the cinema both drew upon and contributed to the increased pace of modern city life, whilst also helping to normalize and cathect the frantic, disadjusted rhythms of the city . . . ; [cinema] reflected and helped to mould the novel forms of social relations that developed in the crowded yet anonymous city streets; and both documented and helped to transform the social and physical space that the modern city represented.[1]

However, the historical, cultural, and geographical specificity of Québec means that Montréal's insertion into such a narrative, and the developments that follow, are both problematic and revealing.

Montréal was founded in 1642, initially as a religious mission, Ville-Marie, an offshoot of the European Counter-Reformation in the territory of New France which had been founded in 1608. By the time of the British conquest of Québec in 1759–60, the city had grown to a population of 5,000, and was located at the center of networks of fur trade and exploration, helped by its position as the most inland oceangoing port in the St. Lawrence basin. Under British imperial rule and then Canadian confederation after 1867, the city expanded and industrialized in the nineteenth century, an expansion based on British (often Scottish) capital and entrepreneurs, and British and

Irish immigration, which momentarily in mid-century made Montréal a majority Anglophone city. However, continued industrialization and a rural exodus created a large Francophone working class, so that by the 1931 Census, of the conurbation's one million people, 60 percent were of French ethnic origin, 26 percent British and Irish, and 13.5 percent "other," the result of mainly German, Italian, and Jewish immigration in the previous forty years.[2] The first question which arises is that relating to the specificities of Montréal's insertion into modernity and modernism.

Certainly, Montréal partook of that general Western and North American process of rural exodus, immigration, technological change, and industrial/urban development at the turn of the century, with the cinema taking its place as a new leisure industry within the new dispositions of capital flow, urban space, and audience patterns, as well as constructing, through shock, montage, and its "virtual presence," the kinds of subjectivity appropriate to the new culture. Walter Benjamin wrote in an essay on Baudelaire in 1939 that "technology has subjected the human sensorium to a complex kind of training. There came a day when a new and urgent need for stimuli was met by the film. In a film, perception in the form of shocks was established as a formal principle."[3] The first film screening in Canada took place in Montréal in June 1896. By 1912 the city had seventy cinemas attracting a quarter of the city's population on Sundays. Although this Sunday cinemagoing was virulently opposed by the Catholic hierarchy, Montréal remained for the first decades of the century the only North American city where it took place.[4]

And yet Montréal's position within Québec/Canada meant that a special inflection was given to the notions of "strangeness" that accompanied modernity. According to this argument, the "intimately related, lived totality" of traditional society was replaced by an abstract space of physical proximity and social distance, so that in the modern city strangers experienced a world populated by strangers.[5] It thus seems odd that a "modernist" depiction of Montréal is so rare in Québec culture and cinema. Arguably, "modernism," understood in its high cultural sense as a response to commodification and reification through the problematization of language, decentering of consciousness, and proclamation of alienation, has existed only sporadically in Canada, for historical and social reasons: an urban life and elite cultural structure different from and peripheral to the experience of Berlin, New York, Paris, and Vienna in the first three decades of the century. In Québec, the first decades of the century were marked by a "clerical nationalist" hegemony in which the Catholic Church in alliance with (often rural) Francophone elites and *notables* was proposing an anti-modern, traditionalist, inward-looking defense of the "French-Canadian" people and its "values." High culture in Québec was subordinated to metropolitan French culture.

Moreover, the lived (political) reality of modernity differed. For the "French Canadians" of the rural exodus just as for the immigrants, Montréal was literally "strange," dominated as it was by the large Anglo population, by Anglo capitalism, and by the English language. In other words, the internalization of the "strangeness" of modernity could at least in part be avoided through displacement on to the Other, as a mere continuation of the experience of British imperialism, and all sorts of appropriations and resistances could be constructed in order to perpetuate a notion of "home." These could take a conservative form such as the role of the Church, but could also be found in the formation of Francophone communities, their outside decks, landings, and courtyards reproducing the communality of village life. For the Francophone *Montréalais* a (provisional) notion of autonomy, of "home," could persist because the disorienting experience of modernity could be compartmentalized in terms of another culture and language.

However, this was a very unstable equilibrium. The "modernizing" force of cinema was always already implicated in a relationship between identity and the flows which would undo it. Montréal intensifies and gives its own specificity to Kevin Robins's observation of the "productive tension" that has been at the heart of urban development, "the city as container and the city as flow," settlement and movement, the bounded and the boundless.[6] The influx of non-British and non-French immigrants, interrupted by economic depression and war, recommenced after 1945. Montréal's role as an Atlantic port in the heart of the continent gave it a unique, "freer" role during American prohibition and the wartime passage of American and Canadian servicemen. The growth of consumer society and the federal government's interventionist social policies in the 1950s all undermined the clerical–nationalist certainties and fixities about "home" and the self-definition of "French Canadians." The new Québec assertiveness and, indeed, nationalism of the 1960s were attempts to reconcile the national idea with modernity, as in other Western nations. This period of reform, known as the "Quiet Revolution," began in 1960 with the provincial election victory, after a fifteen-year gap, of the Liberal Party lead by Jean Lesage under the slogan *"maîtres chez nous/*masters in our own house." A new cinema also emerged.

Until the 1940s, in Québec "the cinema" meant either Hollywood films in English (the vast majority) or films from France. One of the priorities of the Quiet Revolution was to reinvest Montréal with a new Francophone hegemony, that of a new modernizing technocracy, a Francophone business class, and an opening onto the world. The beginnings of a Québec national cinema proper in the 1960s accompany this reappropriation of the city for the Francophone modernizing vision. However, this 1960s cinema usually presented a highly problematizing view of a national idea as fundamentally unfinished and still to be elaborated. For one thing, the modernizing Québec society was located in between two competing models of modernity, namely those of the United States and of Gaullist France. It was the latter which provided the major cinematic resource here, partly because the "American" side of Québec identity implied a dispersed, pre- or post-national continental space, and partly because of the impact on Québec filmmakers and *cinéphile* audiences of the *nouvelle vague*. In the national–allegorical tension between authentication and dispersal, films by major Québec *auteurs* in the 1960s, such as Gilles Groulx, Claude Jutra, and Jean Pierre Lefebvre, represent the new cityscape of Montréal and with it the young urban heterosexual couple, although in a more anxious way than their French equivalents.

The evolution of these visions of Montréal's supposedly triumphant Francophone modernity can be traced in three scenes set in the newly constructed *métro*. In *Valérie* (Denis Héroux, 1968), often dubbed the first Québec pornographic film, the eponymous heroine triumphantly crosses the bridge into the city after escaping from a Catholic orphanage, and lives a reconciling apprenticeship of modernity through (highly sanitized) prostitution and then marriage. The spaces of the city become extensions of her bodily pleasures, including the *métro*, where she caresses the outside of trains and uses the central metal pole as a dancing prop, so that the film comes to be, Benjamin-like, about the new shocks and stimuli of modernity which come to reconstruct the self. The *métro* car also contains different images of women in advertising, and the film attempts to proclaim these as aesthetic, as the nude as opposed to the naked woman, and therefore as non- or post-religious, and continuous with the aestheticizations and sexualizations of consumer society. In contrast, *Sonatine*, directed by Micheline Lanctôt in 1983 (with Montréal in the depths of an economic recession from which it began to recover only in the 1990s), portrays the *métro* as a space of modern alienation and death, as two adolescent girls take an overdose and ride around with a placard proclaiming that they have done so. The national "people" constituted by their fellow-passengers neither act nor react. In a reversal of the Orpheus myth, the girls die underground because no one pays attention, in particular the last *métro* driver, who starts a strike. The "strangeness" of the city, which could be dodged earlier in the century, has overwhelmed its status as "home" now that the Francophones are in charge.

The raising of a specific urban place to the status of mythological space characterizes what is no doubt the internationally best-known film on the city, Denys Arcand's *Jésus de Montréal* (1989). This film continues the diagnostic and denunciatory mode of Lanctôt, underlining the disillusion with the Quiet Revolution generation and legacy to be found in his previous feature, *Le Déclin de l'empire américain* (1986), but here eventually offering potentially ethical solutions to the commodification and moral collapse of contemporary life. The *métro* is the scene of Daniel's (Lothaire Bluteau) last delirium, the quintessential contemporary space of speed, urban crowds, and consumerism (the face of his actor friend glimpsed at the beginning figures here on an advertising poster) now turned into an antechamber of death. Otherwise, Arcand films Montréal here as a generalized *Cité*, a place of sin and corruption possibly interchangeable with other urban spaces, shot from above or at a distance, particularly from the Mount where the passion play is performed. We must look elsewhere for a fuller engagement with the so-called postmodern realities of the city.

Those realities, as summarized by Manuel Castells, intriguingly merge with the specificities of Québec and Montréal. In the Informational City, the national–allegorical tension we have witnessed as always already there in Québec cinema is translated into "the articulation of the globally-oriented economic functions of the city with the locally-rooted society and culture."[7] Montréal has begun to carve an important and distinctive domain within an economic space forged by the 1988 North American Free Trade Agreement and by globalization in general. Much of the Québec film industry is a branch plant for Anglophone Canadian and American productions. This both enables "national" cinema production to take place, and also creates new solidities, new "repatriations," within the migrant or voyaging flows of capital. The clearest example of this is Montréal's recent spatial reconfiguration within the multimedia industry, which is due partly to technical and industrial factors (the branch plant phenomenon, the animation tradition) and partly to cultural factors (Montréal as linguistically rich and as located between European and North American culture). At the end of 1999 there were 850 companies active in this sector, constituting over half of all IT firms in the city.[8] Daniel Langlois, founder of Softimage, which provided animation software for *Jurassic Park* and *Toy Story*, has invested in the Festival of New Cinema and New Media, and sponsored the new CAN$16-million cinema complex on the Boulevard Saint-Laurent devoted to experimental and *auteur* cinema.[9]

One consequence of "the space of flows" superseding "the space of places" is "the increasing differentiation between power and experience, the separation between meaning and function."[10] Thus cultural consumers and Québécois business and political elites become inscribed within a public and media space whose frontiers no longer coincide with the national territory, a leapfrogging from City to World. One cinematic possibility is that of Montréal's metamorphosis into other places, "standing in" in various movies for New York, Paris, even Vienna (*Hotel New Hampshire*, Tony Richardson, 1984), or transformed into a futuristic "no-place" (Robert Altman's use of the old Expo '67 site for *Quintet*, 1979). However, the possibility of the decisive evacuation of "place" by "space" is rarely explored in Québec national cinema. The only major example is that of the director Léa Pool, who as a Swiss–Jewish lesbian has a particularly deterritorializing attitude towards the city. Films such as *Strass café* (1980), *La Femme de l'hôtel* (1984), *Anne Trister* (1986), and *À Corps perdu* (1988) are the nearest Québec feature films have come to Gilles Deleuze's abstract "any-space-whatevers."[11]

What is more, there is a particularly sensitive issue linked to the realities of the Global City, namely immigration. Montréal is, for reasons both of film history and economics, the center of the Québec film industry. The National Film Board moved there from Ottawa in 1956; since the early 1950s it has housed state and private television stations; virtually all Québec's film personnel are there and it is the place which interconnects with the North American and world filmmaking industries. Montréal is the most common setting for a Québec film and would seem, therefore, to play an authenticating role within this national cinema. And yet it is also the "weakest" point for any kind of pure, homogeneous vision of Québec culture to be formed since such a role is immediately contested and contradicted by its insertion within the international flows of both capital and labor. The latter issue is that of immigration and the allophones (those whose "mother tongue" is neither French nor English), and it raises dramatic questions about the future of Québec society. The low birth rate (which plummeted from 26.6 to 14.8 births per thousand from 1961 to 1981) reminds some Québécois of the traditional fear of disappearing in a North American continent in which they are a tiny minority. According to the 1996 census, 9.7 percent of Québec's seven million people are allophones (8.8 percent are Anglophones). To employ another criterion, Greater Montréal is home to 92 percent of Québec's "visible minorities", who form 12.2 percent of the population of the city (significantly smaller, however, than the figures for Toronto – 32 percent – and Vancouver – 31 percent). Of that 12.2 percent, 30 percent are Black, 18 percent are Arab/West Asian and 11.6 percent are Latin American, the second largest such community in Canada. It is a very different place from the rest of the country whose metropolis it is.

   The reconciliation of important sections of these ethnic minorities to the sovereignist project remains the single greatest challenge to the long-term strategy of the ruling *Parti québécois*. The reaction of most Québec filmmakers has been to ignore this dimension when setting their films in Montréal. However, since 1980 a number of filmmakers have placed it at the center of their preoccupations. Some of them have been of immigrant origin (directors such as Paul Tana and Michka Saäl). Others, such as Michel Brault in *Les Noces de papier* of 1989 (a Québécois *Green Card*, with Geneviève Bujold marrying a Latin American refugee), François Labonté in *Manuel le fils emprunté* of the same year, and even J. W. Benoît in his adaptation of the novel by the Haitian writer Dany Laferrière, *Comment faire l'amour avec un nègre sans se fatiguer* (1989), have used the alternative chronotope of the city's multicultural Plateau district as a potential source of more mobile, less stable and, in the case of Labonté's film, potentially less Oedipalized definitions of the Québécois self.

   A group of films in the 1990s began to take on board and attempted to negotiate the new state of affairs of the Global City, which both unbalances that old tension between place and space, container and flow, and creates new possibilities as well as exclusions (Castells's "Dual City" with its polarization between an informational elite and a disempowered locally-oriented population). The *portmanteau* film made for Montréal's 350th anniversary, *Montréal vu par* (1992), can be seen to inaugurate this sequence. All six short films are in fact very oblique, either figuring the city as "elsewhere" or, in their narratives of encounters and combinations, favoring the transversal over the panoptic, the *parcours* over the *carte*. (In Michel de Certeau's work on everyday life, the *parcours* is associated with "the microbe-like, singular and plural practices which an urbanistic system [associated with the *carte*] was supposed to administer or suppress, but which have outlived its decay."[12])

In most of these films, urban space is particularly gendered. To take three examples: in Michel Brault's *La Dernière Partie*, a wife (Hélène Loiselle) announces to her husband (Jean Mathieu) that she is leaving him – this in the recesses of the Forum, where he has dragged her to the Saturday night ice-hockey match. The yellows and browns of the home where she has prepared her departure give way to the gray space of the stadium, a liminal place of transition in a space overwhelmingly coded as masculine, dotted with television screens displaying the match which distract the husband even at this moment. In the end, he is swallowed up by the departing crowd and wakes up alone at home in front of the television. The codifications of space are seen no longer to be operating, as this desperate but now empowered middle-aged woman chooses to pitch herself into displacement and the abandonment of "home."

Léa Pool's *Rispondetemi* relates inner and outer worlds, as a young woman, victim of a car accident with her female lover, is transported by ambulance to hospital. The flashbacks of her past life are juxtaposed with the view of the city from a moving horizontal position, as she "sees" through the ambulance roof, underlining cinema's vocation as here, literally, the vehicle of a mobility that is virtual rather than actual, and creating a non-place and time which blur and render problematic both the notions of destination (will the hospital be reached, and does it matter?) and speed (the slowed-down temporality of her experience). That moving film image is at opposite poles from the panopticism that characterizes the Canadian tradition, since the consolidation of the country with the building of the Canadian Pacific Railway in 1881, of envisioning an east–west line from which to survey the territory – as in the animation of a gull's flight in the closedown sequence on CBC/SRC (Canadian Broadcasting Corporation/Société Radio Canada).

This process is taken further in Patricia Rozema's *Desperanto*, in which Sheila McCarthy reprises her cute, organizationally-challenged role from the director's debut feature *I've Heard the Mermaids Singing* (1987), this time playing Ann Stewart, a Toronto housewife holidaying in Montréal. She too visits the tourist sites in a tourist bus. Enticed by the sexual license of *Le Déclin de l'empire américain*, which she reviews in her hotel room, she decides to make the most of her last night, dresses in a gauche white dress, and crashes a "sophisticated" Francophone party. Her unsuccessful attempts at picking up a man lead to misunderstandings, a squashed strawberry which makes her seem to be menstruating or experiencing some hemorrhage, and a fainting which produces the dream/fantasy sequence which closes the film. Her virtual self is also in white, but has a fairy-queen high collar. She is able to stop time with a remote control in order to flick through her dictionary to translate conversations. The English subtitles become part of the diegesis as she stands between them and the cinema spectator, reading them and appropriating them physically. Even when midnight strikes and the Cinderella fantasy ends, Ann finds herself tended to by ambulance personnel Denys Arcand and Geneviève Rioux, whom she recognizes from *Le Déclin*, and who waft her away to a euphoric dance in the air above Montréal.

The gendered nature of urban space goes to the heart of debates about modernity and its development into the contemporary postmodern. That central modernist figure of the *flâneur*, the detached wanderer playfully and transversally enthralled by the stimuli, the *virtuality*, of the city, has (as Janet Wolff tells us) been so overwhelmingly coded as masculine, that its feminization, if such is the case, would raise important questions for the relationship between modernity and postmodernity.[13] Against Janet Wolff, Elizabeth Wilson has argued that the figure of the *flâneur*, rather than a bastion of male privilege, marked a crisis of masculinity, "a shifting projection of angst rather than a solid embodiment of male bourgeois power."[14] This conglomeration of pleasure ("the *flâneur* appears as the ultimate ironic, detached observer, skimming across the surface of the city and tasting all its pleasures with curiosity and interest"),[15] shopping, and anxiety (because unfixed and nostalgic) has ultimately transmuted itself into new forms which are consistent with the generalized fragmentation and "sensations without consequence"[16] of contemporary consumer society – what David Clarke calls "the *systemic* appropriation of the *flâneur*'s originally *anti-systemic* existence."[17]

Now Montréal can currently be seen as not only a generalized example of that curious representation in the urban scene of a *simultaneous* utopia and dystopia, but also as a particular space in which European nostalgia, melancholy, and alienation coexist with a North American utopianism bound up with the pluralism of consumer lifestyles. The prime emblems for these ambivalences are women and youth, who are precisely the main protagonists of three other 1990s "city films," *Eldorado* (Charles Binamé, 1995), *Cosmos* (Jennifer Alleyn, Manon Briand, Marie-Julie Dallaire, Arto Paragamian, André Turpin, and Denis Villeneuve, 1996), and *2 Secondes* (Manon Briand, 1998). This inflection is not surprising, given the ambivalences both "home" and "outside," or "the street," acquire: for women in terms of their assessment of confinement and freedom, safety and danger; and for "youth" which, in the mobile churning of its lifestyles, is also an embodiment (and object) of anxiety in Québec society, in that this current generation is bearing the full brunt of contemporary instabilities and unfixings (including unemployment or pre-carious employment) that the baby-boomer generation growing up under Fordism and the Quiet Revolution never knew. All three films also pivot round an emblem of movement.

Eldorado renews to an extent the direct documentary tradition in Québec cinema, in its relatively small budget (CAN$1.5 million), use of natural décor and lighting, improvisational dialogues, and the ambition to capture *sur le vif* the lives of its young urban protagonists. On the other hand, it relies a lot on a carefully composed soundtrack of urban noise and rock music, and on montage. Pascale Bussières, twelve years on from *Sonatine*, plays the pivotal figure of Rita, a rollerblading drug-taking marginal still mourning the death of a friend in a suicide pact she survived. She connects briefly with the lives of a lonely neurotic attending psychotherapy; a bourgeois daughter and gen-erous benefactor, whose apartment is wrecked by Rita's drug suppliers; and Lloyd (James Hyndman), a radio shockjock who has a brief sexual encounter in the toilets of the post-punk bar *Les Foufounes électriques* with a barmaid whose live-in relationship is in difficulty.

The film leans toward a modernist dystopia rather than a postmodern uto-pia, and its sexual politics are ultimately rather conventional, despite or be-cause of the character of Rita, mobile but nostalgic. Rita at one point hijacks Lloyd's car to break into an open-air swimming pool at night. This, and her involvement in drug dealing, is emblematic of that destabilizing "agoraphobic space" of the city, tempting, as Elizabeth Wilson puts it, "the individual who staggers across it to do anything and everything."[18] However, it is clear that, while this urban society lacks mental roadmaps, the characters, bereft of "love," are still looking back for some, in particular those which lead to heterosexual couple formation. The frequent shots of aerial telephone lines connote these attempts to connect, to remap the film sentimentally. Astonishingly for a film purporting to be a portrait of contemporary Montréal, there are no characters who are gay or members of ethnic minorities.

Cosmos, a showcase for young directors put together by Roger Frappier at Max Films, does, however, feature both ethnicity (the eponymous Greek taxi driver who links the segments, his black colleague who helps him chase his stolen cab and waxes philosophical about the origins of cities in the last se-quence, *Cosmos et Agriculture*, directed by Arto Paragamian). It also carries the fragmentation of the previous film further, its *portmanteau* structure reinforcing the idea of the city as an assemblage of distinct and separate subjects. This structure recalls Walter Benjamin's notion of the metropolis as labyrinth, in which "we observe bits of the "stories" men and women carry with them, but never learn their conclusions; life ceases to form itself into epic or narrative, becoming instead a short story, dreamlike, insubstantial or ambiguous."[19]

The film produces, within the twenty-four-hour unity of time, notions of simultaneity that are reminiscent of the role of the novel and newspaper in

Benedict Anderson's account of nation-building, but with no overall viewpoint that would allow a position of mastery, and any collective identity that emerges is both provisional and fading.[20] Cosmos himself is a conduit in the literal and figurative senses, the prime connector of this rhizomatic network of relations: an unconsummated sexual re-encounter (André Turpin's *Jules et Fanny*); "transversal" friendships between a woman and a gay man nervous about obtaining the result of his HIV test (Manon Briand's *Boost*), and between a nineteen-year-old budding actress and a wise elderly gentleman (Jennifer Alleyn's *Aurore et Crépuscule*); the rapid montage of a nervous young film director bombarded with screen images as he faces an interview and a compulsory makeover for an internet channel (Denis Villeneuve's *Le Technétium*); and, lurking in the city's labyrinthine depths (echoed in Turpin's hotel corridors), the serial killer, the *M* or Minotaur, first glimpsed and tracked as one of the anonymous crowd in the *métro*, the camera alighting on him as if arbitrarily, as less coded as "strange" than another individual (a cameo from André Forcier) and then following him to his next victim (Marie-Julie Dallaire's *L'Individu*).

Manon Briand's first feature after her contribution to *Cosmos, 2 Secondes* casts Charlotte Laurier as Laurie, a champion cyclist who hesitates at the start of a race, loses, and returns to Montréal to be a dispatch rider. The regulations of this work create a *carte* for the city which Laurie sidesteps to create her own *parcours* both in space and time. Her brother is a theoretical physicist interested in relativity. Her mother has Alzheimer's and has regressed to childhood. Her substitute father-figure is an eccentric Italian bicycle repairman (Dino Tavarone) whose shop is almost in a time warp outside history and commerce, but whose body bears the marks of his long professional cycling career. The woman photographer with whom Laurie eventually forms a sexual relationship is the double of his dream girl left behind to win a race in France decades ago, in a conceit that echoes the account of Einstein and differential aging given by the brother. Above all, the film sets up the bicycle as a supremely cinematic machine, in its echo of the cinematic apparatus, its movement, and the rapid, flickering vision of the city it provides.

Clearly, the diachronic treatment of Montréal in Québec cinema with which we began reveals a set of meanings that is constantly in process but which usefully connects the specificity of the Québec situation with global evolutions and transitions. In his first two feature films, *Le Confessionnal* (1995) and *Le Polygraphe* (1996), Robert Lepage, uniquely, uses Québec City, and not Montréal, to mediate relationships between the local and the global, the global irrupting more surprisingly, poetically, sometimes wrenchingly, amid the labyrinths, secrets, and enclosures of the old founding settlement of the French Canadians. But from cinema's inception, through the postwar era and Quiet Revolution to the dislocations of contemporary globalization, Montréal is peculiar for being in Québec, and peculiar within Québec: "in-between" major spaces, perpetually becoming something else, "minor" in

Deleuze and Guattari's sense of becoming, of innovating, and of questioning norms of mastery and territorialization.[21]

Notes

1 David. B. Clarke (ed.), *The Cinematic City* (London: Routledge, 1997), p. 3.

2 Paul-André Linteau et al., *Histoire du Québec contemporain: De la Confédération à la crise (1867–1929)* (Montréal: Boréal Compact, 1989), pp. 57–64.

3 Walter Benjamin, "On Some Motifs in Baudelaire," in *Illuminations*, ed. Hannah Arendt, trans. Harry Zohn (London: Fontana/Collins, 1972), p. 177.

4 See Germain Lacasse, "Le Dimanche, Montréal va aux vues *ou* la ville aux vues s'anime," in Pierre Véronneau (ed.), *Montréal: ville de cinéma* (Montréal: Cinémathèque québécoise/Musée du cinéma, 1992), pp. 5–11.

5 Clarke, *The Cinematic City*, p. 4.

6 Kevin Robins, "Prisoners of the City: Whatever could a Postmodern City Be?," *New Formations* 15 (Winter 1991): 11.

7 Manuel Castells, "European Cities, the Informational Society and the Global Economy," *New Left Review* 204 (March–April 1994): 28.

8 Data from Jean-Pierre Langlois, Montréal Chamber of Commerce. Montréal also has the highest per capita concentration of high technology jobs of any major North American city (speech by Richard Guay, Delegate General of Québec in London, 28 October 1999).

9 For more on this general topic, see V. Bellemare Brière, "Montréal: capitale multimédia," *Séquences* 197 (July–August 1998): 54.

10 Castells, "European Cities," p. 29.

11 That is, any "space that does not yet appear as a real setting or is abstracted from the spatial and temporal determinations of a real setting." See D. N. Rodowick, *Gilles Deleuze's Time Machine* (Durham: Duke University Press, 1997), p. 63.

12 See Michel de Certeau, "Walking in the City," in Simon During (ed.), *The Cultural Studies Reader* (London: Routledge, 1993), p. 156.

13 See Janet Wolff, "The Artist and the *Flâneur*: Rodin, Rilke and Gwen John in Paris," chapter six in *Resident Alien: Feminist Cultural Criticism* (Cambridge: Polity Press, 1995), pp. 88–114.

14 Elizabeth Wilson, "The Invisible *Flâneur*," *New Left Review* 191 (January–February 1992): 109.

15 Ibid., p. 97.

16 Clarke, *The Cinematic City*, p. 7.

17 Ibid., p. 6.

18 Wilson, "The Invisible *Flâneur*," p. 109.

19 See ibid, p. 107.

20 Benedict Anderson, *Imagined Communities: Reflections on the Origin and Spread of Nationalism* (London: Verso, 1983), pp. 30–1.

21 Gilles Deleuze and Félix Guattari, *Kafka: pour une littérature mineure* (Paris: Minuit, 1975); and *Capitalisme et schizophrénie: Mille plateaux* (Paris: Minuit, 1980), p. 132.

18

(Mis-)Representing the Irish Urban Landscape

Kevin Rockett

As Raymond Williams remarks, "country" and "city" are "very powerful" words.[1] However, in the Irish context, treated as binary oppositions, their ideological resonance is even more pronounced than elsewhere. The "country" as represented within mainstream nationalist historiography, and in much of nineteenth- and early twentieth-century literature and the visual arts, is the site of authentic Irishness. The city in this tradition was negatively regarded – notwithstanding the writings of modernists such as James Joyce and John Eglinton, both of whom applauded the city's romance with technology and modern communications. Lady Gregory, one of the leading figures of the Irish Literary Revival of the late nineteenth century, complained that her imagination was "always the worse for every sight of Dublin."[2] Such was the hostility of the dominant strain of Irish cultural nationalism to modernity and urbanization that Douglas Hyde, the future president of Ireland (1938–45) and founder of the Gaelic League (1893) – an organization dedicated to the replacement of the English language by Irish as the vernacular – was as disturbed at the possibility of a modernized Irish Ireland as much as a modernized anglicized Ireland.

This prejudice, and its corollary, the privileging of the pastoral, was not a product of rural dwellers but of urban, specifically Dublin-based, intellectuals, writers, and artists operating within the context of the colonial experience. While the urban was associated with centers of capitalist concentration and colonial administration, the struggle for the land, literally and figuratively, was fought for a different economic and cultural order, which could be termed self-sufficient and protectionist. Choosing "the country" was a rejection of the trappings of the colonial Other as well as an attempt to enter a romantic Arcadia with man in dialogue with nature, rather than with man. It is unsurprising, therefore, to discover that cinema – a technologically-based modern medium produced in the first instance for the city dweller – should be regarded with suspicion by those who sought to create a mythical Gaelic past.

Two main issues arise in the treatment of cinematic representations of the urban in Ireland. One is how the Irish were represented by foreigners, and by themselves; the other, how images of urban America with its overt secularism and consumerism, and to a lesser extent urban Britain, were received. Ireland's relationship with cinema began when representatives of the Lumière brothers visited the country in 1896 and 1897 to show films and to produce some of the first moving pictures of Ireland. Included in their catalogue as twenty-five items of mostly fifty seconds' duration, these images, which initi-

Figure 18.1 "... some of the first moving pictures of Ireland ..." Sackville Street (now O'Connell Street), Dublin, as filmed by the Lumière brothers, 1897 (*Courtesy of the Film Institute of Ireland*)

ated a new way of seeing the Irish countryside and the city, feature Belfast and Dublin, and the train journeys from Belfast to Dublin, and from Dublin to the port town of Kingstown (now Dún Laoghaire). The scenes of city streets and shots from trains were similar to those filmed throughout the world by the Lumières' cameramen, and likewise are marked by a structured absence of rural life. Even though some of the images in the train-journey films are of the countryside, it has become abstracted, reduced to blurred impressions seen at high speed, giving it a dreamlike, ethereal, or eerie quality. It is as if it is distanced both literally (by the train) and symbolically (by the medium). Compared with the bustling, busy, communal, even aggressive sense of the city – such as in the film of the Dublin Fire Brigade (a popular choice for both cameramen and audiences in all cities) – the countryside is starkly different in its emptiness.

Notwithstanding the argument put forward by the cultural critic Luke Gibbons that Ireland experienced its own form of the "shock" of modernity as early as the Great Famine of the 1840s (akin to that of modernity as experienced by urban dwellers at the turn of the century), one only has to look at the first Lumière films shot in Ireland in the 1890s to realize that there *is* a fundamentally distinct experience of the modern being recorded.[3] It is the difference between the gentle pace of the countryside and the "hyperstimulus" of the city – which, ironically, is formed in Irish cities in part by an agricultural "invasion" of pigs and cattle on their way to export through Dublin port.[4] The sensory assault of everyday life, the defining element of modernity, can be seen even in the fixed camera shots of Dublin, such as in the view of O'Connell Street filmed in September 1897, the oldest surviving moving picture of the capital. Although this sensory assault can also be seen in representations of Belfast, there its meaning is different because of that city's particular relationship to British colonial power.

The popular view of Belfast as underpinned by a work ethic-driven Protestantism is most frequently signified in the towering cranes of the Harland & Wolff shipyards. Serving as a symbolic and actual representation of Protestant–unionist domination of the island's north-east, it sometimes belies the powerful pastoral strain present even within such representations. Certainly, a documentary like March of Time's *The Irish Question* (1944) contrasts "vigorous and aggressive" Belfast with agrarian life in the South, but feature films have been more circumspect in glorifying the work ethic. Indeed, in the British film *Jacqueline* (Roy Baker, 1956), the central character gets "dizzy spells" while working on the cranes and eventually finds solace by leaving the unsympathetic city and relocating with his family to an idyllic farm owned, ironically enough, by the shipyard boss. (As has been well documented, representations of the South are even more thoroughly imbued with a rural romanticism.)[5] If, as John Hill notes, *Jacqueline* had trouble reconciling the Protestant individualist work ethic with Irish romanticism, representations of

Dublin more fully expose the contradictions and suppressions of the Irish urban experience.[6]

In the 1920s and 1930s, the dominant fictional treatments of Dublin centered on the military and domestic events of the period from the 1916 Easter Rising to the 1922–3 Civil War, with most films, such as *Irish Destiny* (George Dewhurst, 1926), concerned with the 1919–21 War of Independence. While John Ford made (in Hollywood) two films dealing with this period – *The Informer* (1935) and *The Plough and the Stars* (1936) – it was Arthur Robison's *The Informer* (1929), based on Liam O'Flaherty's novel and filmed at London's Elstree Studios, which caused controversy by figuring the city as a place of corruption and violence. According to Censor James Montgomery, who refused "this impudent and mischievous distortion" a certificate for public exhibition, the film reoriented *à la* Chicago the social and political events of the novel toward a struggle between the police, gangsters, and prostitutes within Dublin's underworld. He further noted the "pity" that the citizens of Dublin could not "take an action against the producers for a libel" on their city.[7] That Dublin could be regarded as dangerous for both mind and body was likewise suggested in the Irish film, influenced by the Surrealists, *By Accident* (J. N. G. Davidson, 1930). In one scene "the soul-tortured youth" climbs Nelson's Pillar, the city's most prominent monument of the colonial inheritance, but as he attempts to survey the city, he suffers a bout of vertigo. In another scene, which recalls early cinema's fascination with the assault of technology on the human, driving along O'Connell Street he knocks down and kills a pedestrian, who turns out to be himself.

From the 1930s onwards, when modern buildings were being erected in Dublin (the Airport Terminal, for example, completed in 1940), their cinematic representation was largely avoided or denied. In tourist information films, drama-documentaries and independent productions (such as *Portrait of Dublin*, completed in 1951), there was a displacement of the contemporary city in favor of eighteenth-century Dublin. Thus there were celebratory documentaries, March of Time included, which highlighted neoclassical Georgian Dublin: Gandon's Four Courts (1785–1802) and the Customs House (1791), Fitzwilliam and Merrion Squares, Bank of Ireland College Green, and Trinity College. The focus in these documentaries on such major institutional buildings and residential squares had decidedly political implications. As most of the buildings concerned were constructed before the Act of Union (between Britain and Ireland) in 1800, their selective inclusion in these documentaries elided the difficult internal antagonisms between nationalists and unionists which forced political union with Britain had thrown up for over a century. Even when modernization and industrialization were promoted, as in the drama written by Seán O'Faoláin on the Rural Electrification Scheme, *The Promise of Barty O'Brien* (George Freedland, 1951), it was

America, and not Dublin – represented in dark and somber tones – which was used to signify the future.

This, of course, was not unusual. It is one of the peculiarities of urban representations that while New York in particular could inspire awe within Irish popular discourse, at the cultural level, Dublin, as the main Irish urban center, received scant respect. Manhattan, and other New York City locations, were firmly anchored within Irish consciousness as the destination of millions of emigrants, and as such, these not only provided settings for numerous cinematic representations of the Irish, but, in a more general way, came to stand for hope.[8]

The first fiction film shot in Ireland, *The Lad from Old Ireland* (Sidney Olcott, 1910), slides easily from the harsh conditions on the land and the tearful emigration of the hero, to New York, where within ten years he is financially successful and is elected to political office. After he receives word that his sweetheart is to be evicted, he returns to Ireland just in time to pay off the landlord. His modes of transport in Ireland – the train, and the pony and trap – provide a neat summary of the difference between the city and the country. Their juxtaposition of modernity and tradition, or urban and rural, sets a precedent for dealing with (mythic) Ireland, as in the opening sequence of John Ford's *The Quiet Man* (1952). The leaving behind of the train or the breakdown of the motorcar (as in *The Luck of the Irish*, Henry Koster, 1948, and *Hear My Song*, Peter Chelson, 1991) as a symbol of modernity usually allows the hero to enter the harmonious, and often mystical, rural community. In *The Lad from Old Ireland*, the city – New York, which at one level stands in for Dublin – is where the hero is tempted by society women, or "loose" women. The city governed by desire harbors a threat to rural Ireland's sense of community which is established in the film's opening scenes. Only when the hero returns and is greeted by the railway worker are rural values reasserted.

While some information films of the 1940s, 1950s, and 1960s show the foreigner arriving at Dublin (or Shannon) airport in order to indicate that Ireland is part of the modern communications world, after a quick tour of Georgian Dublin (s)he is typically whisked away to the pastoral idyll of the West. Likewise, feature films set in Dublin have characteristically refused a positive or progressive treatment of the city. Indeed, the title of a British thriller set in the capital, *Dublin Nightmare* (John Pomeroy, 1958), perhaps sums this up best. *Another Shore* (Charles Crichton, 1948), also a British film, is about a lazy and woman-shy civil servant lacking in ambition who dreams of leaving Dublin, not for the West, but for the exotic and sunny South Seas. Only when he is trapped in marriage does he resume his job at the Customs House, the administrative headquarters of the Department of Local Government. The film's final image of this (Georgian) building ensures the refusal of modernity, and acceptance – materially and ideologically – of conformity.

With the absence of critical and dynamic representations of Irish cities, both within cinema and official culture, the only images of urban life available to Irish viewers were those produced by foreign cinemas, especially Hollywood. But the Irish did not see Hollywood films in the same form as that in which they were shown either in America or in Britain. Under the provisions of the Censorship of Films Act (1923) the content of films was severely curtailed and films were refused a certificate if they were deemed to be "indecent, obscene or blasphemous." Because the censorship policy was informed by the notion that "the family was the unit of the state," films were banned or cut if they included extramarital affairs, divorce, birth control, abortion, prostitution, homosexuality, and many other "immoral" activities. While Irish audiences were left with cinematic pleasures which in many cases may not have even included the original narrative resolution, they were nevertheless offered images of a modern urban way of life which radically differed from the everyday life experienced by most Irish people. Moreover, many of the cinemas themselves were amongst the few buildings within the state in the International Style, and so, both through their exterior appearance and their un-Irish romantic "atmospheric" interiors, they offered cinemagoers a rare sensuous and exotic experience. As a result, and despite the severity of film censorship which led to about 2,500 films being banned and as many as 12,000 films being cut from the 1920s to the 1970s, the contrast between the joy inherent in the cinematic image (and the "site" of its exhibition) and the dourness of the official culture made going to the cinema the event of the week for many young people during those decades.[9] A recent expression of this is found in Alan Parker's adaptation of Frank McCourt's childhood memoir of urban life and poverty in 1930s Limerick, *Angela's Ashes* (2000). One of the few moments of communal joy shared by the children is their visit to the cinema, where they see, amongst other films, *Angels With Dirty Faces* (Michael Curtiz, 1938), a film, incidentally, whose ending was cut by the Censor because Fr. Barry (Karl Malden) tells a "lie" – that gangster James Cagney was really "yellow" when he was being executed.[10]

Coinciding with the decline of classical narrative cinema from the late 1950s was Ireland's belated engagement with the postwar international world. Finally acknowledging the failure of the economic and cultural protectionist agendas of the post-independence decades, the administrative, business, and political elites promoted more open policies. A byproduct of this was the liberalization in 1965 of film censorship, when the limited certificate provisions of the 1923 Act were adopted and censors could issue "Adults Only" certificates. Also in the 1960s, the Irish urban population increased with, for the first time, a majority of people living in towns with more than 1,500 people. At the beginning of the twenty-first century, the Greater Dublin region has expanded to encompass almost forty percent of the country's population, quite a change from the 6.5 percent living in Dublin City a century ago.

During the transformation of Irish society since the 1970s some of the most innovative work by Irish artists has been concerned with the urban sensibility. However, much of it is marked by two interrelated tropes. First, the old country/city dichotomy is never far away, even if it has been problematized by issues of class, and has been recast in terms of social status with the urban disadvantaged standing in for the rural as the authentic Irish. By celebrating the sense of community within the urban working class, parallels can be made to the putative authentic, earthy life in the Irish countryside. Simultaneously, the ideological "outing" of certain categories of Dubliners as non-Irish has been evident in newspaper columns by social commentators who, by using the "Dublin 4" metaphor (a derogatory reference to a largely wealthy district on the city's south side), have sought to denigrate bourgeois influence in society, and to suggest that *nouveau riche* types, characterized as Europeans, are cut off from true Irishness by virtue of their materialism, and are, in effect, the new Anglo-Irish Ascendancy.[11] The clear implication is that the "authentic" experience of the city is now anchored in the working class, or even amongst recent rural migrants to the city (though many of those, ironically enough, choose to live in Dublin 4). Because of the pressure on the city's housing stock due to the rapid population expansion, people on low incomes are moving to country towns (and cheaper houses) but continuing to work in Dublin, or are being encouraged to resettle in sometimes remote rural areas as a means of reversing the hemorrhage of people from the countryside. This amounts to a reformulation of the traditional urban/rural dichotomy, with working-class culture contrasted with middle-class materialism and social alienation.

Secondly, there continues to be a relative lack of "tangible imagery" of Dublin, or, more correctly, contemporary Dublin, which is in "any real sense distinctive."[12] As Colm Lincoln and others have noted, Roddy Doyle's fictional northside Dublin suburb of Barrytown – made famous in his series of novels (and their film adaptations) including *The Commitments* (Alan Parker, 1991), *The Snapper* (Stephen Frears, 1993), and *The Van* (Stephen Frears, 1996) – lacks "particularity."[13] There is an unremarkableness of place; his suburbia is devoid of history or memory, and it displays the sameness and oneness with other nameless modern working-class estates anywhere else in Europe or, indeed, further afield. But then, as Lincoln states, it is "the people and their sense of community" which constitute place.[14] By concentrating on community and family, the *real* Ireland, at least at the visual or cinematic level, continues to be located in the landscapes of the West and in the rural way of life. As such, foreign films like *This is My Father* (Paul Quinn, 1998) continue an earlier tradition in defining Ireland as rural in opposition to urban America.

The situation in indigenous Irish films is more mixed. The fledgling film industry was a beneficiary of the modernizing and industrializing process of the 1960s, and by the late 1970s films set in Dublin were occasionally produced by Irish filmmakers.[15] The first of these was Joe Comerford's loosely-constructed narrative about five teenage boys, *Down the Corner* (1977), which was set in the West Dublin working-class community of Ballyfermot. (His later film about drug abuse and mental illness, *Withdrawal* (1982), was also based in Dublin.) Likewise, another independent filmmaker, Cathal Black, has explored the darker side of Dublin in *Pigs* (1984). Located in a decaying Dublin Georgian house which is taken over as a squat (symbolically representing the decline of the Anglo-Irish Ascendancy), *Pigs* concerns a disparate group of outsiders, at the margins of urban life: a gay man separated from his wife, a schizophrenic, a prostitute and her black pimp, a disheveled ex-businessman and a drug dealer. However, when compared to representations in many later films, these transients, victims of a newly urbanized Ireland who are seeking emotional or physical stability, are anchored within the street life of the city.

Later in the 1980s came the film which placed Ireland on the international commercial cinema map, the social-realist biography *My Left Foot* (Jim Sheridan, 1989). It tells the real-life story from childhood to adulthood of Christy Brown, a Dublin working-class writer and artist suffering from cerebral palsy who, with the help of his mother (like a Sean O'Casey heroine, she is the long-suffering bedrock of the family), overcomes adversity and finds artistic and personal fulfillment. Despite an uplifting narrative, cast within the affirmative Hollywood mode, the images which predominate are of oppression and poverty, with, again, the middle classes as somewhat less than "real." By contrast, Roddy Doyle's work, notwithstanding a similar interest in working-class existence, is ultimately celebratory. His highly successful novels and their screen adaptations are marked by a modern secular humanism and display a sense of exuberance and pleasure, and delight in their Irishness (if not through place, then through language).

A feature of many Irish urban films is the way in which the rural impinges on the (ubiquitous) working-class community. This is comically seen in the opening of *Into the West* (Mike Newell, 1992), when two boys of a settled traveler family maneuver their horse into the lift of a tower-block of flats in Dublin's northside suburb of Ballymun, in an attempt to bring it into their home.[16] The film, unsurprisingly, ends in the mythic West, even if the boys, following a night in a cinema, are confused as to whether they are Cowboys or Indians. Other films, though less self-consciously, also display this eruption or call of the rural: *Down the Corner* has a key scene played out in an orchard, while *Angela's Ashes*, which is otherwise a grim wallowing in its own representational mire, finds momentary release in the countryside through the walks of father and son, and a fishing expedition by the young Frank and his friend Paddy. One of the images through which the rural and urban have mingled since the 1980s has been that of "urban cowboys" – working-class youths who ride horses bareback through the city's streets. These frequently carry the representational burden of the rural and appear in films as various as the gritty urban drama *Pigs* and the "rags-to-rags" musical *The Commitments*. What is suggested by the image of the urban cowboy is that these youths are outsiders in a concrete jungle and can only achieve authenticity by connecting with their collective rural roots. Indeed, an exhibition and book of photographs by Perry Ogden, *Pony Kids,* starkly demonstrates how these boys can be romanticized.[17] In every case, the boys and their horses are photographed against a neutral white background, with no sense of Dublin or their local environment.[18] One exception to using the trope of the "urban cowboy" as local color is in the modestly-budgeted *Crush Proof* (Paul Tickell, 1999), whose strange mixture of reality and fantasy refuses the romantic clichés of earlier representations and focuses on a teenage gang of horse owners who are pursued by the police.

The version of the rural landscape shot by contemporary Irish filmmakers as they try to challenge the power of the pastoral tradition in Ireland belies the ambition to revisualize the countryside. Many recent films are anchored within a literary tradition of the most stringent kind and are overburdened with speech. The search for a new visual landscape is often half-hearted as it entails a rejection of the standard cultural heritage of Ireland (the landscape of the West) without supplying a viable alternative. Occasionally this act of rejection subverts the earlier tradition of valorizing Ireland as rural, as in films as various as the biker-comedy *Eat the Peach* (Peter Ormrod, 1986) and the generic rip-off crime drama *I Went Down* (Paddy Breathnach, 1997). But even where the Irish city provides the setting – as it does in the latter film – there is a failure to radically revisualize it.

One strategy adopted by Irish and other European filmmakers to counter the dominance of the rural cultural tradition, as well as to compete with American cinema, has been to adapt commercially successful American urban genres to fit the local experience. Exemplary is *The Courier* (Joe Lee/ Frank Deasy, 1988), which was the first indigenous Irish film to represent an Irish city within the generic conventions of Hollywood – specifically the vigilante revenge film. However, *The Courier* was unable to overcome the visual handicap of the modest scale of Irish cityscapes and thus could not provide the same resonances for audiences as its American models. In the face of the powerful urban iconography to which all cinema audiences are accustomed, two recent urban crime dramas – both based on the life of real Dublin gangster Martin Cahill – have devised different strategies. John Boorman has tried to create visually, through black-and-white stock, a more dreamlike vision of Dublin in *The General* (1998), while Thaddeus O'Sullivan's *Ordinary Decent Criminal* (2000) photographs the city at a fast pace to produce a slick, smooth, and witty film which reimagines Dublin as a city of interesting buildings, streets, and people.[19]

While the office in *The Courier* is set at the top of Liberty Hall, still Dublin's tallest building at almost 200 feet, today in Dublin, developers are planning to transform the skyline and the overall relationship of scale of people to buildings – as part of a process through which New York, Chicago, and Los Angeles passed many years ago. (Ironically, Liberty Hall is not the headquarters of a financial institution but of the country's largest trade union, SIPTU, occupying the site from which the Citizens' Army marched to the General Post Office to commence the Easter Rising of 1916.) Developments in the adjacent International Financial Services Center (IFSC) have brought Dublin well within the orbit of global financial market trends. Within a few years, Ireland may have much taller structures if a planned Conference Center project on the North Quays is completed, with office buildings up to 445 feet high. These buildings, like the existing IFSC nearby and similar temples of international finance from Los Angeles to Hong Kong, will no doubt be insulated from the hordes of the working class on their doorstep through high walls, security gates, and mirrored glass.[20] Dublin will perhaps finally get the cityscape that the American urban crime drama has always required it to have.

The recent television police series, *Making the Cut* (1997) and its sequel *DDU* ("District Detective Unit", 1999), set in the city of Waterford, help to illustrate how these developments in finance, and in the economy more generally since the mid-1980s, may be affecting representations of Ireland. It seems fair to suggest that some decision must have been made in making the series to ensure that the city was not recognizably Irish. (It is important to note that British directors were employed.) Little use was made of the specifically local so that the represented version of the city need not be received as uniquely Irish but might function as yet another anonymous location. This issue of "the local," unfortunately, has yet to be fully confronted by Irish filmmakers and by the Irish film industry which, although it has made huge strides during the 1990s in terms of production values, remains primarily concerned with the global audiovisual market, the cultural equivalent of the IFSC.

It may be argued that Irish film producers are trying to achieve what Hollywood has so successfully done since the 1910s: the creation of a narrative with global appeal. Despite its occasional efforts to put a local view on the screen, indigenous Irish cinema, like much of European cinema, has had no sustained answer to the power of Hollywood. As a result, between 80 and 90 percent of the films shown on Irish cinema screens have been American. It is this cinema, and not an Irish one, which has formed the imaginary for generations of Irish audiences. The fact is that more contemporary Irish filmmakers are now embracing, rather than challenging or modifying, the formats of the Hollywood film. Perhaps we have to accept, as Fredric Jameson has observed, that all an indigenous commercial cinema can ever become is a variant of the dominant American form.[21]

Notes

1 Raymond Williams, *The Country and the City* (London: The Hogarth Press, 1985 (1973)).

2 Quoted in Colm Lincoln, "City of Culture: Dublin and the Discovery of Urban Heritage," in Barbara O'Connor and Michael Cronin (eds.), *Tourism in Ireland: A Critical Analysis* (Cork: Cork University Press, 1993), p. 205.

3 Here I have in mind Gibbons's provocative question, "In a culture traumatized by a profound sense of catastrophe, such as Ireland experienced as late as the Great Famine, is there really any need to await the importation of modernism to blast open the continuum of history?" See Luke Gibbons, "Montage, Modernism and the City," in *Transformations in Irish Culture* (Cork: Cork University Press, 1996), p. 167.

4 Ben Singer, "Modernity, Hyperstimulus, and the Rise of Popular Sensationalism," in Leo Charney and Vanessa R. Schwartz (eds.), *Cinema and the Invention of Modern Life* (Berkeley: University of California Press), 1995, p. 75 ff.

5 See Luke Gibbons, "Romanticism, Realism and Irish Cinema," in Kevin Rockett, Luke Gibbons, and John Hill, *Cinema and Ireland* (London: Croom Helm, 1987; 2nd ed. London: Routledge, 1988).

6 John Hill, "Images of Violence," in Rockett et al., *Cinema and Ireland*, p. 237.

7 Film Censor's Reject No. 284, 18 March 1930, National Archives, Dublin. While Ford's version of the novel was also banned by Montgomery, the Censorship of Films Appeal Board passed it for public exhibition.

8 For details of these films see Kevin Rockett, *The Irish Filmography* (Dublin: Red Mountain Media, 1996).

9 A study by the author of Irish film censorship will be published in 2001, entitled *The Los Angelesation of Ireland*.

10 Film Censor's Decisions Reserved, No. 4169, 27 January 1939, National Archives, Dublin.

11 When the first major campaign to save Georgian Dublin was undertaken in 1969 by students who occupied buildings at Hume Street due for demolition, a government minister, Kevin Boland, justified the redevelopment by claiming that such buildings were an expendable leftover of an arrogant and alien ruling class. (See Lincoln, "City of Culture," p. 212).

12 Ibid., p. 219.

13 Ibid., p. 211.

14 Ibid., p. 219.

15 For the history of Irish film production and of representations of the Irish in the cinema see Rockett et al., *Cinema and Ireland*.

16 The term "traveler" refers to a nomadic, gypsy-like, minority population native to Ireland who live partly within and partly outside of the majority, "settled" population of the country.

17 Perry Ogden, *Pony Kids* (London: Jonathan Cape, 1999).

18 For a broader sociological discussion of these photographs see Fintan O'Toole's introduction to Ogden, *Pony Kids*. In his review of the book, Liam Fay cynically remarked that "you know a country is truly rich when photographers produce swish coffee-table books about its underclass." He went on to say, in a comment with which Walter Benjamin would agree, that "removed from their messy, unphotogenic surroundings, the pony kids are intended to appear ethereal, majestic, heroic. Noble savages." This "hopelessly romantic notion . . . is precisely the kind of syrup-hearted, starry-eyed project one would expect from the world of fashion photography," a career Ogden had prior to shooting the "urban cowboys" (Liam Fay, *Sunday Times*, 14 February 1999).

19 In some territories, *The General* was released in a color version.

20 During his presentation to the public inquiry into the proposed scheme, the project's architect, Irish-born but American-based Kevin Roche, described the Spencer Dock development as perfectly appropriate to Dublin's emergence as a node in the circuit of global capital. His intention was to create an international center that would "reflect the character of the new Ireland" and its recent boom in financial services, high-technology, and communications. See Frank McDonald, *Irish Times*, 10 March 2000, p. 6.

21 Fredric Jameson, "Is National Cinema Possible? Remaking the Rules of the Game," conference keynote address to *Projecting the Nation: National Cinema in an International Frame*, Film Institute of Ireland, 15 November 1996.

Part 4

Urban Reactions on Screen

Part 4 returns from urban identity, social crisis, and cinematic production in the postcolonial world to discuss reactions to urban crisis in two paradigmatic former imperial centers – London and Paris. It examines social crisis in these cities in terms of a variety of problems and reactions: utopian projects of postwar urban reconstruction; urban alienation in late Thatcherite Britain; utopian critiques of modernization and corporatization; and the urban–suburban dichotomy as an allegory of the earlier relationship of imperial center to colony.

In the first section, "Idealism and Defeat," Leo Enticknap's chapter "Postwar Urban Redevelopment, the British Film Industry, and *The Way We Live*" examines the production and reception of the 1946 documentary *The Way We Live* as an articulation of the popularization of issues of urban planning and housing development in Britain in the immediate aftermath of World War Two, in opposition to the visionary elitism of prewar urban planning and welfare policies and their expression in the work of the Documentary Film Movement. Mike Mason, in his chapter, "*Naked*: Social Realism and the Urban Wasteland," examines the individual's experience of anonymity, disenfranchisement, and homelessness in contemporary London through the social realism of the film *Naked* (1993) and in opposition to official projections of London as a global, cosmopolitan capital of culture, finance, and material affluence.

In the second section, "Escape and Invasion," Laurent Marie's chapter "Jacques Tati's *Play Time* as New Babylon" draws parallels between the modernist subversion of the French Fifth Republic and bourgeois hegemony in Paris by the agendas of the filmmaker Jacques Tati, the utopian urban planner and architect Constant, and the Situationist International. Adrian Fielder, in "Poaching on Public Space: Urban Autonomous Zones in French *Banlieue* Films," describes the subordination of the suburbs (*banlieues*) of Paris to its city center as an allegorization of the former colonial relationship between France/Paris and its colonies, arguing that recent French youth culture and cinema have revealed the ways in which the class and racial power structures of contemporary France are embedded in the geographical layout of the city.

Idealism and Defeat

19

Postwar Urban Redevelopment, the British Film Industry, and *The Way We Live*

Leo Enticknap

Introduction

In August 1946 a controversial and highly publicized debate took place concerning the social and ethical responsibilities of the British film industry in a peacetime context. The immediate cause of this controversy was somewhat unexpected. That summer, C. A. Lejeune, the film critic of the *Observer*, had begun a campaign intended to draw attention to her belief that the Rank Organization, the largest and most economically dominant distribution outlet then operating in the UK, had decided to abandon the release of a "B"-feature documentary on the grounds that it was likely to prove a box-office failure.[1] The film in question was *The Way We Live* (Jill Craigie, 1946), a dramatized exposition of a town planner's proposal to rebuild the blitzed city center of Plymouth.

Unlike most examples of its genre from this period, *The Way We Live* was not a low-key educational film, produced with taxpayers' money or industrial sponsorship and destined to be shown in classrooms and church halls. It was made with a budget of £40,000 (over twice the average for a feature-length documentary in those days) by Two Cities, another Rank subsidiary which had acquired a reputation for expensive propaganda blockbusters, notably *In Which We Serve* (Noel Coward and David Lean, 1942) and *Henry V* (Laurence Olivier, 1944).[2] The idea of a major, commercial film industry conglomerate producing a documentary about town planning was surprising at the time, and the film remains a unique project in the history of the Rank Organization. More importantly, *The Way We Live* reveals a lot about the nature of and the extent to which the subject it dealt with had become an issue for widespread public debate. The aim of this chapter, therefore, is to examine how the film articulates this debate, to place it in the context of certain important British fiction and nonfiction films dealing with similar issues and to consider whether its unusual (that is, commercial) provenance has any significant bearing on the ideas and arguments it offers.

To begin with, I examine the background to *The Way We Live* in the context of debates about planning during the 1930s and World War Two, and the ways in which they were examined in documentary cinema. I then examine the ideological arguments put forward by *The Way We Live* in the wider context of this background and of the film's industrial provenance, and argue that the film can be seen as the logical culmination of these debates and issues. In conclusion, I suggest that, in the light of the political and ideological issues raised by the film, *The Way We Live* offers a hitherto neglected insight into an important aspect of British politics and society as they affected attitudes toward urban regeneration at the end of World War Two.

Documentary Film and Town Planning

A surprising number of films dealing with urban planning were produced in Britain during the 1930s and 1940s. Interestingly, none seems to have been made during the silent period and very few appeared from the 1950s onwards. Nicholas Pronay and Frances Thorpe's annotated catalogue of government films made during the war lists no less than fifty-four nonfiction films financed by the British taxpayer on this subject, which for Nicholas Bullock constitute "a remarkable testament to the vitality of the discussion and the hopes for reconstruction."[3] Even that figure does not take into account any of the numerous films produced during the 1930s and after the war which address this issue, and non-government productions from the war period itself (for example, fiction films and commercial newsreels).

The idea of "planning" as a means of formulating policy for developing urban and rural communities initially came to prominence in the early 1930s, as did the British documentary film movement. These facts provide a possible reason for the absence of films about planning before this point, and are also connected in terms of the ideological agenda associated with both projects. The town planners and the documentary filmmakers were both motivated by public service imperatives, and as such argued for state intervention in activities that had traditionally been left to the private sector.

Although the Town and Country Planning Association was formed in the early years of the century and promoted a great deal of academic research on the subject, it was not until the 1930s that, in Paul Addison's words, "it first began to influence Government policy in favor of planning the environment."[4] There were two key developments which enabled this to happen. The first was the 1932 Town and Country Planning Act, which enabled local authorities to formulate systematic policies of land use in areas under their jurisdiction. While this approach was politically unprecedented, the planning movement believed that the legislation did not go far enough: two major drawbacks were that it was local rather than national in scope, and that the act's provisions were permissive only and did not enable authorities to overrule existing decisions.[5] The second development was the appointment of a Royal Commission under Sir Montague Barlow, charged with investigating the "distribution of the industrial population," which heard a considerable amount of evidence from the Town and Country Planning Association. Although the immediate context of the report (published in 1940) was defense-related, Barlow recommended that central government should be responsible for planning land use on a national basis, thus boosting the political standing of the town planners.[6] Both as a result of these recommendations and in the light of the realization that war damage would necessitate urban reconstruction on a huge scale, a further commission was set up in January 1941 "to advise, as a matter of urgency, what steps should be taken now or before the end of the War to prevent the work of reconstruction thereafter being prejudiced."[7] The result was the Uthwatt Report, published in September 1942, which recommended that a central planning authority be established in order to oversee the postwar reconstruction program, and that it should have the right to compulsorily purchase land from private owners where necessary.[8] Town planning, therefore, had gone from being an obscure area of academic research to a key element of government policy in the space of a decade.

The growth of the documentary film movement in Britain followed an almost identical trajectory. Although commercially produced newsreels were an established sector of the film industry since before World War One, it was not until 1928 that the Empire Marketing Board formed a film unit (renamed the GPO Film Unit in 1933 and the Crown Film Unit in 1940) intended to produce nonfiction films with a public service agenda.[9] This provided the institutional base for the documentary movement (whose activists also made a small number of films through film industry and other private sponsorship) and its profile grew steadily during the 1930s. But before the outbreak of World War Two, the scope of government film production and the extent of its distribution were restricted by a lack of political impetus: it wasn't until the 1940s that the documentary movement was able to make its voice heard on a national scale and in films that were seen by a significant number of people. As Harry Watt, a prominent documentary director who subsequently established a career at Ealing Studios, recalled in his autobiography, "war was our bonus."[10]

One of the key players in the planning movement before the war was Leslie Patrick Abercrombie, Professor of Civic Design at the University of Liverpool from 1915 to 1935. Abercrombie was subsequently involved in the reconstruction of several blitzed cities – notably London, Coventry, and Plymouth – and also appeared in a number of films on the subject, including *The Way We Live.*[11] The self-styled leader of the documentary movement was John Grierson, an academic who had developed an interest in the reception of mainstream cinema during a period as a research student at the University of Chicago in the 1920s. Upon his return to the UK he campaigned for the establishment of a government film production unit, arguing that the cinema had a potential role to play in education and public information. This, he argued, could not be effectively realized if the medium were left to what he termed the "Woolworth intentions" of the commercial film industry.[12] Abercrombie and Grierson shared the common belief that public-service imperatives were ideologically preferable to private-sector ones, and that centralized policymaking could offset the negative effects of unregulated capitalism.

Given the parallel evolution of the urban planning and documentary film movements, it is hardly surprising that a number of notable documentaries were made about planning and urban regeneration during the 1930s, and still more during the war. Perhaps the best known from the prewar period is *Housing Problems* (Edgar Anstey, 1935), in which an inhabitant of an East London slum tenement describes the unhealthy conditions in her flat.[13] The film condemned the legacy of late Victorian capitalism in creating substandard housing for the working class, and compared the case study in the opening sequence with the modern multistory housing developments which formed the linchpin of the London County Council's slum clearance policy. Similar arguments can be found in other documentaries from the 1930s – notably *New Worlds for Old* (Paul Rotha and Frank Sainsbury, 1938) and *The City* (Alberto Cavalcanti, 1939). These films tended to present the ideas of slum clearance and planning as the product of scientific research, a solution to social problems devised by superior intellects who had a moral right to impose their technologies on the population in pursuit of the greater good. Planners such as the council official in *Housing Problems* and Sir Charles Bressey (an architect and prominent member of the Town and Country Planning Association) in *The City* were shown as implementing "rational philosophy and the socially redeeming virtues of science and technology to cure the problems of society."[14]

Interestingly, these ideas were also explored to some extent in British fiction films from the 1930s and the war period. In *The Tunnel* (Maurice Elvey, 1935), a visionary engineer argues in favor of tunneling across the Atlantic on the grounds that it would promote egalitarianism and international understanding, whilst *Things to Come* (William Cameron Menzies, 1936) describes the reconstruction of a fictional postwar city by a technocraticallyled government: as Jeffrey Richards put it, the creation of "a de-individual-ized, scientific super-state."[15] In addition to fifty-four government documen-taries, a small number of wartime fiction films addressed the issue, notably Basil Dearden's adaptation of the J. B. Priestley play *They Came to a City* (1944), which was rashly described by a National Film Archive cataloguer as "the first attempt to carry out socialist propaganda in the British feature film."[16] This body of films tends to undermine Geoffrey Macnab's assertion that "there was little evidence that enthusiasm for town planning extended to the cinema," although it is worth noting that the bulk of this output was in nontheatrical shorts and Ministry of Information (MOI) monthly releases, not commercially distributed, feature-length productions.[17]

World War Two enhanced the political standing of the town planners and the documentary movement, as both groups found themselves assimilated into the apparatus of government at a much higher level than in the 1930s. As the institutional status of these groups underwent change, so did the arguments being put forward in films about planning. A far greater propor-tion of the public now found itself directly affected by national and interna-tional politics through activities such as Air Raid Protection duty, women working in munitions factories and, of course, compulsory national service. The Army Bureau of Current Affairs (ABCA) held regular lectures and seminars on political issues (including town planning), and after the war it was blamed by the Conservatives for contributing to Labour's landslide vic-tory in the 1945 general election by "spreading socialism in the ranks." As one Army officer observed, "in fifteen months in the ranks I never heard politics mentioned – but [now] the ABCA teaches them that something is wrong and that change is needed. They'll vote Labour, though they couldn't give you the names of three Labour politicians."[18]

Following the winter of 1942, when the victory at El Alamein and the publication of the Uthwatt Report and the Beveridge Report (which pro-posed the establishment of the Welfare State) had shifted public attention toward peacetime and reconstruction, the notion of planning captured the imagination of the population and of filmmakers on a hitherto unprecedented scale. The radical press, led by the *Daily Mirror* and the *Picture Post*, continued to explore the idea in considerable depth, so much so that by the 1945 general election, planning had become an important element of Labour's manifesto.

The Way We Live, the Planning Debate, and the British Film Industry

At first sight, *The Way We Live* seems an atypical example of the genre I have identified in the section above because it was not a product of the documentary movement, but rather of the commercial film industry. As noted above, it was financed by the Rank Organization (then the UK's largest film industry conglomerate, which by the end of the war controlled a third of British cinemas and two-thirds of the UK's production, post-production, and distribution infrastructure) and produced on a relatively high budget by Two Cities, a company well known for high-profile propaganda epics such as *In Which We Serve* and *Henry V*. It is, therefore, rather surprising that the film was researched, written, and directed by a twenty-eight-year-old, Jill Craigie, whose only previous credit was for a three-reel short about Henry Moore and the Blitz (*Out of Chaos*, 1943). Interestingly, the release of *The Way We Live* precipitated a controversy over Rank's apparent reluctance to release the completed film, allegedly because J. Arthur Rank, the owner and chairman of the Rank Organization, feared it would prove unpopular at the box office. (One reviewer commented cynically that "it deals with town planning and is deficient in sex.")[19] However, this issue falls beyond the scope of this chapter.[20]

The film is effectively a dramatized exposition of the Watson–Abercrombie plan for the reconstruction of Plymouth following the Blitz, built around a narrative of a journalist (played by Peter Willes, a moderately well-known character actor of the period) visiting the derelict city to research a newspaper article.[21] This character acts as a conduit through which Abercrombie and the non-professional cast (Plymouth citizens playing themselves) are introduced. A series of scenes describes the shortcomings of interwar housing estates, argues that the Blitz provided an opportunity to wipe the slate clean (literally, in many cases), and goes on to detail Abercrombie's proposals for rebuilding the city center and its outlying environs. *The Way We Live* adopts many of the conventions of a fictional narrative: in a prologue sequence, Willes is seen reading a Ministry of Information poster in Trafalgar Square which quotes King George VI declaring that "the time of destruction is ended, the era of reconstruction begins" and then noticing some books on town planning in a shop window. This prologue provides a clear cause-and-effect scenario, whose aim is to discover how town planning works and its relevance to the spectator. It is followed through by Craigie's casting of an allegedly typical Plymouth family (who were actually played by unrelated Plymouthians chosen through auditions and screen tests), and a series of scenes in which they are shown having to cope with overcrowded housing, derelict and vandalized residential areas, insufficient transport, and a lack of civic amenities.[22]

As the film progresses, scenes illustrating domestic and social problems caused by what the film argues are unplanned interwar housing developments are followed by a description of Abercrombie's plan and a discussion of its likely reception by the people it will affect. A public meeting is shown in which Abercrombie details his proposals and invites responses from the floor. Negative as well as positive reactions are shown: in a montage comprising brief responses from various sections of the community, landowners voice fears that they will lose out by having their property compulsorily purchased by the City Council, while an elderly shopkeeper points out that the City Fathers fought for a freehold system and that the imposition of ninety-nine-year leases on the business and fishing communities would be fundamentally undemocratic.

Set against this, the film repeatedly puts forward the argument that Abercrombie's plan can be seen as an expression of public opinion, emphasizing better living conditions, increased employment, and a revitalized local economy – in short, the creation of a land fit for heroes, but also objectives which the plan can realistically be expected to deliver. In the other major scene featuring Abercrombie, he is seen wandering about the Barbican (the street through the fishing wharves leading to the Mayflower Steps – the only area of central Plymouth left virtually intact after the bombing), pointing out the surviving landmarks. Stressing that his plan for the future must not abandon all links with the past, he assures viewers that those buildings will be retained, "but in the new plan we must not copy them." There then follows a traveling matte sequence in which Abercrombie explains how the new will interact with the old, as architects' drawings are superimposed against the buildings behind him.[23] Scenes are also included of Lord Astor arguing for the plan in Parliament, and of Michael Foot (whom Craigie later married) campaigning in the 1945 general election on the strength of it.

The image of the town planner put forward in *The Way We Live* marks a profound change from that which is presented in 1930s films dealing with the subject. Before the war, planners were depicted as scientist-dictators who were justified in imposing the "de-individualized scientific super-state" of *Things to Come* on the population by virtue of their perceived ability to enhance society.[24] No one at the time, it would seem, seriously questioned the wisdom of their intentions. By the war and its immediate aftermath, the concept of planning had become related to popular opinion and the idea of effecting change according to democratic forces – hence scenes of Abercrombie taking questions at a public meeting and the emphasis on integrating continuity and change.

John R. Gold and Steven V. Ward read these scenes rather differently, noting that the Barbican sequence actually featured designs which Abercrombie had recycled from other projects, and arguing that the public meeting was really intended to convert the uneducated masses rather than generate any meaningful democratic debate, as an exercise in which "doubters are still heard and some of the audience remain confused, but the visionary emerges unbowed."[25] Even if we accept this reading, it remains that the film as a whole was scripted around the idea of planning as an interactive process, driven primarily by the needs of the communities being planned for. A convincing demonstration of this can be found in the closing shots, which show a protest march of Plymouth citizens demanding that the plan be put into action.

The public image of plans and planners, therefore, had undergone considerable change during the war, as had the documentary film. Whereas during the 1930s it had been dominated by Grierson's beliefs, characterized by the fusion of propaganda, education, and the voice of an omnipotent government, the war had forced documentary filmmakers to acknowledge the preferences of cinemagoers, as defined by the commercial performance of films in the distribution and exhibition markets. Thus *The Way We Live*, drawing both on 1930s and wartime influences, offers a complex and intricate combination of the social and political issues involved in the planning debate, and aspects of mainstream cinema (the character development of Willes and the non-professional players, studio aesthetics such as 35mm cinematography and a full orchestral score) which had been found necessary if documentaries were to compete alongside fiction films. The effectiveness with which *The Way We*

Figure 19.1 The closing sequence of *The Way We Live* (*Courtesy BFI Stills Library*)

Live embodies this process of change, both in form and in content, indicates the extent to which the ideas dealt with by the film had come to be accepted by the public at large and the importance with which they were regarded.

Conclusion

Town planning had previously been the subject of a considerable number of films during the 1930s and the war, but, in contrast to *The Way We Live*, their motivation was primarily ideological and they were made primarily in the state sector. A likely reason for this is that the documentary movement and the planning movement shared a very similar background and objectives. *The Way We Live* was a product of the entertainment film industry, which can be seen in the subjective nature of its arguments. Rather than advocating the benefits of a planned society as objective scientific realities in the way that the 1930s planning films tended to, Craigie uses fictional characters to show how Abercrombie"s proposals would improve the quality of life for Plymouth's inhabitants. This is not only consistent with *The Way We Live* having been made by a feature-film studio, but also with the social conditions of World War Two having democratized the notion and public image of planners and planning.

Nevertheless, the ideological reputation of the documentary movement seems to have weighed heavily on the film industry's preconceptions of what would and would not sell to the public, which in turn gave the Rank Organization cold feet when it came to the film's eventual release. Jill Craigie was clearly disillusioned by the experience of working with Rank, concluding that the short-term financial advantages were more than offset by the film industry's lack of commitment to documentaries. In December 1948 she asserted that "film producers who depend directly or indirectly on money from the big distribution organizations cannot be called independent."[26] However, the hybrid nature of *The Way We Live* (and the fact that it has been largely neglected by recent research) makes it a unique and valuable film for historians working fifty years after the event, throwing new light on the popular image of an important element of the postwar reconstruction program and on the work of a number of different elements in Britain's film industry and culture.

Notes

1   C. A. Lejeune, review of *The Way We Live*, in the *Observer*, 28 July 1946.
2   The *Daily Express*, in stories published on 9 July 1946 and 28 July 1946, gives the figure of £40,000; the trade publication *Kinematograph Weekly* estimates that the budget must have been nearer £60,000 (22 August 1946, p. 5).
3   Nicholas Pronay and Frances Thorpe, *British Official Films of the Second World War*

(Oxford: Clio Press, 1980), *passim*; Nicholas Bullock, "Imagining the Postwar World: Architecture, Reconstruction and the British Documentary Film Movement," in François Penz and Maureen Thomas (eds.), *Cinema and Architecture* (London: BFI, 1998), p. 55.

4 Paul Addison, *The Road to 1945: British Politics and the Second World War* (London: Pimlico, 1994, 2nd ed.), p. 42.

5 G. M. Young, *Country and Town: A Summary of the Scott and Uthwatt Reports* (Harmondsworth: Penguin Books, 1943), p. 89.

6 Parliamentary Papers, 1939–40: *Report of the Royal Commission on the Distribution of the Industrial Population* (1940), Cmd. 6153, para. 49, p. 204.

7 Young, *Country and Town*, p. 86.

8 Parliamentary Papers, 1942–3: *Report of the Committee on Compensation and Betterment* (1942), Cmd. 6386.

9 For more on the Empire Marketing Board Film Unit, see Ian Aitken, *Film and Reform* (London: Routledge, 1990).

10 Harry Watt, *Don't Look at the Camera* (London: Elek, 1974), p. 186.

11 For a discussion of Abercrombie's film appearances, see John R. Gold and Stephen V. Ward, "Of Plans and Planners: Documentary Film and the Challenge of the Urban Future, 1935–52," in David B. Clarke (ed.), *The Cinematic City* (London: Routledge, 1997), pp. 73–7.

12 H. Forsyth Hardy (ed.), *Grierson on Documentary* (London: Collins, 1946), p. 80.

13 An indication of the film's enduring reputation can be found in a satirical adaptation, the animated short *Creature Comforts* (Nick Park, 1991) in which zoo animals complain about the uncomfortable conditions in their cages.

14 Gold and Ward, "Of Plans and Planners," p. 66.

15 Jeffrey Richards, *The Age of the Dream Palace: Cinema and Society in Britain, 1930–1939* (London: Routledge & Kegan Paul, 1984), p. 283.

16 Quoted in Charles Barr, *Ealing Studios* (London: Studio Vista, 1993, 2nd ed.), p. 195. For a comprehensive analysis of the fiction films dealing with reconstruction, see James Chapman, "Brave New World? The Projection of Peace Aims in the British Cinema, 1939–45," MA dissertation, University of East Anglia, 1992.

17 Geoffrey Macnab, *J. Arthur Rank and the British Film Industry* (London and New York: Routledge, 1993), p. 158.

18 James Lansdale Hodson, *The Sea and the Land* (London: Victor Gollancz, 1945), p. 349.

19 Paul Holt, *Daily Express*, 26 July 1946.

20 For a full discussion of this controversy, see Leo Enticknap, "The Non-Fiction Film in Britain, 1945–51," Ph.D. thesis, University of Exeter, 1999, chapter 4.

21 James Paton-Watson and Patrick Abercrombie, *A Plan for Plymouth* (Plymouth: Underhill, 1943).

22 William MacQuitty states that Plymouth was not the original choice for the film's location: the initial idea came from Craigie and Sir Charles Reilly, based on his plan for Birkenhead, but Plymouth was eventually chosen after location scouting from a shortlist of cities, including Hull and Coventry. See William MacQuitty, *A Life to Remember* (London: Quartet, 1991), pp. 297–8.

23 At the time *The Way We Live* was produced, this process, in which two or more shots are combined in a way that can take account of camera movements, was

a recently developed and costly optical effect; therefore, its use gives some indication of the budget expended on this film.

24 Richards, *The Age of the Dream Palace*, p. 283.
25 Gold and Ward, "Of Plans and Planners," p. 76.
26 *The Star*, 29 December 1948, p. 6.

20

Naked: Social Realism and the Urban Wasteland

Mike Mason

This chapter will focus on representations of the city offered in the film *Naked* (Mike Leigh, 1993), a film which utilizes aspects of London that are characterized by a sparse anonymity: demarcations between private and public spaces (usually signified by ownership and usage) are blurred. The indices of the capital, such as busy thoroughfares, familiar architectural landmarks, and other conventional cosmopolitan signifiers, are ignored in favor of deserted streets, obscure alleyways, and an empty office block. The main characters in the film inhabit either temporary dwellings (as caretakers for absentee owners) or the desolate spaces that Johnny, the central character, passes through during his "odyssey" in the city. Leigh's vision of the city is thus a partial construction designed to emphasize the fragmented social relationships of his characters and the poverty of their attempts at communication and interaction. Given the environment and conditions in which these must take place, the negative resolution of the narrative seems inevitable.

Of primary concern here are the ways in which *Naked* elaborates on a particular strand of narrative film often referred to, though not unproblematically, as "British social realism," and the way the film reiterates, through structural similarities, an inherent emphasis on causal links between economics, environment, and social behavior. In many ways this project seeks to support and add credence to John Hill's assertion that

> the ideas and attitudes expressed by the social problem film and the films of
> the British "new-wave" do not derive simply from the focus of their subject

matter but also from the deployment of certain types of conventions (in accordance with what an audience "accustomed" to the cinema expects) which, then, inevitably structure and constrain the way in which that subject-matter can be presented in the first place.[1]

To highlight the similarity of these "types of conventions" (but also crucial points of divergence) I want to draw parallels with representations of the urban landscape offered in earlier social-realist films. My aim is thus to illustrate how *Naked* forms part of a narrative intertext that utilizes established narrative codes and typically dialectic strategies to promote a critical discourse on the social conditions of urban existence which may superficially appear to be unified, but which actually embodies a plurality of perspectives.[2] What I am addressing here is how *Naked* promotes a selective construction of the city to further a particular discourse on the fragmentation of personal and communal identities and the coherent social relations that are assumed to follow from these. Through the selective use of locational and temporal zones in the film, emphasis is placed on the isolation and alienation of characters central to the narrative and, through this, typical themes concerning community and economics that may form a generic base for social realist narratives are given a particularly postmodern inflection.

The opening sequence of *Naked* satisfies the requirements of any film aiming to capture and sustain an audience's interest. The audience has an immediate indication of the identity and attitude of the central character (Johnny), the nature of the conflict that will motivate the plot and the backdrop against which this conflict will be played out. Within the first few minutes the main thematic concerns of the ensuing narrative are established. The spectator witnesses what appears to be an act of sexually motivated aggression carried out by Johnny on an unwilling woman in a deserted back alley. The architecture he passes as he makes his escape confirms that the alley is situated in a city. Following the threats visited on him by the assaulted woman, Johnny steals a car and heads for London, the destination of many other social-realist refugees before (and after) him: notably Cathy in *Cathy Come Home* (Ken Loach, 1966), Stephen in *Riff-Raff* (Ken Loach, 1990), and Renton in *Trainspotting* (Danny Boyle, 1996). Arriving in the capital he looks up a former girlfriend from Manchester, Louise, in the flat where she lives. He is welcomed by her flatmate Sophie and later embarks on an uneasy and aggressive sexual relationship with her (much to the annoyance of Louise). Tensions come to a head and he leaves to wander the streets of London. On his travels he encounters, separately, a homeless couple, Archie and Maggie; leaving them reunited he spends a philosophical night with Brian, a security guard, in the empty office block he is guarding. After attempting to seduce the object of Brian's voyeuristic desire in a dingy bedsit opposite the office building, Johnny takes up with an introverted young woman he encounters in the local café where she works. He takes a bath in the flat she is looking after but is eventually thrown out. Back on the streets, he scrounges a lift from a fly-poster but is dispatched with a kick when the man gets tired of Johnny's endless ranting. A gang of youths set on him in an alley and he eventually arrives back at Louise's, where his wounds are tended by Sandra, a nurse and the owner of the flat, who has returned from holiday in Africa. After vaguely agreeing to return to Manchester with Louise he pockets money left by Jeremy, a yuppie acquaintance of Sandra, and departs in a quiet moment to limp off to an unspecified future.

The sequences involving Johnny's lone odyssey in the capital provide the most crucial material in terms of Leigh's partial treatment of the city. Within this complex montage of sequences one of the key thematic strands, beyond Johnny's incapacity to connect with people, is that of possession and dispossession. The locational iconography in *Naked* supports this theme through the juxtaposition of the order and stability of the residential and mercantile areas of the city with a polluted and decaying urban wasteland. Relatively affluent exteriors and interiors are placed against and between the architectural poverty, squalor, and degradation of a domain hidden behind hoardings and shopfronts. The organizational and exploitative capabilities of those who own the former is set against the fragmented social interaction and impo-

Figure 20.1   Johnny's lone odyssey in the capital . . . (*Naked*) (*Courtesy of Thin Man Films Ltd*)

tence of those who inhabit the latter; in this way characteristic behavior is apparently linked to characteristic surroundings. Residential areas, when shown, are noticeably devoid of people. The hustle and bustle and to-ing and fro-ing associated with the capital city's inhabitants are reduced to an indifferent silence. All of the people in the more affluent sector with whom Johnny has extended dialogues carry out caretaker roles for absentee owners of the buildings they inhabit. The empowered are literally distanced, removed from the interpersonal battlefield with which Johnny engages.

The treatment of *mise-en-scène* used for the initial rape in the alley is mirrored toward the end of the film when Johnny receives his comeuppance from a gang of youths. In the prologue, Manchester is signified by claustrophobic, somber night shots of obscure alleys and narrow streets, providing a stark contrast to the spacious, daylit streets Johnny encounters on his arrival in London. The optimism intimated by this contrast is finally negated when he meets his nemesis through a beating that takes place in an alley as dismal as the one used to signify Manchester. What is important here is the irony set up by the intratextual relationship of event and location. Johnny receives the punishment he attempted to evade by fleeing to London in a location that has resonances of the place where he committed the original misdeed; an irony that doesn't escape commentary from Johnny toward the end of the film. As the following examples will illustrate, the use of back alleys and passages as settings for deviant action (invariably in night shots) forms a convention in social-realist film narrative that both mobilizes and reinforces dominant connotations of such spaces. A further crucial observation is that locations such as these provide anonymous transitional zones between the private domain of house and garden and the public areas of trade and transport; the actions that take place are not permissible in the domestic sphere of the family or the ordered and constrained arena of social interaction.

To understand the development of this convention requires a historical digression. The particular use of this type of location for scenes of violent beatings in other films with social-realist themes is typified in *Room at the Top* (Jack Clayton, 1958). Joe Lampton, the central character, is beaten up on a canal towpath, ostensibly for poaching someone else's girl but more acutely, in terms of the narrative thematic, for betraying Alice, his true love who has just previously met a solitary death in the car she was driving. This crucial death follows the announcement of his engagement to Susan Brown, the daughter of a wealthy and influential industrialist. In the final instance the beating can be read as punishment for the act of class betrayal signified by this engagement. The exchange of community that the act implies is marked in the scene that precedes and directly motivates the beating. In a pub situated in a working-class area he procures the attentions of a local girl by assuming the name and mannerisms of Jack Wales, his "middle-class" rival in the narrative. In doing so, he affirms his acceptance of the exchange and inevitable alienation from the environment and company he finds himself in. Equally, Frank Machin's fight with the rugby team captain in *This Sporting Life* (Lindsay Anderson, 1963) forms the crucial turning-point in his aspirations to become a professional rugby player and escape the daily oppression of the coal mine. During a gala ball celebrating the local rugby team's achievements he provokes the captain into a fight in an adjacent alley, hoping through this to attract the attention of the team's scouts – a strategy that immediately results in his recruitment to the team.

As these two examples illustrate, an essential narrative problematic in social-realist work is the central character's conflict of loyalties in relation to particular, clearly defined communities. Within the narrative structure of many British social-realist films, significant actions such as "the beating" or "the death" serve pivotal functions relating to the resolution of this problematic. Following an historical trajectory, many films evidence the influence of such structural strategies: for example, *The Loneliness of the Long Distance Runner* (Tony Richardson, 1962), *Scum* (Alan Clarke, 1979), *Riff-Raff* (Ken Loach, 1990), *Raining Stones* (Ken Loach, 1993), *Trainspotting* (Danny Boyle, 1996), and, most recently, *Nil by Mouth* (Gary Oldman, 1997).

Of course, there are many interesting parallels here with earlier American "social problem" films such as *On The Waterfront* (Elia Kazan, 1954), in which the central character, Terry, is caught between loyalties to Charlie, his brother who is a bookkeeper for "the mob," and Edie, his true love but also the sister of a man he helped to murder for the mob.[3] Terry is finally turned against the mob, and toward the interests of the honest but oppressed working-class community that Edie represents, when the mob kills his brother and leaves the body hanging on a meat-hook in a tenement alley for Terry to discover. The stylistic treatment of event and location in this American "social problem film" – using sparse, high-contrast lighting resonant of *film noir* to represent the city – compares clearly with the stylistic strategies of the above British social realism, while, on a formal level, we might also note the intertextual placing and significance of event (the death). Terry is lured from Edie's apartment into the same alley from which he earlier lured Edie's brother to *his* death: a locational link between crime and punishment reiterated forty years later in *Naked*.

In between the rape that opens *Naked* and the beating that precipitates the conclusion, we find similar and equally resonant treatments of location. Johnny encounters Maggie and Archie separately in one of the two busy thoroughfares depicted in the film. After meeting Maggie, Johnny is quickly drawn into the realm of the homeless, a realm presented as an extreme opposition to the bustling mercantile sector and the tranquil residential areas encountered up to this point in the film. Leigh's treatment of this area is, as with the alley, made significant though an excessive, non-naturalistic use of light that renders the squalor of the surroundings subservient to the kind of aesthetic considerations typical of its social-realist predecessors. Andrew Higson has noted that the city in *A Taste of Honey* (Tony Richardson, 1961) provides "the spectacular object of a diegetic and spectatorial gaze – something precisely "to-be-looked-at" – it is emptied of socio-historical signification in a process of romanticization, aestheticization (even humanization)."[4] Of John Grierson's Documentary Film Movement of the 1930s (often cited as the foundation on which the British New Wave was built), Brian Winston asserts that:

> The "movement" usually thus concentrates on surfaces, even while managing to run from the social meaning of those surfaces. Given the aesthetic preferences of these filmmakers, camera and editing style always tended to mannered composition and baroque image flow. . . . The slums are nearly always photographed in elegant compositions and become, in consequence, settings as exotic as the North West Territories or Samoa.[5]

In the first sequence in which Johnny and Maggie enter the location, arched recesses are illuminated from within to intensify both their architectural splendor and to trace a perspective orthogonal, followed through by a line of suspended lights to a vanishing point right of frame. The inferred spatial infinity is accentuated by Johnny and Maggie's movements to the foreground and augmented by a group of extras walking to the background along this diagonal axis. An additional burst of directed light, emanating off-screen right, picks out a ceiling of steel girders in *chiaroscuro* detail. Apart from the obvious connotations implied by the scale of these and similar artifacts that follow, the spectator is presented with an emphatic combination of architectural detail that, while implying railway viaducts and part-demolished warehouses, has resonances of a decayed Victorian neoclassicism defiled and rendered obsolete by the intrusion of postwar functionalist modernism. This comparison is made more blatant as the film progresses by the inclusion of Brian's office block. A pertinent parallel can be found in Derek Jarman's dystopian vision of an economically divided, post-Thatcherite London in *Last of England* (1987). Markedly similar aspects of *mise-en-scène* (delivered more persuasively on Jarman's materially downgraded film stock) include distressed brickwork, the selective use of light and smoke and, inevitably, graffiti. Together these produce what has become a typically postmodern cliché (certainly when augmented by one or two burnt-out cars) that features regularly in contemporary British film and television drama and provides a shorthand signification of urban decay and, as a seeming inevitability, the domain of the disempowered and usually criminal underclass.

This visual cliché has taken some time to establish its validity. A critical period in its emergence can be found in the British documentary movement from the late 1930s onwards: typical are Edgar Anstey's much-lauded documentary film *Housing Problems* (1935) and Humphrey Spender's photographic work in Bolton carried out under the auspices of Mass Observation.[6] Delving further into the past, we could also consider the pioneering documentary photography of Lewis Hine and Jacob Riis and their images of American urbanization from the beginning of the twentieth century.[7]

Returning to narrative fiction film and, specifically, social realism, some of the most potent renditions of the urban wasteland that have entered the vocabulary of cultural production can be found in the cinema and television films of Ken Loach. The most pertinent of these in terms of themes and use of location is *Cathy Come Home*, particularly where this deals with the regressive narrative spiral that Cathy and her family find themselves in. Through a series of misfortunes, precipitated by her husband's unemployment after an accident, they descend the housing ladder and are eventually split up, the film ending with Cathy's children being taken into care. Toward the end of their tortuous road, the penultimate stage of their degradation, before institutionalization, is set against the same ruinous backdrop still evident in *Naked* and *Last of England* some thirty years later. Before *Cathy Come Home* we find the urban wasteland cropping up wherever filmmakers need a definitive signifier of the working-class environment. In *Room at the Top*, Joe Lampton, as a bribe to take him away from Susan, is offered a job in the small town where he grew up. During the painful trip back to the *milieu* from whence he came Joe revisits the bombed home of his childhood and, through an encounter with a child who has claimed the ruins as a makeshift garden and playhouse, is confronted with the squalor of the working-class existence he is trying to escape. The wasteland is also evident, albeit minimally, in *This Sporting Life*, when Frank Machin is driven to seek the anonymity of the dosshouse. Here, through in-frame montage, Lindsay Anderson shows simply but directly how far Frank Machin has come, his white S-type Bentley providing a stark signifier of conspicuous materialism against the gray brutality of the littered dereliction surrounding it.

Leigh's montage shares the same graphic contrast as Anderson's almost subliminal statement but is painted with a much larger brush. The architectural and civic degradation of Maggie and Archie's domain is mirrored later in the film by the equally redundant shabbiness of the fly-poster's canvas: a canvas situated in obscure streets and back alleys that are littered with the detritus of the city and lined with boarded-up shopfronts that signify the demise of the localized trade that formed (and still forms) the focus of romanticized representations of traditional urban working-class communities. Between these, Leigh has sandwiched the modernism of Brian's empty monolith and the stylized but kitsch classicism of the homoerotic Greek souvenirs in the flat cared for by the introvert woman. The opposition of these two spheres is purposefully accentuated by pastel colors (beige in the office, blue in the flat) and, certainly in the office building, by a camera that lingers on any available reflective surface to stress connotations of clinicism and purity. These direct, if not necessarily eloquent, metonymic signifiers of the decadence of cultural tourism and the perverse logic of speculative development are placed in an overarching montage against the dystopia of the wasteland.

To abate the risk of running foul of Christian Metz's criticism of Sergei Eisenstein and seeing "montage everywhere and extending its boundaries disproportionately," we could distinguish between editing that indicates intentional montage strategies and occasions where meanings may be generated by the audience that were possibly not intended by the makers.[8] Given the particularly obvious oppositions presented through the structure of *Naked* and Leigh's long experience as a filmmaker, it is difficult to accept that he was not aware of how these would be read by an audience and that intention had no play. A further consideration is whether montage should be considered within the parameters of strictly contiguous visual images or whether all audiovisual elements may be considered, even when separated by lengthy periods of screen-time. According to Eisenstein in *The Film Sense*:

> In such a case, each montage piece exists no longer as something unrelated, but as a given *particular representation* of the general theme that in equal measure penetrates *all* the shot-pieces. The juxtaposition of these partial details in a given montage construction calls to life and forces into the light that *general* quality in which each detail has participated and which bonds together all the details into a whole, namely, into that generalized *image*, wherein the creator, followed by the spectator, experiences the theme.[9]

The distinction stressed here is that the interaction between the constructs offered by the maker (the juxtaposed representations) and the spectator's reading (the image of the theme), emphasized by Eisenstein through his use of "*particular representation*" and "generalized *image*," allows for a broader and more open interpretation of the role and implications of montage across entire film narratives than would a purely sequential and momentary shot-by-shot analysis. Applying this to Leigh's construction in *Naked*, we can assume from the obvious oppositions presented through the chosen locations that the arrangement of sequences is by no means arbitrary or accidental and that the underlying rationale that motivates both the syntagmatic and paradigmatic axes of the narrative is a purposeful attempt to prioritize a particular theme above others.[10] This dialectical presentation of an economically and often physically divided city (also present in *Last of England*) is apparent throughout the social realist *oeuvre* but its parameters extend to include such fantastic science-fiction epics as *Blade Runner* (Ridley Scott, 1982), *Soylent Green* (Richard Fleischer, 1973), *Things to Come* (William Cameron-Menzies, 1936), *Metropolis* (Fritz Lang, 1926), and many more. Indeed, we could pursue the path further and include the literary works of H. G. Wells (which provided the basis for scripts of some of the above) and the later work of Charles Dickens (particularly *Hard Times* and *Bleak House*).

In *Naked* this well-trodden dialectic is reiterated, but the crucial difference lies in a repetition that is significantly bleaker than other social-realist works where representations of the urban are more resonantly characterized by an iconography laden with socialist sentiment. In the latter, issues of community and class loyalty are played out against domestic townscapes and interiors that signify the great economic and social divide. Joe (in *Room at the Top*), Frank (in *This Sporting Life*), and Terry (in *On the Waterfront*) are clearly punished for their betrayal of the communities that inhabit the neighborhoods containing the urban wasteland. In *Naked* the working-class townscapes common to its predecessors have all but evaporated. Their place in the urban landscape has been engulfed, as in Jarman's vision, by the wasteland, the survivors left to scrape out a niche in the domain of the middle class or, like *Naked*'s Archie, lose their sanity. Johnny has no ties, no affiliations. No community can fully claim his loyalty or offer him the narrative resolution of a unifying, if threatened, ideological stasis. In keeping with the postmodern condition, Johnny has, literally as well as metaphorically, no home to call his own.

Notes

1   John Hill, *Sex, Class and Realism* (London: BFI, 1986), p. 54.
2   The terms "intertext" and "intertextuality" used in this chapter acknowledge that an audience's comprehension of a particular narrative film may be enhanced by its relationship to other works which evidence distinct similarities of form and/or content. Intertextuality will play a role both in the reception and understanding of a film by audiences, as well as in its production ("creation") by the filmmaker. For further information, see Robert Stam, Robert Burgoyne, and Sandy Flitterman-Lewis, *New Vocabularies in Film Semiotics* (London: Routledge, 1992), pp. 203–10.
3   For a useful history of the American social problem film, see Peter Roffman and Jim Purdy, *The Hollywood Social Problem Film* (Bloomington: Indiana University Press, 1981).
4   Andrew Higson, "Space, Place, Spectacle," *Screen* 25, nos. 4/5 (1984): 2–21.
5   Brian Winston, *Claiming the Real* (London: BFI, 1995) p. 38.
6   For examples, see Jeremy Mulford (ed.), *Worktown People by Humphrey Spender* (Bristol: Falling Wall Press, 1982).
7   For examples, see Robert Doherty, *Social-Documentary Photography in the USA* (New York, Photographic Publishing Co., Inc., 1976).
8   Christian Metz, *Film Language* (New York: Oxford University Press, 1974), p. 32.
9   Sergei Eisenstein, *The Film Sense*, trans. Jay Leyda (London: Faber & Faber, 1977, 3rd ed.), p. 18.
10 The terms "syntagmatic" and "paradigmatic" are used here in the sense that

the representation of London in *Naked* – both in the way it orders and combines its imagery from shot to shot and from sequence to sequence (the *syntagmatic*), and in the way certain images of London are selectively included and others left out (the *paradigmatic*) – is constructed in order to prioritize the theme of the urban wasteland. See Stam et al., *New Vocabularies in Film Semiotics*, p. 9; James Monaco, *How to Read a Film* (New York: Oxford University Press, 1981, 2nd edn.), pp. 142–6.

Escape and Invasion

21

Jacques Tati's *Play Time* as New Babylon

Laurent Marie

The illusion has been shattered that a work of art has
a fixed value: its value is dependent on
the creative ability of the onlooker, which in turn
is stimulated by the suggestions the work of art arouses.
Only living art can activate the creative spirit,
and only living art is of general significance.
For only living art gives expression to the emotions,
yearnings, reactions and ambitions which
as a result of society's shortcomings we all share.

Constant, *COBRA manifesto*, 1948[1]

In an interview for *Les Lettres françaises* in May 1958, after the release of *Mon Oncle*, Jacques Tati explained that he had not made up his mind as to what his next film would be about, adding that, instead of shooting a film, he would not mind constructing a building: "My building might not be perfect, but it would still be great putting it together."[2] Ten years later, Tati would talk of *Play Time* (1967) as the film of which he was proudest: "It's exactly the picture I wanted to make . . . I've suffered a lot because of it, physically and financially, but it's really the film I wanted to do" – a film for which he devised not only a building but a whole town.[3] *Play Time* was released in December 1967 after three years spent building the set and shooting the film.[4] Critical reaction was mixed and the public did not visit *Play Time* in great numbers.

Play Time has since often been considered an *avant-garde* film mostly for its *mise-en-scène* and its modification of the comedy genre in terms of narrative and characterization.[5] Little has been written about its political dimension.

What I propose to do here is to point out the relevance of *Play Time* to the 1960s in the light of Situationist writings. More specifically, I shall examine Situationist theories on urbanism with particular reference to *New Babylon*, the utopian urban project devised by the Dutch artist Constant who, after his participation in the *avant-garde* art movement COBRA, became a member of the Situationist International.[6]

Two months after Tati received the Academy Award for Best Foreign Film for *Mon Oncle*, Charles de Gaulle returned to power in May 1958, and in November the French voted overwhelmingly in favor of the new constitution which marked the birth of France's Fifth Republic. In July 1961, Tati was awarded the newly established *avance sur recettes* (a public grant based on the film scenario) for *Play Time* by the *Centre national de la cinématographie* (CNC; the French National Film Center). Tati's interest in urbanism, already apparent in *Mon Oncle*, was not merely incidental. It coincided with a wave of new housing projects made necessary by France's shortage of housing stock and rapid urbanization. Although they began before de Gaulle's era, these new developments took on a new impetus under the Gaullist regime. A total reorganization of the French capital and its vicinity was made possible by a new law (2 August 1961) which created the "district of Paris," an institution which was responsible for the preparation, development, and financing of new urban projects across 1,305 towns. Thus a number of high-rise estates were created in the outskirts of Paris. These *Zones à Urbaniser en Priorité* (ZUPs; Priority Urbanization Zones) were "based on the notion of the separation of accommodation, industry and offices, and increasing use of the car."[7] Moreover, the new regime, which Louis Chevalier described as "the reign of the technocrats," set about the construction of the business district of La Défense, a project on which De Gaulle was particularly keen.[8] Alongside rapid urbanization, France was beginning to enjoy the benefits of the affluent society, as evidenced by the steep increase in the ownership of cars and television sets.[9] Tati was not the only one concerned with the evolution of French society. The genesis of *Play Time* also coincided with the birth of the Situationist International.

The Situationist International was founded in 1957 by members of previous *avant-garde* movements, among them COBRA, the Lettrist International and the Movement for an Imaginist Bauhaus.[10] Its aim was quite simply to "change life," putting forward both a comprehensive attack on art and a radical critique of society as a whole. Its main outlet was the *Internationale Situationniste*, of which twelve issues were published between June 1958 and 1972. Most articles in the first three years of the *Internationale Situationniste* tackled issues such as automation, urbanism, town planning, politics, and games theory, as well as cinema. While Situationists complained that "everyone was hypnotized by work and by comfort, by the lift, by the bathroom, and by the washing machine, and that young people everywhere had been allowed to choose between love and a garbage disposal unit and everywhere they had chosen the garbage disposal unit," they also believed that mechanization and automation could lead to a new leisure-based society.[11] For the Situationists, the new urban space represented the perfect arena where "scientific knowledge and technical skill could be brought into play" since "art and technology could become one" and "reveal the true dynamic and shape of *the city*."[12] Lifts, garbage disposal units, and technology are all present in "Tativille," the city of *Play Time*.

Before looking at the way Tati criticizes the alienating impact of technology on Tativille's citizens, it is worth examining the technology its director availed himself of in the making of the film. *Play Time* was shot in 70mm, color, and stereophonic sound. Tati was always keen to keep in touch with the latest technical innovations on offer. This is not only true of *Play Time*. *Jour de fête* was shot in color in 1947, and in 1974 Tati was among the first to use video when he directed his last film, *Parade*. Tati's use of state-of-the-art film technology in *Play Time* does not serve any spectacular purpose, but instead contributes to the revolutionary aspect of the film. In fact, his handling of technical innovations echoes the way Situationists saw new film techniques as a means to change the role of cinema in society. In an article in *Internationale Situationiste* entitled "For and against cinema," film is described both as a passive substitute for the artistic activity which modernization has made possible and as an enslaving art form.[13] Yet it also "acknowledges interesting and valuable new technical applications such as stereophony or odorama" and states that "the progressive aspects of industrial cinema should be developed and put to use in the same way that an architecture based on the psychological function of ambience should allow the hidden treasure to come out of the manure of absolute functionalism."[14]

Tati was always adamant that he was not against modernization or modern architecture *per se*.[15] He told students at the *Institut des hauts études cinématographique* (IDHEC) that he was

> not against modern architecture if it is properly and effectively put to use, if it brings us something good. I am not very intelligent but I am not going to tell you that we should build small schools with tiny windows so that the pupils won't seen the sun, and that hospitals with dirty sinks, where one was badly looked after, were brilliant. . . . [16]

What he criticizes in *Play Time* is the use to which modern architecture is being put: "The film's satire is not about the place where we live but about the way we use it."[17] Tati explains that he is "against a certain way of life, a sterile homogenization which affects the way we think as much as the place where we live."[18] This denunciation takes place mostly in the first part of the film where repetition, homogenization, and banalization are the central themes.[19] Among other things, Tati makes fun of what traveling has become in the modern world. The spectator cannot help pitying the group of American tourists who desperately try to catch sight of the real Paris but always end up in the most nondescript places. What should have been a unique experience has turned into a non-event. In thesis 168 of *Society of the Spectacle* (1967), Guy Debord, the most prominent Situationist, analyzes the place of tourism in modern society and his comments seem perfectly appropriate to the obvious poverty of the Americans' Parisian sightseeing experience:

> Human circulation considered as something to be consumed – tourism – is a by-product of the circulation of commodities; basically, tourism is the chance to go and see what has been made trite. The economic management of travel to different places suffices in itself to ensure those places' interchangeability. The same modernization that has deprived travel of its temporal aspect has likewise deprived it of the reality of space.[20]

Among a number of Situationist concepts, that of "psychogeography" strikes a chord in relation to *Play Time*. Psychogeography is defined as "the study of the specific effect of the geographical environment, consciously organized or not, on the emotions and behavior of individuals."[21] Whether it be outside or inside buildings, the way the film's characters, including M. Hulot, wander about Tativille is often determined by the geography or the architecture of the place in which they find themselves. Thus M. Hulot is swallowed by the lift and spat out on the wrong floor, and glass partitions prevent him from meeting M. Giffard whom he came into town to see. In the first part of the film, characters are isolated from each other, either as the result of the deliberate organization of the workplace (as in the cubicles of the office block) or by the organization of the city itself. The civilization of the car is also targeted in *Play Time*. There are many scenes at the beginning of the film which echo the view of traffic circulation as "the organization of universal isolation," and indeed many more in Tati's subsequent film, entitled precisely *Trafic* (1971).[22] In Situationist terms, the car is "the sovereign good of an alienated life and an essential product of the capitalist market," while "the development of the urban *milieu* is the capitalist domestication of space."[23] The bland and alienating characteristics of modern architecture and urbanism mocked by Tati were ceaselessly reviled by the Situationists: "We have no intention of contributing to this mechanical civilization, to its bleak architecture, to its inevitably catatonic leisure."[24]

Society of the Spectacle, which was published in November 1967, a month before *Play Time*'s release, remains the key Situationist text. In it, Debord develops a radical and complex critique of capitalism and "pseudo-anti-capitalism" (that is, Eastern Europe, China, or Cuba). In the wake of Lukács's *History and Class Consciousness* (1923), which became available in French in the

1950s, Debord considers that capitalist society has reached such a degree of alienation and separation that "what is now missing in life can only be found in the spectacle in the form of separated independent representations."[25] Since "the economy has subjected all aspects of human life to its own rules," all aspects of human life have been commodified, the final stage being both the fetishization of these commodities and the reification of their producers, this phenomenon affecting every aspect of everyday life.[26] It is this very impoverishment of daily life which Tati portrays in the first part of *Play Time*. The spectacle of consumer society is clearly targeted in the sequence in the chain store when the American tourists look ecstatically at the garbage bin. Nevertheless, Tati pushes his critique furthest in the scene in which Hulot is invited to visit his friend's apartment. The conversations inside cannot be heard. Hulot's friend makes a display of his material possessions (he is even proud of his parking meter), including a homemade film of his skiing holidays, which he is unable to show because he cannot work the projector. Tati shows the spectacularization and reification of life itself through a shot of identical flats seen through their glass front.

However humorously they are depicted in the sequence, these identical flats, in which the inhabitants watch the same television program, illustrate Debord's insistence that

> the question of the use of technological means, in everyday life and elsewhere, is a political question. . . . The new prefabricated cities clearly exemplify the totalitarian tendency of modern capitalism's organization of life: the isolated inhabitants (generally isolated within the framework of the family cell) see their lives reduced to the pure triviality of the repetitive combined with the obligatory absorption of an equally repetitive spectacle.[27]

When Tati criticized "the need of our civilization to make a show of itself," he seemed to be putting in simpler words Debord's first thesis, which reads: "The whole life of societies in which modern conditions of production prevail presents itself as an immense accumulation of *spectacles*. All that once was directly lived has become mere representation."[28] Yet *Play Time* is not all doom and gloom. Jacques Tati not only reports a worrying state of affairs, he helps his spectators to find a way out. I would like to look at the way out devised by Tati in the light of Constant's *New Babylon* project.[29]

The ex-COBRA artists, Asger Jorn and Constant Newhenhuis, belonged to the first group of Situationists in 1957. Constant developed a special interest in urbanism and architecture, and, with Guy Debord, worked on the notion of Unitary Urbanism, defined as "the theory of the combined use of arts and techniques for the integral construction of a *milieu* in dynamic relation with experiments in behaviour."[30] It asserts that "man's environment can be totally unified and that all forms of separation – between work and

Figure 21.1   Spectacularization and reification in Jacques Tati's *Play Time*
(*Courtesy of Specta Films CEPEC*)

leisure, between public and private – can finally be dissolved. But even
before this, the minimum program of unitary urbanism is to extend our
present field of play to every kind of building we can wish for."[31] I believe
Play Time to be a filmic illustration of this minimum program.

Constant was to develop Debord's point further. The Dutch artist devised
New Babylon thanks to Unitary Urbanism and other Situationist concepts
such as the already mentioned psychogeography, and two others, the *dérive*
and the "constructed situation." The *dérive* ("drift") is a "mode of experimental behavior linked to the conditions of urban society: a technique of transient passage through varied ambiences." A constructed situation is "a moment
of life concretely and deliberately constructed by the collective organization
of a unitary ambience and a game of events."[32]

As a city/society for *Homo ludens*, Constant explains, *New Babylon* rejects the
utilitarian rationale which governs our present society. *Homo faber* has left very
little room for *Homo ludens*. Yet, thanks to technological progress, it is foresee-
able that all activities of production might be automated. This would free
humankind from the constraints experienced in a utilitarian society and would
result in a classless society in which freedom is a lived reality. In such a
context, the inhabitants of New Babylon would be able to develop, expand,

and fulfil their creative potential in an environment in which they enjoy freedom in terms of time and space. New Babylonian culture is not the result of isolated activities or exceptional situations: instead, it is the result of the global activity of the entire population. The new form of urbanization thus created implies a new relation between the urban and the habitat, with human beings necessarily living a nomadic way of life. In New Babylon every place is accessible to everyone. Everyone changes places as they wish, when they wish. Life becomes an endless journey through an ever-changing world. *Homo ludens* finds, in New Babylon, the ludic city befitting a new way of life.

The long central sequence in the Royal Garden restaurant constitutes the turning point of *Play Time*. As a location, the Royal Garden becomes the psychogeographic vortex toward which drift a variety of people of diverse social and national origins. At the beginning, the customers tend to look like the clientele one would expect to see at the opening of a posh new nightspot. From the moment the glass front door is broken inadvertently by M. Hulot, there are more and more passersby who drift aimlessly inside the restaurant and start wandering about. Once inside, the drifters and some of the original customers become participants in a "constructed situation." The destruction of the Royal Garden, either provoked or spontaneous, and the resulting ambience show people coming, going, drinking, dancing, and singing together. From the dysfunctional place it was at the beginning of the evening, the restaurant has become a communitarian area in which unconscious desires come into the open: even M. Hulot starts flirting. Lucy Fischer is right to stress that "only when the restaurant décor is totally destroyed, do people begin to relax and enjoy themselves, and begin to *play*."[33] This is when and where order gives way to disorder, functionalism to chaos and a new form of harmony. But above all else, it is where people unite with their surroundings, where their behavior is no longer controlled by their environment, where they are no longer separated from it, but take hold of the place. Whereas, before, the city prevented people from meeting one another, the Royal Garden has now become a social place in the New Babylonian sense of the term: "For us, social space really means the concrete space where people meet, come into contact. Spatiality is social. In New Babylon, social space is social spatiality."[34]

Like the inhabitants of New Babylon, the people of *Play Time* seem to wander about the Royal Garden, looking for new experiences, unknown ambiences, not with the passivity of tourists but instead with the full awareness of their ability to act on the world, to transform it, to re-create it; and they do create a new social space in sharp contrast with the town depicted in the first part of the film. This happens because the space and the ambience have been altered by a succession of factors triggered by a number of occupants of the premises. Once more, the customers' behavior illustrates that of the New Babylonians as imagined by Constant:

> At every moment of their creative activity, the New Babylonians are in direct contact with one another. Each of their actions is public and each of them may in turn provoke new ones. All of these interventions form a chain reaction which only ends when a situation, which has reached a "critical" phase, explodes and transforms into a new situation. This process is not controlled by a single person, it does not matter to know who has triggered it and who will modify it in the future. In a way the critical moment is truly a collective creation.[35]

It is worth noticing that in order to make his explanation clearer, Constant uses the example not of a restaurant but of a café: "In New Babylon, at any moment anyone can change the atmosphere of the café by changing the noise level, the light, the temperature, the smells. A small group arrives and the configuration of the place will be altered. With a minimum of effort, all wished-for modifications can take place."[36] This strikingly echoes what happens in *Play Time*'s Royal Garden.

The metamorphosis of the city happens as a result of the destruction of the old setup and the creation of a new social format. It is in the aftermath of the wild night at the Royal Garden that a brighter morning dawns. The last sequence then takes on its deepest sense and should be read as a sign of optimism on Tati's part, as he himself acknowledged.[37] In this scene, a roundabout jammed with circling cars becomes a merry-go-round activated by what was once a parking meter, as a passerby blows a trumpet: the city is transformed into a fairground attraction park. In Tati's world, the merry-go-round, reminiscent of the circus floor, evokes childhood, fun, and games. In this ultimate scene, Tati brings play into the heart of the city. Furthermore, the props which compose this last sequence and the fashion in which they are used remind us that "all the constituents for a freer life are already at hand, both in the cultural as well as in the technical domains. They simply need to be given a new meaning and be differently organized."[38] Thus in *Play Time*, a new function is added to the means of transport: "from being simply tools," the cars "become instruments of play."[39]

In Situationist terms, cinema is the central art form of the society of the spectacle, since it depends on the separation of the spectator from the work of art. For the Situationists, no matter how much *Play Time* seemed to attack modern society in its content, it would always be merely another passive substitute for real artistic activity. The film would, therefore, lack any true political dimension. But *Play Time* is as political in form as it is in content. The revolutionary narrative aspect of the film stems from two deliberate decisions on Tati's part. On the one hand, Tati dilutes the notion of the film hero. On the other hand, he endows his spectators with a very active role in the viewing event. Tati refuses to show M. Hulot as the main character. The use of long takes, deep-focus and the 70mm format, as well as the absence of closeups, allows Tati to turn every character into an extra – including Hulot himself – or, better still, to allow every extra to achieve Hulot's status. Tati refuses the fetishization of M. Hulot as character, and consequently Tati's own reification as filmmaker.

The main consequence of Tati's doing away with the notion of the film hero is that it gives the spectator more agency. This is probably where the film was most disorienting for its public. Tati may have been too confident of his audience's ability to participate in the viewing event. For without this participation, there is little point in watching Tati's favorite film. *Play Time* was Tati's "gift" – another Situationist key word – to his public: "The images are designed so that after you see the picture two or three times, it's no longer my film, it starts to be your film. You recognize the people, you know them and you don't even know who directed the picture."[40] In a very fine analysis Lucy Fischer describes what is required of the spectator for a full appreciation of *Play Time*. Tati's "democracy of gags and comics" rests, Fischer argues, on a dialectic of game and play: "The comic work as game, and the spectator's response as play."[41] This directorial decision is on a par with the thematic content of the film:

> Because of his formal emphasis on a gamelike mode, Tati's films can be seen not only to present, on a narrative level, the problem of passive leisure, but also, in their very structure, to inspire in the viewer a playful response. Hence they act as palliatives for the very problem they depict. Clearly the relation of structure and signification in Tati's work is extraordinarily tight – the form of his films addressing the issues of content.[42]

Play Time requires a dynamic and creative spectator. Just as the New Babylonians move about their cityscape, the watchers of *Play Time* must do likewise in the screenscape devised by Tati. Thanks to his use of the 70mm format and extreme depth of field, Tati creates a kind of dynamic maze through which the spectator must wander. His or her gaze must acquire a nomadic quality so as to err freely in Tativille in search of new discoveries. The spectator's gaze is therefore no longer controlled by the film's narrative. On the contrary, s/he has acquired a high degree of freedom: the spectator who watches *Play Time* circulates through the screen and each new viewing is therefore a new experience. Each new visit to Tativille leads to new pleasures.

If, for Constant, "a fulfilling life can only be achieved through continuous creation and re-creation" and "Man can only fully realize himself by creating his own life," for Tati a successful film is one which allows the spectators to create and re-create the viewing event at will.[43] *Play Time*'s *raison d'être* rests on the spectators taking charge of the narrative, playing with it. Both New Babylon and *Play Time* represent an intensification of the urban and filmic spaces open to their respective residents and visitors. Tati refuses his specta-

tors mere contemplation of the film but encourages them to become actively
involved in the same way Constant wants the inhabitants of New Babylon to
be the active creators of their city. They both share Debord's belief that
there "can be no freedom apart from activity, and within the spectacle all
activity is banned."[44]

When it was released in December 1967, Tati played down the political
overtones of his latest film. Yet in an interview in 1976 with Penelope Gilliatt
he was much more explicit as to his own political inclination:

> Hulot is not the hero of *Play Time*. The main character is the décor and the
> heroes are the people who break it up. I am not a Communist. I could have
> been, if Communist history were not so sad. It makes me sound old-fashioned,
> but I think I am an anarchist. Great things were done by the historical anar-
> chists.[45]

Gilliatt wrote that *Play Time* epitomized Tati's politics. Far from being reactionary, Tati in *Play Time* "'read' May before it happened," to use Keith
Reader's phrase about the Situationists and May 1968.[46] The film promoted
a playful, festive, and poetic revolution, on a par with the "revolutionary *fête*"
of the Situationists.[47] It is in this light that the reference to "la Bastille" – one
of the landmarks of the French Revolution and a square known since for its
large popular gatherings – must be read when the inebriated customers start
singing "*A la Bastille, on aime bien Nini Peau de chien*" in a restaurant which bears
the name "*Royal* Garden."[48] Tativille is thus more akin to Pinot-Gallizio's
playful machines and Constant's New Babylon project than to the "grids" of
Mondrian, who has been mentioned in relation to *Play Time*.[49]

In Truffaut's *Les Quatre Cents Coups*, shot in 1958, the headmaster shouts at
his pupils: "I dread to think of France in ten years' time, it won't be a pretty
sight!" Truffaut wrote to Tati after he saw *Play Time* to comfort him in view
of the poor reception of the film. "*Play Time* is the Europe of 1968 shot by the
first Martian filmmaker," Truffaut wrote.[50] *Play Time* did indeed predict May
1968, but it was not shot by a Martian but by someone acutely aware of the
society of which he was a member. It is as if Tati were talking to Truffaut's
schoolboys, now in their early twenties, showing them that one of the ways to
build a better place in which to live was through a "reappropriation" of the
urban environment. In the aftermath of the events, Louis Chevalier wrote
that "May 68 was also an attempt on youth's part to regain the city, which
had been a place of freedom for so long but which had changed so much in
the 1960s."[51] A few months earlier the inhabitants of Tativille had also
reclaimed their city.

Notes

1 Constant, in Willemijn Stokvis, *COBRA* (New York: Rizzoli, 1988), p. 30, originally published in "COBRA manifesto," *Reflex* I (Amsterdam, September–October 1948).
2 Marc Dondey, *Tati* (Paris: Ramsay Cinéma, 1989), p. 180.
3 Jonathan Rosenbaum, "Tati's Democracy", *Film Comment*, May–June 1973, p. 40.
4 For a complete account of the film's early stages, see Brent Maddock, *The Films of Jacques Tati* (Metuchen, NJ and London: The Scarecrow Press, Inc., 1977), pp. 76–8; and Dondey, *Tati*, pp. 185–96.
5 See Rosenbaum, " Tati's Democracy," pp. 36–41; Lucy Fischer, "*Play Time*: the comic film as game," *West Virginia University Philological Papers* 26 (August 1980): 83–8; Kristin Thompson, *Breaking the Glass Armor: Neoformalist Film Analysis* (Princeton, NJ: Princeton University Press, 1988); Paolo Bertotto, "Magic City," in *Paris vu par le cinéma d'avant garde, 1923–1983* (Paris: Paris Expérimental, 1985), pp. 43–8.
6 Published after this chapter was written, David Bellos refers to the Situationist International in his biography of Tati, but he does so in a rather dismissive way, without mentioning Constant. See Bellos, *Jacques Tati, His Life and Art* (London: Harvill Press, 1999), pp. 268–77.
7 See Robert Gildea, *France since 1945* (Oxford and New York: Oxford University Press, 1997), pp. 80–2; and Bernard Marchand, *Paris, histoire d'une ville, XIXᵉ-XXᵉ siècle* (Paris: Éditions du Seuil, 1993), pp. 280–320.
8 Louis Chevalier, *L'Assassinat de Paris* (Paris: Calmann-Levy, 1977), p. 129; on La Défense, see Marchand, *Paris, histoire d'une ville*, p. 303.
9 See Kristin Ross, *Fast Cars, Clean Bodies, Decolonization and the Reordering of French Culture* (Cambridge, MA: MIT Press, 1995), pp. 15–70.
10 See Marie-Hélène Colas-Adler, *Groupes, mouvements, tendances de l'art contemporain depuis 1945* (Paris: École Nationale Supérieure des Beaux-Arts, 1990), p. 97.
11 Christopher Gray (ed.), *Leaving the 20th Century* (London: Free Fall Publications, 1974), p. 2.
12 Ibid.
13 *Internationale Situationiste (IS)*,1: 9, reprinted in Ken Knabb (ed.), *Situationist International Anthology* (Berkeley: Bureau of Public Secrets, 1981).
14 Ibid.
15 See Jacques Tati in Michel Mourlet, "Tati ou pas Tati," *Les Nouvelles Littéraires*, 30 November 1967.
16 Jacques Tati in Jean-André Fieschi, *La Voix de Tati* (Mulhouse: Limelight/Éditions Ciné-fils, 1996), p. 20.
17 Claude-Marie Trémois, "Play Time: le temps de s'amuser. Jacques Tati donne une leçon de 'mieux vivre' aux spectateurs pendant deux heures vingt minutes," *Télérama*, 17 December 1967.
18 Tati in Mourlet, "Tati ou pas Tati."
19 Rosenbaum, "Tati's Democracy," p. 40.
20 Guy Debord, *Society of the Spectacle*, trans. Donald Nicholson-Smith (New York: Zone Books, 1994), p. 120.

21 *IS* 1, p. 13, reprinted in Knabb (ed.), *Situationist International Anthology*, p. 45.

22 Attila Kotyani and Raoul Vaneigem, "Program élémentaire du bureau d'urbanisme unitaire," *Internationale Situationniste* 6 (August 1961): 16, reprinted in Knabb (ed.), *Situationist International Anthology*, p. 66.

23 Guy Debord, "Positions situationnistes sur la circulation," *IS* 3 (December 1959): 36–7, reprinted in Knabb (ed.), *Situationist International Anthology*, p. 65.

24 Gilles Ivain (Ivan Chtcheglov), "Formulaire pour un urbanisme nouveau," *IS* 1 (June 1958): 16 (reprinted in Gray (ed.), *Leaving the 20th Century*, p. 18).

25 On Lukács and Debord, see Anselm Jappe, *Guy Debord* (Pescara: Via Valeriano, 1995), pp. 40–55, 22.

26 Ibid, p. 22.

27 Guy Debord, "Perspectives de modifications conscientes dans la vie quotidienne," *IS* 6: p. 23, reprinted in Knabb (ed.), *Situationist International Anthology*, p. 71).

28 See Tati in Mourlet, "Tati ou pas Tati"; Debord, *Society of the Spectacle*, p. 12.

29 For a comprehensive analysis of New Babylon, see Jean-Clarence Lambert, *New Babylon, Constant, Art et Utopie* (Paris: Éditions du Cercle d'Art, 1997); and Simon Sadler, *The Situationist City* (Cambridge, MA: MIT Press, 1998), pp. 105–55.

30 *IS* 1, p. 13.

31 Debord, "Positions situationnistes sur la circulation," p. 36.

32 *IS* 1, p. 13.

33 Fischer, "*Play Time*," p. 87.

34 Constant, "New Babylon, une ville nomade," in Jean Duvignaud (ed.), *Nomades et vagabonds* (Ser. cause commune, collection 10/18, Paris: UGE, 1975), p. 205.

35 Ibid., p. 218.

36 Ibid., p. 228.

37 Tati in Mourlet, "Tati ou pas Tati."

38 Jappe, *Guy Debord*, p. 95.

39 Constant, "New Babylon," p. 211.

40 Rosenbaum, "Tati's Democracy," p. 34.

41 Fischer, "*Play Time*," p. 87.

42 Lucy Fischer, *Jacques Tati: A Guide to References and Resources* (Boston: G. K. Hall & Co., 1983), p. 38.

43 Constant, "New Babylon", p. 229.

44 Debord, *Society of the Spectacle*, p. 21.

45 Penelope Gilliatt, *Jacques Tati* (London: Woburn Press, 1976), pp. 55–8.

46 Keith Reader, *The May 68 Events in France* (New York: St. Martin's Press, Inc., 1993), p. 53. For examples of negative views of *Play Time* as reactionary, see Dominique Noguez, *Le Cinéma autrement* (Paris: Les Éditions du Cerf, 1987), p. 182; Albert Cervoni, "L'air du temps," *France Nouvelle*, 27 December 1967, p. 14; and Robert Benayoun, "Dullsville, Funless, Borecity, Snoretown and Lullabygrad," *Positif* 93 (March 1968): 61–2.

47 Pascal Dumontier, *Les Situationnistes et Mai 68* (Paris: Éditions Champ Libre, 1989), in Reader, *The May 68 Events in France*, p. 53. Tati himself acknowledged that *Play Time* was quite violent; see Fieschi, *La Voix de Tati*, p. 20.

48 My emphasis. *Nini peau de chien* is a song written by Aristide Bruant, a famous Parisian popular singer at the end of the nineteenth century.

49 See, for example, Emmanuel Abela, *Présence(s) de Jacques Tati* (Schiltigheim:

LimeLight/Les Éditions Ciné-fils et la Ville de Schiltigheim, 1997), p. 19. See also Noguez, *Le Cinéma autrement*, p. 182.

50 François Truffaut, quoted in Dondey, *Tati*, p. 211.
51 Jappe, *Guy Debord*, p. 86.

22

Poaching on Public Space: Urban Autonomous Zones in French *Banlieue* Films

Adrian Fielder

Our taverns and our metropolitan streets, our offices and furnished rooms, our railroad stations and our factories appeared to have us locked up hopelessly. Then came the film and burst this prison-world asunder by the dynamite of the tenth of a second, so that now, in the midst of its far-flung ruins and debris, we calmly and adventurously go traveling.
Walter Benjamin, "On the Work of Art in the Age of Mechanical Reproduction" (1936)[1]

You may make a rupture, draw a line of flight, yet there is still a danger that you will re-encounter organizations that re-stratify everything, formations that restore power to a signifier, attributions that reconstitute a [re-territorialized] subject . . . micro-fascisms just waiting to crystallize.
Gilles Deleuze and Félix Guattari, "Rhizome" (1980)[2]

This chapter examines a body of films (tentatively labeled as a genre by *Cahiers du Cinéma* in 1995) issuing from a cultural space that, until the mid-1980s, was not a locus of cinematic production: the *banlieues* of major French metropolises.[3] Although *banlieue* is usually translated into English as "sub-urb," this type of urban space has little to do with the associations evoked by the English term. The contemporary term *banlieue* has quite a long history, as it comprises two Latin roots (*banni* + *leuga*) first borrowed by Middle French around the twelfth century and transformed into *ban* + *lieue*. *Lieue* means "place," but in medieval France, *ban* had a special meaning: it designated a judicial proclamation issued by the feudal authority in a given town, which all of the manor lord's subjects were obliged to observe under penalty of law. The *banlieue* was the space surrounding the town, inhabited by the lord's vassals, in which the *ban* was proclaimed and over which it had jurisdiction.[4] The term *banlieue*, then, has historically designated a very specific type of inhabited space: a place literally excluded from the terrain inside what Mazzoleni calls a city's "somatic membrane," but which is nevertheless subject to the authoritative dictates of the power structure(s) located in the center of the city.[5]

The current meaning of the term emerged in the years following World War Two, when immigrants from former French colonies (especially North Africans) began erecting shantytowns (or *bidonvilles*) on the margins of French cities in which they comprised the labor force for Reconstruction efforts. The *bidonvilles* came to be perceived in the French media and political discourse as mini-*casbahs* inscribed on French soil, dangerous zones of indeterminacy into which the forces of law and order could not completely penetrate.[6] Much like the Bunker Hill evoked by Mike Davis in chapter 3 of this volume, these areas were soon targeted for "urban renewal."[7] Starting in the mid-1960s, low-rent, high-rise apartment complexes called HLM (*Habitations à Loyer Modéré*) were built on the sites of these squatter communities, which were thus effectively displaced.[8] These new neighborhoods became known as *les banlieues*, since they are located *outside* the "urban periphery" in cities such as Paris, Lyon, and Marseille, and today they are home to the majority of immigrant families living in France. In the last two decades, socially- and spatially-marginalized subjects in the *banlieues* have been obliged to cope with a faltering educational system, extremely atrophied vocational training, and an unemployment crisis of epic proportions.

The relation of these communities to the "city proper" (that is, in the Parisian example, those institutions centered within the legal boundary delimiting the twenty *arrondissements*) has thus become an increasingly conflictual one which bears witness to a curious coincidence between the etymology of the word and contemporary state policies towards *banlieue* inhabitants.[9] Indeed, in many ways it seems that the imposed hierarchies once given metaphorical "shape" in the colonial imagination by the distinction between *métropole* (as the center and locus of power, culture, hegemony) and *périphérie* (those subjugated terrains at the frontier of "civilization"), have now been literally spatialized within the contemporary French cityscape. In the wake of recent urban riots, the *banlieues* have been subjected to increased police surveillance (particularly the aggressive campaigns of the CRS, the *Compagnie républicaine de sécurité*, a state-funded police agency) and to daily media coverage (most often in the form of "crisis reporting"). This chapter examines four films featuring the struggles of emergent urban subcultures within these communities: Thomas Gilou's *Raï* (1993), Matthieu Kassovitz's *La haine* (*Hate*, 1995), Jean-François Richet's *État des lieux* (*State of Places*, 1989), and *Ma 6-T va cracker* (*My C-T is Gonna Crack*, 1997) – all of which are set in the *banlieues* north of Paris.[10] Starting from the premise elaborated by Michel de Certeau, that the city is a zone of cultural conflict whose individual citizens inhabit a textual system of which they themselves are not the authors, my analysis will concentrate on the various tactics available to *banlieue* inhabitants attempting to "poach" on the urban system in/through these films.[11]

Urban Space and the "Writing Machine of the Law": Visibility and Marginality in the *Banlieue*

Drawing from Foucault and Bourdieu, de Certeau suggests that a given social regime can be understood as a constellation of interwoven "orders" (whether spatial, technological, or political) organized much like language itself; in other words, as a *textual system* which attempts to interpellate individuals into the established networks of a "scriptural economy." In effect, the subject's body is seen as a blank page on which "the writing machine of the Law" attempts to inscribe a sign with a fixed meaning, so as to turn it into "a symbol of the Other, something *said, called, named*."[12] At times, this virtually immemorial effort to forge a binding, uniform law (a social body) out of the infinite heterogeneity of individual human bodies is articulated in symbolic form: as in the legal obligation to carry documents of identification, "parchment and paper are put in place of our skin . . . [and] form a sort of protective coating around it."[13] However, in times of crisis (as, for example, when inmates of concentration camps are literally branded so as to "mark" them as parts of the camp system), the dominant order is inscribed in a more direct and violent manner: "paper is no longer enough for the law, and it writes itself again on the bodies themselves."[14] Whatever the means of inscription, the scriptural enterprise aims to regulate the circulation of all the bodies within its demarcated purview and thus to assure the maintenance of its own strategic site (as well as the extension of that site through an appropriation of external space).

Throughout the corpus of *banlieue* films, the various forms of this "writing machine of the Law" loom as a constant and omnipresent menace. As representatives of ethnic and cultural minorities which have been targeted in recent years by ever-stricter regulations to carry identity papers, and subjected to ever-increasing police surveillance aimed at controlling the underground economies through which many *banlieue* inhabitants pay the rent, the characters in the films in question seem keenly aware of the mechanisms of surveillance by which the French state attempts to identify and regulate "disruptive" elements of the population. This becomes apparent through the recurrent use of the phrase *en carton* ("in a box") as a derogative modifier added onto a description.[15] The term has several meanings in current French slang, including "shelved," "pigeonholed," or "in sights" (as in the cross hairs of a rifle). The way it is used in these films seems to combine elements of these different significations to produce a metaphorical sense of the term: as in *Raï*, when Nordine jokingly calls Djamel "pauvre reubeu en carton" ["poor Arab in a box"] while pointing an imaginary handgun at his friend's head. In such uses, the person being described is ridiculed because he lacks power. He has been recognized and named, "boxed" and categorized ("put on a shelf"), immobilized, and even targeted. His lot is laughable. He is not free.

What makes this concept (as used in the *banlieue* films) extremely important in relation to the characters' use of urban space is that this unenviable position of being "within the enemy's field of vision" is consistently equated with the exterior spaces of the Parisian cityscape.[16] Richet's films are especially concerned with staging the street as a zone of conflict circumscribed by institutional mechanisms of territorial control (whether ground patrol or helicopter surveillance), in which both individuals and gatherings of people constantly run the risk of being identified as "deviant bodies" in need of immobilization or incarceration. The main character Jean in *État des lieux*, an unemployed blue-collar type who rides around town on his motorcycle, has a humiliating confrontation with a police officer, who stops him for no apparent reason other than the fact that his bandanna makes him look like a gang member. Throughout *Ma 6-T va cracker*, the repeated sound of helicopters acts as an audible signifier of the panoptic modes of surveillance mobilized by the CRS – much as in John Singleton's *Boyz N the Hood* (1991), in which the lights of police choppers continually survey the streets of South Central Los Angeles. As a result, the protagonists know that when they descend from their apartments and move through the streets of their *banlieue*, they necessarily move through specular fields exerted by the institutional sight/site of "discipline" (surveillance). In other words, they know that their own bodies will be readable (because visible) elements of the city-as-text: potential sites of inscription for the "writing machine of the Law."

Yet the city's panoptic systems are maintained not only by state-run police agencies, but also by the ubiquitous eyes of television and security cameras. In *Raï*, Nordine, who is constantly in search of semi-private enclaves (such as movie theaters) where he can "shoot up" without being harassed, becomes adept at covering security cameras with his hat while prying open locked doors in alleyways. This kind of encounter is portrayed humorously in a scene from *La haine*, when the three main characters (Saïd, Vinz, and Hubert) try to gain admittance into a posh apartment complex in downtown Paris. Obliged to speak into a security camera to ask the tenants if they know Saïd's friend (whom he only knows by the guy's nickname), Saïd (who is "Beur," or second-generation Arab) fails to gain entrance and tells Vinz (who is ostensibly of Sephardic Jewish heritage) to speak into the camera because Vinz's white skin makes him less suspicious to the eyes peering at them through the

camera lens. By presenting the spectators of the film with the point-of-view
of those positioned inside the building, Kassovitz emphasizes that the characters' visibility within the urban exterior is precisely that which places them *en
carton* and thus allows them to be identified, categorized as potentially unruly
bodies, and excluded from the interior space contained by the edifice.

An earlier scene from *La haine* highlights the ways in which the state
television news apparatus becomes yet another roving extension of *l'oeil du
pouvoir* ("the eye of power") into the *banlieue*. As the three characters are
sitting in an empty playground, a van drives up in the background. Positioned above the characters, a female news reporter and a man holding a
television camera hail them and then ask if they participated in the previous
night's riots (which were represented by the news clips shown during the
film's opening credits). This elicits a violently negative reaction from the
three characters:

> *Reporter*: Hooo! Hello sirs, it's for TV! Did you take part in the riots last night?
>   Did you break something? Or burn some cars?
> *Saïd*: Were we lookin' like looters to you, lady?
> *Reporter*: Oh no, I never said that . . .
> *Vinz*: Oh yeah, well what were we lookin' like to you, lady?
> *Reporter*: Oh, nothing . . .
> *Hubert*: Why don't you come down out of the car, this ain't Toiry!
> *Reporter*: No, listen: we have work . . .
> *Vinz*: Yeah, yeah, you have a lot of work, like what for example? What, like
>   finding a nice juicy story? Stirring up some shit? Getting a good scoop?

Saïd accuses the news team of having automatically labeled them as *voyous*
("hoodlums," or in this case, "looters") because of their physical appearance,
and they demand that the camera be switched off. With his comment, Hubert
emphatically (and somewhat ironically) maintains that their neighborhood is
not a zoo designed for the viewing pleasure of paying consumer-spectators
expecting to see the "wild beasts" of the *banlieue* jungle (as we learn at the end
of the scene, Toiry is a drive-through zoological park outside Paris).

While this scene further underscores the ways in which mainstream perceptions of *banlieue* inhabitants have been informed by alarmist discourses on
the "problem" of immigration, it also indicates that the characters are conscious (in some sense) of the ideological ramifications of being seen – and, by
extension, of being interpellated. Indeed, the intrusive presence of the camera in their "turf" is enough to cause Vinz to hurl a rock at the news team.
Their behavior and their comments express both a consciousness of their
confinement within the space delimited by the eye of the camera, and a
desire to escape the scrutiny of this reifying gaze. In this light, the frustration
they feel at their own powerlessness in this situation seems to be provoked
not simply by being equated with beasts in a cage or by being categorized as

unruly looters. More importantly, it is the very fact of being visually identified and labeled, or "tagged" – and this by a system of representation/
classification which is *not their own* – that signifies (to them) their subjection to
the dominant social order.

Poaching on the *Hors-Carton*: The Search for Urban Autonomous Zones

Based on the evidence presented thus far, the *banlieue* films under investigation bear witness to the saliency of the kind of approach Foucault outlines in
Discipline and Punish, in which he considers Bentham's model of prison architecture as emblematic of the ways in which the organization of social space
(and urban space in particular) comes to determine not just the distribution
and circulation of bodies in space, but most fundamentally, the modalities of
exchange through which power relations are elaborated throughout society.[17] Yet this is precisely where de Certeau's framework proves to be a
useful intervention, insofar as his basic project is to conceptualize the tactical
performative modes by which individual subjects (who must reside within
spatial and cultural fields regulated by the "writing machine" of this prevailing scriptural economy) may attempt to reappropriate "the right to name"
wielded by dominant institutions.

This immemorial struggle between established order(s) and creative appropriation is literally spatialized, for de Certeau, on the penultimate "battleground" of technocracy: "the city." As conceived by city planners, the
boundaries of a particular architectural edifice are designed not only to
circumscribe an "inside," but also to reduce the opportunities which individual users of the urban system (for example, walkers in the street) may
tactically "seize on the wing." Yet, while the city is given shape by "an
ensemble of interdictions" (walls, fences, barricades), it simultaneously presents
"an ensemble of possibilities" (sidewalks, staircases, roofs) which can be actu-
alized by pedestrians in either conventional or unpredictable ways.[18] According to de Certeau's formulation, those individuals who navigate this text by
maximizing its possibilities are described as "trailblazers in the jungles of
functionalist rationality . . . [who] trace 'indeterminate trajectories' . . . within
the space ordered by the organizing techniques of systems."[19] From this, we
get a new way of reading these "trajectories":

> One can analyze the microbe-like . . . practices which an urbanistic system was
> supposed to administer or suppress, but which have outlived its decay; one can
> follow the swarming activity of these procedures that, far from being regulated
> or eliminated by panoptic administration, have reinforced themselves in prolif-
> erating illegitimacy, developed and insinuated themselves into the networks of

surveillance, and combined in accord with . . . tactics to the point of constituting . . . surreptitious creativities that are merely concealed by the frantic mechanisms and discourses of the observational organization.[20]

The operative word he suggests to describe this process is "poaching," which
serves as a metaphor for the ways users of pre-established orders come to
inhabit (whether illicitly or not) textual systems of which they are not the
authors.

What I would like to suggest is that, as second- and third-generation
offspring of immigrant families (who for the most part were born and/or
raised in the neighborhoods they inhabit), the youths whose struggles are
featured in *banlieue* films are especially adept at maximizing the "possibilities"
presented by the urban topography. Thus it is significant that, while all of
these films explicitly thematize the many forms of territorial control to which
banlieue inhabitants are subject, they also suggest that the characters are, in
fact, capable of escaping and/or subverting that control (even if only temporarily) – that is, of finding spaces within the city which are, so to speak, *hors-
carton* ("outside the box"). The characters in *Raï* transform a number of
locations throughout the neighborhood "outside" of police surveillance (most
often in the basements of HLM and other apartment complexes, actually
called "caves") into underground trading posts where all manner of illicit
goods are exchanged, where deals are negotiated, and debts settled. The
neighborhood youths in *La haine* gather on the roofs of HLM towers, as well
as in *espaces marchands* (covered areas which are supposed to remain empty
except on market days), where they chat, exchange stories and insults, break-
dance, and listen to music – a composite of activities they call "zoning." The
protagonists in both *État des lieux* and *Ma 6-T va cracker* congregate in "caves"
and abandoned warehouses to perform rap music and even to traffic in
automatic weapons. In such created communal spaces, the youths cannot be
visually located and identified by "the eye of power" (at least for the time
being). By extension, neither can they can be named, labeled, and read. The
"writing machine of the Law" cannot inscribe its order onto their bodies and
thus make them into classified elements of its own textual system.

Another way to read these improvised spaces would be through Deleuze
and Guattari's notion of "autonomous zones" (or "indeterminate zones")
first elucidated in *A Thousand Plateaus*, where they describe such zones as
pockets of activity toward which individual "bodies-in-becoming" gravitate
in order to escape (however fleetingly) those "apparatuses of capture" aimed
at regulating the forces contained within a given social (or molecular) field.[21]
These "zones" are not necessarily demarcated as a continuous space: in fact,
they are most often constituted by a *constellation* of areas which are *spatially
separated* and yet linked together as nodes on a shifting network – in other
words, deterritorialized areas which are nevertheless assembled into an iden-

Figure 22.1   The *banlieusards* articulate another line of escape (*La haine*)
(*Copyright Les Films Lazennec*)

tifiable modality of occupying space. Conceived as one instance of what
Deleuze and Guattari call *lignes de fuite* ("lines of escape"), the migration
routes communicating between and among these nodes are by no means
fixed and are themselves also in constant flux.[22]

While such lines are determined in part by the spatial coordinates of the
zones they access, the bodies circulating through these networks may at any
moment improvise the logic of their movement in response to changing
environmental conditions (for example, by deciding to stop frequenting one
or another of the nodes, or discovering other enclaves as yet "undiscovered"
by the forces of order), thus articulating new lines of escape. It is through
such tactics of nomadism that the constituents of autonomous zones may
attempt to occupy a "smooth space" within the interstices of a field organized by state-regulated mandates to control bodies in circulation ("striated
space").[23]

In one way, the necessarily migratory trajectories of those who constitute
such autonomous zones affirm the conceptual distinction de Certeau articulates between, on one hand, strategically-minded entities with the power to
demarcate territories and thus to striate space according to their own models
(for example, city planning), and on the other hand, those subjects or com-

munities who lack *un espace propre* ("a space of their own") and thus must depend on *tactical* modes of operation. However, the added dimension offered by the theory of Nomadology to analyses of the cultural production of marginalized urban subcultures is what Deleuze and Guattari conceive to be the dynamic and incessant interrelations between periods of *deterritorialization* (during which, as I'm reading them here, a smooth space is temporarily constituted through the occupation of autonomous zones) and *reterritorialization* (in which deterritorialized subjects are again obliged to negotiate within the bounds of striated space).

In this light, it is extremely significant that the narrative of each film ends with an immobilization or reterritorialization which serves as a reminder that the characters do not, in fact, have the luxury of *un espace propre.* In *État des lieux,* Jean becomes stranded in the middle of a seemingly deserted industrial zone when his motorcycle breaks down after his encounter with the police, depriving him of his means of transport and thus effectively sedentarizing his trajectory. In the culminating scene from *Raï,* which seems a deliberate quote of Scorsese's *Mean Streets,* Nordine (who, in his constant attempt to avoid or escape from people to whom he owes money, corresponds to De Niro's character, Johnny, throughout that film) finds temporary solace by firing a handgun aimlessly from a roof and shouting obscenities at passersby below, only to find – once his brother convinces him to descend from his lofty perch back to street-level – that the police are waiting for him (a confrontation that costs him his life).

Yet the errant wanderings of the protagonists in *La haine* seem most emblematic of the oscillating patterns between nomadic and state-sanctioned modes of occupying space theorized by Deleuze and Guattari. At one point during the morning, they climb a neglected staircase to the roof of an HLM tower, where forty or so other youths are already congregated, eating *merguez,* listening to music, "zoning" together. Physically raised above the street, this created communal space is temporarily outside the gaze of police or media surveillance. However, not long after they arrive, the sound of a helicopter is heard passing overhead and soon a group of CRS officers appears to stop the party. The institutional mechanism of territorial control thus attempts to bring these individuals *back down into* the city-as-text, where their behavior can be easily monitored (that is, where they can be "read" as visible and comprehensible signifiers), and where their use of the urban semiotic system can be regulated and stabilized. In effect, they must move to another position if they want to remain *hors-carton.* Vinz, Saïd, and Hubert thus spend most of their day traversing the city in search of "undiscovered" locales. Of course, at each location the arrival of the CRS disperses the gathered youths, who then attempt an escape by following another line of flight out of disciplinary reach (for the time being).

The inevitability of such reterritorializations is then allegorized in the well-known roof scene towards the end of the film. After Vinz, Saïd, and Hubert miss the last *banlieue* train of the evening, they are forced to spend the remainder of their night in the streets of downtown Paris. Repeatedly excluded or expelled from interior spaces (including Astérix's apartment, a night club, and an art gallery) and incapable of finding a way back home, the three misfits climb another roof (again, to escape from the police). With the Eiffel Tower illuminated in the background, Hubert tells Vinz the "joke" first heard from his off-camera voice at the very beginning of the film: "Hey Vinz, you know the story of the dude falling from a fifty-story building? And at each floor, the dude keeps repeating to assure himself, 'So far so good, so far so good, so far so good . . . '". Whereas at the beginning of the film, the allegorical significations of this story are left unarticulated, this time Hubert provides an interpretation that resonates directly with their experiences throughout the day and night. He says: "You see, it's like us in the 'hood – the important thing's not how you fall, it's how you land."

Life in the *banlieue*, then, as Hubert explains it, is a constant descent from the detached perspective from which one can survey the world below without being seen, from which one can read and interpret the urban text without being written into it. One must be prepared at all times to "operate"

Figure 22.2 Hubert allegorizes the Icarian fall they all must take (*La haine*) (*Copyright Les Films Lazennec*)

within the striated space imposed by others, as one must traverse the meta-phorical page upon which is inscribed the signifiers of the social text. Such an Icarian fall, he assures us, is as sure as the force of gravity itself.

Seen through the conceptual categories elaborated within de Certeau's theoretical framework and within Deleuze and Guattari's Nomadology, Hubert's allegory, like the *banlieue* films I have examined in this chapter, seems to be advocating a (tactical) performative mode of inhabiting the city, through which emergent urban subcultures might attempt – even within the most striated of state-regulated spaces – to constitute an *urban body nomadism*.

Yet if the films discussed above resonate with contemporary cultural theo-ries devoted to conceptualizing the relations between urban space and the subjectivities (both individual and collective) constituted within it, in the final analysis it is the films that speak for themselves. What all of these films make clear is that the "real city" in which they take place is situated within the fields of cultural struggle given shape by the postmodern/postcolonial me-tropolis. This "anti-Paris" is depicted not as some liberating ontological es-sence in which to immerse oneself in order to better represent it, but rather as a place that doesn't matter: *un espace quelconque*, to use Deleuze's term, from which to escape, or an "any-place-whatever" in which marginalized human subjects are nevertheless endeavoring to reinvent communal and cinematic spaces.[24]

Notes

1   Walter Benjamin, *Illuminations*, ed. H. Arendt (New York: Schocken, 1967), p. 239.

2   Gilles Deleuze and Félix Guattari, *Capitalism and Schizophrenia, vol. 2, A Thousand Plateaus*, trans. Brian Massumi (Minneapolis: University of Minnesota Press, 1987), pp. 464–70. [orig. *Capitalisme et schizophrénie, vol. 2, Mille Plateaux* (Paris: Minuit, 1980)]

3   Although many films have been shot in these areas since World War Two, a "banlieue-film" is unique in that it purports to provide spectators with an "in-sider" portrayal of social life in the communities localized within the "suburbs" of French cities. For concise discussions of the rubric "banlieue-film," see T. Jousse, "Le banlieue-film existe-il?," *Cahiers du cinéma*, 492 (Juin 1995): 37–9; and B. Reynaud, "Le 'hood: Hate and its Neighbors," *Film Comment*, 32, no. 2 (March–April 1996): 54–8.

4   Cf. "banlieue," *Le Robert Dictionnaire historique de la langue française* (Paris: Dictionnaires le Robert, 1994).

5   "The city has a somatic . . . membrane, which may be palpable (in the case for example of city walls), or impalpable, and which both surrounds and limits its somatic individuality"; Donatella Mazzoleni, "The City and the Imaginary," *New Formations* 12 (1990): 97.

6   Mireille Rosello provides a suggestive reading of French interpretations of the *bidonvilles* during this era: in effect, growing paranoia about the presence of foreigners in France found expression through the mainstream's insistence on these areas as "atypical pockets of disorder that contrasted with the imaginary perfection and visible straightforwardness of Haussmannian boulevards." See "French Bidonvilles in the 1960s: Urban and Individual Initiatives," *Renaissance and Modern Studies: Reading the City*, 40 (1997): 99.

7   See chapter 3 in this volume.

8   For a concise account of this "upgrade" to the era of the HLM, see Alec Hargreaves, *Immigration, "Race" and Ethnicity in Contemporary France* (London: Routledge, 1995), pp. 66–76; and for autobiographical accounts of the process, see Azouz Begag, *Le gone du Chaâba* (Paris: Éditions du Seuil, 1998 (1986)), and Mehdi Lallaoui, *Du bidonville au HLM* (Paris: Syros, 1993).

9   For a comprehensive account of the transformations in French postwar immigration policies, see Maxim Silverman, *Deconstructing the Nation: Immigration, Racism and Citizenship in Modern France* (London: Routledge, 1992).

10   Other films that can be considered under the rubric "banlieue films" include Malik Chibane's *Hexagone* (1988), Karim Dridi's *Bye Bye* (1995), and Medhi Charef's *Le thé au harem d'Archimède* (1985), which is based on Charef's novel, *Le thé au harem d'Archi Ahmed* (Paris: Mercure de France, 1983).

11   This approach most directly draws on Michel de Certeau, *The Practice of Everyday Life*, trans. Steven F. Rendall (Berkeley: University of California Press, 1984); *L'invention du quotidien*, vol. 1, *Arts de faire* (Paris: Gallimard, 1980).

12   de Certeau, *The Practice of Everyday Life*, p. 140.

13   Ibid.

14   Ibid.

15   Cf. "carton," in *Harrap's Slang French* (Paris: Harrap, 1993, 2nd ed.).

16   This is General von Bülow's definition of the space of tactics (cited in de Certeau, *The Practice of Everyday Life*, p. 212).

17   Michel Foucault, *Discipline and Punish*, trans. Alan Sheridan (New York: Pantheon, 1977 (1975)).

18   de Certeau, *The Practice of Everyday Life*, p. 98.

19   Ibid., p. 34.

20   Ibid., p. 96.

21   These ideas are perhaps most clearly sketched out in Deleuze and Guattari, *A Thousand Plateaus*, pp. 167–91, 280–2, 333–4.

22   For various conceptualizations of "lignes de fuite," see ibid., pp. 205–31.

23   Ibid., p. 469.

24   Gilles Deleuze, *Cinema 2: The Time-Image*, trans. Hugh Tomlinson and Robert Galeta (Minneapolis: University of Minnesota Press, 1989), p. 272.

Index